Welcome, Holy Spirit

Welcome, Holy Spirit

Garrie F. Williams

REVIEW AND HERALD® PUBLISHING ASSOCIATION
HAGERSTOWN, MD 21740

Texts credited to Amplified are from *The Amplified Bible.* Copyright © 1965 by Zondervan
Publishing House. Used by permission.

Texts credited to MT are from *The Holy Scriptures According to the Masoretic Text: A New
Translation,* Jewish Publication Society of America, 1917.

Scripture quotations marked NASB are from the *New American Standard Bible,* © The Lockman
Foundation 1960, 1962, 1963, 1968, 1971, 1972, 1975, 1977.

Texts credited to NEB are from *The New English Bible.* © The Delegates of the Oxford University
Press and the Syndics of the Cambridge University Press 1961, 1970. Reprinted by permission.

Texts credited to NIV are from the *Holy Bible, New International Version.* Copyright © 1973,
1978, 1984, International Bible Society. Used by permission of Zondervan Bible Publishers.

Texts credited to NKJV are from The New King James Version. Copyright © 1979, 1980, 1982,
Thomas Nelson, Inc., Publishers.

Bible texts credited to NRSV are from the New Revised Standard Version of the Bible, copyright
© 1989 by the Division of Christian Education of the National Council of the Churches of Christ in the
U.S.A. Used by permission.

Bible texts credited to RSV are from the Revised Standard Version of the Bible, copyright ©
1946, 1952, 1971, by the Division of Christian Education of the National Council of the Churches of
Christ in the U.S.A. Used by permission.

Bible Texts credited to TEV are from the *Good News Bible*—Old Testament: Copyright ©
American Bible Society 1976; New Testament: Copyright © American Bible Society 1966, 1971, 1976.

Verses marked TLB are taken from *The Living Bible,* copyright © by Tyndale House Publishers,
Wheaton, Ill. Used by permission.

This book was
Edited by Richard W. Coffen
Designed by Patricia S. Wegh
Cover design by Helcio Deslandes
Cover illustration by Paul Salmon
Typeset: 9.8/11.8 Times

PRINTED IN U.S.A.
98 97 96 95 94   5 4 3 2 1

Library of Congress Cataloging in Publication Data
Williams, Garrie, F., 1940–
    Welcome Holy Spirit / Garrie F. Williams.
        p.   cm.
    1. Holy Spirit—Meditations. 2. Devotional calendars—Seventh-day
Adventists. 3. Holy Spirit—Biblical teaching. 4. Spiritual life—Seventh-day
Adventist. I. Title
BT121.2.W544 1994
231'.3—dc20   94-22331
                                                                CIP

ISBN 0-8280-0852-3

Dedication

To my mother,

Joan Winifred Downes,

a lady who, in the midst

of seemingly overwhelming troubles,

always "remembered the morning watch"

and taught me to have faith

in an unfailing God.

Meet the Author

*G*arrie Fraser Williams joined the Seventh-day Adventist Church in New Zealand as a teenager and began to preach as a young carpentry apprentice when he was 18. His dedication to Jesus led him to witness as a lay preacher and literature evangelist for 10 years until he graduated from Avondale College in 1968.

Full-time gospel ministry has been varied and fruitful for Garrie throughout the past 25 years. He has pastored churches in Australia and the United States; taught practical theology at Avondale College; worked as an inter-union evangelist for the South Pacific Division; led study tours through the Middle East and South Pacific; completed a master's degree from Andrews University; and served as a conference departmental director.

In 1987 Garrie Williams founded the Homes of Hope small group ministry and has been used mightily by the Holy Spirit as he has addressed revival meetings, seminars, camp meetings, and pastors' retreats across North America as well as in many countries overseas. In 1991 he became president of Trinity Power Ministries, an international, church supporting, nonprofit organization dedicated to prayer and small group ministries, emphasizing the power of the Holy Spirit and the gospel of the Lord Jesus Christ.

Garrie is the author of a number of best-selling books, including *How to Be Filled With the Holy Spirit—and Know It, Give the Holy Spirit a Chance,* and *Window to Revelation.* His interests also include walking—anywhere from beaches to mountain trails, collecting miniature churches, and using his practical building skills. Garrie and his wife, Barbara, have three beautiful daughters—Carolyn, Lyndell, and Sharon—all of whom are married and live in Australia.

From the Author

et me introduce you to a wonderful friend—the Holy Spirit. The two years of research and prayer through every Bible verse that mentions the Holy Spirit and in scores of books about Him as I have prepared this devotional book have helped me come to know Him better than ever before. You do not have to be nervous about the Holy Spirit. He is not just a mighty person of power. He is a gentle Comforter and a friend who will never embarrass or hurt you. Every day this year as you welcome the Holy Spirit to have complete access to every part of your life, you will not only enjoy a beautiful friendship with Him but you will also see Jesus more clearly.

The Pentecostal emphasis on tongues has sometimes frightened others regarding the Holy Spirit. Although Adventists never have or never will agree with the Pentecostal position, they have always been interested in the Holy Spirit and His ministry. Throughout these readings I have tried to take a biblical approach that will avoid fanaticism and will discourage any unbalanced extremes. I stand firmly on the side of historic Adventism and pray that this book will reflect the balanced approach to the Holy Spirit found in the more than 40,000 references in the Spirit of Prophecy.

There is no doubt that God wanted this book to be written, and I am also sure that the enemy of souls did not. He tried every trick to stop it. There were times when it was almost impossible to continue, and my faith nearly failed as did Elijah's when he ran away to a cave and wished to die. I am sorry that I cannot profess to have been a living example of all that I have written, and God knows that it is only by His grace and love that I was able to complete this work. He used faithful prayer partners, friends, and family members to keep a light shining in the darkness. People who recognized my human weaknesses helped me not to forget that love never gives up. Penny Estes Wheeler, acquisitions editor of the Review and Herald Publishing Association, also encouraged me to carry on when the task seemed overwhelming.

I thank all who consented to have their experiences included in this book. All the stories are true, although a few names have been changed. I thank those who helped me with resources and my wife, Barbara, for suggesting the title of this book. What a wonderful way to begin each day, saying "Welcome, Holy Spirit. Welcome to my life again today. Welcome to complete control of every part of me. Thanks for making Jesus real to me today!"

As you spend a year studying everything in the Bible on the Holy Spirit, make this also a year when the Holy Spirit can lead you into ministry. Join together in small groups in your community or church to pray through the verses of the week's readings. Nurture one another in the groups, and reach out to others in love. Share this book with friends and neighbors. In this way your groups will grow, your church will grow, and you will be amazed to see the miracles of grace and healing that will take place through the power of the Holy Spirit. Jesus will be glorified as never before.

Overview

I.
The Holy Spirit in the Old Testament
Welcome to Saving Power

II.
The Holy Spirit in the Gospels
Welcome to Mighty Ministry

III.
The Holy Spirit in Acts
Welcome to Complete Filling

IV.
The Holy Spirit in the Epistles
Welcome to Spiritual Growth

V.
The Holy Spirit in Revelation
Welcome to Final Victory

SPIRIT LIGHT

The earth was without form, and void; and darkness was on the face of the deep. And the Spirit of God was hovering over the face of the waters. Gen. 1:2, NKJV.

*I*t has been stated that negative events occur infrequently in most lives, and that's why those events often stand out. Do you agree? Sometimes I feel like strongly disagreeing, but then as I consider my life even in its hardest times, I can see that much good and blessings have always been present.

The Holy Spirit is the joy bringer who enables us to see the multiplied points of light in our lives even through the darkness of emotional, physical, or material trouble. Look again at Genesis 1:2. Out of the initial chaos the Holy Spirit's power brought incredibly beautiful cosmic order. The word translated here as "hovering" is found only once more in the Bible. You may want to take time to study how Moses pictures in Deuteronomy 32:11 the hovering flight of an eagle over the young in her nest. He uses this to illustrate God's care for His people.

The Spirit can work a miracle of true joy and beauty in you now.

Wondering what God's Word could possibly have for him in Genesis 1, a pastor began to pray through the Bible. Suddenly verse 2 jumped out with stunning reality. *This is what my life is like,* he thought. *It is secretly in darkness and chaos. I don't know what will happen to my home and ministry.* Then the Spirit of God hovered over the chaos. "Please, Lord, bring help to me by Your Spirit," he prayed. "Please enable me to see meaning and joy again." And the Lord who said "Let there be light" created new hope and beauty in the life of a burned-out pastor.

Let the Holy Spirit turn on the light in your life. Just as the pastor's life was illuminated by Jesus' love, so your life can be enlightened today. If a letter, telephone call, or personal comment throws you into unexpected darkness, reach out to the Holy Spirit. He is Jesus' special gift to you.

✄ *A Prayer for Today* ✄

Lord, I claim the joy of Your Holy Spirit today. I trust You because I believe that chaos, darkness, and even deep distress do not frighten You away. I ask You not only to "hover o'er me, Holy Spirit," but also to fill me completely now.

DOES THE SPIRIT GIVE UP?

And the Lord said, "My Spirit shall not strive with man forever,
for he is indeed flesh; yet his days shall be one hundred
and twenty years." Gen. 6:3, NKJV.

Not long after the Creation story, the same Spirit who had conquered chaos seemed to be surrendering to it. Under no circumstances does the Holy Spirit violate human free will. A life or world once illuminated by the light of Jesus' love may force its way through all the Holy Spirit's loving influences and switch into darkness. Even so, the Holy Spirit always inspires the building of an ark of hope.

The Steinfield family had come to know the Lord during an evangelistic series. They soon became bright lights in the church, leading and teaching in many areas, until one day suddenly they were gone.

"What happened?" asked many church members who had taken the Steinfields for granted during the past two years.

A pastoral visit disclosed that this family had gradually slipped back into old habits. Personal prayer and family worship had been neglected; the light had gone out. The Holy Spirit had tried every means possible to nurture the Steinfields, but fellow church members had not shared the Holy Spirit's commitment to fellowship and love.

Years have past, and the Steinfields' three boys and one girl have grown up away from the faith they had known so briefly as children. Their parents have known floods of personal tragedy and materialistic disillusionment without the support of a loving church family.

"My Spirit shall not strive with man forever." Has the Holy Spirit really given up on the Steinfields? Fortunately, no. God has Noahs now who, through His grace, are building arks of love and care. The Steinfields may live in your neighborhood today. You may not find them with this name, but they are there. Yes, there are thousands of Steinfields who are recipients of the Holy Spirit's special concern and Jesus' unfailing love.

❦ *A PRAYER FOR TODAY* ❧

Lord, I'm so encouraged to know that Your Holy Spirit still surrounds the unsaved with Your wonderful love. Even those who have slipped away from You are still objects of Your special care. Please use me as a Noah today to build an ark of nurture in which all who respond can feel safe and secure.

RECOGNIZING THE SPIRIT

And Pharaoh said to his servants, "Can we find such a one as this,
a man in whom is the Spirit of God?" Gen. 41:38, NKJV.

Can you recognize the Spirit's ministry in the life of a fellow believer? If you find that hard, think about a polytheistic Egyptian king seeing such dramatic evidence of Joseph's God that he was prepared to make this former young prisoner the prime minister of the greatest nation then on earth!

Pharaoh saw what New Testament Christians would call spiritual gifts. Joseph apparently displayed gifts of prophecy, wisdom, and leadership (see 1 Cor. 12). No doubt Joseph was one of God's anointed (Ps. 105:15). We do not often use the word "anointed" today, but it simply means to apply oil. In biblical times the term was used for setting a person apart for a special religious or secular office, or in connection with healing or cleansing. In each case the oil symbolized the Holy Spirit's ministry.

Look for Josephs where you work, study, or live. You may not find them surrounded by Egyptian pyramids, but in the shadow of pyramid-like business structures—the multistoried, high-rise obelisks scraping the sky in the massive ultramodern cities that encompass more than half the world's population today. You will not find a Joseph by looking for a faultless man, woman, or young person. But you will recognize a Joseph when you find someone revealing the love of Jesus amid the famine or affluence of modern life.

When I was introduced to Tereza Satelli, the owner of a vegetarian restaurant in Brazil, I knew that I had met a Joseph. Despite many pressures from family, church, and business, Tereza was filled with the Spirit in such a way that she was able to lead, inspire, and minister to the leaders of 20 small groups, which in turn ministered to more than 200 people in the busy city of Campinos.

❧ *A PRAYER FOR TODAY* ❧

Lord, so often we see the frauds and fakes—people who deceive and hurt.
But today I pray that You will help me meet a Joseph full of Your love and
wisdom in this Egypt of confusion in which I live. Yes, Lord, help me
remember that I also may be a Joseph whom someone,
even a non-Christian, may recognize today.

BUILDING IN THE SPIRIT

And I have filled him with the Spirit of God, in wisdom, in understanding, in knowledge, and in all manner of workmanship. Ex. 31:3, NKJV.

Construction on the new church building proceeded slowly as volunteers tried to overcome the hurdles of limited time and knowledge. The idea of building this way had seemed an exciting challenge to the members of the small congregation as they met weekly in a rented schoolroom. Funds were also limited, but enthusiasm was bountiful.

Eighteen months of evenings and weekends on the job left able-bodied members exhausted and discouraged. It seemed impossible that the work would ever be completed. Then one beautiful day that will live forever in the memories of that little congregation, Mark, Darleen, and their young family visited the rented schoolroom for a worship service.

Mark and Darleen were not public speakers or singers, but it was soon obvious that Mark had exceptional building skills, which he had recently dedicated to the Lord, and Darleen was gifted as an interior decorator. God used Mark and Darleen in a remarkable way, and it seemed that in no time at all the congregation was meeting in its beautiful new church building.

Apparently the Spirit who created the world and blessed Bezaleel as he built the sanctuary can gift people in a way that will affect buildings, machinery, and electronics. Perhaps the television production director can be more gifted by the Spirit than the television preacher. Perhaps the artisan of the stained-glass window can be actually gifted by the Spirit to a greater extent than the Bible class teacher or church administrator.

Don't feel discouraged today if within the setting of the Christian church you feel less gifted because you excel with computers, needlework, or engineering but are not able to take an active role in public leadership within the church. Whatever your spiritual gift is, God will give you creative energy as you use it for His glory.

✎ *A PRAYER FOR TODAY* ✎

Thank You, Lord, that You are not bound by religious stereotypes.
You see value in every person's ministry. Today help me use
everything You have given me to build beauty in a world
that needs to see trophies of Your wonderful love and care.

SHARING LEADERSHIP IN THE SPIRIT

Then I will come down and speak with you there, and I will take
of the Spirit who is upon you, and will put Him upon them;
and they shall bear the burden of the people with you,
so that you shall not bear it all alone. Num. 11:17, NASB.

*H*ave you ever felt that you were bearing a burden alone? That's not God's plan for any person, not even for a Spirit-filled Christian.

"Please kill me here and now," Moses prayed (Num. 11:15, NKJV) as the load of leading a large group of complaining people finally seemed about to crush him into the desert sand of the Sinai Peninsula. Moses was leading the Israelites in the power of the Holy Spirit, but even Spirit-filled people can become discouraged when they try to accomplish everything all alone.

Just as the light of one candle is not diminished when several others are lit from it, so when the Holy Spirit, who was upon Moses, was shared with other leaders, they all revealed the fullness of the Spirit's power.

Pastor Rod had tried to minister alone to the 250 members of his congregation, but the task seemed impossible, and he considered the possibility of taking up some other type of employment. Knowing, though, that God had called him to the ministry, he pleaded for wisdom rather than simply giving up and dropping out.

In answer to that earnest prayer, the Lord led Pastor Rod to understand the value of small groups and prayer partner ministry. Soon he had the assistance of more than 20 Spirit-filled lay pastors who were able to share the blessings and burdens of nurture and outreach ministry.

Not only did the lay pastors minister to their small groups, but also the Holy Spirit led them to minister to their pastor and his family. Pastor Rod's ministry was greatly enhanced, and he became a much more effective spiritual leader than before.

Who is bearing the burden with your pastor? Criticism may kill a dedicated pastor's ministry, but watch your pastor flourish when he or she has a team of Spirit-filled members working together.

❦ *A PRAYER FOR TODAY* ❧

Whatever my occupation or ministry is, Lord, I'm acknowledging today that I
need help. In fact, I need help in every area of my life. I accept this help not
only from You, Lord, but from all whom You will lead into partnership with me.

Seventy New Prophets

Then the Lord came down in the cloud, and spoke to him, and took of the Spirit that was upon him, and placed the same upon the seventy elders; and it happened, when the Spirit rested upon them, that they prophesied, although they never did so again. Num. 11:25, NKJV.

The Old Testament records a number of incidents when the coming of the Holy Spirit was made evident by a supernatural spiritual experience. When the 70 elders received the same Holy Spirit who was upon Moses, they all prophesied. What form this prophesying took we do not know, but it certainly must have unequivocally confirmed the 70 as Spirit-filled leaders.

Obviously the elders' prophesying was not predictive of the future, or else long periods of time would have been necessary to judge the accuracy of each statement. The 70 elders must have spoken "edification, and exhortation, and comfort" (1 Cor. 14:3) with such fervor and clarity that it was obvious they spoke for God. It is possible that their messages were in music, as was the prophesying of David's young musicians (1 Chron. 25:1-3).

When the assorted Christians who became known as Moravians gathered on the estate of Count Zinzendorf of Saxony at the beginning of the eighteenth century, God again chose to pour out His Spirit on His people. The fruitage of prayer, Bible study, fellowship, and complete surrender to God's will became evident at the Wednesday morning Communion service at Berthelsdorf on August 13, 1727. The Holy Spirit came upon the people with such power that they hardly knew whether they were in heaven or on earth. The effect was so earthshaking that community members working 20 miles away and unaware that the meeting was taking place were deeply conscious of the Holy Spirit filling their own lives.

So it was in the Israelite camp at Taberah. Two of the elders, Eldad and Medad, who were not at the tabernacle, began to prophesy in the camp in a way that was recognized immediately by the people (Num. 11:26, 27).

❦ *A Prayer for Today* ❦

Lord, help me discern Your Spirit and be open to the prophetic voice of Your Word. As the Spirit comes upon people around me, please give me spiritual wisdom and the readiness to be filled and speak for You today.

RIGHT SPIRIT, WRONG PLACE

But two men had remained in the camp: the name of one was Eldad,
and the name of the other Medad. And the Spirit rested upon them.
Now they were among those listed, but who had not gone out to the
tabernacle; yet they prophesied in the camp. Num. 11:26, NKJV.

We are not told what delayed the two "dads" from meeting their
appointment with the other 68 elders, but apparently the outpouring of the Holy Spirit was not restricted to one geographical location. No sooner had Eldad and Medad been empowered to prophesy
when a young talebearer rushed to Moses with the startling news that resulted
in Moses' assistant, Joshua, wanting to silence this unauthorized display of
spiritual power.

Have you ever noticed how threatened some Christians are by reports of
the Holy Spirit filling and using people of other churches or denominations?
Jesus' disciples struggled with the same tension, but their Master had a very
important answer. " 'Teacher,' said John, 'we saw a man driving out demons
in your name and we told him to stop, because he was not one of us.' 'Do not
stop him,' Jesus said. 'No one who does a miracle in my name can in the next
moment say anything bad about me, for whoever is not against us is for us' "
(Mark 9:38-40, NIV).

When teenage Adventist pioneer Ellen Harmon received her gift of
prophecy, mature Christians of various church groups condemned it as the
work of Satan. But Joseph Bates, a retired sea captain who was then an active minister, came to a different conclusion than did Joshua, the ancient
Israelite assistant commander. In fact, Bates said: "I can now confidently
speak for myself. I believe this work is of God and is given to comfort and
strengthen His scattered people."

As Paul said: "Do not despise prophecies [no matter where the Holy Spirit
may cause them to happen, we may add]. Test all things; hold fast what is
good" (1 Thess. 5:20, 21, NKJV).

✥ *A PRAYER FOR TODAY* ✥

You don't always act according to my preconceived ideas, Lord,
and I'm glad about that. But please help me not feel threatened by the
working of the Holy Spirit in other places and people. I'm open today
to be used by the Spirit in whatever way You choose.

STOPPING THE SPIRIT'S WORK

Then Moses said to him, "Are you zealous for my sake?
Oh, that all the Lord's people were prophets and that the Lord
would put His Spirit upon them!" Num. 11:29, NKJV.

Y ou may be shocked by this, but even God's most sincere and dedicated leaders may try to stop the Holy Spirit's work. I was surprised
to read that it was no less a person than the great Joshua who tried
to stop the prophetic ministry of the Spirit-filled elders. Joshua was jealous
for Moses' leadership. His motives were good, but his vision was limited and
would have stifled God's work.

Moses was not at all threatened by being surrounded by Spirit-filled people. In fact, he expressed his heartfelt desire that they all receive the spiritual
gift of prophecy. Most church leaders I know would be very excited to find
all the members of their denomination or congregation filled with God's
Spirit. But there may be surprising and unexpected results when the Holy
Spirit moves with power in fully surrendered lives.

In eighteenth-century England most church leaders believed that the
gospel was effective only when presented in a church building. Following the
Spirit's filling of about 70 Moravians and Anglicans on January 1, 1739, in
London, George Whitefield, who had been present that night with John and
Charles Wesley, began to preach to thousands in the fields of England. Notice
John Wesley's surprise at this unexpected working of the Holy Spirit. "In the
evening I reached Bristol, and met Mr. Whitefield there. I could scarce reconcile myself at first to the strange way of preaching in the fields, of which
he set me an example on Sunday; having been all my life . . . so tenacious of
every point relating to decency and order, that I should have thought the saving of souls almost a sin, if it had not been done in a church" *(Journal,* Mar.
29, 1739).

A Joshua or a Moses. Which will you be like when the Spirit takes possession of willing lives today?

❧ *A Prayer for Today* ❧

Lord, You do the unexpected because You are not bound by the traditions we
have created. Thank You for being willing to surprise me with Your Holy Spirit
today, bringing a new revelation of ministry and service for Jesus.

CAN THE SPIRIT USE SINNERS?

And Balaam raised his eyes, and saw Israel encamped according to their tribes; and the Spirit of God came upon him. Num. 24:2, NKJV.

The Holy Spirit can use only those people who are fully obeying God. I really believe that."

No one doubted that Chuck was sincere about his very definite and authoritative statement, but Connie disagreed. "What about Balaam? The Spirit came upon him, and he spoke for God, even though he had fallen away from being a man of integrity and consecration. In fact, he was mixed up in sorcery."

Connie was right. The Holy Spirit did use Balaam in a special way despite all his problems, but that did not mean that God in any way approved of Balaam's sins. In fact, Balaam became a byword for the tragedy of religious mercenary greed and evil (see 2 Peter 2:15; Jude 11; Rev. 2:14).

There is an ever-present risk when God uses sinners in His service. Unless hearts and minds are fully surrendered to God, the Holy Spirit's working through a sinner's life can be taken as evidence that God is turning a blind eye to sin. Nothing could be further from the truth. The Holy Spirit always works to bring holiness to each life He fills.

A young man was brought to Jesus through the ministry of a famous TV evangelist. Another lady received genuine physical healing as the same preacher prayed for her. Later people questioned this young man and woman when the immoral life of the evangelist was publicly exposed. Yes, God had honored these people's faith even though the instrument He had used went, like Judas and Balaam, into moral and spiritual tragedy.

If God waited to use only totally obedient people, His work would be long delayed. What He does look for are people of all ages who are fully surrendered to Him and open to the wonderful privilege and joy of being Spirit-filled Christians in His service.

Don't wait until you feel sinless before you begin to use your spiritual gifts for God. Remember, the spiritual gifts that make your ministry effective are gifts of grace.

☞ *A PRAYER FOR TODAY* ☜

Father, I can serve You only because of the forgiveness that Jesus makes possible. If You choose to use me in some special way today, do not in any way allow that privilege to weaken my resolve to have victory over every sin.

HOW LONG DOES IT TAKE?

And the Lord said to Moses: "Take Joshua the son of Nun
with you, a man in whom is the Spirit, and lay your hand on him."
Num. 27:18, NKJV.

*W*hat will you be like 40 years from now? If you are young enough to ask that question, the answer is fairly simple. You will probably be much like you are now—only more so. Personality and even character do not change a great deal throughout the years. Practice does not make perfect, as the saying goes, but practice usually does make our habit patterns and personality traits permanent. Radical changes are possible only as we allow the Holy Spirit to fill our lives with the power of Jesus' love.

Although Joshua was always respected as a courageous, dedicated leader, 40 years did make a positive spiritual difference in his life. At Taberah, Joshua had tried to stop the prophesying of the Spirit-filled elders (Num. 11:28). After four decades of wilderness wandering on the part of His people, God acknowledged that Joshua himself was a man filled with the Holy Spirit.

Don't, however, make the mistake of thinking that it takes God 40 years to change people sufficiently so that they can be filled with His Spirit and reveal His gifts. Peter was filled with the Holy Spirit on the day of Pentecost, only about 50 days after he had denied Jesus with cursing and swearing. Paul was filled with the Holy Spirit only three or four days after being a killer of Christians. The Roman military officer Cornelius was filled with the Spirit the very moment he accepted Jesus as Lord. God doesn't need time. He is willing and able to fill any life the moment it is open to Him.

Before Joshua was publicly recognized and inaugurated as a Spirit-filled leader, God recognized him as such. In the same way, as God fills your life He will immediately acknowledge your gifts, even though other people may take a little longer to recognize the uniqueness you have to offer. Evil forces will try to delay your ministry indefinitely, but God is calling you now. All the special gifts of the Spirit are available today.

❧ *A PRAYER FOR TODAY* ❧

Thank You, Lord, for being able to accept me and fill me as I open my life to You. I'm glad that You don't need a long time to work in my life. You can use me as Your servant right now.

THE SPIRIT OF DELIVERANCE

When the children of Israel cried out to the Lord, the Lord raised up a deliverer for the children of Israel, who delivered them: Othniel the son of Kenaz, Caleb's younger brother. The Spirit of the Lord came upon him, and he judged Israel. Judges 3:9, 10, NKJV.

*W*hat image does the word "judge" bring instantly to your mind? Think about it for a moment. Do you picture a courtroom or a prison? Do you think of stern justice or hard retribution? Perhaps you have a positive image of judges that encompasses joyful acquittal, mercy, or abundant financial compensation. Have you imposed your contemporary attitude toward judges onto the Bible book with that name? If this is the case, you may be surprised to find a different emphasis altogether.

"I'm excited about the book of Judges," a young pastor recently told me. "This book really shows the power of God's Spirit in a remarkable way over the enemies of His people."

Pastor Kevin Wilfley had been making a careful study of the Holy Spirit for a number of years when he discovered the connection between judgment and the Holy Spirit in Judges. "In the original languages of the Bible, judgment can be understood in many places as deliverance as well as vindication and justice," Kevin explained. "In the book of Judges, God records the deliverances of Israel to show what He can do for us by His Spirit. We can have victory over the enemy as the Holy Spirit brings judgment on evil in us or around us today."

No wonder we find God's people in the Bible looking forward to judgment. They knew and trusted the Judge.

Othniel was apparently not a man of prestige in the community, but when God's Spirit came upon him, God used him to free His people from Mesopotamian oppression. Hebrew scholars say that the verb and preposition combination "came upon" means to be "actively present upon." In other words, the Holy Spirit inspired and gifted Othniel continually so that the fruit of deliverance and victory brought 40 years of peace in the land of Israel.

✿ *A PRAYER FOR TODAY* ✿

In the midst of spiritual struggle I trust in the victory power of Your Holy Spirit, Lord. Help me accept Your deliverance today so that the peace of Jesus can fill my life with confidence and hope.

YOU ARE WORTH A LOT

But the Spirit of the Lord came upon Gideon; then he blew the trumpet, and the Abiezrites gathered behind him. Judges 6:34, NKJV.

*D*o you have a healthy, positive self-esteem? Gideon didn't. When God asked him to lead Israel to victory, Gideon was full of excuses, all of which seemed to be based on factors indicating an inferiority complex. "He said to Him, 'O my Lord, how can I save Israel? Indeed my clan is the weakest in Manasseh, and I am the least in my father's house'" (Judges 6:15, NKJV).

While egotism and arrogance have no place in Christian leadership, it is often surprising what excuses people make for *not* allowing God's Holy Spirit to use them in some special way. "I hold only a very insignificant position in the church." "I'm only a new Christian." "I haven't been to the seminary." "I'm the only church member in my family." "I'm too young [or old]." "I'm an introvert." So the list goes on.

Gideon's excuses, however, did not excuse him from God's service. In fact, as the Holy Spirit came upon Gideon, he was used to lead out in one of the greatest victories in the history of God's people. The word in Judges 6:34 for "came upon" literally means "clothed." Gideon was clothed with the Holy Spirit, or the Holy Spirit clothed Himself with Gideon. Either way, the effect was the same. The amassed armies from Midian were defeated by the Lord through Gideon and his 300 men. The New International Version uses "clothed" again in Luke 24:49, where Jesus told His disciples to "stay in the city until you have been clothed with power from on high."

God often uses people who consider themselves of little value. It is easier for Him to equip them for service than people who are intoxicated with their own importance. Once those who consider themselves of little value see that they are worth so much that Jesus would have died for them alone, and as they realize that they are the dwelling place of the Holy Spirit, the effect is explosive. Myths are shattered, and enemies are scattered and defeated.

❦ *A PRAYER FOR TODAY* ❧

Lord, I thank You for the value You place on me and that You are willing to clothe me with Your enemy-conquering Spirit. Help me today to accept the total victory that You have made possible for me through Jesus.

From Triumph to Tragedy

Then the Spirit of the Lord came upon Jephthah, and he passed through Gilead and Manasseh, and passed through Mizpah of Gilead; and from Mizpah of Gilead he advanced toward the people of Ammon. Judges 11:29, NKJV.

The story of Jephthah again knocks the props out from under any high-and-mighty ideal that we might have constructed of the type of men and women God's Spirit can use to deliver His people. Jephthah, the son of a harlot, led a band of worthless raiders and apparently ended up killing his only child as a human sacrifice. Amazingly, the sacrifice of his daughter happened *after* Jephthah was filled with the Holy Spirit. It is incredible but true. The thought of it makes us sick.

There is no doubt that this story illustrates the danger of following the unbiblical impulses of sinful human nature, even when those impulses seem to have a spiritual emphasis. Although God's Spirit came upon Jephthah and he led his people to defeat the overwhelming Ammonite army, Jephthah did not think of the potential implications of his hasty and dangerous vow. When he saw his pretty young daughter dancing with timbrels out of his house, his feelings must have turned from lighthearted joy to the heaviness of lead. No way would God have condoned this senseless loss of a young life. Nonetheless, it seems that Jephthah fulfilled his vow.

We may wonder why God would allow stories like this to be recorded in the Bible. But they do certainly keep before us a flashing red light of warning. While the Spirit can mightily use any life which has become open to God's will, that does not preclude that life slipping again into actions which in no way reflect God's character. In fact, Satan delights in bringing dishonor to God in this way.

Such a tragic turn of events, illustrated at least six or seven times in the Old Testament, is a sobering lesson that we can learn today as we acknowledge our need to stay close to Jesus at all times.

A Prayer for Today

Lord, help me avoid the trap of impulsive decisions that may have tragic consequences. May I be led by Your Spirit as I pray and accept counsel from Your Word and from people of experience in the ways of truth and rightness.

CHILDREN IN THE SPIRIT

So the woman bore a son and called his name Samson;
and the child grew, and the Lord blessed him. And
the Spirit of the Lord began to move upon him at Mahaneh Dan
between Zorah and Eshtaol. Judges 13:24, 25, NKJV.

*H*ow young is too young for the Holy Spirit to fill a person's life? One thousand eight hundred people were gathered for the Saturday afternoon meeting in the beautiful church on the campus of the Adventist academy in Hortolandia, Brazil. Toward the end of the meeting I invited people who wanted to pray during a special season of prayer to make their way down to one of the six microphones near the front.

Many earnest prayers were offered, but none inspired me as much as that of an 8- or 9-year-old girl who began to pray with an eloquence that was obviously from the Holy Spirit. She prayed for those present in the meeting and also for the conversion of her father, who had not yet committed his life to Jesus. Later I learned that the father was so deeply moved by his daughter's prayer that he came forward during the call and surrendered his life fully to Jesus Christ.

The Holy Spirit, who "stirred up" Samson (as "moved upon" can be translated), can stir up children even younger than the 8-year-old Brazilian. At a seminar in Oregon a boy of about 4 years of age came forward to the microphone to pray. He led his father with him, and as I listened to this little child I knew that the Holy Spirit was using him to lead us into God's presence.

Apparently John the Baptist was filled with the Holy Spirit even before birth (Luke 1:15). This unborn baby leaped with joy in his mother's womb as there was contact with Jesus about six months before Jesus' birth.

Pray today for young children, babies, and even the unborn so that they may be filled with the Holy Spirit.

At a camp meeting where I spoke a few years ago, I heard a young pastor tell a large audience how he placed his hand on his pregnant wife's abdomen and prayed and sang to their unborn baby. If the baby could hear, it was certainly receiving a great start in life!

❧ A PRAYER FOR TODAY ❧

No life is too young or old to be filled with the Spirit, Lord. I pray today
for the very young so that they may leap for joy in the Spirit
and so that You will use them to minister somehow to me.

WHEN THE LION ROARS

*And the Spirit of the Lord came mightily upon him, and he tore the
lion apart as one would have torn apart a young goat,
though he had nothing in his hand. Judges 14:6, NKJV.*

As we drove through the Wild Animal Safari in Queensland, Australia, we commented on how docile the lions looked. One even slept like a giant cat on the roof of a car, to the delight of my daughters. Suddenly a steel cage on wheels was towed into the central grassy area, and a man in the cage began to throw out pieces of raw meat. The lions were transformed instantly into snarling beasts, tearing at the meat and leaping at the cage with fierce intensity.

"You wouldn't get *me* into that cage!" exclaimed my oldest daughter, Carolyn. "Not even for thousands of dollars would I be shut up in there with those beasts only inches away."

It's unlikely that you have ever been attacked by a lion, as Samson was, although the "devil walks about like a roaring lion, seeking whom he may devour" (1 Peter 5:8, NKJV).

Apparently lions were common in Palestine during Old Testament times. In fact, they are mentioned more than 150 times in the Bible. But lions certainly were not as common as the violent and destructive attacks of the forces of evil on people everywhere today.

Sometimes even a docile characteristic of our own personality can be changed by a "raw meat" situation into an uncontrolled, peace-destroying emotion. External circumstances that seem benign and innocuous can suddenly change into a turmoil of hurricane-like intensity.

As the young, energetic lion rushed its attack on Samson, the Holy Spirit came mightily upon Samson. It can be translated that the Spirit "rushed" upon Samson. Samson would ultimately be destroyed by his own uncontrolled passions, but at this time God chose to save Samson by the power of the Spirit, because there was yet a great work of deliverance for Samson to accomplish.

Never underestimate the victory power of the Holy Spirit as Satan the lion roars today.

❧ *A PRAYER FOR TODAY* ❧

*Lord, You know the attacks that Your people face today. The lion pounces in the most
unexpected ways. Thank You for the assurance of inner peace as I trust in You right now.*

DESTROYING THE ENEMY

Then the Spirit of the Lord came upon him mightily,
and he went down to Ashkelon and killed thirty of their men,
took their apparel, and gave the changes of clothing to those who had
explained the riddle. So his anger was aroused,
and he went back up to his father's house. Judges 14:19, NKJV.

E ven before Samson's birth God had chosen him to deliver His people from the Philistines. This young man had dedicated parents. His diet was uncontaminated by unclean foods or addictive substances. He was a superman physically, but he had a fatal flaw—moral weakness. And this weakness led him to desire a woman from the enemy nation. Soon he saw her treachery, and, as the Holy Spirit came upon him, God was able to turn Samson's foolishness into a triumph that destroyed some of the enemy and turned Samson toward his home.

The new birth experience, which brings the Holy Spirit into a Christian's life (Eph. 1:13; Eze. 36:25-27), is the beginning of the Holy Spirit's work of destroying the enemy that had held authority in that person's thoughts, words, and actions since the time of natural birth. Unfortunately, like Samson, there are enemies that even a Spirit-filled Christian may fall in love with. One famous television evangelist revealed mighty gifts of the Spirit, but fell in love with lust. Another satisfied his desires with the love of material prosperity. Both discovered the treachery of the enemy, and one eventually wrote from prison, "I ask all who have sat under my ministry to forgive me for preaching a gospel emphasizing earthly prosperity."

In the tragic circumstance of this former evangelist's confession, God led this disgraced preacher to destroy more than "30 Philistines." People, through his testimony, saw the terrible danger of a Spirit-filled Christian being attracted to such enemies within as pride, egotism, self-sufficiency, dishonesty, lust, greed, church politics, and criticism.

❧ A PRAYER FOR TODAY ❧

Lord, if I become enamored of the enemies within and eventually know the
heartache of their treachery, please help me remember that Your Spirit
can still give me victory. There's no bondage so strong that
it cannot be broken by Your mighty power. Holy Spirit,
I ask You to lead me always back to my Father's house.

BREAKING THE BONDAGE

When he came to Lehi, the Philistines came shouting against him.
Then the Spirit of the Lord came mightily upon him; and the ropes that
were on his arms became like flax that is burned with fire, and his
bonds broke loose from his hands. Judges 15:14, NKJV.

*A*lbert's addiction to nicotine kept shouting at him like an angry Philistine army. For 40 years he had suffered from the taunting cries of this enemy. It had broken his health and his self-esteem, and had always seemed to defeat his desire to witness as a victorious Christian.

I did not know Albert or his history of addiction, but I did hear his cry for help as I led a prayer season at a spiritual retreat in northern California. "I have to have a cigarette every 20 minutes. I've been through every stop-smoking program and method. I've been in the hospital two times, and I just cannot quit."

A number of pastors and lay leaders immediately gathered around Albert and laid hands on him as they prayed for his full surrender to the power of the Holy Spirit. "Jesus loves you, Albert," one pastor said. "Please remember that your salvation is dependent on the blood of Jesus, not on your victory over smoking. But this victory will enable you to have a glorious testimony of His great power and give you a freedom to share the love of Jesus in ways that you have not had before."

Two days later, at the last meeting of the retreat, Albert jumped to his feet. "I just can't keep quiet!" he exclaimed. "For the first time in 40 years I've not had a smoke for 48 hours. Praise God, the bondage is broken! I'm free."

Albert's testimony of the Spirit "coming mightily upon him" opened the way for many others to tell of bondages they were struggling to break. Intercessory prayer culminated in a concert of praise as those who had been set free from specific physical, emotional, social, and spiritual problems celebrated their victory through the Holy Spirit's power.

❧ A PRAYER FOR TODAY ❧

The enemies that shout, Lord, are sometimes depression, fear, bad temper,
moodiness, and negative thoughts. May they be like ropes as weak
as burned flax as their tyranny is broken by Your great power.

SUPER STRENGTH

Then Samson called to the Lord, saying, "O Lord God,
remember me, I pray! Strengthen me, I pray, just this once,
O God, that I may with one blow take vengeance on the Philistines
for my two eyes!" Judges 16:28, NKJV.

Samson asked for physical strength because he was fighting flesh-and-blood enemies. Christians ask for spiritual strength because they "do not wrestle against flesh and blood," but against evil spiritual forces that attack from within them and from the outside (Eph. 6:12, NKJV).

The source of strength for Christians of all ages is always the same. They are "strengthened with might through the Spirit in the inner man" (Eph. 3:16, NKJV). Greater is He who is in the Spirit-filled person than he who is in the world (1 John 4:4).

Like Samson, it is possible to be blinded by the enemy so that we grope around in the spiritual darkness of this world, wondering where to turn for help and healing. "If the Good News we preach is hidden to anyone, it is hidden from the one who is on the road to eternal death. Satan, who is the god of this evil world, has made him blind, unable to see the glorious light of the Gospel that is shining upon him" (2 Cor. 4:3, 4, TLB).

This blindness may happen even in just one area of an otherwise enlightened Christian life. A person may be a prominent leader in institutional Christianity and yet be blinded by pride, political wrangling, Laodiceanism, or some other "acceptable" sin.

If you are feeling the grip of darkness descending upon your soul today, you can ask the Holy Spirit to lead you again, not to the pillars of a pagan temple, but to the cross of Jesus. Samson asked to be led again, and the Lord heard his prayer and restored his strength. At the cross you will see the light that will dispel the darkness that has surrounded a particular area of your life. This is the great work of the Holy Spirit, who not only leads the blind to the source of light but also gives the strength to destroy the enemy, the power of darkness, who has gained authority over some area of life.

❦ A PRAYER FOR TODAY ❧

Lord, I believe that Your strength is made perfect only in people
who realize their own lack of spiritual power. Holy Spirit, thank You
for leading me again to renew my vision at the cross.

WELCOME TO A NEW MAN

You will meet a group of prophets coming down from the high place with a stringed instrument, a tambourine, a flute, and a harp before them; and they will be prophesying. Then the Spirit of the Lord will come upon you, and you will prophesy with them and be turned into another man. 1 Sam. 10:5, 6, NKJV.

A life that is supernaturally changed is always a remarkable testimony to God's power.

Ron grew up in a Christian home in which legalism led him to turn away from God to the demon powers of drugs and alcohol. Years of his young life were sacrificed before Ron again surrendered to the Holy Spirit's power. One Sabbath afternoon Ron sat in front of the fire in our family room as he quietly played the guitar and led us in singing beautiful Christian songs. We could truly testify as we enjoyed Ron's fellowship that here was a person who had been "turned into another man."

The same possibility of dramatic change is available to every person.

Strangely, when God promised to change the future Israelite king into another man, Saul was not displaying characteristics of evil addictions, greed, lust, or violence. Rather, he was showing evidence of a lack of self-confidence, limited assertiveness, and low self-esteem. He was the tallest and most handsome man in Israel (1 Sam. 9:2), yet when his great moment came he was found hiding in the baggage (1 Sam. 10:22, NRSV).

As the Holy Spirit came upon Saul, God made a radical change in the man's life. Although Saul was little in his own eyes (1 Sam. 15:17), the Holy Spirit gave him bigness of spiritual power to lead the new monarchy. Tragically, though, the changes made in Saul's life when disconnected from the Holy Spirit became the very means by which his kingship crashed and his life crumbled. Saul eventually thought of himself as so big that he did not need to obey the word of the Lord. His rebellion was as dangerous as witchcraft (verse 23) because it aligned him with the powers of evil.

❦ A PRAYER FOR TODAY ❧

Father, help me see bigness and smallness in relationship to You rather than in comparing myself to other people. Through Your Holy Spirit, make the "size" changes necessary in my life to enable me to be Your subject and a servant of Your people.

January 20

A BRAND-NEW HEART

*And so it was, when he had turned his back to go from Samuel,
that God gave him another heart; and all those signs
came to pass that day. 1 Sam. 10:9, NKJV.*

The Holy Spirit always begins by working on the heart. In biblical literature the heart is the very core of personal being. It is seen as the center of character and religious and moral conduct, and the source of all physical vitality and spiritual life. The heart is acknowledged as the seat of the will, intellect, reflections, feelings, and passions. When God explained to Samuel that humans look on the outward appearance but the Lord looks on the heart (1 Sam. 16:7), He was trying to explain His intimate knowledge of who a person really is.

With our modern understanding of anatomy, physiology, and psychology, we try to explain that the Bible is not talking about the organ that pumps the blood around the body when it zeroes in on the heart as the center of our being. We realize that this refers to what we would call today a combination of emotions, thoughts, motives, desires, ambitions, and reasoning, all of which determine who we are in God's sight. These factors are what a "soul" really is.

Some scholars believe that when God spoke of turning Saul into another man He was referring to a conversion experience. It is at conversion that the Holy Spirit performs His radical heart surgery. Not just a quadruple bypass, but a completely new heart. "I will give you a new heart and put a new spirit within you; I will take the heart of stone out of your flesh and give you a heart of flesh" (Eze. 36:26, NKJV).

Sadly, Saul's history indicates that he allowed the old heart to keep beating, and eventually it destroyed him. But on this glad day of great festivity, as the signs of the Holy Spirit were made evident, Saul's new heart was so open to the anointing of the Holy Spirit that the people recognized him as a servant of God.

❧ *A PRAYER FOR TODAY* ❧

*Lord, at conversion You created in me a new heart representing
the new soul center, direction, and power in my life. Today,
by Your Holy Spirit, please keep that heart alive and strong
so that my life may be a reflection of Your will.*

AN UNLIKELY PROPHET

*When they came there to the hill, there was a group of prophets
to meet him; then the Spirit of God came upon him, and
he prophesied among them. 1 Sam. 10:10, NKJV.*

No one but Samuel knew yet that Saul had been anointed as king, so it was rather a shock to the people when Saul began to prophesy. You can hear the people saying with a tone of incredulity in their voices, "Is Saul also among the prophets?" (verse 11, NKJV). As the news spread across the country like a warm Chinook wind on the Canadian prairies, the Israelites could have said, "Do you know that tall, shy Benjaminite, the one who is so self-conscious that he hides when company comes to his house? Well, he has become a spokesperson for God."

It was apparently like announcing that a teenage mother of two preschoolers from Harlem, New York, had suddenly become president of the United States.

God loves to surprise us by showing what He can do through the power of the Holy Spirit. Billy Bray was an uneducated Cornish miner whose reputation as a foul-mouthed drunkard was unrivaled in his home village. When Billy was converted he came from the "lowest hell of evil." "In an instant the Lord made me so happy, that I cannot express what I felt," Billy testified. "I shouted for joy. I praised God with my whole heart. . . . They said I was a madman, but they meant I was a glad-man. Glory be to God" (F. W. Bourne, *Billy Bray—the King's Son,* p. 20).

God used Billy as a mighty prayer warrior to heal the sick, build chapels, and preach the gospel in England.

Most prophetic ministry does not foretell the future, but brings words of "edification and exhortation and comfort" (1 Cor. 14:3, NKJV). That's why all Christians are to pray that they may prophesy (verses 1, 39). Some of your friends may be surprised when you, like Billy Bray and Saul, speak to them a message of "strengthening, encouragement and comfort" (verse 3, NIV) from the Lord, but your ministry in the Holy Spirit's power will bring warning and blessing to all who listen. The people whom God uses are often surprised themselves when they see the power of the Holy Spirit ministering through them.

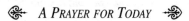 *A PRAYER FOR TODAY*

*Lord, I love the way You often do what is unexpected. I'm open
to whatever You have planned for my life and ministry.*

ANGER IN THE SPIRIT

And Nahash the Ammonite answered them, "On this condition
I will make a covenant with you, that I may put out
all your right eyes, and bring reproach on all Israel." . . .
Then the Spirit of God came upon Saul when he heard this news,
and his anger was greatly aroused. 1 Sam. 11:2-6, NKJV.

*A*s the Holy Spirit fills a life, there is not only joy and assurance of salvation but also anger against evil. Like the Ammonite enemy of ancient Israel, evil seeks to humiliate, disfigure, and destroy Christians today. Evil arises in the most unexpected places and at the most inopportune times, and threatens to put out our "right eyes, and bring reproach on all" the church. Evil specializes in dirty trick tactics.

Tony was a lay leader in his local church and often spoke to the congregation on Sabbath mornings. In his work as a builder, Tony was in the habit of explaining to prospective customers, "You can trust me; I'm a Christian. My company will build you a house that you will be very pleased with." But Tony was secretly doing inferior work. In fact, his building practices were deceptive and dishonest, and customers were treated badly. Tony's pastor tried in a loving way to pray and reason with him, but Tony would not listen. In fact, he became angry with the pastor and tried to destroy his ministry.

Eventually the newspapers published the story, and this crooked businessman was punished by the law. However, in the eyes of many customers and newspaper readers, great reproach was brought upon all the church, and God's character was misjudged.

The Holy Spirit brings anger against sin in all its devious forms because He shows sin to be ultimately and eternally destructive. Just as Saul battled the Ammonites, so Christians who are filled with the Spirit find themselves involved in spiritual battles. People are not the enemy, but the evil principle of sin must be dealt with on all levels so that there can come the great rejoicing of victory.

❧ A PRAYER FOR TODAY ❧

Help me discern evil, Lord, and confront it in the power of Your Spirit.
May my anger be against sin, not against sinners or even against myself,
for people are the objects of Your love.

ANOINTING A KING

Then Samuel took the horn of oil and anointed him in the midst of his brothers; and the Spirit of the Lord came upon David from that day forward. So Samuel arose and went to Ramah. 1 Sam. 16:13, NKJV.

*D*o you have the heavenly unction?" the preacher asked in a Sabbath sermon not long after I had become a Christian. "Unction" was not a word I understood, but the pastor read it in the King James Version of the Bible. I had heard my Catholic friends speak of "extreme unction," but I certainly did not understand the "extreme" version of this term either, and was not interested in knowing what it meant.

Later I discovered that the word "unction" comes from a Latin translation of a term meaning to apply oil. Modern Bibles use the word "anoint," which has its origin in Middle French.

The anointing of David represented the Holy Spirit coming upon him and empowering him for spiritual leadership. David's anointing differed from that of the other national leaders of Israel in that the Holy Spirit came upon David "from that day forward." Not until the Messiah and the outpouring of the Holy Spirit on New Testament Christians would the continuous result of anointing again apply. "Now He who establishes us with you in Christ and has anointed us is God, who also has sealed us and given us the Spirit in our hearts as a deposit" (2 Cor. 1:21, 22, NKJV). This anointing by the Holy Spirit abides, or remains, in the Christian (1 John 2:20, 27).

If the preacher were to ask me that question today, I would jump to my feet and shout, "Amen!"

I was first conscious of the anointing of the Holy Spirit when I was 18. I had been converted shortly before, but I later became aware of the mighty power of the heavenly "unction." That power enabled me, as a young carpentry apprentice, to begin publicly preaching the gospel in a way that would eventually lead many to Jesus. Unfortunately, after becoming a professional minister I gradually forgot about the divine anointing until 20 years later, at which time I realized my desperate need.

❦ *A PRAYER FOR TODAY* ❦

Father, I now would again like to answer yes joyfully to the preacher's question. Thank You that through Jesus I do have the anointing of the Holy Spirit. Praise the Lord!

BATTLING AN EVIL SPIRIT

*But the Spirit of the Lord departed from Saul, and a distressing spirit
from the Lord troubled him. 1 Sam. 16:14, NKJV.*

There is absolutely no doubt that God never sends evil spirits to oppress or possess any person. But it is also certain that when someone totally rejects the Holy Spirit, he or she becomes open to harassment by evil powers. I believe that it is only in this way that the Old Testament says the "distressing spirit" was from the Lord. In Scripture God is often given responsibility for things He allowed because of human free will.

Speaking of Saul's situation, Josephus, the Jewish historian who wrote in the first century A.D., suggested: "The divine power departed from Saul, and removed to David. . . . But as for Saul, some strange and demonical disorders came upon him, . . . for which the physicians could find no remedy but this, that if any person could charm those passions by singing, and playing upon the harp, they advised him to inquire for such a one, and to observe when these demons came upon him and disturbed him, and to take care that such a person might stand over him, and play upon the harp, and recite hymns to him" *(Antiquities,* 6. 8. 2).

The powers of evil cannot remain active in the presence of the beautiful "psalms, hymns, and spiritual songs" that can be sung by God's children. These spiritual weapons are powerful and effective in the voice and heart of a Spirit-filled Christian. David used this music method most effectively for Saul (1 Sam. 16:23), but eventually the powers of evil were so strongly entrenched in Saul that they led him to destruction.

Sometimes friends will send me a Christian music cassette and encourage me to listen especially to one or two songs. From Kim and Jim came "Refiner's Fire"; from Janet, "He Knows What to Do"; from Michael, "You Gave Me Love." Often as I drive I will listen to these songs again and again, until they become part of my praise and spiritual weaponry.

❦ A PRAYER FOR TODAY ❧

*Lord, do You have a music ministry for me? Somehow, even though
I may not be a talented singer, let me be an agent of deliverance
to someone who needs victory power over evil—power that
can come through the words and melody of Christian music.*

EVEN THE ENEMY PROPHESIES

So [Saul] sent men to capture [David]. But when they saw a group of prophets prophesying, with Samuel standing there as their leader, the Spirit of God came upon Saul's men and they also prophesied. 1 Sam. 19:20, NIV.

When Ellen Harmon was 15 years old, she was deeply earnest about her relationship with the Lord but was surprised when it appeared that God was giving her some very vivid dreams of Jesus and the great temple in heaven. As she came into an even closer fellowship with her Lord, Ellen felt convicted to share her faith, and at some of the small group meetings in Portland, Maine, the Holy Spirit would come upon her with such power that her strength would be taken. This supernatural sign gave great courage to some, but provoked strong opposition from others.

A family who had been leaders in this opposition attended a meeting, and one of the men voiced doubts about the genuineness of Ellen's experience. "But he had scarcely stopped speaking when a strong man, a devout and humble Christian [Brother R], was struck down before his eyes by the power of God, and the room was filled with the Holy Spirit." Following this experience, Ellen testified of her great love for Jesus. Then the man who had come to destroy the young David began to prophesy with tears of genuine repentance.

"Sister Ellen, I will never again lay a straw in your way. God has shown the coldness and stubbornness of my heart, which He has broken by the evidence of His power. I have been very wrong."

Like the prophets in the time of Saul, this former enemy, after telling of his truly miraculous answer to prayer, began to glorify Jesus and shout praises to God. In fact, he became a strong witness in the power of the Holy Spirit. "I offered a silent prayer, that, if this [Ellen's falling prostrate] was the holy influence of God, Brother R might experience it this evening. Almost as the desire went up from my heart, Brother R fell, prostrated by the power of God. . . . Welcome, light! Welcome, Jesus!" *(Testimonies,* vol. 1, pp. 44-47).

❧ *A PRAYER FOR TODAY* ❧

Praise Your name, Father! Evil opposition can be turned to Your glory by the power of the Holy Spirit. Thank You for this assurance that God will always triumph over evil.

PROSTRATED BY THE SPIRIT

But the Spirit of God came even upon [Saul], and he walked along prophesying until he came to Naioth. He stripped off his robes and also prophesied in Samuel's presence. He lay that way all that day and night. This is why people say, "Is Saul also among the prophets?"
1 Sam. 19:23, 24, NIV.

*I*n the house at Ramah, Saul was overcome by the Holy Spirit, as had been his three groups of messengers. All day he lay on the floor as a strange and humbling testimony to God's power. Unfortunately, however, the humility was dramatic but temporary.

Unlike Saul, whose experience did not signify a new and lasting relationship with God, many of the people who opposed young Ellen Harmon came into unity of purpose and effort by an unusual revelation of the power of God. "In a prayer meeting soon after, the brother who had confessed that he was wrong in his opposition experienced the power of God in so great a degree that his countenance shone with a heavenly light, and he fell helpless to the floor. . . .

"A few weeks after, while the large family of Brother P. were engaged in prayer at their own house, the Spirit of God swept through the room and prostrated the kneeling suppliants. My father came in soon after, and found them all, both parents and children, helpless under the power of the Lord" (*Testimonies*, vol. 1, p. 47).

More than 30 years later this same experience was still happening. James White wrote in 1874: "At one time, while we were knelt in prayer [in the Loughborough home in Santa Rosa], and Mrs. White took my arm and bade me rise and go free, as I arose, the Holy Ghost came upon us in such a measure that we both fell to the floor" (A. L. White, *Ellen G. White: The Progressive Years*, pp. 428, 429).

While Saul's experience warns us that being "slain in the Spirit" is no substitute for daily surrender to God and His revelation to truth, it is important to know that in every age the Spirit's power can bring supernatural evidences of God's presence.

❧ A PRAYER FOR TODAY ❧

I bow low in Your presence, Almighty God. In weakness or in strength, enable me to be a cup running over with Your indescribable power.

SPEAKING THROUGH A SINNER

These are the last words of David: "David, the son of Jesse, speaks.
David, the man to whom God gave such wonderful success;
David, the anointed of the God of Jacob; David,
sweet psalmist of Israel: the Spirit of the Lord spoke by me,
and his word was on my tongue." 2 Sam. 23:1, 2, TLB.

What a powerful testimony at the end of an anointed, Spirit-filled life! Yes, David had made his mistakes, and one of them was sung about from the hymnbook of Israel, Psalm 51. Nevertheless, the Holy Spirit always remained with David, and he was conscious that he had been used as a spokesperson for God.

If you have feared that the Holy Spirit will leave you because of your sin, the story of David is God's message of encouragement to you today. David's acts of adultery and murder were tragic and inexcusable, but his deep, sincere repentance revealed that he in no way had repulsed the Holy Spirit from his life. In fact, it is the Holy Spirit who draws sorrowful sinners to repentance and inspires them with new hope, no matter what they have done.

Just as God's words were on David's tongue, so can you and I, repentant sinners, still speak for God as we proclaim the revelation of truth and love that He gives us to share. As you pray and study the Bible, God may bring to your mind a message to communicate with an individual or group of people. Evil angels may try to convince you that you are unworthy to be a spokesperson for God. If this happens, remember David.

I visited Jack in a maximum security prison where he was serving 15 years for murder. He had become a born-again Christian, but many people wondered whether it would last when he was on the outside. After Jack's release, the Holy Spirit continued to move with great power in his life. The Word of God on Jack's tongue was used mightily to lead many to Jesus in the year or two he lived with his new wife before he died of cancer.

Some of God's most effective witnesses today are people who have come in contact with prison ministries while behind bars. Jesus not only came to set the captives free, but wants them to represent Him to those who need to hear the good news of the gospel.

❧ *A PRAYER FOR TODAY* ❧

Thank You for not giving up on me, Holy Spirit, even in the most difficult times. May Your Word, Lord, be on my tongue today. Hallelujah!

WELCOME, A GREAT PROPHET

*But as soon as I leave you, the Spirit of the Lord will carry you
away, who knows where, and when Ahab comes and can't find you,
he will kill me; yet I have been a true servant of the Lord all my life.
1 Kings 18:12, TLB.*

*H*ave you ever wished that you could fly away rather than face a
confrontation with evil? Obviously Obadiah assumed that the
Holy Spirit would take Elijah on a comfortable escape route
through the "friendly skies" rather than meet a king who wanted to kill him.

As I visited some of the luxury tourist hotels on the island of Maui, I noticed intriguing water slides that twisted and turned down through caves and beautiful gardens to the pool below. Israel, however, in the 50 years after King David, had descended not a water slide but a wickedness slide that had ended in a dust bowl of religious, political, and moral corruption.

But God loved Israel, as He does all sinners, so He chose to use a Spirit-filled prophet to bring them to their senses. Elijah had warned Ahab, and now more than 40 months later Elijah was back to break the drought by the mighty power of the Holy Spirit.

No, the Spirit did not take Elijah away as Obadiah had feared. Instead the Spirit led the prophet into the presence of the king, who immediately blamed Elijah for all the trouble. "Is that you, you troubler of Israel?"

Unfortunately but predictably, Spirit-filled Christians still face this same attitude today. On fire with the love of Jesus, a young mother returned home from the worship service. Her drug-addicted, physically abusive husband launched immediately into a tirade of accusation. "Your Christianity is breaking up our marriage. You're to blame for the trouble in this home."

Tanya knew that what he said was untrue and was able to confront the evil with the spirit of truth and discernment.

When Holy Spirit revival comes to a community, the effect is often so dramatic that opposition is immediately aroused. All the great revivals in British and early American history closed taverns, gambling halls, and houses of prostitution. But the revivals also emptied the law courts and filled the churches.

❧ *A PRAYER FOR TODAY* ❧

*Lord, it seems so natural to want the Spirit to take me away from trouble.
Today I ask for the strength to face the evil in me and around me,
and to stand firm for truth in the love of Jesus.*

WELCOME TO THE FIRE

Then the fire of the Lord fell and burned up the sacrifice, the wood,
the stones and the soil, and also licked up the water in the trench.
When all the people saw this, they fell prostrate and cried,
"The Lord—he is God! The Lord—he is God!" 1 Kings 18:38, 39, NIV.

*W*inter in many parts of the Northern Hemisphere during January draws people to the fire. A fire looks cheerful and bright; it warms and comforts; it makes food palatable; it eliminates the possibility of hypothermia. Fire also has the power to sterilize and destroy.

Elijah, filled with the Holy Spirit, called down the fire of God on the altar at Mount Carmel. Fire is one of the great symbols of the Holy Spirit. Jesus, looking forward to Pentecost, said, "I have come to bring fire on the earth, and how I wish it were already kindled!" (Luke 12:49, NIV). When Pentecost finally came, there were tongues of fire that burned so warmly that thousands were led to fall at the foot of the cross and cry out, "The Lord—He is God!"

When Samson was filled with the Spirit, the ropes that bound him were like flax burned in the fire. At Mount Carmel and on the day of Pentecost the fire of the Holy Spirit set thousands free from the bondage of false religion and human traditions. The ropes of sin were broken, and satanic forces were routed.

Many times people would ask Billy Bray why he leaped, danced, and shouted for joy in the Lord. "I was born in the fire and cannot live in the smoke," he would reply. "The devil would rather see us doubting than hear us shouting."

The fire of the Spirit burned so brightly in Billy that he was likened to a blazing candle. He did not want to be like a miner's safety lamp, used only at certain working times, nor like a church lamp, used only once or twice a week. Day and night he proclaimed with holy joy, "The Lord—He is God!"

A fire attracts attention. When you see something blazing brightly, you look to discover what is happening. "What is fire?" I asked my chemistry teacher years ago. "It's a change of state," he replied. So when Christians blaze with the fire that changes their lives, others will look and learn of God's love.

❧ *A PRAYER FOR TODAY* ❧

May the fire of Your Spirit burn the dust and stones in my life,
and enable me today to be a blazing witness for You, Lord.

January 30

A WELCOME VOICE

And after the earthquake, there was a fire, but the Lord was not in the fire. And after the fire, there was the sound of a gentle whisper. 1 Kings 19:12, TLB.

Sometimes the Holy Spirit is represented by an earthquake (Acts 4:31) and sometimes by fire (Acts 2:3); but in his time of deep depression Elijah needed, more than anything else, to hear the Spirit as a delicate whispering voice.

Elijah had run away after his triumph at Mount Carmel because he had apparently mistakenly concluded that Ahab and Jezebel would also be defeated and destroyed. But not so. Instead, they issued a death degree for him. Now in his depression and exhaustion he had escaped to Sinai and had hidden in misery, self pity, and suicidal despair.

In that state of mind a person does not need booming thunder, fierce fire, or violent wind. Elijah felt numb with emotional pain, and it was only a gentle, sweet voice that could speak to his heart. That was the voice of the Comforter, the Holy Spirit. He assured Elijah of continued ministry and ultimate victory, and in that moment of tender loving care Elijah the prophet was reborn.

Pastor Freeman had just finished a very successful series of evangelistic meetings in his church. More than 40 people had been baptized, and many conversions and rededications had taken place. Secretly, though, like Elijah, the pastor was now feeling very depressed. He had thought that the success of the meetings would have silenced his critics and eliminated the group of dissidents trying to take control of the church board. It was not so, however, and Pastor Freeman was thinking of resigning.

"What you need is a good rest," his wife told him. "You've worked seven days a week, 12 hours a day, for the past six weeks. Take some time now to enjoy some recreation, quiet walks, reading, prayer, and fun with the family. You'll soon feel much better."

She was right, and God did use this pastor mightily again after he had listened to the Spirit's "still small voice" or "gentle whisper."

❦ *A PRAYER FOR TODAY* ❦

Lord, open my ears to hear Your loving voice today. I thank You that You do not desert the discouraged, but surround them with Your arms of strength and turn them back to ministry and joy again.

SPEAKING THE TRUTH

Then Zedekiah the son of Chenaanah came near and struck Micaiah on the cheek and said, "How did the Spirit of the Lord pass from me to speak to you?" 1 Kings 22:24, NASB.

*I*sn't it easy to like people who always tell you the things you want to hear? Ahab had about 400 of these "yes men" whom he called prophets. They prophesied peace and safety, but sudden destruction was coming.

Micaiah was willing to speak the truth even in the face of unpopularity and imprisonment. Zedekiah, one of Ahab's prophets, slapped Micaiah on the face and questioned the Spirit who was in God's man. The false prophets were so deceived that they believed they possessed the Spirit of God and failed to recognize the lying spirit that was speaking through them.

Jody was a college student who had fallen in love with a handsome young man from a nearby city. He often arrived with beautiful gifts at the girls' dormitory and wanted to take her out to exciting and romantic places. There was a major problem, however. This young man did not share Jody's faith in God. In fact, he was not only an unbeliever but practiced a lifestyle that was totally different from this young lady's upbringing.

A number of Jody's friends encouraged her to marry Dave, telling her that she could change him and enjoy an exciting life with him. One or two others warned of consequences that could be filled with heartache and trouble.

As a young pastor I received a call from Jody about four years after she had married Dave. I hardly recognized her as the girl I had known at college. "I've aged 10 years," she told me. "Dave was in trouble with the law and with other women. He has left me now, and I can hardly support our 3-year-old twins. What can I do?"

I could have asked Jody about the false prophets who had encouraged her to marry Dave, but instead I turned her to the practical help of the Holy Spirit. He could not undo the past, but He did bring courage and hope for the future.

❧ *A PRAYER FOR TODAY* ❧

Father, I ask that You will lead me to friends and advisors who have a true spirit of discernment rather than to those who will always seek to please me with their opinions.

February 1

DOUBLE BLESSING

*When they had crossed, Elijah said to Elisha, "Tell me, what can I do
for you before I am taken from you?" "Let me inherit a double
portion of your spirit," Elisha replied. 2 Kings 2:9, NIV.*

A miracle worker, a mighty man of God, asks what he can do for you
before he leaves you to carry on in his place. What do you request?
Money, supernatural power, popularity? Solomon asked God for
wisdom and received it in a package deal with everything else he needed. But
why did Elisha ask for a double portion of the Holy Spirit? Why not 100
times the amount that had rested on Elijah?

Double portion did not mean twice as much, as if the Holy Spirit is given
in measurable doses. Rather, this request meant that Elisha was asking for the
right of a firstborn son (Deut. 21:17). He was asking for recognition that he
was to be Elijah's spiritual heir.

Of course, Elijah was not able to make the choice of his heir. Only God
had that power. So Elijah did not make any rash promises, but suggested a solution that would leave the outcome in God's hands. It is rare that an equally
great successor can follow exactly in the footsteps of a mighty man of God.
Usually God will have to begin a new work of the Spirit under different circumstances.

At the Moody Bible Institute in Chicago I looked at the life-size picture
of the evangelist Dwight L. Moody, whom the Lord used to bring Jesus to
millions. When Moody died, other men took his sermons and preached them
word for word. They spoke with equal eloquence and prayed for the Spirit to
fill them as He had filled Moody. Yet the results were never the same. God
did, however, have a man whom He used mightily in a different way—
Reuben Torrey, a scholar, writer, and evangelist who developed the great ministry of the Moody Bible Institute.

A new pastor cannot be a carbon copy of his much loved predecessor, but
the Holy Spirit gives him a unique ministry to bless his congregation.

❧ *A PRAYER FOR TODAY* ❧

*As Your child, Lord, and a joint-heir with Jesus, I claim a double portion
of Your Spirit right now. Fill me so that I may serve You
in the special way You have chosen for me.*

February 2

DOUBLE DIFFERENCE

When the young prophets of Jericho saw what had happened, they exclaimed, "The spirit of Elijah rests upon Elisha!" 2 Kings 2:15, TLB.

*I*n the state of Washington a widow who had just experienced the filling of the Holy Spirit in her life was amazed when some Christian friends recognized immediately what had happened to her. "You have the anointing of God on you," they told her as they all praised the Lord together.

Similarly, Elijah's students, not knowing where he was, discerned the Spirit so strongly in Elisha that they fell down before him under the influence of God's power.

Bible scholars state that Elisha's request was for a double portion "in the form of your spirit," and this request was granted when Elisha saw his master taken up in the chariot of fire. The young men from Prophecy College, Jericho, where Elijah had been the principal, recognized that it was actually the Holy Spirit who "rested," or "settled upon," Elisha as He had on the 70 elders in the time of Moses (Num. 11:25) and as He would on Jesus (Isa. 11:2).

Jesus promised His disciples that the Holy Spirit would also come upon them (Acts 1:8), and His pledge was dramatically fulfilled on the day of Pentecost. In every case in which the Holy Spirit comes upon a person, it is recognizable to others who have a spirit of discernment, as happened to the widow and her friends 20 centuries later in Washington.

As Elisha now wore the cloak of his glorified master, so Spirit-filled Christians today are covered by the righteousness of Jesus as they reveal the miracle-working power of their Master. That is why you need not be afraid to ask Jesus for a double portion of His Spirit today.

❧ A PRAYER FOR TODAY ❧

Give me joy today, gracious Father, by bringing me to the feet of someone in whose life the Spirit has made a double difference. Perhaps I will meet him or her in person, in a book, on the telephone, or in the media. Let me praise You for Your miraculous power in that life.

RUNNING AWAY

"Sir," they said, "just say the word and fifty of our best athletes
will search the wilderness for your master; perhaps the Spirit of the
Lord has left him on some mountain or in some ravine."
"No," Elisha said, "don't bother." 2 Kings 2:16, TLB.

*A*s soon as I'm 65 I'm out of here," the 60-something pastor exclaimed to some of his peers. "I'm going to retire, get away from ministry, and grow strawberries."

Perhaps the students from Prophecy College thought that Elijah had also gone to grow strawberries. Once before he had departed in depression and had ended up in a cave. So the young prophets suggested a rescue mission with 50 college athletes.

John Loughborough and John Andrews were young preachers who eventually became itinerant Adventist evangelists. By 1856 they had both become discouraged and had ended up in the little town of Waukon, Iowa. On December 9 Ellen White, who was not yet 30, received a vision that she must go and find those young "Elijahs." She saw that there was a spirit of witchcraft and divination at Waukon. "I call upon all who have the cause of God one particle at heart," she wrote, "to rise in the name of the Lord and put down the manifestations among them" *(Manuscript Releases,* vol. 11, p. 352).

When they finally reached Waukon, Ellen White and her party discovered Loughborough working as a carpenter. Reluctantly he went down to her sleigh, only to be greeted three times by the question "What doest thou here, Elijah?"

The young carpenter was soon convicted by the Holy Spirit and reentered the gospel ministry for a lifetime of distinguished service.

Where are you today? Have you slipped away from your ministry? You may be able to serve God growing strawberries or carpentering, but perhaps the Spirit is convincing you that you should be leading a small group or ministering as a full-time gospel worker, literature evangelist, medical missionary, teacher, or Community Services worker.

Praise God for the Spirit's rescue mission.

☘ *A PRAYER FOR TODAY* ☘

Thank You for always searching for me when in my own mind I've wandered
to Waukon and am not serving You as You know I can.
Today with joy I accept my ministry once again.

DIGGING TRENCHES

"But now bring me a musician." And it happened, when the musician played, that the hand of the Lord came upon him. And he said, "Thus says the Lord: 'Make this valley full of ditches.' For thus says the Lord: 'You shall not see wind, nor shall you see rain; yet that valley shall be filled with water, so that you, your cattle, and your animals may drink.'" 2 Kings 3:15-17, NKJV.

The hand of the Lord on Elisha represented the Holy Spirit coming upon him (Eze. 3:14; 8:3). In the midst of the music he prophesied concerning water—another symbol of the Spirit (John 7:38, 39). Wherever in a community pools of revival are found, we should dig trenches between them so that they can flow together as a great reservoir of Holy Spirit power available to supply those in desperate need of the water of life.

Ellen White's vision concerning the brethren in Waukon indicated that she was to dig a trench through which the Spirit could again pour into the lives of the discouraged workers in that town. The trench to Waukon was not easy to dig. But prayer and persistence made it possible. First the snow began to melt, making traveling by sleigh very difficult. Brother Hart, who owned the sleigh, said that it would be a miracle if they reached their destination that December. Then, in answer to prayer, snow began to fall—just enough to start the journey. Partly along the way a snowstorm struck, delaying the journey almost a week. Eventually Ellen White and her party reached the Mississippi River and were told that it was impossible to cross. A foot of water was flowing over the ice, and several teams had broken through. The drivers had barely escaped with their lives.

But the Holy Spirit had pointed the faithful "trench diggers" to Waukon. "Go forward, trusting Israel's God," Ellen White directed Brother Hart. What praise there was as they ascended the bank safely on the Iowa side!

Is the hand of the Holy Spirit upon you to dig a trench today so that water may flow into dry and discouraged lives? Then go forward in faith, joining small groups of praying people together into a congregational reservoir of love.

✎ A PRAYER FOR TODAY ✎

I'm thirsty again, Lord. I lift my cup up to You so that Your hand may open the spring of living water. May my cup overflow with blessing and love.

WELCOME HEALING

Then the prophet went down and walked back and forth in the house a few times; returning upstairs, he stretched himself again upon the child. This time the little boy sneezed seven times and opened his eyes! Then the prophet summoned Gehazi. "Call her!" he said. And when she came in, he said, "Here's your son!" 2 Kings 4:35, 36, TLB.

*I*t is surprising how often the Holy Spirit reveals His power in healing miracles. The birth of the Shunammite woman's son had been a miraculous event, but a few years later he wilted and died in the heat of the day. Now the Holy Spirit revealed His resurrection power and delivered the young man from premature death.

God also had an Elisha in the early Adventist movement, and the miraculous power of the Holy Spirit was revealed when two of the movement's most prominent young men wilted in the heat of ministry. After meeting John Loughborough soon after her arrival at Waukon, Ellen White attended an evening meeting that had been called especially for this occasion. At that meeting the power of the Holy Spirit fell on the whole company, and Ellen White received a vision from the Lord. It contained a message of healing. "Return unto me, and I will return unto thee, and heal all thy backslidings."

The result was as dramatic as seven sneezes from a dead boy. Confessions were made, and it was as if "the flood gates of heaven seemed suddenly opened," she reported. "I was prostrated by the power of God." The meeting continued until past midnight, and then resumed at 10:00 the next morning and continued until 5:00 p.m. The brethren and sisters at Waukon "labored for each other with zeal and with the power of God upon them" (*Life Sketches,* pp. 160, 161).

If your dreams of ministry have died in the heat of negative circumstances, take heart. In the power of the Spirit you can pick up your ministry again and see the miraculous take place. Spiritual gifts will also enable you to be a healer of other ministries, as you bring edification, exhortation, and comfort to workers who are in the forefront of the battle.

✎ *A Prayer for Today* ✎

When the sun seems hot, You are my shade, Lord. When life is gone, You are my resurrection. When my hopes crash, You untangle the mess and get me started again. Praise the Lord!

WHY THIS, LORD?

And Elisha sent a messenger unto him, saying,
Go and wash in Jordan seven times, and thy flesh shall come again to thee,
and thou shalt be clean. 2 Kings 5:10.

*D*o you feel a need for spiritual healing? If so, the Lord may give you some very unexpected instructions, just as He surprised Naaman with a strange formula for removing his leprosy.

This is the second time the number seven is mentioned in connection with Elisha's service for God. The young man had sneezed seven times, and now Naaman was to dip seven times into the Jordan River.

Although Naaman did not know it, seven is significant in the symbolism of the Spirit. For instance, a prophecy of the Holy Spirit upon Jesus emphasizes seven aspects of the Spirit's power. He is the Spirit of the Lord, wisdom, understanding, counsel, might, knowledge, and fear of the Lord (Isa. 11:2). When the Spirit of the Lord is poured out, it is upon seven specific groups of people: all flesh, sons, daughters, old men, young men, servants, and handmaids (Joel 2:28, 29). Five times in Revelation the Holy Spirit is represented by the number seven. Seven is a symbol of spiritual perfection, and this is certainly an important part of the Holy Spirit's unique representation of the character of the Father and the Son.

Naaman was annoyed by simple requirements that he did not understand, as we often can be when the Holy Spirit asks us to do something seemingly mundane or unusual. He led Mother Teresa to minister in Calcutta, not Croatia. He sent David Livingstone to Africa, not Aberdeen; Adoniram Judson to Burma, not Birmingham; James Hudson Taylor to China, not Africa.

To bring about your complete healing from the leprosy of sin, He may be asking you to do something much different from what you have ever imagined. "I've been asked to be the youth leader in my local church!" a man exclaimed. "I can't believe it! I wanted to be an elder." A few months later he rejoiced with some friends over the great changes this unexpected ministry had made in his life.

  ❧ *A PRAYER FOR TODAY* ❧

All right, Father, I will follow the leading of Your Spirit with gladness,
even though the direction You lead is not to the pleasant
places I would choose for myself.

Welcome Army

And Elisha prayed, "O Lord, open his eyes so he may see." Then the Lord opened the servant's eyes, and he looked and saw the hills full of horses and chariots of fire all around Elisha. 2 Kings 6:17, NIV.

You may know what it is like to feel alone while surrounded by opposing forces. At work or school—or even in your church or home—it may seem that the pressures of evil are overwhelming. Amid this tension you meet a Christian who calmly states, "Don't fear. Those who are with you are more than those who are with the enemy." You are tempted to think, *It's easy for this person, who is not experiencing what I am, to say this. He or she can have great faith, but what about me? How will I survive?*

Early one morning Elisha and his young servant found themselves surrounded by a great army with horses and chariots—the top military equipment of the time. Elisha had the spirit of discernment plus unwavering faith in God's power, so he did not need to see any sign or evidence of the presence of Yahweh Sabaoth—the Lord of the armies of heaven. But the prophet wanted his young friend to witness a sight he would never forget. As his eyes were opened so they could see beyond the natural to the supernatural, he caught a glimpse of the firepower of the great God of heaven. He saw the evidence of the Spirit of the Lord of hosts (Zech. 4:6).

Very often God will reveal miraculous evidence of His power to those whose faith is just beginning to grow or is not yet firmly established. This is why new Christians are usually able to tell remarkable stories of amazing answers to prayer. When, however, you have experienced many evidences of the Holy Spirit's leading and nurture in your life, you will be able, without any visible evidence, to assure others that "those who are with us are more than those who are with them."

A number of times in my life I have experienced what appeared to be direct angelic intervention. This really confirmed my belief in the presence of these supernatural agents of God, but I do not need that confirmation now in order to believe.

A Prayer for Today

Don't let me become overly impressed by visible numbers, Lord. Give me confidence in the unfailing superiority of Your power.

A NURTURING SPIRIT

*Then the Spirit came upon Amasai, chief of the captains, and he said:
"We are yours, O David; we are on your side, O son of Jesse!
Peace, peace to you, and peace to your helpers!
For your God helps you." So David received them,
and made them captains of the troop. 1 Chron. 12:18, NKJV.*

*A*ffirmation. We all like it when it genuinely expresses appreciation and support. As the Holy Spirit ministers comfort and nurture among the members of a small group, He often leads them to affirm each other and give assurance that, as prayer partners, they will stand by each other in the intensity of spiritual battle.

A young mother, whose positive self-image in Jesus had been almost obliterated by an abusive husband, found new hope as her small group told her how much she meant to each of them. Later she was able to affirm and encourage many others.

Pastor Rod (January 5) was greatly blessed in his ministry by the prayer partners who had become his supportive team. One Friday the pastor was particularly tired after a week that had been unbelievably busy. It seemed that there had been no time to think of a sermon for the worship service on Sabbath. Now on Friday evening Pastor Rod put his head in his hands and prayed as some tears fell on his open Bible, "Lord, what can I do? I'm too tired even to think."

At that moment his phone rang. "Please answer that for me," he called to his wife, Linda. "I just can't handle another problem."

But this was not a problem but a solution. "As we were praying together," a prayer partner who had been meeting with another of the prayer team informed Pastor Rod, "the Holy Spirit impressed me to call you and tell you that we love you. We're glad that you're our pastor. We'll have a team of 10 people praying for you tonight as you prepare your sermon."

The next morning as the pastor preached, there was unmistakable evidence that the Holy Spirit had anointed this servant of God and his message for the people.

☙ A PRAYER FOR TODAY ❧

*Is there someone I can affirm today, Lord? I'll do it as You have
encouraged me with Your unfailing support
and the assurance of salvation given me by Jesus.*

February 9

BUILDING IN THE SPIRIT

Then David gave his son Solomon the plans for the vestibule,
its houses, its treasuries, its upper chambers, its inner chambers, and
the place of the mercy seat; and the plans for all that he had by the
Spirit, of the courts of the house of the Lord, of all the chambers all
around, of the treasuries of the house of God, and of the treasuries
for the dedicated things. 1 Chron. 28:11, 12, NKJV.

*I*n the Old Testament the Holy Spirit gave detailed instructions for building the Temple. This structure and its ceremonies were to point forward to various phases of Jesus' ministry. In the New Testament the Holy Spirit gave all the vital information for building the church. The church was not to be a structure of stone and gold like the Temple, but a group of people who had been saved by Jesus' blood. They were to be bonded together with the mortar of love.

Both the Temple and the church were to glorify God and to serve as object lessons that the Holy Spirit could use to teach all nations the wonders of God's saving grace. But the Temple became a center of powerless traditionalism, and the institutional church became a series of brick, wood, and stone structures, replicating the ceremonialism of the Temple.

The Holy Spirit is, however, still giving building instructions for the true church. Even now He is gathering people together as they are filled with the rich treasures of God's grace.

Let me give you some of the Spirit's building instructions: Join together with other born-again Christians for prayer, breaking of bread, fellowship, and Bible study (Acts 2:42). As you meet, admonish one another with psalms, hymns, and spiritual songs (Eph. 5:19). Let everyone in the fellowship minister to each other as led by the Holy Spirit (1 Cor. 14:26).

Now you will begin to see the church grow. It will be a much more magnificent structure than the ancient Temple because it will be made up of living stones—people who are alive in Jesus. And you will be in the very place planned for you by the Holy Spirit.

❦ *A PRAYER FOR TODAY* ❧

Draw me into the beautiful fellowship of Your church, Father, and bind me
with the mortar of love to the other parts of this beautiful structure.

SEEK AND ALWAYS FIND

Then the Spirit of God came upon Azariah (son of Oded), and he went
out to meet King Asa as he was returning from the battle.
"Listen to me, Asa! Listen, armies of Judah and Benjamin!" he shouted.
"The Lord will stay with you as long as you stay with him!
Whenever you look for him, you will find him.
But if you forsake him, he will forsake you." 2 Chron. 15:1, 2, TLB.

*W*ill the Spirit ever leave you? No. But it is possible for you to leave the Spirit. If you go away from Him, He will soon seem to be far away from you.

"I don't feel close to God anymore," a friend confided.

"Remember," I replied, "that God hasn't moved. It is you who has wandered away. God is always in the same place."

It is not by our feet but by our affections that we slip away from God. Distance from God is not spacial but spiritual. It is not geographical but attitudinal. When the Holy Spirit calls us back to God, He asks us not to move our location, but to renew our total allegiance. The gulf between the "far country" and the Father's house can be bridged by one step of faith.

As the Spirit prophesied through Azariah, it is true that if you seek the Lord you will certainly find Him.

A young man who had brutally molested and murdered three children began to seek God shortly before his execution. A new light began to dawn in his mind, and in his last few hours of life he gave his testimony. "There is hope; there is peace," he said. "I find both in the Lord Jesus. Look to the Lord, and you will find peace."

People eagerly awaiting the young man's hanging were skeptical of his conversion, but the Spirit also led a thief on a cross next to Jesus to seek and find the promise of eternal hope.

It is remarkable how the Father accepts all who respond to the Holy Spirit's invitation to come back to God. People often will not accept someone who has treated them badly and then comes back because there is nowhere better to go. God, however, is not like that. He just opens His arms and says, "Come."

❧ *A PRAYER FOR TODAY* ❧

Lord, I give You permission to hold me close and never let me go.
To stay with You is even better than having to come back.
But I know that You always are ready to welcome a wanderer home.

HANDLING INSULTS

*Then Zedekiah the son of Chenaanah came near and struck Micaiah
on the cheek and said, "How did the Spirit of the Lord
pass from me to speak to you?" 2 Chron. 18:23, NASB.*

*I*t is not unusual for Spirit-filled people to find themselves, for no fault
of their own, the objects of insult, suspicion, and ridicule. Amid the
great controversy between good and evil, true Christians know what it
is to be the subjects of satanic attack. Jesus was taunted by people in high
places who wanted Him to perform miracles as some cheap exhibitionist
would do. He never succumbed to this temptation because the Holy Spirit
was ministering through Him to meet the needs of hurting humanity, not to
satisfy the curiosity of cantankerous people.

A young carpenter's work associates scoffed at him, "Why don't you pray
now? It might do some good and get you out of the problem you face."

A lady who had been used by God as His agent for many healing miracles was told when she became sick, "Why don't you heal yourself if you
have such amazing healing power?"

A pastor who became depressed was asked, "Why don't you practice
what you preach?"

If you have received such spiritual insults, it is important for you not to
react or become discouraged. Micaiah was thrown into prison and given the
bread and water "of affliction" (verse 26), but he was not deterred from his
Spirit-given conviction: "Whatever my God says, that I will speak" (verse 13,
NKJV).

The young carpenter's prayer did not solve his work problem at that time,
much to his scoffers' delight. It did, however, give him the wisdom to handle
the problem in a way that ultimately brought glory to God.

The sick lady herself was not healed, but she continued to help others in
spite of her own affliction.

If you are insulted and misunderstood today because of the Holy Spirit in
your life, go forward in faith, knowing that even though "some may love you;
some may hate you," you can "trust in God and do the right."

❧ *A PRAYER FOR TODAY* ❧

*Father, forgive those who scoff at my faith and the power of the Holy Spirit
in my life. Just let me somehow sow a seed of Your love in their hearts.*

February 12

WELCOME, SINGING SOLDIERS

Then the Spirit of the Lord came upon Jahaziel . . . , a Levite and descendant of Asaph, as he stood in the assembly. He said: "Listen, King Jehoshaphat and all who live in Judah and Jerusalem! This is what the Lord says to you: 'Do not be afraid or discouraged because of this vast army. For the battle is not yours, but God's.'" 2 Chron. 20:14, 15, NIV.

This chapter has become one of my favorites in the Old Testament. The Holy Spirit moved with such power upon the musicians that the choir went out praising God for victory even before the battle started.

Can you sing in the face of impending trouble? Do you praise God even as the enemy advances? It is not natural; it is supernatural. It is the work of the Holy Spirit to make this possible as He convinces you that the battle is not yours but the Lord's.

If you lose your job, get a serious illness, or attend a funeral for one of your closest relatives or friends, you do not usually sing the "Hallelujah Chorus" or give a vigorous rendition of the doxology. But the Holy Spirit's message is sure: "Believe His prophets and you shall prosper." "Stand still and see the salvation of the Lord."

When Corrie ten Boom and her sister Betsie arrived at the dreaded concentration camp for women at Ravensbruck, it seemed that they had entered the cruelest place on earth. The Nazis had incarcerated these Dutch ladies for aiding Jews in Haarlem. Sitting outside in the sleet and rain, lying in lice-infested beds, stripped naked before leering male guards, these two ladies of faith would quietly sing and praise the Lord. One of their favorite gospel songs was "Lead, kindly light, amid th' encircling gloom. . . . I do not ask to see the distant scene, One step's enough for me." Eventually Betsie quietly joined the more than 95,000 women who died at Ravensbruck, but Corrie was miraculously released to go and witness around the world.

❧ *A PRAYER FOR TODAY* ❧

Lord, with the help of Your Spirit I sing a song of praise in the midst of the chaos and calamities of life, knowing that the battle is in Your hands.

OBEYING THE SPIRIT

Then the Spirit of God came upon Zechariah the son of Jehoiada the
priest, who stood above the people, and said to them, "Thus says God:
'Why do you transgress the commandments of the Lord,
so that you cannot prosper? Because you have forsaken the Lord,
He also has forsaken you.'" 2 Chron. 24:20, NKJV.

A few days before Betsie ten Boom died in the Ravensbruck concentration camp near the end of World War II, she spoke softly to her sister Corrie, telling her of a vision that God had given her in the night. It was pitch dark in Barracks 28, where 700 women tried to sleep on lice-infested bunks. Betsie was weak and frail as she told Corrie that, after the war, she must return to Germany and tell the people that the Holy Spirit would fill their hearts with God's love.

"The Germans are the most wounded of all the people in the world," Betsie whispered. "Think of the young girl guard who swore in such filthy language yesterday. She was only 17 or 18 years old, but did you see how she was beating that poor old woman with the whip? What a job there is to do after the war!" Corrie had no desire to return to Germany, but wanted to go back to her quiet job as a watchmaker in Holland.

When Corrie realized that God had a worldwide ministry for her, she thought *I will go anywhere but Germany.* After about 10 months visiting and speaking for Jesus in America, Corrie felt the hand of God on her, calling her specifically to Germany. Soon she realized that her attitude toward Germany was one of disobedience to God. Listen to Corrie explain her decision: "F. B. Meyer said, 'God does not fill with His Holy Spirit those who believe in the fullness of the Spirit or those who desire Him, but only those who obey Him.' More than anything I desired to be filled with God's Spirit. I knew I had no choice but to go to Germany" *(Tramp for the Lord,* pp. 40, 46).

Perhaps, like Corrie, you have been resisting a ministry that God has placed before you. Today, in the power of the Spirit, you can answer the call.

❧ *A PRAYER FOR TODAY* ☙

Father, I know that I received Your Spirit at conversion, but I pray
that no act of deliberate disobedience
will hinder me from receiving Your fullness today.

THE GOOD SPIRIT

You gave your good Spirit to instruct them.
You did not withhold your manna from their mouths,
and you gave them water for their thirst. Neh. 9:20, NIV.

*I*n the midst of a great revival, people often recognize the character of the Holy Spirit. Would you like to "stand up and bless the Lord" (Neh. 9:5) today? Experiencing the mighty moving of the Holy Spirit in revival, as the people did in chapter 8 of Nehemiah, you review God's past actions in your life and acknowledge that God's Spirit is good. He is the Spirit of love, acceptance, and forgiveness.

Corrie ten Boom often thought back over the horrors of Ravensbruck and realized that it was hard to find anywhere in her heart the true Christian attitude for the former Nazis that would reveal through her the Spirit's goodness. Where was love, acceptance, and forgiveness in a horror camp where allegedly more than 95,000 women died? How could she ever forget the horrible cruelty of the guards and the smoke constantly coming from the chimney of the crematorium?

Then in 1947 Corrie was speaking in a church in Munich, and when the meeting was over she saw one of the most cruel male guards of Ravensbruck coming forward to speak to her. He had his hand outstretched. "I have become a Christian," he explained. "I know that God has forgiven me for the cruel things I did, but I would like to hear it from your lips as well. Fräulein, will you forgive me?"

A conflict raged in Corrie's heart. The good Spirit of God urged her to forgive. The spirit of bitterness and coldness urged her to turn away. *Jesus, help me. I can lift my hand. I can do that much.*

As their hands met it was as if warmth and healing broke forth with tears and joy. "I forgive you, brother, with all my heart." Later Corrie testified that "it was the power of the Holy Spirit" who had poured the love of God into her heart that day. Once again the "good Spirit" had triumphed *(Tramp for the Lord,* pp. 56, 57).

❧ *A PRAYER FOR TODAY* ❧

Good Spirit, I am not like You by nature but want to be instructed in Your beautiful characteristics of forgiveness and true love.

WELCOME, ADMONITION

Yet for many years You had patience with them, and testified against them by Your Spirit in Your prophets. Yet they would not listen; therefore You gave them into the hand of the peoples of the lands. Neh. 9:30, NKJV.

I just can't understand those people in Bible times," Charlie exclaimed. "They had so much warning from God, yet they still messed things up and ended in trouble."

"I don't think we're any better," Doris replied. "Look at the mistakes we make, and we've been brought up in the church and have learned all the doctrines and heard the Bible stories since cradle roll."

Bible knowledge and information have little value unless one makes a definite commitment to God. That is why the Holy Spirit speaks to the heart. Even though He is concerned that we learn the great truths and teachings of the Bible, He is much more concerned that we come every day into a heart relationship with God. When a crisis arrives in our life, the Holy Spirit does not seek to activate proof texts for abstract doctrines, but He brings to our minds a picture of Jesus and His great love for us and the consequences of hurting Him.

A lady had an urge to shoplift even though she did not have financial problems and could have easily paid for the things she wanted. Often when she was tempted to slip something into her bag, she would remember, "Thou shalt not steal," but it did not make any difference. One day she allowed the Holy Spirit to introduce her to Jesus, and she came to love and trust Him. Christian friends admonished her, not with the threats she had heard a thousand times but with a beautiful picture of the cross of Calvary. Today she is so honest that she could be trusted with the crown jewels of England.

To be part of ancient Israel or modern Christianity was or is in itself no guarantee of deliverance from evil. But to allow the Holy Spirit to testify of God's great love is the strongest motivation for good that a mind can ever grasp.

❧ A PRAYER FOR TODAY ❧

Open my eyes, Lord, to see beyond the rules of a religious system to a personal relationship with You.

WELCOME, BEAUTY

By His Spirit He adorned the heavens;
His hand pierced the fleeing serpent. Job 26:13, NKJV.

*D*o you enjoy beauty? Some people travel all around the planet as they search for the loveliest place on earth, while others find it near to home. The Holy Spirit loves beauty, and as the agent of power in the Trinity Creation team, He made the breathtaking adornment of the heavens and the earth. He garnished the Creation so that it glistened in glorious color and pleasantness to the human eye.

Just as the Hebrew bride and groom adorned themselves with ornaments and jewels, so the Holy Spirit beautifies God's people with the wonderful "robe of righteousness" (Isa. 61:10). The anointing of the Spirit of God brings "beauty for ashes" and "the garment of praise for the spirit of heaviness" (Isa. 61:3).

No wonder God's redeemed people shout for joy and are full of praise—all the ugliness of sin is covered, just as the chaos at the beginning of Creation was replaced by the adorning work of the Holy Spirit. And it was then that "the sons of God shouted for joy" (Job 38:7). If you have looked out on breathtaking beauty, you may have experienced the overwhelming urge to shout for joy. Mountains, lakes, forests, autumn leaves, sunset, tropical lagoon, flowers, birds—hallelujah! What would you add to that list? Think about it, and shout hallelujah again.

The Bible not only begins but also ends with the Holy Spirit's adorning work. The New Jerusalem descends "as a bride adorned for her husband" (Rev. 21:2). The Holy Spirit shows God's people the incredible beauty of the Holy City at the center of the new earth (Rev. 21:10). This earth He re-creates, along with the new heavens, in which will dwell eternal righteousness (2 Peter 3:13). In the sight of the New Jerusalem, once again there is joy in God's glorious adorning of His creation (Isa. 65:18).

Trust Him today. He understands our brokenness and strife and can make our lives beautiful.

❦ *A Prayer for Today* ❦

Holy Spirit, I'm open to Your work of creating true beauty.
May the beauty of Jesus be seen in me—radiant and joyful.

WELCOME, NEW CREATION

The Spirit of God has made me, and the breath of the Almighty
gives me life. Job 33:4, NKJV.

Why is it so important to believe that God created the world?" the university student asked. "We know that the earth is here and the universe is out there, and although I do not understand the biblical record of Creation, I do believe that God set everything in motion so that it could gradually evolve."

This theistic evolutionary approach is quite common and is sometimes thought of as a compromise between Creation and the theory of evolution. The question for today, though, is how does this idea affect your possibility of vibrant Christian living now and in the future?

Not only does Scripture recognize the power of the Holy Spirit as He activated in the beginning that which the Father had designed and Jesus had made (Gen. 1:2, 26; Heb. 1:1-3), but salvation itself involves the definite creative power of the Trinity. In Christ we are a new creation (2 Cor. 5:17). Our new spiritual being is "created in righteousness and true holiness" (Eph. 4:24). This new life is the work of the Holy Spirit in resurrection power (Rom. 8:11). He, through Jesus, is able to create a new heart in born-again Christians (Eze. 36:26, 27), and this creation enables them to be involved in a lifestyle of good works (Eph. 2:10).

Now it is easy to see why evil forces do not want you to have complete faith in God's creative power. They want to rob you of the assurance that you can have of salvation and victorious living.

God's creative power is also displayed in His future actions and is the foundation of your future destiny. He creates a new heavens, a new earth, and a new Jerusalem (Isa. 65:17, 18; 2 Peter 3:13; Rev. 21:1). The forces of evil do not want you to believe in God's future creative power because they are committed to giving you the impression that this life is all you have. Today, praise the Lord, you can claim the amazing benefits of the Holy Spirit's past, present, and future creative power. Your destiny is with the Creator God.

✦ *A PRAYER FOR TODAY* ✦

Holy Spirit, I now open my heart to Your creative power. Make me new,
make me whole, through the blood of Jesus,
which guarantees forgiveness and eternal life.

February 18

TRULY ALIVE

If He should set His heart on it, if He should gather to Himself
His Spirit and His breath, all flesh would perish together,
and man would return to dust. Job 34:14, 15, NKJV.

*H*ave you ever felt as if you were out of breath? If your breath is taken away from you even for a short time, your physical life is gone. When the Holy Spirit is taken away, spiritual life dies, because the Holy Spirit is the Spirit of life in Jesus Christ and His righteousness (Rom. 8:2, 10). Without Him Christianity and the church are dead.

One of the most widely read Christian authors today, almost 80 years after his death, is Oswald Chambers. I regularly gain new blessings from his best-selling devotional *My Utmost for His Highest.* Oswald Chambers, however, did not always have the dynamic, thought-provoking Spirit-life found in that volume. As a young man he had transferred from the University of Edinburgh to Dunoon Bible Training College, and it was at that institution, in the midst of spiritual turmoil, that a hungering and thirsting for the complete filling of the Holy Spirit was created in him.

On one occasion, as he was working as a tutor in philosophy at the college, Chambers heard F. B. Meyer speak about the baptism of the Holy Spirit. Still Chambers did not become conscious of this wonderful experience happening in his life. "The Bible was the dullest, most uninteresting book in existence, and the sense of depravity, the vileness and bad motiveness of my nature was terrific. I see now that God was taking me by the light of the Holy Spirit and His Word through every ramification of my being. I knew no one who had what I wanted; in fact, I did not know what I did want. But I knew if what I had was all the Christianity there was, the thing was a fraud" (cited by V. Raymond Edman, *They Found the Secret,* p. 33).

As Oswald Chambers said, without the Holy Spirit Christianity is a fraud, but with true Spirit-life it is the most dynamic force in the world.

❧ *A PRAYER FOR TODAY* ❧

Breathe on me, Holy Breath of God. Fill me with new life.
Holy Spirit of life, enable me today to live in true righteousness and joy.

DO NOT LET HIM GO

Do not cast me away from Your presence,
and do not take Your Holy Spirit from me. Ps. 51:11, NKJV.

O nce you know what it means to be alive in the Holy Spirit and develop a friendship with Him, there is no way you would want to
lose that fellowship and life. Of course, God will never take His
Holy Spirit away from any person, although a person may take herself or
himself away from the Holy Spirit.

It is possible to grieve the Spirit (Eph. 4:30) or to quench the Spirit
(1 Thess. 5:19). David no doubt vividly remembered the tragic consequences
of Saul's turning away from the Holy Spirit. In the Old Testament we find the
Holy Spirit coming upon individuals, anointing them, clothing them, and
guiding them. David had sinned in a way that brought terrible dishonor to
God, but he did not want the Holy Spirit taken away from him; and God never
removed His Spirit from clothing the repentant king.

Young Dunoon college tutor Oswald Chambers had not yet tasted life in
the Holy Spirit as King David had, but somehow Chambers realized that he
needed true spiritual life more than anything else. He began to claim the
promise of Luke 11:13 and was convinced that he needed to testify that he
was praying for the Holy Spirit.

When the opportunity finally came, Oswald Chambers gave his testimony
at an aftermeeting during a mission in Dunoon. The people sang the prayer,
"Touch Me Again, Lord," and Chambers knew emphatically that his time had
come. He rejoiced in receiving the awareness of the Holy Spirit in his life.
Looking back later on the transition, he said: "If the four previous years had
been hell on earth, these five years have truly been heaven on earth. Glory be
to God, the last aching abyss of the human heart is filled to overflowing with
the love of God. Love is the beginning, love is the middle, love is the end.
After He comes in, all you see is 'Jesus only, Jesus ever.'" Little wonder that
king David did not want to lose the Spirit.

❦ A PRAYER FOR TODAY ❧

Praise You, heavenly Father, for life in the Spirit.
I never want to lose that life or treat it lightly in any way.

February 20

WELCOME, GENEROUS SPIRIT

*Restore to me the joy of Your salvation, and uphold me with
Your generous Spirit. Ps. 51:12, NKJV.*

*I*t is easy to like generous people. Isn't it exciting to find out that the
Holy Spirit is generous? That is true because every person in the Trinity
is generous—not mean, miserable, or cheap. King David had lost the
assurance of salvation and the joy of the Holy Spirit's witness (Rom. 8:16).
He knew, however, that with forgiveness would come a bountiful, generous,
overflowing outpouring of the Holy Spirit that would result in singing, praise,
and the spiritual gifts necessary to lead others to conversion (Ps. 51:13-15).

A few years ago I sat beside Egyptian troops who were guarding the Suez
Canal. It was strange to see huge ships appearing to sail through the desert
sands. More than 60 years earlier Oswald Chambers, who had begun teaching at Dunoon Bible Training College in 1911, was appointed by the YMCA,
in July 1915, to spiritual service for the British troops at the Suez Canal.

After Chambers had been filled with the Holy Spirit at Dunoon, he had written: "When you know what God has done for you, the power and the tyranny of
sin is gone and the radiant unspeakable emancipation of the indwelling Christ is
come, and when you see men and women who should be princes and princesses
with God bound up by the show of things—oh, you begin to understand what the
apostle meant when he said he wished himself accursed from Christ that men
might be saved" *(They Found the Secret,* pp. 34, 35).

In fulfillment of Luke 11:13 Oswald Chambers had received the fullness
of the generous Spirit and now, at Zeitoun, by the Suez, he was used in the
same generous way to bring sinners to repentance and conversion. And it was
there at Zeitoun, in November 1917, that the breath of life left this man who,
although he was only in his 40s, would be a powerful witness for God's generous Spirit through his writings even at the end of the twentieth century.

❧ *A PRAYER FOR TODAY* ❧

*Lord, as Oswald Chambers once prayed, in simple dependence on
Your Holy Spirit indwelling me and uniting me with Your nature,
I look to You. Cause me to be all You would have me to be.
Generous Spirit, help me also be a generous Christian.*

February 21

CREATING NEW PARTS

*You send forth Your Spirit, they are created; and You renew
the face of the earth. Ps. 104:30, NKJV.*

Our God states that no one else in the universe is like Him. He has powers that no other beings possess (Isa. 45:9-11). God's creative power, which He exercises through the Holy Spirit, is unique, and the Bible keeps emphasizing it because of its incredible importance, not only in our origin but also in our present life and future destiny.

Divine healing is a very clear example of the Holy Spirit's creative work. No satanic force or human medicine can re-create in living form a diseased or disabled body part. People sometimes attribute healing miracles to Satan, and while it is true that he may cause pain and then take it away, he certainly cannot produce a new living part or organ of the human body.

Earnest Minns, a dedicated lay leader who later became my father-in-law, entered a hospital in 1951, and during the course of an operation it was discovered that he had terminal, inoperable cancer of the liver. The surgeon sewed him up and gave him just a few months to live. After a camp meeting Sabbath of prayer and fasting, Mr. Minns was immediately and totally healed. Surgeons who later examined him stated that he, miraculously, now possessed the healthy liver of a young man.

Only God can perform an act like that. It was not the psychological removal of some abstract pain or some cheap trickery, but an undeniable demonstration of the Holy Spirit's application of God's creative power. That miracle liver functioned healthily and normally for 35 more years, until Mr. Minns died of other causes.

No satanic power or scientific genius can do what your God can do. He is the Spirit of life—your life today and eternally. Look at the evidences of God's creative power around you and in you, and praise Him now. Allow Him to work creatively in situations in which there seems to be no human solution. You will be surprised at the results!

❧ A PRAYER FOR TODAY ❧

*My Father and God, I rejoice in the works of Your hand. Thank You
that my existence is not an accident or my future an eternal
nothingness. With You there is life and healing power.*

February 22

REPLACING REBELLION

They angered Him also at the waters of strife, so that it went ill with Moses on account of them; because they rebelled against His Spirit, so that he spoke rashly with his lips. Ps. 106:32, 33, NKJV.

When church members resist the Holy Spirit and allow a spirit of criticism and negativeness to control their lives, the results can be very devastating for a good pastor. Many pastors, like Moses, have been pushed into destructive behavior because of the resistance to true spirituality that moves with subtle militancy through some congregations.

Moses was not excused because of the Israelites' rebellion. Neither can we today excuse a pastor who reacts in an unchristian way. It is a tragedy, however, when in both church members and church pastor the powers of evil supersede the Spirit of Jesus.

Right in your church family you can be an agent of positive change today through the Holy Spirit's power. Begin by coming to God personally in total surrender to Jesus. Ask the Holy Spirit to reveal any problem or attitude that needs to be dealt with in your life and to give you complete victory even if you do not understand the circumstances that originally initiated your negative attitude. As the love of Jesus begins to pour into your heart by the Holy Spirit (Rom. 5:5), ask God to reveal to you whom you should call to join you in a prayer team. You may be surprised whom the Lord will suggest.

Make an appointment to meet with this prayer team before the week is ended, and come together in surrender, confession, and repentance. If your pastor is not part of this team, call him or her and arrange a time to gather around the pastor, laying on hands and allowing the Holy Spirit to move in a mighty way.

You may see resistance among some church members, because the enemy of souls wants to fuel the fires of rebellion, but you will also discover you and your pastor moving into the promised land of miraculous Spirit-filled ministry in your congregation and community.

☙ A PRAYER FOR TODAY ☙

Lord, I'm opening my heart to You for the elimination of any rebellion, resistance to Your Spirit, or rejection of Your pastors and church leaders that may have been festering in my life.

February 23

EVEN ON DEATH ROW

Where can I go from Your Spirit? Or where can I flee from Your presence? If I ascend into heaven, You are there; if I make my bed in hell, behold, You are there. Ps. 139:7, 8, NKJV.

Years ago I was told that if you go to certain places the angels will wait outside, and you will be on your own. Not so with the Holy Spirit. Even in the lowest hellhole on earth He will be there ready to hear the slightest hint of a prayer. He is not restricted by walls, international boundaries, glass or steel barriers, or sin- and crime-infested environments.

At a seminar on the Holy Spirit, I listened to Sondra Brewer tell a tragic but triumphant story. When Sondra and her husband, Spencer, took a new step forward in the Christian faith, they did not realize what hellish attacks from the enemy lay ahead for them. The greatest tragedy came a few years later when one of their sons, Dennis, was involved in a scuffle with a police officer and shot him with his own gun.

After the officer's killing, Dennis had run away in fear and had taken a hostage, with whom he held off police during a nightlong siege. Many times through the night Sondra had knelt down and prayed on the phone with her son. After the arrest a pastor had given Dennis a Bible, which he began to read, along with other Christian literature.

Dennis was convicted of first-degree murder and sentenced to death. Would the Holy Spirit be present with him on death row in San Quentin prison? Was there any hope for the more than 300 men waiting for the fateful day when they would face the executioner?

Once on death row, Dennis realized that God had a special ministry for him, and even in that unlikely place the Spirit led men into small group Bible studies. "'I am with you always' is my favorite verse of Scripture," Sondra told me recently. "I know that we can always believe in the presence of God to hear and answer our prayers—even in San Quentin."

You can be sure today that you are never more than a prayer away from the Holy Spirit.

❧ A PRAYER FOR TODAY ❧

Thank You, Lord, for the assurance of Your ever-present availability. I fellowship with You now because You are an unfailing friend.

THE OTHER PRISONER

*If I take the wings of the morning, and dwell in the uttermost parts
of the sea, even there Your hand shall lead me,
and Your right hand shall hold me. Ps. 139:9, 10, NKJV.*

Sondra Brewer's visits to her son on death row in San Quentin led her to learn the tragic story of the lives of many of the more than 300 men awaiting execution. Some had been there almost 10 years. Others were new. But most of them had someone outside—a mother or father, a wife or child—who was hurting deeply. Not only in the prison but on the streets and in the ghettos people needed to know that God's hand can hold and lead them.

Do you remember what it was like to hold the hand of someone you trusted when you were very young? It was warm and reassuring. It was a source of strength and courage. That is why the Bible uses God's hand as one of the most comforting symbols of the Holy Spirit (Eze. 3:14; 8:3).

When Sondra and her husband, Spencer, visit Dennis in San Quentin, they have to talk to him by phone through a panel of glass. They cannot touch him, but the Holy Spirit does. He is holding and leading Dennis with His right hand. "For as many as are led by the Spirit of God they are the sons of God" (Rom. 8:14).

As the Spirit moved on Sondra's heart she was convicted to begin a ministry for the hurting families of the prisoners on death row. The families are prisoners also—prisoners of circumstances and tragedy. So this ministry, called The Other Prisoner, reaches out its hand to the people who are waiting and wondering about a loved one on death row. Some people feel God's hand in small groups, in support at court trials, in personal prayer, visitation, or telephone calls. Many have said, "I could not have carried on without this help. It has meant so much to me to know that there are friends who care."

Yes, you too can trust God's hand to hold you and lead you always in the presence of the Holy Spirit.

There is heartening assurance in the grip of a special friend's hand. To hold the hand of someone you love means that you are near and dear to each other. That's what God's love is like.

❧ *A PRAYER FOR TODAY* ❧

*I'm reaching out to You today, Lord. I'm grateful for
Your strong hand and Your gentle touch.*

WELCOME, LIGHT

*If I say, "Surely the darkness shall fall on me," even the night shall be
light about me; indeed, the darkness shall not hide from You,
but the night shines as the day; the darkness and the
light are both alike to You. Ps. 139:11, 12, NKJV.*

The young lady expressed her innermost fears as she visited her psychologist. "I fear my shadow. I fear it most of all at night when it turns everything to darkness."

Only in God's strength can any person walk through the valley of the shadow of death and yet fear no evil.

As I listened to Sondra Brewer tell her experience during a testimony time at a seminar on prayer and the Holy Spirit that I was teaching in California, I detected a note of fear and tiredness in her voice. "About a week ago another prisoner was executed in San Quentin," she explained sadly. "My son had ministered to him, and I had talked and prayed with him, yet it has really affected me, because his death in the gas chamber was a long and painful process."

Dennis had been six years in the valley of the shadow on death row, and often Sondra had to remind herself that darkness and light are both alike to the Holy Spirit. "For the past few nights I have not slept for more than a half hour," she said as she came forward for anointing and healing prayer. Tom, Carolyn, Janet, Doris, and others gathered around and laid hands on Sondra as we earnestly prayed and anointed her with olive oil.

Next morning at the seminar Sondra was very excited as she shared with the group what had happened. "Last night I slept for more than three hours. I had a wonderful assurance that the darkness had not hidden me from God and that He has given me light and peace." Since then Sondra's sleep has returned completely to normal, and so has the sleep of many of the "other prisoners" to whom the Holy Spirit ministers through Sondra and her friends. The Holy Spirit transforms the darkness of long, lonely nights into the shining brightness of God's love.

❦ *A PRAYER FOR TODAY* ❦

*Lord, I come to You today with inexpressible relief as You illuminate everything
around me with the soft, clarifying light of Your Spirit's presence.*

GOOD SPIRIT

Teach me to do Your will, for You are my God; Your Spirit is good.
Lead me in the land of uprightness. Ps. 143:10, NKJV.

Not only is God's Spirit generous (Ps. 51:12), but He is also good. Of course, that is just what we would expect, because the Father and the Son are good, and it is the goodness of God that leads sinners to repentance (Rom. 2:4). Repentance is one of the most important gifts from God (Acts 5:31), and it is the good Spirit who delivers the gift beautifully wrapped in acceptance and forgiveness.

When Sarah was very young her parents, she claims, involved her in satanism and ritual abuse. Body scars and other objective evidence seem to substantiate her memories of bad spirits leading deceived people into degradation and despair. Sarah says that she was forced to watch human sacrifice, was involved in sexual rituals with adults, and was buried alive with only a small tube through which to breathe. As she grew into an adult, memories of the actions of evil spirits almost destroyed Sarah's sanity. They affected her health and destroyed her marriage.

But God's good Spirit was also working with Sarah. Christian friends surrounded her with prayer, and a Christian counselor helped her work through the painful memories. "I know God's Spirit is helping me and blessing me in many wonderful ways," Sarah told me. "I'm feeling much better, and I'm going to take a new name and make a new start as God continues His healing in my life."

You may not have been damaged as deeply as Sarah, but all of us have been hurt by sin and its subtle trickery. While satanic forces concentrate on oppression, harassment, and accusation, God's good Spirit repeatedly makes available the love, acceptance, and forgiveness that enable us to rise above negative circumstances and unhappy memories so that we can really flourish as fully functional Christians.

Rejoice in the presence of the good Spirit today. You can be happy and have absolute trust in God's leading. He can bring good out of the most difficult circumstances.

❧ *A PRAYER FOR TODAY* ❧

Father, You know how much all people need someone who is totally
dependable and uncompromisingly good, and I accept You today
as the One who meets the criteria of an unfailing friend.

WELCOME, TRUE SPIRIT

Turn at my reproof; surely I will pour out my spirit on you; I will make my words known to you. Prov. 1:23, NKJV.

Wisdom promises to pour out her spirit, and it is the Holy Spirit—the Spirit of wisdom—who opens minds and hearts to understandings that form the basis of good decisions and right actions.

"I have made a lot of poor choices and have done some very stupid things," the businessman admitted as his empire began to crumble around him. "I made a crazy mistake," the teenager acknowledged as she left the abortion clinic. "I can't believe how foolish I was," the young man whispered from his hospital bed after wrecking the car he had driven while under the influence of alcohol.

While the Holy Spirit does not make a person 100 percent infallible, He does enable the people He fills to avoid many of the tragic pitfalls that have ruined countless lives.

First, the Holy Spirit leads people to be open to God's will. This attitude of submission to God causes a person to look at a situation from God's perspective—a spiritual perspective, an eternal perspective.

Second, Spirit-filled people surround each situation with a lot of prayer. This gives time to look at all the implications involved rather than making a poorly thought-through, hasty decision.

Third, Spirit-filled people know what it is to have a small group of nurturing friends whose counsel they trust and respect. They ask for and carefully weigh the advice of these spiritually gifted people.

Fourth, the Holy Spirit combines truth and encouragement. He not only inspires you to take the right road, but also gives you a map so that you are aware of the intersections and detours.

As I review some of my own painful mistakes, I can see that I neglected one or more of these four steps. When, however, as Spirit-filled Christians we have met all the conditions of spiritual wisdom and then things still go wrong, we are not hurt by self-recrimination but can move ahead in faith to our next venture with God.

✥ A PRAYER FOR TODAY ✥

Shake me out of my self-confidence, Lord, and open my eyes to see with the clear perception of Your Spirit.

THE SEVENFOLD SPIRIT

*The Spirit of the Lord will rest on him—the Spirit of wisdom and of
understanding, the Spirit of counsel and of power, the Spirit of
knowledge and of the fear of the Lord. Isa. 11:2, NIV.*

*F*or the first time in Scripture Jesus and the Holy Spirit are shown to
be the team that will conquer evil and exalt righteousness. Like the
seven-branched Jewish menorah, these seven descriptive terms reveal the brilliant character of the Holy Spirit's ministry in the life of Jesus and
His followers.

The Holy Spirit is the Spirit of the Lord, who draws people to glorify
God. He is the Spirit of wisdom, who enables the people He fills to make
good decisions. He leads them to discern between right and wrong, so He is
the Spirit of understanding. He is the Counselor, the Comforter, who guides
God's people through the most difficult problems. As the Spirit of might He
gives miracle-working power and also leads into all truth as the Spirit of
knowledge.

The Holy Spirit brings deep respect and devotion to God, so He is the
Spirit of reverence or piety, as the ancient Jewish scholars and the Latin
scholar Jerome translated this phrase. On the basis of this description the
Holy Spirit is spoken of in Revelation as the seven Spirits of God, not because
He is more than one but because of the sevenfold characteristics of His won-
derful ministry.

Are you walking in the seven-lux brilliance of the Holy Spirit's life as
Jesus did, or are you just looking at the light?

Peter Hamilton, the teenage son of Tom and Carolyn, explained to his
academy teacher the difference between looking at the light and being in the
light. He took a flashlight to school and shone the bright beam onto the ceiling of his teacher's darkened office. "You can see the light very clearly," Peter
explained, "but you are not yet in the light until you put at least your finger
in front of the light bulb. Now, even though it may be just the tip of your fin-
gernail, you are in the light."

❧ *A Prayer for Today* ❧

*Father, I'm eager for the Holy Spirit not only to shine around me today but
also into me and through me in the sevenfold brightness of Jesus' love.*

PLANNING WITH THE SPIRIT

"Woe to the obstinate children," declares the Lord, "to those who carry out plans that are not mine, forming an alliance, but not by my Spirit, heaping sin upon sin." Isa. 30:1, NIV.

The addition of sin to sin multiplies trouble and brings division between families, friends, congregations, and communities. On the other hand, to plan with the Holy Spirit subtracts the devil's devious ways from any situation and guarantees the sum total of God's bountiful blessings.

A plan is a pattern of action that is worked out beforehand. When I was a teenager, I became an apprentice builder and had to learn how to draw and read house plans. On a scale of one inch to one foot all the details of the future structure were carefully worked out on paper. Copies of the paper—usually called blueprints—were taken to the job, and preplanned actions were precisely followed so that eventually a lovely house was built.

Without plans, life operates on a day-to-day basis, and very little of significance can be achieved. No structure, program, or event of any substance can be built without plans, because that which is above is dependent on the construction or preparation that is below it. As it has been said: "To fail to plan is to plan to fail."

Planning with the Holy Spirit enables us to activate God's plans for our lives. When we come in surrender to God, foundations are laid for future actions and events that would be the very things we would choose ourselves if we could see the end from the beginning. "For I know the thoughts that I think toward you, saith the Lord, thoughts of peace, and not of evil, to give you an expected end" (Jer. 29:11). This expected end is the future that is planned for and the hope that is realized through the Holy Spirit as He releases His people from the captivity of sin by Jesus' blood. As Paul says, you can be part of God's eternal plan as you are "strengthened with might" by the Holy Spirit within (Eph. 3:16).

❧ *A PRAYER FOR TODAY* ❧

Father, I'm totally open to Your plan for my life because I trust You and believe that You will reveal it to me as I take each step.

WATERFALL OF POWER

Till the Spirit is poured upon us from on high, and the desert becomes a fertile field, and the fertile field seems like a forest. Isa. 32:15, NIV.

Think of the most spectacular waterfall you have ever seen. When the Holy Spirit is poured out, the results are always as obvious as Niagara Falls. The Spirit does not come as an insignificant trickle but with mighty power, and there is soon formed a pool of love that is poured out from God "by the Holy Spirit" (Rom. 5:5). There is also the noise of rejoicing and praise, shouts of victory and new streams of living water (John 7:38, 39).

In Oregon we walked with Larry and Carolyn through a beautiful forest toward a distant waterfall. Occasionally we would stop and listen, trying to determine whether we were near our destination. After walking a few miles without hearing the falls, we turned back, concluding that it was farther than we expected.

On my first visit to Niagara Falls I was surprised when a few miles from our destination another passenger on the bus said, "Do you see that cloud of spray in the distance? That's the location of the falls."

In the same way people today are looking and listening for the evidences of the outpouring of the Holy Spirit.

Multnomah Falls, dropping more than 600 feet, is one of the highest in the United States. In the middle of one winter we heard that these beautiful falls were falling no more because they had frozen into a solid column of ice. As we photographed the falls we saw a very graphic illustration of the Christian church. The outpouring of the Holy Spirit began at Pentecost, but within a few decades a spiritual winter descended on the church, leaving only a frozen memory of past Holy Spirit power. Now, praise the Lord, a new day has dawned when the water is beginning to pour down again. We are living in the time of the last-day latter-rain refreshing that will result in fruitful fields and flourishing forests of spiritual life.

❦ *A PRAYER FOR TODAY* ❦

Father, I stand today at the foot of the falls, asking to be soaked and filled with the overflowing presence of the Holy Spirit. Pour out Your love so that I may be clearly identified as a Spirit-filled Christian.

AN ANCIENT CITY TESTIFIES

Search from the book of the Lord, and read: Not one of these shall fail; not one shall lack her mate. For My mouth has commanded it, and His Spirit has gathered them. Isa. 34:16, NKJV.

For years I studied the archaeology and ancient history of the Bible lands, noticing the uncanny accuracy of the predictions of the Spirit-inspired prophets. Through the prophets God foretold the destiny of nations, cities, and peoples. And the present status of all these places indicates that He was stating an indisputable fact when He claimed that there is no god like Him, who is able to tell the end from the beginning (Isa. 46:9, 10).

For instance, the wonders of ancient Petra, in the land of Jordan, continue to amaze the travelers who take the nearly two-mile walk down the siq, between the towering cliffs, where the narrow path leads to a sudden, stunning view of the stone city that is half as old as time.

Early one morning I set out to climb Umm el Bayyârah, the 1,000-foot fortress rising from the rocky valley floor in the heart of Petra. In the time of Isaiah the prophet this was a great capital of the Edomite empire, which had defied Israel and their God and had sunk into the depths of pagan corruption. Our group was led on the difficult climb by Musa, a local Bedouin guide.

After hours of scrambling up the rocks, we reached the place where earlier this century archaeologist Crystal Bennett had spent seven weeks on the flat summit of Umm el Bayyârah looking for new evidence of the Edomite empire.

Through six ancient prophets dozens of precise prophecies were written about Edom, such as those we find in Isaiah 34. As archaeologists have discovered, not one word of these prophecies has failed. Peter Stoner, professor emeritus of science at Westmont College, and Robert C. Newman state in their book *Science Speaks* that the probability of just three of these specific prophecies being fulfilled by accident would be 1 in 10,000 (p. 93).

Remember this: If the Holy Spirit can be so sure about cities and nations, you can absolutely trust Him with all the details of your life.

☙ *A PRAYER FOR TODAY* ❧

Lord, I want to continually search Your Word, giving the Holy Spirit the opportunity ever to increase my confidence in You.

WELCOME, TRUE PERSPECTIVE

Who has directed the Spirit of the Lord,
or as His counselor has taught Him? Isa. 40:13, NKJV.

*D*o you enjoy reading great literature? That is what you will find in the second part of Isaiah's book, which begins with chapter 40. This part is so different from the first that some scholars have suggested that it was written by a different author. However, the New Testament clearly identifies Isaiah as the prophet who so beautifully and vividly wrote these words by inspiration of the Spirit (Luke 3:4-6; 4:16-19).

You may want to read prayerfully through Isaiah 40, underlining the approximately two dozen promises that the Holy Spirit will reveal to you there.

In this chapter, and throughout the remainder of this book of consolation, the Holy Spirit blends together many details of Jesus' two advents.

From near my home in Oregon I can look north and see Mount St. Helens and Mount Rainier. They appear very close to each other, with Mount Rainier, which towers more than 14,000 feet, appearing slightly to the right and much smaller than Mount St. Helens, which, since 1980, is only about 8,000 feet high. Yesterday, however, as I flew into Portland from Chicago I could see the mountains from the east, and their true perspective appeared, with the two mountains obviously almost 100 miles apart and Mount Rainier towering much higher.

In the same way, in the beautiful literature of Isaiah 40, the First and Second Advents seem to be together, while in other prophecies the Holy Spirit will show them from a perspective that will reveal their distance apart and relative glory. Isaiah, the gospel prophet, is used also to reveal God's comfort and good tidings. God has the gentle care of a good shepherd. He understands the whole universe, so He does not need the advice of any counselor to understand every perspective of your life. The reward He has for you is not one you would wish to return, like an unsuitable Christmas gift. It is exactly what one would choose who knows the innermost secret longings of your heart.

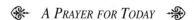

A PRAYER FOR TODAY

Lord, my spiritual horizons are often so foggy that I sometimes want
to instruct You and tell You what You should do in my life.
Help me recognize that You know more about me than I myself do.

THE HEART OF A SERVANT

See my servant, whom I uphold; my Chosen One, in whom I delight.
I have put my Spirit upon him; he will reveal justice
to the nations of the world. Isa. 42:1, TLB.

*A*t a midweek prayer meeting more than 100 people, as they knelt before God, sang a prayer in which they asked Him to make them like Him—a servant. It is not natural for educated, sophisticated, cultured people to want to be servants. This is the work of the Holy Spirit.

Jesus took "the form of a servant" (Phil. 2:7). He came to earth to serve humanity (Matt. 20:28). He applied the prophecy of Isaiah 42:1 to Himself. Paul felt honored to consider himself "a servant of Jesus" (Rom. 1:1) and commended those who, like Phoebe, became servants of the body of Jesus, His church (Rom. 16:1).

In 1909 a fiery, Spirit-filled Irish preacher proclaimed the gospel in Melbourne, Australia. With humility and power William Nicholson journeyed around the world more than 10 times and, like Paul, served his God as a winner of souls. After Nicholson, as a young Presbyterian, had been filled with the Holy Spirit, he learned in a Salvation Army street meeting what it meant to have a servant's heart. "The wonder to me was that all the fear of what men might say or do had vanished, and now I was willing to do anything or go anywhere. . . . As I walked down the street that Saturday it seemed as if every friend and relative I ever had were out and about. When I came to the open-air meeting and saw the two wee Salvation Army girls singing and rattling tambourines and poor daft Jimmy holding the flag, I nearly turned back. Talk about dying, I was dying hard that night" (cited by V. Raymond Edman, *They Found the Secret,* p. 103).

After praying and sharing the Word with those gathered around, William marched down the street as, with a tambourine in his hand, he led the group. He was naturally shy and timid, but of that night he said, "I lost my reputation and fear of man and found the joy and peace of the overflowing fullness of the Spirit. Hallelujah!" *(ibid.).*

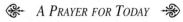

  A PRAYER FOR TODAY

Lord, I'll serve You today because I love You. You've given life to me.

WELCOME, FLOOD

*For I will give you abundant water for your thirst
and for your parched fields. And I will pour out my Spirit
and my blessings on your children. Isa. 44:3, TLB.*

William P. Nicholson was thirsty for the victory power of the Holy Spirit in his life. Many times as a young sailor he had thirsted for fresh water, but now, seven months after his conversion, a deep longing had grown within him for the mighty endowment of the Holy Spirit that would enable him to be truly a servant of God. A local businessperson in Bangor, Northern Ireland, had arranged a "Convention for the Deepening of the Spiritual Life," and William was invited to attend. As a Presbyterian, he explained, he would have considered these meetings wildfire and fanaticism if he had known what the real emphasis would be.

The Holy Spirit gently led William into the convention, and there his hunger and thirst greatly increased. "At last I became desperate," he said as he recounted his experience many times during great evangelistic meetings. Finally, walking outside the convention, he told the Lord that he was willing to give the Holy Spirit unconditional permission to fill his life. "Hallelujah! what a thrill, what a peace, what a joy! Although an old-fashioned Presbyterian, I began to weep, and sing and rejoice like an old-fashioned Free Methodist."

Writing of Nicholson's subsequent experience with the Lord, V. Raymond Edman, chancellor of Wheaton College, said: "On street corners and in cottages, in the city and in the villages, in his place of employment on the railroad and in the churches, Nicholson became a fearless and flaming winner of souls" *(They Found the Secret,* p. 103).

Before beginning his worldwide evangelistic ministry with Dr. Wilber Chapman and Charles M. Alexander, William Nicholson was mightily used by the Holy Spirit in many parts of Britain, especially in the coal mining villages. Edman tells of the wonderful fruitage of these floods of water on the dry ground: "Many came to a saving knowledge of the Lord Jesus and many yielded themselves fully to the Saviour and became Spirit-filled, soul-saving Christians" *(ibid.,* p. 104).

❧ *A PRAYER FOR TODAY* ❧

*Father, it's flood time for me today. I'm thirsty and am praising You
for the glorious blessing of Your Spirit.*

March 7

IN WHOSE IMAGE?

Come near to Me, hear this: I have not spoken in secret from the beginning; from the time that it was, I was there. And now the Lord God and His Spirit have sent Me. Isa. 48:16, NKJV.

Originally God created man and woman in His own image. Since then people have been trying to create God in *their* image. Through Jesus, the One who was sent to be our Redeemer, the Holy Spirit has revealed a glimpse of what God is really like so that we can be re-created in His image.

As a young man William Nicholson had been saved from shipwreck but still not saved eternally. Back home on May 22, 1899, he was reading the paper and smoking as he waited for his godly mother to prepare breakfast. Suddenly without warning a voice spoke to his heart, "Now or never. You must decide to accept or reject Christ."

In response he cried out, "Lord, I yield. I repent of all my sin and now accept Thee as my Saviour." At that moment William was conscious that he was saved. "I never have had any doubts about my salvation. The blood has been applied, and the Spirit answered to the blood" *(They Found the Secret,* p. 99). Although the grosser sins, he testifies, dropped from his life, William was still plagued by a sense of helplessness as far as living a totally committed life.

When William learned of the convention where he would later be introduced to the Holy Spirit, he tried in fear to create God in the image of his denomination. "I didn't want to be anything or do anything a Presbyterian ought not to be or do. I tried so hard to make the Lord see and understand my fears and feelings, but He had no sympathy for my fears. I couldn't make Him a Presbyterian!" *(ibid.,* p. 102).

Perhaps you are trying to make God a Seventh-day Adventist or a member of some other denomination. But you need not fear the Holy Spirit. As He is poured out in your life today, He will lead you, as He did William Nicholson, in the wonderful way you should go.

Often we pray for the Holy Spirit but want Him to come in a way that is according to the image of God's power that our denomination has given us. But God is God, and He will pour out His Spirit in His own best way.

❧ A PRAYER FOR TODAY ❧

Lord, stop me trying to adapt You to what I am like and help me not fear the molding and empowering of Your Holy Spirit in me.

March 8

WELCOME, VICTORY BANNER

So shall they fear the name of the Lord from the west, and His glory from the rising of the sun; when the enemy comes in like a flood, the Spirit of the Lord will lift up a standard against him. Isa. 59:19, NKJV.

*W*hat a wonderful promise! You will find this verse translated in different ways in various versions of the Bible because of the ambiguity of the Hebrew words. The meaning, however, in all translations is the same—no matter what forces of evil sweep in upon us, we can be victorious through God's mighty power.

Are you being flooded by the enemy today? Floodwaters are not usually pure and clean. They are contaminated by pollution and junk. Many dreams are washed away in the swirling rush of a flood. The enemy flooding you may be impure or negative thoughts, bad memories, depression, or even external persecution. You may feel swamped by financial pressures or marital problems. Remember, when the enemy comes in like a flood, the Holy Spirit will lift a standard against all evil. Hallelujah!

Because this is one of my favorite verses about the Holy Spirit, I have thought and prayed a lot about this word "standard." It appears only in a couple of English versions of the Bible, but one can gain real confidence from its biblical usage, which seems to be based on a Hebrew word that can be translated "a battle standard" or "banner raised as a signal."

I like the double emphasis on this great victory word in Psalm 60:4: "You have given a banner to those to fear You, that it may be displayed because of the truth" (KJV).

Claim this promise now and wave the banner with spiritual energy.

One of my favorite names for God, which I use in prayer each day, is Yahweh Nissi—the Lord my banner, my victory. He lifts up the victory banner—the banner of love—and the forces of evil are pushed back. They cannot stand in the face of the Holy Spirit's declaration of power. Lift up the banner now, and wave it in the face of whatever evil threatens to flood you. You are a child of God. You are on the winning side.

⟡ *A PRAYER FOR TODAY* ⟡

I praise You, Yahweh Nissi, for Your glorious banner, and I ask now that You raise it up in the midst of my fears and temptations.

SPEAKING WITH NEW COVENANT POWER

*"As for me, this is my covenant with them," says the Lord. "My Spirit,
who is on you, and my words that I have put in your mouth will not
depart from your mouth, or from the mouths of your children,
or from the mouths of their descendants from this time on
and forever," says the Lord. Isa. 59:21, NIV.*

Seven hundred years before Isaiah's prophecy Moses had wished that "all of the Lord's people were prophets, and that the Lord would put his Spirit upon them" (Num. 11:29). Now, in the only Old Testament verse directly linking the Spirit and new covenant, the promise is given that God's redeemed people from the time of the Messiah forward can individually be filled with the Spirit and proclaim His Word in fulfillment of Moses' heartfelt desire.

Read Isaiah 59:21 again and thank God that it includes you. If you have accepted Jesus as your Saviour, you are a child of the new covenant, and just as Isaiah prophesied that the Holy Spirit would be upon the servant Messiah (Isa. 11:2; 42:1; 61:1) so the Holy Spirit is always available to fill you and to give you God's message to speak.

The charismatic word in the mouth of each redeemed, Spirit-filled person is the word of prophecy, the word of wisdom, the word of knowledge, the word of true tongues and interpretation (1 Cor. 12). These gifts of the Spirit, which are speaking gifts, have their foundation in that which is the basis of the new covenant, namely, the written Word—the Bible—and the Word made flesh—Jesus.

Through the speaking gifts of the Holy Spirit in the New Testament, the Scriptures are not merely written words that give intellectual knowledge but words with living relevance in the reality of life today. Now it is time for you, if it has not already happened, to speak as a Spirit-filled servant of God. You may be able to do it one on one, in a small group, or in a large meeting. Whatever way God chooses, you will rejoice that His promise of powerful communication has been fulfilled.

❦ A PRAYER FOR TODAY ❦

*Lord, implant in my mind a word of edification, exhortation, or comfort
that I can speak today as the Holy Spirit enables me to glorify Jesus.*

WELCOME, NEW ANOINTING

*The spirit of the Lord God is upon me, because the Lord has anointed
me to bring good news to the suffering and afflicted. He has sent me
to comfort the broken-hearted, to announce liberty to captives
and to open the eyes of the blind. Isa. 61:1, TLB.*

The stunning extent of Jesus' anointed ministry unfolds in the first
three verses of Isaiah 61. His evangelism would slash the restric-
tive red tape and racial, religious prejudice of traditional Judaism.
Instead of their being reeds blowing in the wind, the good news from the
Anointed One would enable heartsick, hurting, lost human beings to become
strong oaks of righteousness and heirs of God's eternal kingdom.

On a plane from San Francisco to Burbank I read again Ann Kiemel's little book *I'm Out to Change My World.* I have listened to Ann speak and am
always deeply moved by the beautiful simple testimony of "an ordinary girl
in a big world."

"You see, I am a Christian and Jesus is the Lord of my life," she explains
to those who will listen. "He laughs with me and cries with me and walks the
lonely roads with me. . . . He and I are out to change the world. And . . . He
can change your world" (p. 23).

On a flight home from San Antonio, tired after a week of speaking to 500
teenagers, Ann sat alone as she quietly sang praises to God. From behind, a
young man began to speak to her, asking her if she minded leaving San
Antonio. Then he explained that he was returning to Vietnam, where he had
seen his two best buddies die. He had come home on leave and had found that
his wife had left him.

Could the Spirit now use Ann to bind up the brokenhearted and proclaim
good news to the poor?

Quietly she shared her testimony and wrote out a little prayer. As the
plane neared its destination the GI leaned over and spoke to Ann again: "I
wanted to thank you," he told her. "I prayed that prayer, and I don't feel alone
anymore. And Ann, I think God and I—we can make it" (p. 24).

❦ *A PRAYER FOR TODAY* ❧

*Lord, I praise You that Your anointed ministry has reached me,
bringing healing and hope. In the brokenness of this world
let me be an agent of strength and stability.*

WELCOME, REMINDER

Yet they rebelled and grieved his Holy Spirit. So he turned and became their enemy and he himself fought against them. Isa. 63:10, NIV.

*D*o you like being reminded of past mistakes? It won't happen in heaven, because God apparently erases them from the memories of all who are saved. But this life is different. As painful as it may be, it is important for us to remember—at least occasionally—the ways in which we fell into sin, disappointed God, and hurt others.

It is not the duty of other people to do this reminding. Satan loves to do it in his destructive way, but we should not listen to his gloating accusations. The Holy Spirit is the one who handles God's reminders and in a way that constantly safeguards us from falling into the same trap again. The Spirit reminds, not to make us feel guilty again, but to activate in our consciousness the assurance of forgiveness and our constant need of total dependence on His victory power. The Israelites grieved the Holy Spirit and unfortunately reached the place where they could hear God's voice no more.

"I don't think you can understand what I'm going through," a young man said to me as he discussed a very hard situation he was facing because of some of his own foolish actions. I hesitated for a few moments before I surrendered to the Holy Spirit's prompting to share with him a little of a similar situation that I had passed through years before when I was a teenager. He listened carefully as I briefly told him about my experience. It was painful for me to have to remember what it was like returning to a restaurant owner the money I had stolen.

As we prayed together I realized the value of the Holy Spirit's reminder of a past but forgiven sin. "Thank You for the assurance You have given me today," the man prayed. "I'm so glad that the pastor understands what I'm going through and that he has given me hope that I can know You will forgive me and give me power to be victorious."

❧ A PRAYER FOR TODAY ❧

Father, don't let me become one who drags up the past of others but remind me constantly of Your forgiveness and love in my life.

WELCOME MEMORIES

*Then he remembered the days of old, Moses and his people, saying:
"Where is He who brought them up out of the sea with the
shepherd of His flock? Where is He who put
His Holy Spirit within them?" Isa. 63:11, NKJV.*

The Holy Spirit wants to help you remember the way God has led in your life. Never forget God's past leading no matter how rough the present may be. There are a number of ways you can keep the positive past alive and powerful in your memory, and if you allow the Holy Spirit to activate these principles, you will find that your strength in present situations will increase greatly.

First, write out a list of experiences that you consider are evidences of God's leading. Pray through your life right from your earliest memories, and look for the good. The enemy wants you to concentrate on bad memories, but God wants you to exalt and treasure the good. List your good memories, whether they be 10 or 100, and keep the list in your Bible or some other place where you can review it often and add to it. Talking to old friends or family members may stimulate long-forgotten indications of God's providence.

Second, take the opportunity often to share your stories. Make sure, though, that you do not tell the same people the same story more than once or bore others with complicated details. Make the stories concise, and give glory to God. If you have children, they will hear you tell the stories to different people and will eventually know them so well that they will tell your stories to their own friends or children should time last.

Third, write out in full the stories that have had the most impact on your life and send them to a Christian magazine for publication. There is no guarantee that they will be accepted, but you may be surprised. You may want to share the manuscript with your pastor and ask him if he would like to use it as a sermon illustration.

Remember, in all things to give glory to God. Praise God and recount what He has done. Even the smallest blessings are to be treasured like tiny pearls.

❧ *A PRAYER FOR TODAY* ❧

*Lord, I forget the good so easily, but I ask You for an experience today that I
can add to my list of evidences of Your leading in my life.*

WELCOME REST

Like cattle that go down to the plain, they were given rest by the Spirit of the Lord. This is how you guided your people to make for yourself a glorious name. Isa. 63:14, NIV.

When the Holy Spirit gives rest, it does not necessarily mean sleep. In fact, some Spirit-filled people need to be counseled at times to ease up a little and "come . . . apart . . . and rest a while," as Jesus said.

Yesterday the Spirit led me to suggest to a friend whom God is using mightily, "Please don't take on so many things all at once. I think you need some more sleep." Unfortunately I do not always practice what I preach. For ministers, even the Sabbath is not a time of rest, but often a very stressful day.

The rest that God gives, however, is primarily spiritual rest. Isaiah says that God is leading the people to whom He promises rest, which indicates activity. But it is not activity to earn or merit salvation. There is no rest for anyone who is in the grip of salvation by works. Spirit-filled people know that their salvation is certain in Jesus Christ. "For as many as are led by the Spirit of God, these are sons of God" (Rom. 8:14, NKJV).

The rest that is promised to us in the gospel is beautifully explained in Isaiah 61:1-3. Read again those wonderful words. There is rest from the weakness of spiritual poverty, which is followed by rest from the agony of brokenheartedness. Hallelujah! There is rest from the prison bondage of evil habits and addictions, and the future takes on the new perspective of God's eternal purpose. Comfort, beauty, and joy take the place of mourning and sorrow, which deplete energy and destroy vitality. Praise and security flourish like a mighty oak tree as the Holy Spirit leads us to the One who says: "Come unto me, all ye that labour and are heavy laden, and I will give you rest" (Matt. 11:28).

Today, as you open your heart to the Holy Spirit, He will give you the glorious assurance that filled the heart of the psalmist who testified: "My soul finds rest in God alone; my salvation comes from him" (Ps. 62:1, NIV). Do not leave your home without this certainty, or you will face a restless day.

❦ *A PRAYER FOR TODAY* ❦

Lord, I'm restless until I rest in You.
Today again I accept the fullness of Your salvation.

BACK ON YOUR FEET

*Then the Spirit entered me when He spoke to me, and set me
on my feet; and I heard Him who spoke to me. Eze. 2:2, NKJV.*

*H*ave you ever felt that you needed help to get back onto your
feet? Ezekiel had fallen down before the presence of the Lord,
who appeared in a glorious scene of symbolic majesty.
Sometimes we fall in the presence of discouragement, evil, or overwhelm-
ingly difficult circumstances.

No matter, however, what the reason may be, the Spirit of God will
get us back on our feet so that we can carry on.

Brenda had been a highly successful flight attendant for many years when
her back and shoulder were badly injured in sudden violent turbulence during a long flight. The resulting pain and emotional suffering were complicated by very difficult workers' compensation cases in which it seemed that
Brenda would not receive the justice she deserved.

In the midst of Brenda's deep depression and financial ruin she asked her
church for help, but there was no response. On the other side of the country,
however, the Holy Spirit was moving on the heart of a friend to call Brenda
and speak the very words that were needed. "She told me to read the story of
John the Baptist in Luke 1:41," Brenda explained to me. "I was just amazed
that someone would call me long distance to encourage me and pray for me
as my friend did. Like John, I began to leap for joy as I realized that the Spirit
was getting me up on my feet again."

Since that time God has used Brenda to write many wonderful Christian
songs, some of which have been sung publicly many times. One of these
songs, entitled "Face-to-Face," points out that we need not worry about our
woes when we can simply envision being face-to-face with Jesus.

Yes, Brenda now sees herself face-to-face with the loving God who has
lifted her up and has established her feet firmly on solid ground.

You can be one of the Holy Spirit's lifting agents today. While some people seem to concentrate on knocking others down, God and His children are
in the business of lifting up the fallen.

❦ *A PRAYER FOR TODAY* ❧

*Father, I kneel at the foot of the cross, knowing that Jesus' love and
forgiveness lift me higher than I have ever been lifted before.*

STANDING UP AGAIN

*Then the Spirit lifted me up, and I heard behind me a loud
rumbling sound—May the glory of the Lord be praised
in his dwelling place! Eze. 3:12, NIV.*

God has many exciting and different ways that He can use to get us
spiritually onto our feet. As a young teenager Ellen Harmon would
sometimes spend almost all night in prayer. She was earnestly
seeking God, yet her mind was gripped with a sense of hopelessness as she
despaired of eternal salvation. In the midst of this situation Ellen dreamed
that she saw a great temple.

The temple in her dream was vast and was supported by one immense pil-
lar to which was tied a mangled and bleeding lamb. All who entered the temple came before the lamb and confessed their sins. Just in front of the lamb
Ellen saw elevated seats on which the happy forgiven people sat. "The light
of heaven seemed to shine upon their faces, and they praised God and sang
songs of glad thanksgiving that seemed like the music of the angels" *(Life
Sketches,* p. 33).

Before Ellen could bring herself to come in humility before the lamb, a
trumpet sounded, and all became darkness. Now she felt that the Spirit had
left her forever, never to return.

But God certainly was not going to leave Ellen in that state. As He lifted
up Ezekiel, so He would lift up this earnest young teenager. Soon after her
first dream Ellen received another, in which she was invited into Jesus' presence. As she looked into His beautiful countenance, He seemed to smile and
place His hand upon her head. He told her to "fear not." In her joy many
scenes of beauty and glory seemed to pass before her, and she felt that she
had reached the safety and peace of heaven. Jesus' presence filled Ellen with
holy reverence and an inexpressible love *(ibid.,* pp. 32-36).

The hope that filled Ellen's heart as the beauty and simplicity of trusting
in God began to fill her soul can also lift you onto your feet again today. The
Holy Spirit will give you a vision of the reality of the truths of God's Word
that will enable you to see beyond the mundane discouragements of this life.

❧ *A PRAYER FOR TODAY* ❧

*Lord, as I come into the presence of Jesus now I praise You for the wonder
of Your salvation and the certainty of Your love.*

LIFTED BY FIRE

*So the Spirit lifted me up and took me away, and I went
in bitterness, in the heat of my spirit; but the hand of
the Lord was strong upon me. Eze. 3:14, NKJV.*

God's Spirit does not operate in our lives on the basis of our feelings but rather in response to our willingness to be the Lord's servants. Ezekiel was full of bitterness and anger because of the unfriendly looks and rebellious attitude of the people. He had, though, a surrender to God that often caused him to fall on his face in the Lord's presence.

When meetings were first held in the Harmon home, in Portland, Maine, young Ellen Harmon did not attend, because she was still in a state of despondency and distress. The church, however, made Ellen the subject of special prayer, and even a leading brother whom they called Father Pearson, an early opposer of Ellen's visions, now joined in the prayer for her.

Let's listen to Ellen tell in her own words what happened at one of the meetings in her parents' home. "While prayer was offered for me, that the Lord would give me strength and courage to bear the message, the thick darkness that had encompassed me rolled back, and a sudden light came upon me. Something that seemed to me like a ball of fire struck me right over the heart. My strength was taken away, and I fell to the floor. I seemed to be in the presence of the angels. One of these holy beings again repeated the words, 'Make known to others what I have revealed to you.'

"Father Pearson, who could not kneel on account of his rheumatism, witnessed this occurrence. When I revived sufficiently to see and hear, he rose from his chair, and said: 'I have seen a sight such as I never expected to see. A ball of fire came down from heaven, and struck Sister Ellen Harmon right on the heart. *I saw it! I saw it!* I can never forget it. It has changed my whole being. Sister Ellen, have courage in the Lord'" *(Life Sketches,* p. 71). Then young Ellen began to move ahead like Ezekiel to proclaim the word of the Lord.

Years ago my college theology teacher, Alfred Jorgenson, reminded his class, "Be my feelings as they will, Jesus is my Saviour still." In the same way the Holy Spirit is always available.

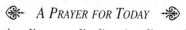

❀ *A PRAYER FOR TODAY* ❄

Father, I'm open. I'm listening. I'm ready.

March 17

WELCOME, INSTRUCTION

Then the Spirit came into me and raised me to my feet. He spoke to me and said: "Go, shut yourself inside your house." Eze. 3:24, NIV.

The Spirit's instructions can occasionally seem rather unusual. Two of my prayer partners, Tom and Carolyn, felt impressed that the Holy Spirit was giving them some special instructions for me, and Carolyn was surprised when she felt that the Lord was directing her to go and clean out their clothes closet. When the task was completed, Carolyn prayed, "Lord, what does this task have to do with the message that you want Tom and me to give Garrie?" Soon the Spirit led her to understand that I needed, at that time, to be clothed in a much deeper and more intimate relationship with God and that some of the fears I was clothed with needed to be sorted out and cast aside.

The next day Tom and Carolyn called and made an appointment to visit with me, and as we talked and prayed together I quickly discerned the accuracy and pertinency of the message that they shared. With tears we acknowledged God's goodness and the joy that we can have as we come into a trusting relationship with Him.

I am not one who professes to hear God's voice speaking to me, apart from in His Word, except on very rare occasions, but inside my house as our small group has met each week I have often been deeply impressed as the Lord has given special messages for me from the Word. Occasionally we have had friends from overseas join our group, and the Lord has used them to exhort and comfort, even in situations among our group members of which the visitors had no foreknowledge.

The Holy Spirit gave Ann Kiemel the strange instructions to sing a Christian song to a gnarled old cab driver in Miami Beach. He rolled up the windows as she sang of God's ability to make "something beautiful" out of our "brokenness and strife." After it was over, this old, lonely man said with tears in his eyes, "I want your God. He and I could ride together."

Welcome and be willing to follow the Holy Spirit's instructions today.

⚘ *A PRAYER FOR TODAY* ⚘

Lord, I'm listening to Your Word and request strength to obey
Your voice as it leads me in the path of truth.

A HELPING HAND

He stretched out the form of a hand, and took me by a lock of my hair;
and the Spirit lifted me up between earth and heaven,
and brought me in visions of God to Jerusalem. Eze. 8:3, NKJV.

One of the most exciting discoveries about the Holy Spirit that I made in the Old Testament was His association with the symbolism of the hand of God. Ezekiel uses this expression a number of times, including verse 1 of this chapter, in which he says: "The hand of the Lord God fell upon me there."

The power of the Spirit in the New Testament was often pictured by the hand of the Lord in the Old. It was the strength of the hand that brought Israel out of Egypt. The children of Israel sang, "Your right hand, O Lord, has become glorious in power" (Ex. 15:6). Joshua acknowledged that the hand of the Lord is mighty (Joshua 4:24).

Nehemiah connects the hand of God to the redemption of His people. "Now these are Your servants and Your people, whom You have redeemed by Your great power, and by Your strong hand" (Neh. 1:10). It is this same hand of God that brings His people out of the bondage of sin. It enables them to accept Jesus as the One who redeemed them when He died in their place on the cross of Calvary. The Holy Spirit constantly reveals that born-again Christians are not only the children of God (Rom. 8:16), but can also have victory over sin by His mighty power (1 John 4:4). God has tattooed the names of His children on the palms of His hands, and He will never let them go (Isa. 49:16).

One of the greatest Holy Spirit passages, Psalm 139:7-10, reminds us that God's hand leads us and holds us even in the most inaccessible places of life. As Paul says: "For as many as are led by the Spirit of God, these are the sons of God" (Rom. 8:14).

Many Christians today are beginning to recognize the amazing confidence that they can have as they become aware of the hand of the Lord upon them. That hand is strong for you. That hand is right for you. You can take that hand again today by reaching out in faith and giving your life in full surrender to Him who is glorious in power.

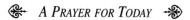 *A PRAYER FOR TODAY*

Please lift me up by Your hand today, Lord, and give new confidence
in Your merciful greatness.

March 19

WELCOME, NEW LIFE

Then the Spirit lifted me up and brought me to the gate of the
house of the Lord that faces east. There at the entrance
to the gate were twenty-five men. Eze. 11:1, NIV.

The most miraculous lifting that the Holy Spirit can do is when a person who has accepted Jesus' death on the cross is raised up to walk in resurrection life. This experience comes when we allow the Holy Spirit to make us alive together with Jesus (Eph. 2:5; Rom. 8:11).

For many months Esther experienced increased feelings of spiritual despair. Eventually she was getting very little sleep and wondered at times if the only escape would be death. The devil's lies multiplied as he tried to destroy her and the wonderful prayer ministry that the Lord had given her. But God has promised a way of escape (1 Cor. 10:13) so that each of His children can know what it is to move from the cross to the empty tomb.

"I feel that I've been nailed on the cross for months, and I have to get off," Esther said to the friend who was praying with her. "It seems that the whole weight of the world is on my shoulders."

"Just accept the resurrection power of the Holy Spirit," her friend explained. "Come off the cross and out of the tomb now, and be alive in Jesus. You will know the joy of resurrection life."

There was a struggle in Esther's mind for a few minutes, and then she finally took the step of faith, giving the Holy Spirit permission to lift her up just as Jesus was raised from the dead. For some time Esther had been trying to understand a deep emotion that seemed to be taking the place that God should have in her heart. Now as she opened her eyes she exclaimed to her friend, "It's in the right place. My feeling has now moved aside so that God is filling the central place in my heart."

What a joy! What a victory!

"I wish that every Christian could know about this deep healing and experience it for themselves!" Esther exclaimed as she later shared the good news with her other prayer partners.

❧ *A PRAYER FOR TODAY* ❧

My Father and my God, I accept now the beautiful
resurrection life that You offer me today.

March 20

A READER OF MINDS

Then the Spirit of the Lord fell upon me, and said to me, "Speak!
'Thus says the Lord: "Thus you have said, O house of Israel;
for I know the things that come into your mind."'" Eze. 11:5, NKJV.

This morning as I prayed I felt strongly impressed to call some people in New York whom I had met briefly in Florida. It was by a series of "mistakes" that the Lord had led James and Joan, together with their daughter Debbie and her two children, to my seminar. They were all visiting Fort Lauderdale, and on Sunday morning they looked in the yellow pages to find a church to attend. Although the family is Roman Catholic, James and Joan wanted to attend a church that was teaching about the Holy Spirit and healing. Debbie did not really want to attend church at all but said if they did, it should be a Catholic church.

The family "mistakenly" arrived at the Seventh-day Adventist Church that Sunday morning as I was teaching about the Holy Spirit, prayer, and healing. I saw them enter and sit on the back row about 10:45 but did not realize that they were not part of the congregation. Toward noon the seminar broke into small groups, and it was then that I met James, Joan, and Debbie and had the opportunity to hear of their experience and, together with the church pastor, to minister to them.

This morning when I called to talk to James and Joan, who had now returned home, Joan was very surprised. "James is in the hospital with a serious heart condition," she explained to me sadly. "One of our eight stores has just been burned, and business is very difficult because of the recession. Last night I read the story of Peter sinking in the Sea of Galilee and felt that I myself was going down. This morning as I prayed I asked that the Lord would have someone who would reach out to me as Jesus did to save Peter."

Three thousand miles away in California the only One who can read minds and thoughts helped me speak the needed words of edification, exhortation, and comfort.

The Bible was written long before the age of telephones, but the Holy Spirit can use this technology to great advantage today. Not only does He move people occasionally to call a friend at the right time, but He also gives to some a full-time telephone ministry.

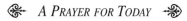

❧ *A PRAYER FOR TODAY* ❧

Lord, I entrust You with the thoughts and intents of my heart.

WELCOME VISION

*Afterwards the Spirit of God carried me back again to Babylon,
to the Jews in exile there. And so ended the vision of
my visit to Jerusalem. Eze. 11:24, TLB.*

The Holy Spirit not only gives visions of dramatic events affecting great nations and powerful cities but also of amazing changes that can take place in people's lives through God's mighty power.

As Pastor Altermatt and I spoke to Debbie, who had arrived by "accident" with her parents and children at my seminar in Fort Lauderdale, it seemed that the Spirit immediately gave us a vision that this young lady's life would be dramatically changed by hearing and accepting the wonderful gospel of our Lord Jesus Christ. In a few minutes that vision was very positively confirmed.

Step by step Pastor Altermatt led Debbie through the gospel presentation as she acknowledged her need of Jesus. She recognized that Jesus' death on the cross was for her and that all she needed to do was to open her heart in full surrender to Him. At the appropriate moment the pastor asked Debbie if there was anything stopping her from accepting Jesus as her Saviour. We were all happy when she answered no, and we knelt with her as she prayed the sinner's prayer, welcoming Jesus as the Lord of her life.

The glow on Debbie's face and the new joy in her heart was easily recognized as she later shared her experience with the whole group. "I did not want to come to a church today," Debbie admitted, "but my parents' prayers have been answered. I'm so happy that I now know that I became a born-again Christian just a few minutes ago."

The whole congregation praised God and rejoiced with this new member of the family of God. It was a miracle that a soul was saved on a Sunday morning in an Adventist church. Debbie's father summed up how he and his wife felt when he said, "We couldn't have bought this experience for thousands of dollars."

As with Ezekiel, God gives to His people a vision that the captives can be free. All who are prisoners in the Babylon of fear, rebellion, guilt, or sin can, like Debbie, return to the promised land of joy and peace.

⸎ A PRAYER FOR TODAY ⸎

*Lord, open my eyes to see the souls who are ready to accept You as their
Saviour and help me be Your servant to introduce them to Jesus.*

GOD'S SPIRIT DISPLACES IDOLS

I will put My Spirit within you and cause you to walk in My statutes, and you will keep My judgments and do them. Eze. 36:27, NKJV.

*I*t was the grip of idolatry in the lives of the ancient Jewish people that finally led them into their Babylonian captivity. In the midst of a number of prophetic messages that reveal the plan for the restoration of a remnant, God spoke of spiritual renewal as the basis for the people's future ability to stay free from the iniquity and defilement of idol worship.

Idolatry is loving anyone or anything more than God. Perhaps you think that you are not affected by idols, so here is a quick test: Whom or what do you think about the most? Whom or what do you talk about the most? Whom or what has your warmest affections and best energies? If you are really honest with yourself about this and if you do not find God in the number one place, then a red flag should be waving in your mind. It says: Take heed to the Lord's warnings against idolatry, and implement the cure, or else the idol will destroy you in the end.

God deals with our guiltiness of idolatry by making it possible for us to accept by faith Jesus' death on our behalf and to receive His forgiveness as we come to Him with confession and repentance. God deals with our inability to live free from idolatry by filling us with the Holy Spirit's indwelling presence. It is the Spirit who causes those He fills to live according to all the principles of God's Word. With the Holy Spirit within you, then all of God's biddings become enablings and all His commands become promises that delight the heart.

Ezekiel 36:25-28 is definitely a new covenant promise, even though Ezekiel does not use that term. He does, however, use the new covenant formula to describe your position in relationship to God as the Holy Spirit fills you today: "You will be my people and I will be your God" (verse 28). The dearest idols have been destroyed.

❧ *A PRAYER FOR TODAY* ❧

Reveal to me, Lord, anything that may have become an idol to me, and help it come into its rightful place in my life by the power of Your Spirit.

LANDING AMID THE BONES

*The hand of the Lord was upon me, and he brought me out by
the Spirit of the Lord and set me in the middle of a valley;
it was full of bones. Eze. 37:1, NIV.*

The Lord gave some rather unusual visions to His prophet so that He might impress on the minds of His people their spiritual condition and their only source of true revival. I have had the opportunity to visit the Monastery of St. Catherine at Mount Sinai. Here in the famous library are more than 3,000 ancient manuscripts, many of them as dry and battered as the bones seen by Ezekiel in his strange vision. Yet among these manuscripts have been found the words of eternal life.

For instance, it was here, in 1844, that Count Tischendorf found the A.D. 340 manuscript that became known as the Codex Sinaiticus. This document contains not only parts of the Old Testament but also the complete New Testament, with the beautiful account of the gospel of life through the sacrifice of Jesus and the mighty resurrection power of the Holy Spirit. Yes indeed, the bones can live.

Also at St. Catherine's is the richly adorned Byzantine Church of the Transfiguration. This church contains the Chapel of the Burning Bush, which is said to have been built by the mother of Constantine in A.D. 342. Some beautiful icons here show how the dead bones can live. Jesus is seen being baptized by immersion in the Jordan River. He is pictured as dying on the cross and rising from the grave. He provides the free gift of eternal life.

About 12 monks live at St. Catherine's. When they die, they are buried for one year in the 15-foot-square burial ground, and then their skeletons are taken to the charnel house and added to the heaps of bones that are already there. As I have looked at these disconnected bones and the skeleton of St. Stephanos, who has been sitting there fully clothed since A.D. 580, I was reminded again of Ezekiel's vision. Yes, it is possible, through the resurrection power of the Holy Spirit, that these bones shall live!

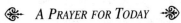

✦ *A PRAYER FOR TODAY* ✦

*Father, when life seems dry and disjointed
help me remember that there is life in You.*

March 24

RATTLING THE BONES

I will put my Spirit in you and you will live, and I will settle you in your own land. Then you will know that I the Lord have spoken, and I have done it, declares the Lord. Eze. 37:14, NIV.

I listened to a good young preacher give a very meaningful modern application of this prophecy. "The valley," he explained, "represents the church. Without the Holy Spirit it is full of lifelessness and people who are dead in trespasses and sins. All the doctrines and teachings of the church can be presented as church members 'hear the word of the Lord' (Eze. 37:4), but that is not enough to bring the necessary life.

"The bones rattle together and are covered with flesh. However, all the organization, ceremonies, policies, and institutionalism—no matter how successful they may look—cannot open the graves (verse 12). It is only as the Spirit of God fills each life that the church can rise up like a mighty army (verse 10) and move forward in conquering power for Jesus."

Even though I knew that the primary application of this prophecy related to the Jews in exile in Babylonia and God's desire to bring them back to their homeland where again a remnant could live in spiritual vitality, I agreed wholeheartedly with the pastor's modern application. There have been times in my own Christian experience when, even as a minister, I have had no living relationship with the Lord. I knew how to do and say everything right, but true spiritual life was lacking.

A person in this situation usually is not aware of what has happened, because the dead do not know anything (Eccl. 9:5). But God in His love and mercy is constantly leading His people to places where they can be exposed to prayer ministries, revival, and a new awareness of the gospel. It is exciting to see the dramatic changes that take place when a person rises from the grave of spiritual deadness. I praise God for His resurrection power in my own life, and I invite you to ask the Holy Spirit to fill you completely with His life today.

✥ A PRAYER FOR TODAY ✥

Lord, I ask You not only to rattle the bones of my life but also to raise me up to be part of Your great army. Fill me with Your Spirit again today so that Your life can be revealed through me.

WHAT MIGHT HAVE BEEN

And I will never hide my face from them again, for I will pour out my Spirit upon them, says the Lord God. Eze. 39:29, TLB.

*I*t is a tragedy that national Israel failed to meet the conditions that would have made it a great object lesson of the mighty power of their God to all the surrounding nations. Ezekiel 39:29 concludes a series of restoration prophecies that began in Ezekiel 33:23. It is the bridge into the concluding chapters, where the Holy Spirit pictures life-giving streams of water that would have poured from the great temple, bringing sustenance of healing for all people (Eze. 47:12).

It is imperative that all Christian organizations and denominations learn the lesson of ancient Israel. It is not enough to know truth, work for God, believe prophecy is fulfilling in their ministry, or receive the promise of the Holy Spirit. Unless there is continual surrender to God's will and leading; willingness to fulfill the conditions of faith, grace, spiritual growth; and sincere obedience to the Word, God can certainly replace the unfaithful ones by raising up others who can fulfill His eternal purpose.

It is because of the principle of conditional prophecy (Jer. 17:7-10) that God now ministers to the world through a nation of faith, spiritual Israel. Prophets of the new covenant, such as Paul and John the revelator, picture a scenario in which the final outpouring of the Holy Spirit and the resultant battle between good and evil take place. John draws from the imagery of Ezekiel 38 and 39 when he sees those who try finally to destroy the city of God as Gog and Magog (Rev. 20:8).

As always, victory for God's faithful remnant is made possible because God pours out His Spirit upon them in latter-rain power (Joel 2:23, 28-32). Do not rely on your denominational affiliation or your past or present ministry for your salvation. Come into a face-to-face, daily relationship with God's Spirit, and grow in grace and in the knowledge of your Lord and Saviour Jesus Christ. Then denomination and ministry will take their rightful place.

✎ *A Prayer for Today* ✎

Father, as You have poured out Your Spirit upon me,
so enable me to walk in the light of Your eternal Word.

VISION OF GLORY

Then the Spirit took me up and brought me into the inner court;
and the glory of the Lord filled the Temple. Eze. 43:5, TLB.

*E*llen Harmon was only 18 when she married James White, an energetic young preacher. During their first months of married life the Holy Spirit revealed to Ellen some more of the glories of the heavenly temple, and these glories transformed her vision of heaven and earth forever.

When I visited the Howland home in Topsham, Maine, with conference president Elmer Malcolm, we talked of some of the wonderful experiences the Lord had given the early Adventist pioneers in that place. Telling of a vision she received on April 3, 1847, Ellen White says: "We felt an unusual spirit of prayer. And as we prayed, the Holy Ghost fell upon us. We were very happy. Soon I was lost to earthly things, and was wrapped up in a vision of God's glory." She goes on to tell of the glories of the holy and Most Holy places in the great heavenly temple and the exceeding brightness of the glory of the throne of God (in A. L. White, *Ellen G. White: The Early Years,* p. 120).

This great experience of glimpsing God's glory was given to Ellen White many times. For instance, almost 19 years after the experience in the Howland house, the Whites were visiting in Rochester, New York, where James's health became so bad that he began to think about death. Again Ellen White tells what happened: "Christmas evening, as we were humbling ourselves before God and earnestly pleading for deliverance, the light of heaven seemed to shine down upon us, and I was wrapped up in a vision of God's glory. It seemed that I was borne quickly from earth to heaven, where all was health, beauty, and glory. Strains of music fell on my ear, melodious, perfect, and entrancing" *(Life Sketches,* pp. 171, 172).

Little wonder that Ellen White would shout, "Glory! Glory! Glory!" as she was taken into vision. Like Ezekiel of old, this young lady was privileged to catch a glimpse of the magnificent glory that is in store for all the redeemed.

&-- *A PRAYER FOR TODAY* --&

Train my eyes, Lord, to look in faith beyond the darkness of this world
to the enduring brightness of Your eternal kingdom.

NOT DAZZLED BY BABYLON

But at last Daniel came before me (his name is Belteshazzar,
according to the name of my god;
in him is the Spirit of the Holy God). Dan. 4:8, NKJV.

N ebuchadnezzar was right. Daniel was a man who gave dramatic evidence that the Holy Spirit of God was in him, as Theodotion said in his second-century Greek translation. Although Daniel was a prisoner in a foreign land, he was not in a dark, damp dungeon but surrounded by affluence and opulence in the palace of the king. Sometimes Satan does that to us to confuse our minds and weaken our resistance to evil. Sin's pleasures can seem comfortable, exciting, and rewarding—for a time. They can nurture our egos until we feel important in the land of the enemy. Our money, our good looks, our intellect, our wit, our personality, make us popular, and we revel in it until the day of reckoning shows up the emptiness of it all.

Daniel did not make the mistake of being dazzled by the glamour of his surroundings. Even in the relatively small issue of diet he had refused to compromise his determination to remain undefiled by the subtle deceptions of Babylon. Out of Daniel's decision to do right came the stirring temperance song we taught our children years ago. "Dare to be a Daniel, dare to stand alone! Dare to have a purpose firm! Dare to make it known!"

Fortunately, apart from his lions' den experience, Daniel was not alone, but was blessed with a small group of praying friends. The Holy Spirit led these men into prayer fellowship as they faced a series of severe tests (Dan. 2:13-18). In this way the Holy Spirit was able to place hedges around them in their beautiful but hostile environment. They saw the glory of God, and it showed up the darkness of their earthly surroundings.

Dare to be a Daniel. Don't let your guard down in the presence of an attractive person, a glittering environment, a glamorous business deal, an exciting opportunity, or a rest and recreational delight. Be strong in the Spirit of the Holy God.

❦ *A PRAYER FOR TODAY* ❦

Father, help me remember that the gods of this world may sometimes
appear good, but only You are totally and eternally reliable.

March 28

NOT A MAGICIAN

*"Belteshazzar, chief of the magicians, because I know that
the Spirit of the Holy God is in you, and no secret troubles you,
explain to me the visions of my dream that I have seen,
and its interpretation." Dan. 4:9, NKJV.*

There are so many mystics, religious visionaries, New Age psychics, and so-called prophets today that I doubt whether we can ever know whom to trust," Romona, a 40-something graduate student of philosophy and psychology, said to me.

"Let me tell you about a man who lived more than 500 years before the time of Jesus," I replied.

"Why go back so far? Why not tell me about someone living today?" she countered as her face betrayed her obvious interest.

I asked the Holy Spirit for wisdom and then began to tell her the story of Daniel and King Nebuchadnezzar. "It happened a long time ago, but it gives us the unique opportunity to verify all the details and see that in the midst of all types of counterfeits God's truth is clearly revealed."

I went on to explain how Nebuchadnezzar had confidence in Daniel because he had heard the amazing word of God concerning the dream of a great image, which is found in Daniel 2. "Romona, this dream predicted the rise and fall of nations," I said. "We can check all the historical information and can confirm that Daniel's prophecies were written long before the final events they portray. Sources such as the Dead Sea scrolls and the famous manuscript that Count Tischendorf found at the Monastery of St. Catherine show that Daniel is indeed an authentic Old Testament book.

"Nevertheless, objective facts are not all that God wants us to know. Daniel was not a magician but a Spirit-filled child of God. So, as an understanding of prophecy came to Daniel, he blessed the name of God. He acknowledged that true wisdom came only from Him. Daniel glorified, praised, and worshiped as he recognized God's greatness and omnipotence (Dan. 2:20-23). This is the difference you must look for," I explained to Romona. "In the heart and life of a true prophet, you will find that only God is exalted and praised. There is unmistakable evidence of genuine devotion to Him."

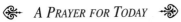

✎ *A PRAYER FOR TODAY* ✎

Lord, establish my confidence firmly upon Your wisdom and might.

March 29

TRYING THE FAILURES FIRST

"This dream I, King Nebuchadnezzar, have seen. Now you, Belteshazzar, declare its interpretation, since all the wise men of my kingdom are not able to make known to me the interpretation; but you are able, for the Spirit of the Holy God is in you." Dan. 4:18, NKJV.

*D*o you have a problem with the Nebuchadnezzar syndrome? This is the third time that Nebuchadnezzar confessed his confidence in Daniel's connection to the Spirit of God, but although Nebuchadnezzar testified to the wonders that God worked for him (Dan. 4:2), he still turned to his magicians and astrologers first (verse 7). Old habits and allegiances are hard to break.

"If this program is going to succeed," the church administrator said, "the main thing we need to do is organize some committees and raise some money."

"Haven't we learned in the past that money and committees can't do the work?" a young pastor replied. "Let's go to the Lord in prayer. Let's earnestly seek for the outpouring of the Holy Spirit. Perhaps we can spend a few days in prayer and fasting, and then we'll see miracles take place as God blesses His humble servants."

The young man was right. Committees and funding have a place, but to depend upon them is a dangerous habit, because it is God who supplies us with the simple means that the Holy Spirit can use.

"When I get tired and overworked, I start drinking a lot of coffee," a Christian lady confessed. "It seems, however, that coffee is just not solving my problems anymore."

Maria was amazed at the difference that came into her life when she attended a Holy Spirit seminar and learned to spend time in communication with God through meaningful prayer and devotional study of the Word. "I heard about this years ago," she said, "but have neglected God in recent years."

We see multiplied examples of the Nebuchadnezzar syndrome. So I ask you to examine your attitudes and actions today and turn to the Holy Spirit, knowing that you can always look first to the source of true wisdom and understanding.

✎ A PRAYER FOR TODAY ✎

Father, You are able to reveal the deepest meaning of all life's mysteries, so again I turn to You for the direction I need.

March 30

KNOCKING KNEES AT THE PARTY

"There is a man in your kingdom in whom is the Spirit of the Holy God. And in the days of your father, light and understanding and wisdom, like the wisdom of the gods, were found in him; and King Nebuchadnezzar your father—your father the king—made him chief of the magicians, astrologers, Chaldeans, and soothsayers." Dan. 5:11, NKJV.

The socialites of Babylon were partying the night of their kingdom's downfall. They had taken the golden vessels from God's Temple in Jerusalem, and now they were using them in a drunken revelry in honor of corrupt pagan gods. In the midst of this scene, which in various ways is repeated often as the world nears its twenty-first century after Christ, part of a bloodless hand was seen writing on the wall, and its message was not welcome.

Belshazzar's knees knocked together as he shook with uncontrollable fear. In desperation the young king reenacted the generational sin of his grandfather Nebuchadnezzar. He called first for the wise men of the kingdom—psychics who have always failed. Belshazzar's mother, however, remembered the Nebuchadnezzar syndrome and finally called for help from Daniel, the Spirit-filled man of God.

"Life is a party," someone has said, but it never seems to end up like a beer commercial. Apart from Jesus, fun turns quickly to fighting, singing to sickness, delight to depression. Sooner or later the Holy Spirit's writing appears on the "wall" of the mind. A human body that has been made for true rejoicing with God finds itself fearfully facing the consequences of unforgiven insobriety, immorality, and impropriety. The "knees" of the mind begin to knock together with uncontrollable regret, and the countenance changes to one of exhaustion and suspicion. There is no more trust. The fun gods have failed again.

In the midst of today's confusion are still Daniels who can interpret the signs of the times. God's will is that His Holy Spirit speaks to the partygoers before they lose the kingdom forever. Listen carefully for His voice today as He still brings light, understanding, and wisdom, connected, as always, to love, acceptance, and forgiveness.

❈ *A PRAYER FOR TODAY* ❈

Lord, with You life is great, and when fellow Christians come together,
they can have a true festival of joy without regret.

March 31

AVOIDING UNREASONABLE FEAR

*"I have heard of you, that the Spirit of God is in you,
and that light and understanding and excellent
wisdom are found in you." Dan. 5:14, NKJV.*

When humanity's party is finally over, the lost call for the rocks and mountains to fall on them and hide them from the wrath of the Lamb (Rev. 6:15-17). Only people in deep fear could be intimidated by a lamb, but those in the ultimate depression of their final rejection of God's Spirit even fear the One who could help them the most.

While I was visiting Iraq, I sat in the ruins of ancient Babylon and read again the clear and concise message that the Holy Spirit gave to Daniel. Here, in Babylon's last hours, are revealed all the clues to avoiding the fear that is self-destructive in the end. Listen now as Spirit-filled Daniel fearlessly deals with the king.

Notice first that Daniel would not be bribed to accept the gifts of the world (Dan. 5:17). If we remember this, the powers of evil can have no ultimate claim on us. Second, Daniel recognized that honor and authority are actually in God's hand (verse 21). Committees, boards, or electorates can be manipulated or make mistakes, but God is the final decider of our eternal destiny. Third, there is only madness and foolishness until God's rule is recognized in the kingdom of the heart (verse 27). Fourth, true greatness comes through sincere humility before God (verse 22). Kneeling at the cross of Jesus, we are at the highest place possible in this life. Fifth, the desecration of true worship results in manipulation by false gods (verse 23). If we do not worship in Spirit and in truth, we are open to religious materialism, empty emotionalism, or cold formalism. Sixth, unless we recognize God's ownership of our life through the blood of Jesus and unless He is glorified in our body and spirit (verse 23; 1 Cor. 6:19, 20), our only future is the tragedy of eternal destruction (Dan. 5:30).

Praise the Lord that we can allow the Holy Spirit to write the wonderful words of life on our hearts today! Jesus has been "weighed in the balances" and found sufficient for all.

✿ *A PRAYER FOR TODAY* ✿

*Father, I acknowledge You as the giver and sustainer of all that I have,
and in You only do I glory.*

April 1

A RAIN OF RIGHTEOUSNESS

Be glad then, you children of Zion, and rejoice in the Lord your God;
for He has given you the former rain faithfully, and He will cause
the rain to come down for you—the former rain, and the
latter rain in the first month. Joel 2:23, NKJV.

*I*t's beginning to rain." What is your first reaction to those words? In a drought area they are cause for celebration. In a waterlogged valley you may reply, "Oh no! We've had enough."

In the Israelite agricultural economy rain was essential for survival, and the sequence of early, midseason, and final (or latter) rains was vital for the growth and abundance of the harvest. It is not hard to see why, then, the symbolism of the seasons of rain is used so effectively to illustrate the mighty pouring out (Joel 2:28, 29) of the Holy Spirit.

Actually "former rain" in this verse may be translated "teacher of righteousness," and it is the great ministry of the Holy Spirit to magnify and teach the righteousness of Jesus in the lives of God's people. Righteousness and rain are connected in the messages of the prophets. Isaiah says: "Rain down, you heavens, from above, and let the skies pour down righteousness" (Isa. 45:8). Hosea is even more helpful in explaining the symbolism of righteousness, rain, and the Holy Spirit. "Sow for yourselves righteousness; reap in mercy; break up your fallow ground, . . . till He comes and rains righteousness on you" (Hosea 10:12).

Open your heart in surrender to that wonderful rain of righteousness today.

We can understand Joel's latter-rain prophecy as having special significance now during the dramatic times in which we live. We are by no means waterlogged with God's Spirit, and we are beginning to see the drought break. Around the world there is coming such a revelation of Jesus' righteousness in the beautiful message of the gospel that more people are reportedly becoming new Christians than ever before in human history—more than 78,000 a day. It is exciting not only to be part of this great movement of the Spirit but also to experience the latter rain of victory power in your own life right now.

 *A PRAYER FOR TODAY*

Father, soak the dryness of my life with the full outpouring
of Your Spirit of righteousness and truth.

RED-HOT FIRE

After I have poured out my rains again, I will pour out my Spirit upon all of you! Your sons and daughters will prophesy; your old men will dream dreams, and your young men see visions. Joel 2:28, TLB.

*H*ave you ever seen red-hot metal being poured out like liquid fire? That is the way the word "pour" can be translated in Joel 2:28. At Pentecost the Holy Spirit literally appeared like tongues of red-hot fire, and the disciples began a blazing ministry in the power of the Spirit.

Dr. Lilia Beer is a Florida physician whom the Spirit of God used in a special way during a year of community medical service in Tijuana. Through her Bible studies a whole new church of more than 50 members was raised up. A few years later Lilia was led by the Lord to study and pray about the Holy Spirit, and as a result she found in her heart a deep thirsting for a new outpouring of the fire in her life and church.

Lilia was encouraged by Linda, who had come back to the Adventist Church after a number of years in a Pentecostal denomination. "I believe that the Adventist Church has the right teachings," Linda had said to Dr. Lilia, "but why do we have so little of the Holy Spirit?"

As these two earnest ladies began to pray together with their pastor and a small group of earnest church members, the Spirit implanted a vision in their minds. It began to burn within them like red-hot fire. "We will have a seminar on the Holy Spirit in our church, and this will be the beginning of a great work of the Spirit in this part of Florida."

The God who gives visions and dreams honors the faith of those who are obedient to His direction. I was privileged to lead the seminar and see the outpouring of the Spirit take place. A Baptist who had been brought to the seminar by an Adventist friend testified, "My pastor has been teaching on this topic, but I have never heard anything as clear and certain as I have learned here this weekend. Praise God that I have actually experienced what it means to be filled with the fire of the Spirit!"

&- *A PRAYER FOR TODAY* -&

*Give me a burning vision, Lord, of what can happen
as Your Spirit is poured out.*

April 3

WELCOME POWER FOR SERVANTS

*Even on my servants, both men and women, I will pour out
my Spirit in those days. Joel 2:29, NIV.*

Peter explained the supernatural events on the day of Pentecost by quoting Joel's prophecy. He interpreted the word "afterward" as meaning "in the last days" (Acts 2:17), and other New Testament writers concur that the whole Christian era is indeed the last days of salvation history. This age of the Holy Spirit was inaugurated at Pentecost and will culminate at the second coming of Jesus, when the "sun will be darkened, and the moon will turn red as blood" (Acts 2:20, TEV).

Not all people in the age of the Holy Spirit and in the time of the great latter rain will receive the outpouring of the Spirit. It is reserved especially for those who are willing to be God's servants. Through the fruit and gifts of the Spirit, the servants of God are able to reflect His character and minister for Him. This is why I encourage you again to pray the servant's prayer of total surrender, renewing each day God's power in your life. "Make me a servant, as You were a servant, Lord."

"The results of the Holy Spirit seminar in our church have been miraculous," Dr. Beer told me as she talked to me on the phone from Florida. "Yesterday at the conclusion of the Sabbath service the pastor asked if any would like to wait behind for special prayer. More than 100 came forward, and we prayed together for more than one hour. People laid hands on the sick as they prayed for them, and some wonderful healing took place. We sang quietly together in prayer, and church members told of great blessings that they had received."

Dr. Lilia Beer reminded me of a number of people we had anointed during the seminar and then concluded, "One of my patients was suffering from a swollen leg for which I could find no cure. After the anointing this lady discovered that her leg was completely healed, and she has had no recurrence of the disease. Others who had been skeptical of the work of the Holy Spirit gave similar amazing testimonies of the mighty ministry of the Spirit through His servants today."

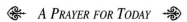

A PRAYER FOR TODAY

*Lord, I thank You that I can live at this time when Your servants
can serve with super spiritual power.*

PATIENT SPIRIT

Is it being said, O house of Jacob: "Is the Spirit of the Lord impatient?
Are these His doings?" Do not My words do good to
the one walking uprightly? Micah 2:7, NASB.

*H*ave you ever felt like attacking the mail carrier when you received a letter that you didn't like? It is unlikely, but often the messengers of God are treated this way. Being God's spokesperson is not always a path to popularity.

After preaching a positive, Spirit-filled message one Sabbath morning a young pastor was surprised when an angry church member accosted him in the foyer. "You had no right to speak to me the way you did in that sermon," the man shouted.

The pastor explained to the skeptical member that he knew nothing of the man's situation but had merely spoken the words of Scripture that the Holy Spirit had impressed on his mind for that day.

Micah the prophet faced a similar situation. He had faithfully given his message of warning to Judah in a time of national apostasy, and as a result the people were angry with him. Why did he not preach about peace and safety as did their own false prophets? Was God's Spirit impatient because He warned of judgment to come?

A week ago some friends called and explained that as they had been praying the Lord had impressed them to fax me some parables that they had written regarding a problem I was struggling with. As soon as the fax arrived I realized how accurately the parables illustrated the deceptions and dangers of my situation. I would much rather have heard that everything was all right, but their timely warnings also convinced me of the Holy Spirit's patience as He deals with God's children in a firm but loving way.

God's Spirit will never act impulsively or impatiently with you. He will do all He can to keep you on the right path without violating your free will. However, never think that the Spirit's patience with you will allow Him to leave you to walk unwarned into the place where the enemy of your soul can have final authority over you.

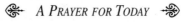

❧ *A PRAYER FOR TODAY* ❧

Father, I ask You today for the patience and loving firmness
in dealing with others that You consistently show to me.

NO DOUBT ABOUT IT

But as for me, I am filled with power, with the Spirit of the Lord,
fearlessly announcing God's punishment on Israel for her sins.
Micah 3:8, TLB.

*M*any Christians feel that it would be a matter of pride to acknowledge that they are saved by Jesus' blood or are filled with the Holy Spirit. If you find that hard to believe, then stand up in your church some Sabbath morning and ask, "How many here are born-again Christians?" or "How many of you are Spirit-filled Christians?"

But to admit a fact about who you are is not sinful pride but simple reality. If in an American church you asked, "How many are Americans?" most people would raise their hands. They would acknowledge reality.

After a worship service I asked those who would like certainty about being filled with the Holy Spirit to remain. A large portion of the congregation came to the front, and I explained the steps to this complete assurance.

"First, ask the Holy Spirit to create within you a deep longing for this experience. You have remained here to pray because this thirsting has already begun to happen, so recognize this as the first step. You are coming in total surrender to Him. While this earnest desire is in your heart take the second step—the step of faith—and believe that He has heard your prayer for His filling, and begin to thank Him and praise Him that He has now taken possession of every part of your being. Following this, He will give you the absolute certainty that you are a child of God (Rom. 8:16)."

After we had sung and praised the Lord together, many people stood with tears of joy in their eyes and testified that it was wonderful to have an assurance they had never known before. A few weeks later I met one of the men who had been present. "I'm renewing my experience with the Holy Spirit every day," he was quick to tell me. "Jesus has become special to me. I know that I'm a Spirit-filled Christian."

That's not sinful pride. That's the reality you can have each day.

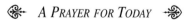

✖ *A Prayer for Today* ✖

Thank You, Lord, for fulfilling the promise of Luke 11:13 again today.
I know that I have Your gift of the Spirit.

HE IS ALWAYS HERE

According to the word that I covenanted with you
when you came out of Egypt, so My Spirit remains among you;
do not fear! Haggai 2:5, NKJV.

This church does not look as impressive as the one I used to belong to. I wonder if the Lord is really working here?"

I have met people who have been worried about that question when they have moved to a new city or denomination and have been very concerned about worshiping in an insignificant little structure. When the Jews who had seen Solomon's Temple compared it with the new Temple of Zerubbabel, they almost panicked. Surely God could not do much with a place like that!

The prophet brought great courage to the people. He affirmed that the Holy Spirit would remain with them and that the Messiah would grace this humble structure with His presence.

However small your house of worship is, it can be a powerhouse of Holy Spirit ministry through the love and presence of Jesus, the desire of all nations.

One of the traps into which Christianity has fallen has been to become building-centered rather than people-centered. From the time of Constantine until the present, vast fortunes have been spent on elaborate structures, while funds for ministry have been scarce. Early Christianity did not have this problem. Believers and seekers met in houses or outdoors, and all knew that they would be nurtured and fed in these households of faith as the Holy Spirit ministered through the people He filled.

"I'm so excited about this church!" a retired physician said to me as I was conducting revival meetings with Pastor Eoin Giller. I knew that he wasn't talking about the building. "My wife and I moved across the country to be members here," he continued. "We needed the love that we have felt in this place; the people are friendly; the pastor really feeds us from the Word of God; the Holy Spirit is moving here in a wonderful way."

Whatever building you may assemble in for public worship this week, you can trust that God's Spirit remains among you and will enable you to glorify Jesus.

⚜ *A PRAYER FOR TODAY* ⚜

No matter how externals appear, I'll open my heart
to Your presence, love, and power, Lord.

WELCOME, TRUE STRENGTH

Then he said, "This is God's message to Zerubbabel: 'Not by might, nor by power, but by my Spirit, says the Lord Almighty.'" Zech. 4:6, TLB.

This verse is one of the great favorites of Christians who are constantly looking to the Holy Spirit to accomplish the things that human wealth and ability cannot do. He is the source of true power (Acts 1:8) and supernatural might (Eph. 3:16).

Zerubbabel faced seemingly insurmountable mountains of obstacles, but God showed Zechariah through eight visions that he would be successful because of the work of the Holy Spirit.

The Holy Spirit is again building a temple. As He comes to dwell in us at conversion we become the temple of the Holy Spirit (1 Cor. 6:19, 20). The temple He builds is not the human body, however, but a character that reflects God's glory.

"I've let God down so badly," a friend told me. "How is it ever going to be possible for me to be a Christian whose heart is fully right with God?"

I reminded my friend of God's promise to Zerubbabel. "It can be done only as you let the Holy Spirit do the work. Remember, we 'are being transformed . . . by the Spirit of the Lord' (2 Cor. 3:18, NKJV)."

Please do not be discouraged by obstacles today. Just as the Temple in Jerusalem was being built not in order to bring the Jews back from captivity but because they were back, so God's Spirit is working in you not to save you but because you are saved already by accepting the gift of eternal life from Jesus.

In some parts of the world are beautiful cathedrals that have remained unfinished for centuries. While one part is being completed, another part is crumbling. Sometimes I have felt like that myself, but then I look at some victory gained and remember not to despise the day of small things (Zech. 4:10). The work that has begun through the mighty power of the Holy Spirit will be finished when Jesus comes. Then we will shout, "Grace, grace" (verse 7), recognizing that it was not our work that saved us but that salvation is a gift from our wonderful God.

❦ A PRAYER FOR TODAY ❧

Master Builder, keep on working with me so that I can more perfectly display the beauty of Your handiwork. Make the repairs and new additions necessary for my continued ministry.

REST IN ENEMY TERRITORY

And He called to me, and spoke to me, saying,
"See, those who go toward the north country have given rest
to My Spirit in the north country." Zech. 6:8, NKJV.

No territory of the enemy is more fearful today than AIDS. It is like the Assyrians, Babylonians, and Persians whom Jerusalem faced from the north.

A few years after Sally discovered that her husband was gay, she was diagnosed as dying of AIDS. After leaving her husband, Sally had sunk into a lifestyle of drinking, heroine, and cocaine, and she had hung out with a motorcycle gang. Now, following the diagnosis, she was filled with anger and wanted to die as soon as possible.

Juanita Kretschmar, of the New York SDA Community Health Services, tells what happened next in the "north country" of the enemy. Sally decided to jump out in front of a bus and commit suicide, but just as the fast-moving vehicle approached, it was slowed down by a van that stopped beside her. Van ministry worker John stepped out and said to Sally, "Excuse me, but you seem upset. Would you like me to pray for you?" For the first time Sally was able to talk about what had happened to her and the terrible anger that filled her life. After prayer John gave her a *Steps to Christ* and explained that he was not even scheduled to be at that place that day.

"I came home and read the book. Something different happened to me. It was like my whole life turned around. I got close to the Lord, and He answered all my prayers." Later Sally told Juanita about the powerful ministry of the Holy Spirit in the "north country." It was as though He said to her through *Steps to Christ,* "Get up; let's go. You don't have much time."

Six months later Sally had gained 52 pounds, and her body was functioning normally. Others say that she looks fit enough to run the marathon, and her doctors cannot explain what has happened. Now she brings rest, through the Holy Spirit, to the hurting in the land of the enemy as she visits and prays with other AIDS patients.

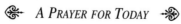

A PRAYER FOR TODAY

Lord, as Sally says, You are my Father, my Brother, my Healer,
my Counselor, my Friend.

April 9

HEARING THE SPIRIT

*They made their hearts as hard as flint and would not listen to
the law or to the words that the Lord Almighty had sent
by his Spirit through the earlier prophets. So the Lord
Almighty was very angry. Zech. 7:12, NIV.*

Y ou're very stubborn," a work associate said to me when I refused to
follow some advice he was giving. I called it not stubbornness but
determination. I couldn't see a problem, so why should I change?
Later I discovered that even though he was not quite right in what he said, I
was also unwise not to have listened to a friend's counsel.

Your friend the Holy Spirit knows how it feels to have His advice ignored.
He is always right, and in love He warns and teaches. But do we listen? When
we don't, the resulting trouble we find ourselves in is not His fault but our
own.

Ricki and Phillis had been warned not to marry. Both had been married
once or twice before and had serious personality problems that were certainly
not compatible in any way. Their pastor had prayed and reasoned with them
at length but all to no avail. Now, one year later, everything was in a mess.
Their arguments had become violent. When "hearts as hard as flint" clash, the
sparks begin to fly. Ricki had punched Phillis a few times, and she was afraid
of him. She had left Ricki and was filing for divorce. He was constantly ha-
rassing her and telling her that he loved her, but nothing worked.

There is only one solution for a heart of flint, and that is to allow the Holy
Spirit to work a conversion that will result in "a heart of flesh" (Eze. 36:26,
27). This means understanding the gospel, repentance, and daily surrender to
God. A heart of flesh will be strong for truth but soft and submissive to the
direction of the Spirit, who will often lead through the counsel and concern
of trusted friends and respected spiritual leaders.

I can say from experience, as you may also have discovered, that it is better to follow the Holy Spirit's leading than it is to ask God to help you pick
up the pieces later.

❦ *A PRAYER FOR TODAY* ❦

*Soften my heart with oil, Lord; make it ready to do Your will.
Give me wisdom to listen to spiritual counselors.*

April 10

WELCOME, SPIRIT OF GRACE

And I will pour on the house of David and on the inhabitants of Jerusalem the Spirit of grace and supplication; then they will look on Me whom they have pierced; they will mourn for Him as one mourns for his only son, and grieve for Him as one grieves for a firstborn. Zech. 12:10, NKJV.

The next-to-last verse about the Holy Spirit in the Old Testament is one of the most meaningful in the whole Bible. It is a prophecy concerning the outpouring of the Spirit after Jesus' crucifixion. Here for the first time Spirit and grace are linked together. He is called the Spirit of grace in Hebrews 10:29, and many New Testament references indicate that "grace" can often be understood as the mighty power of the Holy Spirit. When, in Acts 4, the disciples received a great outpouring of the Spirit, "great grace was upon them all" (verse 33). Later the Lord confirmed to Paul: "My grace is sufficient for you, for My strength is made perfect in weakness" (2 Cor. 12:9, NKJV).

"I have been praying for the Holy Spirit to fill me," a young man said, but he looked puzzled about the first effect of this earnest prayer. "Now I seem to feel worse than ever. I see my own sinfulness more than I ever have before and feel really bad about how I've treated Jesus."

He was surprised when I replied, "Praise the Lord!" Then we read together Zechariah 12:10, and I explained that the Holy Spirit's first work is to show us Jesus and that the Spirit leads us to deep sorrow for the way our sins pierced our wonderful Saviour.

The Spirit of grace does not leave us mourning, however. As Isaiah has said, He gives us "the oil of joy for mourning, the garment of praise for the spirit of heaviness" (Isa. 61:3).

What a great God we have!

Even while we were sinners Jesus was pierced and died to pay the penalty not only for our sins but for the sins of the whole world. "The Spirit of grace and supplication," I told my young friend, and I remind you today, "makes it possible for you to praise God for forgiveness, salvation, and the certainty that you are a child of God."

❧ A PRAYER FOR TODAY ❧

Hallelujah! Thank You, Jesus, for being willing to be crucified so that I can have the indescribable joy of eternal life.

THE SPIRIT OF TRUE MARRIAGE

But did He not make them one, having a remnant of the Spirit?
And why one? He seeks godly offspring. Therefore take heed
to your spirit, and let none deal treacherously with
the wife of his youth. Mal. 2:15, NKJV.

*A*fter praying through almost 100 wonderful Old Testament verses concerning the Holy Spirit, we find ourselves considering the last biblical references that would be written for more than 400 years. Now there would be four silent centuries of expectancy and hope, during which time the people must live in strength and purity as Israel's remnant of the Spirit.

God was deeply concerned that His people remain true to their marriage vows to Him and not become ensnared by the adultery of idolatry. Just as a husband has a responsibility to be faithful to his wife, so God desired His people to be faithful to Him. Unfaithfulness always brings its own punishment: heartache, loneliness, self-blame, physical and emotional sickness, separation from family and finances, guilt and grief, loss of assurance of salvation. This was not the "offspring" that God wanted for His beloved. His destiny for them through the power of His Spirit was to be His special treasure—His jewels (Mal. 3:17).

God's desire for us, as part of His remnant of the Spirit today, is exactly the same as He had for His people at the end of the Old Testament. We are waiting with hope and expectancy for the return of Jesus. This event is coming as surely as did the first advent of Jesus, but are we living in the Spirit or are we in unfaithfulness turning to love other gods?

When my youngest daughter Sharon was small I used to call her Treasure. Now that she herself is a mother, she sometimes reminds me of that and how special it was to her. Let the Spirit remind you today that you are one of God's treasures. The enemy of souls will try to rob you of that joy by constantly tempting you into unfaithfulness to God and those with whom you are united in special relationships. Let Jesus' love and forgiveness encircle you with the complete assurance of your oneness with God today.

☙ A PRAYER FOR TODAY ❧

Great is Your faithfulness, Lord, unto me. Thank You
for showing me how special I am to You.

BEGINNING THE NEW TESTAMENT

These are the facts concerning the birth of Jesus Christ: His mother,
Mary, was engaged to be married to Joseph. But while she was still
a virgin she became pregnant by the Holy Spirit. Matt. 1:18, TLB.

The Holy Spirit is introduced with stunning suddenness at the beginning of the New Testament. Without a word of warning or introduction, we find Him credited for the pregnancy of a young woman. While it was obviously expected that the original readers of the Gospels would be familiar with the work of God's Spirit from their reading of the Old Testament, the same does not necessarily apply through the subsequent centuries. Even the disciples at Ephesus had not so much as heard of the Holy Spirit (Acts 19:2).

Jesus' ministry as recorded in the four Gospels provides the bridge between the Holy Spirit in the Old Testament and the age of the Holy Spirit that begins with the first 28 chapters of the book of Acts. In the Gospels Jesus models the team ministry with the Spirit that will characterize true Christianity between Pentecost and the Second Coming.

As with the incarnation of Jesus, true Christianity is conceived by the Holy Spirit wherever it begins to grow and flourish. The seed for the great missionary movements has always been planted and nurtured by the Spirit rather than by the will of missionaries. The most successful workers for God have always recognized that the Spirit has gone before them. If that has not happened, then no amount of preaching or teaching can bear fruit.

That which happened at the Incarnation and the establishment and spread of Christianity in general is also true for each individual. The Holy Spirit begins a miraculous work in our hearts so that we can learn of Jesus and accept Him as our Saviour. Without the Spirit's beginning work, which comes as suddenly and unexplainedly as the Incarnation, we can never grasp or accept the wonderful plan of salvation. It will be to us just another theory, another intellectual possibility. That is why it is so important that the unsaved are open to the gentle ministry of the Spirit of the living God.

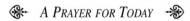

A PRAYER FOR TODAY

Holy Spirit, create within me the fertile soil that will enable
the love of Jesus to grow and flourish.

WELCOME, SPIRIT OF JESUS

As he lay awake considering this, he fell into a dream, and saw an angel standing beside him. "Joseph, son of David," the angel said, "don't hesitate to take Mary as your wife! For the child within her has been conceived by the Holy Spirit." Matt. 1:20, TLB.

I stood by the grave of Sojourner Truth and marveled again at the miracle of a life transformed by a vision of Jesus. Following her conversion, Sojourner Truth, who had been born a slave in New York and had served several masters before her emancipation in 1828, began to speak to large crowds about her experience with the Lord. On one occasion, though, when she realized that she had forgotten the presence of the Holy Spirit, she was filled with deep fear and "shrunk back aghast from the awful look" she perceived as coming from the One she had thought of as a friend.

Just as God gave a dream to take away Joseph's fear, so this young lady caught a new glimpse of Jesus. Listen as she tells the story in her autobiography. " 'Who are you?' was the cry of her heart, and her whole soul was in one deep prayer that this heavenly personage might be revealed to her, and remain with her. At length, after binding both soul and body with the intensity of this desire, till breath and strength seemed failing, and she could maintain her position no longer, an answer came to her, saying distinctly, 'It is Jesus.' 'Yes,' she responded, 'It is *Jesus.*'

"Previous to these exercises of mind, she heard Jesus mentioned in reading or speaking, but had received from what she heard no impression that He was any other than an eminent man, like a Washington or a Lafayette. Now He appeared to her delighted mental vision as so mild, so good, and so every way lovely, and He loved her so much! And how strange that He had always loved her, and she had never known it!" *(Narrative of Sojourner Truth, p. 67)*.

Little wonder Sojourner Truth had such a powerful ministry. She became a strong voice opposing slavery, spoke eloquently for women's rights, and worked to make her country a place where freedom was a reality for all. She not only loved to preach the gospel, but she lived the gospel in the power of the Holy Spirit, who had made possible the birth of the One who set the captives free.

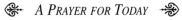

❦ *A PRAYER FOR TODAY* ❧

Calm my fears, Lord, with new insights of my loving Saviour.

SPIRIT AND FIRE

I baptize you with water for repentance. But after me will come one who is more powerful than I, whose sandals I am not fit to carry. He will baptize you with the Holy Spirit and with fire. Matt. 3:11, NIV.

*I*t is tempting to think of the fire as the tongues at Pentecost or as the enthusiasm the Spirit produces in those He fills. It appears, however, that the fire that accompanies the infilling of the Holy Spirit symbolizes the purifying and refining effect of suffering and trouble in the life of the believer. I know that does not sound like good news, but it is a reality of spiritual life.

As the Holy Spirit works mightily in our life, the "chaff" of selfishness and sin can be burned up (Matt. 3:12). Please remember that this is not the basis of your salvation but the fruitage that enables you to reflect the character of Jesus.

At a revival meeting in the South Bay area of Los Angeles I listened to Beth sing the beautiful "Vineyard Song," in which she told of the divine Refiner's fire and of her heart's sole desire—holiness. As she sang I remembered a book that Beth's small group leader, Janet, had given me a few months earlier—*Gold Tried in the Fire.* This had helped me understand that it is the Holy Spirit's work during the fires of affliction that helps produce in me true Christian character (1 Peter 1:7; Rev. 3:18).

If you are like me, you naturally want to escape the fire, but to go through it now as a saved person and in the power of the Holy Spirit means to escape the final fires that do not refine but destroy (Rev. 20:9).

The coming of the Holy Spirit is not neutral. It often causes fiery conflict as it arouses the opposition of the enemy. Jesus said that He came to send fire on the earth, and at His baptism of fire on the cross Jesus was immersed in the suffering caused by a sinful, rebellious world (Luke 12:49, 50). Remember, however, that when you are baptized with the Holy Spirit and fire you have, through Jesus, the survival capabilities of the three Hebrews in the Babylonian fiery furnace.

❧ A PRAYER FOR TODAY ❧

My Father and my God, in the heat of battle I accept the insulation of Your robe of perfect righteousness.

WELCOME, GENTLE DOVE

After his baptism, as soon as Jesus came up out of the water, the heavens were opened to him and he saw the Spirit of God coming down in the form of a dove. Matt. 3:16, TLB.

*W*hy a dove? I have watched bald eagles in Alaska. They are powerful and majestic. In Australia I have sat and studied the noisy and fascinating cockatoos. But this week in Tucson, Arizona, I have noticed the doves eating the ripe olives on the trees surrounding veterinarian Paul Neff's house. Like lambs, doves are gentle and unassuming. They are quiet and nonaggressive.

The dove was the rabbinic symbol for national Israel. Now it would become the symbol of the Holy Spirit's presence in the Christian church. Although the Spirit would sometimes come like a mighty rushing wind or violent earthquake, He is most like a dove in His interpersonal relationships with the people He fills. He does not force Himself on anyone but comes only when invited. He does not assume control of any life unless He is specifically requested to do so. He does not make a lot of noise about Himself, but always glorifies Jesus. He can be grieved away by unfriendly actions but is always quickly willing to return.

"I was so nervous about the Holy Spirit that I didn't invite Him into my life," a very successful pastor confided. "However, I have now found Him to be a wonderful friend personally and a very important partner in my ministry."

At a camp meeting an elderly lady expressed to me the joy that she had discovered in fellowship with the Holy Spirit. "He draws me close to Jesus and is always there to aid me in my prayers and Bible study. He doesn't push me to do anything but gently leads me to minister to others."

A young man who attended a Friday evening prayer fellowship with about 30 other young people shared with the whole group, "The Holy Spirit is very special to me. It seems that He always assures me that I'm a beloved son of God and that I can be confident that Jesus is my personal Saviour."

You can relate to the Holy Spirit as a special friend who will never hurt or embarrass you in any way.

❦ A PRAYER FOR TODAY ❧

Gentle Spirit, fill me again with Your quiet confidence and strength. Thank You for the assurance of my place in Your family.

UNWELCOME TEMPTATION

Then Jesus was led out into the wilderness by the Holy Spirit,
to be tempted there by Satan. Matt. 4:1, TLB.

That Jesus was led into the wilderness indicates a certain reluctance on His part. We can understand His feelings, because we know that temptation is no picnic. Jesus' three and a half years of intense conflict with the enemy was beginning, and His humanity was not looking forward to it. I can imagine Him saying to the Holy Spirit, "I need Your help now to get out to the place of battle and start the final countdown to Calvary."

But the enemy waited for the most vulnerable moment to attack. After 40 days of fasting, Jesus' body was crying out for food and recognition with an intensity as demanding as the craving of an addict.

I read some time ago about new glass security doors that were installed in the Washington suite of a high-ranking U.S. cabinet official. The Secret Service had stated that the $58,000 doors were very necessary, but when an official who monitored government spending checked the value of the new security doors, he discovered that they were always open and unguarded. In other words, they were a waste of money.

In the wilderness of temptation Jesus used a security system that the Holy Spirit makes available to every child of God. He shut the doors on temptation by saying, "It is written," and the resulting victory for Jesus was the beginning of Satan's ultimate defeat.

Although, after our baptism by water or the Spirit, the enemy will usually intensify his attacks upon us, we can be sure that the Holy Spirit will not lead us into any situations of temptation. In fact, Jesus taught us to pray that we will not be led into temptation, but will be delivered from the evil one. If by our foolishness we reach the place where temptation seems irresistible, then the Holy Spirit can still bring to our minds the words of Scripture that will function as a powerful security system. The wilderness of depression can blossom with the flowers of victory and joy.

❧ *A Prayer for Today* ❧

I thank You, Lord, that You were willing to understand the intensity of
temptation and were able to be victorious with the same weapons available to me.

HIS WORDS IN YOUR MOUTH

But when they arrest you, do not worry about what to say or how to say it. At that time you will be given what to say, for it will not be you speaking, but the Spirit of your Father speaking through you. Matt. 10:19, 20, NIV.

*E*ven the words that the Holy Spirit will give in a crisis do not guarantee that the speaker's life will always be spared (Matt. 10:21). Two thousand years of Christian history tells us of millions who have died for their faith in Jesus Christ. But the Holy Spirit's words do guarantee that persecutors will hear a faithful witness of truth that may later bear fruit. The Holy Spirit gives a "power of utterance and a wisdom which no opponent will be able to resist or refute" (Luke 21:15, NEB). Praise the Lord!

Armando Valladares spent 22 years in Cuban prisons. He was starved, tortured, and threatened with execution. Only his faith in God miraculously sustained him. In his book *Against All Hope* Valladares tells the story of a Protestant preacher, Gerardo, whom the prisoners called the Brother of the Faith. Each evening at Boniato he would lead the men in prayer and singing, and as the guards came to beat the prisoners and stop the meeting, he would sing out "Glory, glory, hallelujah!" "The Brother of the Faith had been at La Cabana and at Isla de Pinos," Valladares says. "He was his own most moving sermon. He always cheered us up, called us to prayer meetings, washed the clothes of the sick—and helped many men face death with strength and serenity. Above all he taught us not to hate; all his sermons carried that message."

The Holy Spirit gave Gerardo many faithful words to speak to his captors, and when they beat him, "the eyes of the Brother of the Faith seemed to burn; his arms opened to the sky, seeming to draw down pardon for his torturers." He was still forgiving his tormenters as their machine-gun bullets ripped into his chest in 1975. Like the Spirit-filled deacon Stephen, Gerardo had spoken the words that the Holy Spirit had placed in his mouth, and now in peace he fell asleep to await the great morning of resurrection (see Acts 6:10; 7:54-60).

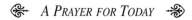

❦ *A Prayer for Today* ❧

Even if this is a day of peace and relative prosperity,
help me be faithful in speaking Your word of wisdom, Lord.

MONOPOLY ON THE SPIRIT

*Behold, My Servant whom I have chosen, my Beloved in whom My soul
is well pleased; I will put My Spirit upon Him, and He will declare
justice to the Gentiles. Matt. 12:18, NKJV.*

*I*t does not take long to recognize the mighty working of the Holy Spirit
in Jesus' life and ministry. At least 15 times in the Gospel of Matthew
the prophecies of Isaiah are quoted or referred to, showing that Jesus
was certainly the fulfillment of the predictions that were given concerning the
amazing work of the Messiah.

This Spirit-filled ministry, however, was not for Jesus alone. Although
Jesus moved fully in the Spirit, He did not claim a monopoly on the Holy
Spirit. He entrusted most of His work for the Gentiles, as mentioned in this
prophecy, to His followers who would be Spirit-filled from the time of
Pentecost.

Years ago some pastors were meeting together to plan a large evangelistic campaign in their city. As possible speakers were discussed, many of the
pastors agreed that the very successful evangelist, Dwight L. Moody, would
be the man to invite. A young pastor, who was rather negative, commented,
"From the way some of you talk, you'd think Mr. Moody has a monopoly on
the Holy Spirit."

Silence filled the room for a moment, and then one of the pastors replied,
"No, Mr. Moody doesn't have a monopoly on the Holy Spirit. But the Holy
Spirit does have a monopoly on Mr. Moody."

Because of this monopoly, Moody's ministry reached millions for Jesus
in his lifetime of Spirit-filled service.

Like Jesus, Mr. Moody, and countless other Spirit-filled Christians
through the ages, we can open our lives today to the wonderful monopoly of
the Holy Spirit. There is no monotony in this ministry. It is the most exciting
work on earth. As His servants and the beloved of God, we can find joy in our
ministry and worship, knowing that the Lord is working out His prophetic
plans for the world through us. We can be as surely a part of prophecy as was
Jesus Himself.

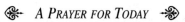

A PRAYER FOR TODAY

*I come again in full surrender, Lord, asking You to take
complete possession of my life.*

DEFEATING DEMONS

But if I cast out devils by the Spirit of God,
then the kingdom of God is come unto you. Matt. 12:28.

*A*s Jesse and Tom walked out of the room where they had been pray-ing for more than an hour following a revival meeting, Jesse asked, "Are you a minister?"

He was amazed when Tom replied, "No, Jesse, I'm an attorney."

But Tom has a ministry that the Holy Spirit had used that night to bring great victory in Jesse's life. Jesus, through the Holy Spirit, always sets the captives free when they come to Him for help.

At a meeting the next day I interviewed Jesse as he told his story of demon possession, drugs, gang warfare, and family heartaches. He had be-longed to an infamous motorcycle gang that had been involved in demonic ritual sacrifices and crime and violence of every kind. In fact, a few nights be-fore, he had come to the church with a gun to kill the pastors whom he con-sidered responsible for his wife's leaving home. That night someone had called the police, and it had taken four officers to control him. Pastors Eoin and Mitch had prayed for Jesse, and he had found some relief, but in his meeting with Tom the evil was finally conquered.

As Jesse testified to the group, everyone could see how powerfully the Holy Spirit had moved in the life of this man whose blood had stained the church carpet at the time of his fight with the police. He cried as he intro-duced his son, who was with him for the first time in 17 years. He praised God that he had found freedom in Jesus. The devil had not wanted to give up his territory, but the victory was as sure as when Jesus healed the demon-pos-sessed man in Matthew 12.

Although you may not be confronted by a demon-possessed person like pastors Eoin and Mitch or attorney Tom were, you may experience times when you feel Satan tempting and accusing you. When this happens remem-ber that you can always be victorious by Jesus' blood and the Holy Spirit's power.

☙ A PRAYER FOR TODAY ❧

Lord, I recognize Jesus as my almighty Saviour,
who has supreme power over all of the agencies of darkness.

BLASPHEMY AGAINST THE SPIRIT

Therefore I say to you, every sin and blasphemy will be forgiven men,
but the blasphemy against the Spirit will not be forgiven men.
Matt. 12:31, NKJV.

Religious leaders had accused Jesus of casting out demons by the power of Satan, and Jesus did not take this accusation lightly, because He knew where this type of thinking could lead. He saw that those who reject the clear evidence of the power of God will find themselves on the side of one who never leads a soul to repentance and forgiveness but only to destruction.

I do not know what Brother P had done, but he wrote to Ellen White because he was deeply concerned that he was guilty of the unpardonable sin. She wrote to him many words of great encouragement. She explained that our God is loving and forgiving and saves the repentant sinner by His grace, always making available His righteousness by faith. This wonderful fact she illustrated by the actions of the father when the prodigal son returned home. Ellen White explained to Brother P that we must never place ourselves on Satan's side by not believing in God's acceptance when we, through the power of the Holy Spirit, come to the light shining from the cross.

Read now part of this letter that relates to Jesus' discussion in today's text. "Brother P, you ask if you have committed the sin which has no forgiveness in this life or in the life to come. I answer, I do not see the slightest evidence that this is the case. What constitutes the sin against the Holy Ghost? It is willfully attributing to Satan the work of the Holy Spirit" *(Testimonies,* vol. 5, p. 634).

It is easy, but extremely dangerous, to judge the work of the Holy Spirit wherever it is taking place today. If it does not fit into our system or preconceived opinions, we are inclined to say that it is of Satan. Revivals have often been rejected because they cut across the status quo of church organizations. Rather than making this mistake, let us leave the judgment to God and be fully open to Spirit and truth in our own hearts and lives.

❧ A PRAYER FOR TODAY ❧

Father, help me be slow to judge others and quick to open my heart
again to the loving ministry of Your Spirit.

WELCOME FORGIVENESS

Anyone who speaks a word against the Son of Man, it will be forgiven him; but whoever speaks against the Holy Spirit, it will not be forgiven him, either in this age or in the age to come. Matt. 12:32, NKJV.

*H*ave you experienced the agony of thinking that you have committed a sin that can never be forgiven? Sometime in life most Christians find themselves in the position of wondering if their sins are too bad for Jesus to deal with. Take courage. Anyone who has caught a glimpse of Jesus and His love cannot bear the thought of being eternally separated from Him. On the other hand, those who have no concern for spiritual things seem little troubled about the eternal consequences of unforgiven sin.

That is why I always take courage when someone approaches me—as Dale did. "I'm addicted to pornography," he confessed with tears in his eyes. "I'm deeply concerned that I have committed the unpardonable sin."

Dale was surprised when I responded, "Praise the Lord! This is a sign that the Holy Spirit has access to your heart, Dale, and is still able to convict you of sin. Your deep concern is a sure indication that the Holy Spirit is leading you to victory and assurance of salvation in Jesus."

Mrs. McCutcheon asked if I would speak to her daughter, Betty. "What is the problem?" I asked.

"She's living in sin and is not at all concerned about it."

"We can pray that Satan will be restricted and that the Spirit of the Lord will be able to speak to her heart," I explained. "But God will not force Himself on Betty. She must be open to Him."

Christians are often surprised to learn that there are sins that lead to death and sins that do not lead to death (1 John 5:16, 17). Earlier John said that the sins that do not lead to death are those that are confessed to God and cleansed by the blood of Jesus (1 John 1:7-9). So we can quickly discover that the only unforgivable sin is that which is not confessed and covered by the blood.

Praise God for the Holy Spirit, who will once again today convict of sin and lead us gently to our lovely Saviour.

❧ *A PRAYER FOR TODAY* ❧

Search me, O God, and then give me a clear picture of my hope in Jesus.

THE SPIRIT SHOWS WHO IS LORD

He said to them, "How is it then that David, speaking by the Spirit,
calls him 'Lord'? For he says, 'The Lord said to my Lord:
"Sit at my right hand until I put your enemies under your feet."'"
Matt. 22:43, 44, NIV.

Who is your Lord, your Master? When you recognize Jesus not only as Saviour but also as Lord of your life, you will have taken a giant step toward understanding and experiencing the true power of Christianity. This recognition is possible only through the Holy Spirit's ministry.

When Adolf Hitler rose to power, a large part of the German church recognized him as the "Führer," but Protestant Evangelical pastor Martin Niemöller said, as the Spirit of the true God filled his heart, "Not you, Herr Hitler, but God is my Führer." Niemöller had learned the tragic mistake of silence against the enemy. "In Germany, they came first for the Communists, and I didn't speak up because I wasn't a Communist. Then they came for the Jews, and I didn't speak up because I wasn't a Jew. Then they came for the trade unionists, and I didn't speak up because I wasn't a trade unionist. Then they came for the Catholics, and I didn't speak up because I was a Protestant. Then they came for me, and by that time no one was left to speak up."

Niemöller spent eight years in the dreaded Sachsenhausen and Dachau concentration camps. One of Hitler's last orders was for the execution of this faithful pastor who proclaimed in the Spirit, as David did, the Lordship of Jesus Christ and the right of the church to be separate from the control of the state. Fortunately, Niemöller was liberated by the Allies before his execution was carried out. His fellow patriot for the Lordship of Christ, Dietrich Bonhoeffer, author of *The Cost of Discipleship,* was not so fortunate. He was executed just before the surrender of Germany in May 1945.

If you have accepted Jesus as your Saviour, affirm again today your willingness for Him to be the Lord of your life whatever the cost may be. Then His Spirit will lead you to walk in a path of victorious Christianity.

❦ A PRAYER FOR TODAY ❦

Father, I willingly and joyfully give You the right to have full authority
over every aspect of my life today.

April 23

WELCOME, ALL NATIONS

Therefore go and make disciples of all nations,
baptizing them in the name of the Father and of the Son
and of the Holy Spirit. Matt. 28:19, NIV.

*L*ike many other Christians, I have stood in Westminster Abbey a number of times, praying at the grave of the great missionary David Livingstone. This man had taken seriously the gospel commission to carry into all the world the message of salvation and the personal freedom of all people. Livingstone had first thought that he might go to China, but the Lord closed that door and opened another to the great continent of Africa. His ministry has inspired thousands to follow the great commission.

Livingstone was born in Blantyre, Scotland, and at the age of 10 he began working in a cotton mill to help support his family. His parents, he says, had taught him the theory of free salvation by the atonement of our Saviour, but the change that came in his life when the Holy Spirit led him to accept this personally was dramatic.

"This change was like what may be supposed would take place were it possible to cure a case of 'color blindness,'" he wrote in his best-selling book. He continued, "The fullness with which the pardon of all our guilt is offered in God's book drew forth feelings of affectionate love [in me] to Him who bought us with His blood, which in some small measure has influenced my conduct ever since" (quoted in Mrs. J. H. Worcester, Jr., *The Life of David Livingstone,* p. 8).

For more than 30 years in Africa, amid terrible personal hardships, Livingstone made disciples and baptized in the name of the Father, Son, and Holy Spirit. He recognized that the whole Trinity was included in this great gospel ministry and that it was the Holy Spirit who was empowering him to fulfill the commission.

But never far from his thoughts was his love for Jesus. On his birthday, March 19, 1872, not much more than a year before his death, Livingstone wrote: "My Jesus, my King, my life, my all; I again dedicate my whole self to Thee. Accept me and grant, O gracious Father, that ere this year is gone I may finish my task" *(ibid.,* p. 97).

✎ *A PRAYER FOR TODAY* ✎

Holy Trinity, I know that it is possible to fulfill Your gospel commission only as
I have a personal relationship with You. Today again
I make that full surrender and commitment.

April 24

RECEIVING THE SPIRIT

"I baptize you with water but he will baptize you
with God's Holy Spirit!" Mark 1:8, TLB.

T he Bible clearly teaches that the Holy Spirit comes to dwell in you
at conversion (see, for example, Eph. 1:13; Eze. 36:27; Rom. 8:9).
In New Testament times conversion and water baptism usually followed closely together, so water baptism and accepting the gift of the Spirit
were sometimes linked.

But a study of the biographies of Christians whom God has used mightily, even in modern times, reveals that there was inevitably a time in their experience when they became fully open to the total power and control of the
Holy Spirit in their life, and they often called this event the baptism or receiving of the Spirit.

I like the way Dennis Bennett explains the difference between *having* the
Spirit and *receiving* the Spirit. "A man may push his way past my secretary
and come into my office and sit down while I am very busy at my desk. I
know he is there, but continue working, not acknowledging his presence.
After a few minutes my telephone rings and someone on the other end of the
line asks, 'Have you a man in your office?' and proceeds to describe my visitor. I reply, 'Yes, he's here, but I haven't laid aside my work to welcome him.
I haven't received him yet.'

"But then suppose I lay aside my work and give my visitor a cordial welcome and devote to him my undivided attention and ask him, 'Why are you
here and how may I serve you?' Then my visitor may rise to his feet with a
glad smile and shake my hand and say, 'Oh, I'm so glad you finally received
me, for I have a check for you for one million dollars and I want to give it to
you. And I have an important message from a friend whom you haven't seen
in a long time, plus so many other good things I want to share with you, now
that you have received me'" (*The Holy Spirit and You,* p. 18).

If you have been converted and consequently have the Holy Spirit in your
life, I encourage you to receive Him today by giving Him your full attention.
You will be surprised at the results.

❧ *A PRAYER FOR TODAY* ❧

Welcome again today, Holy Spirit.
Please take control of every part of Your dwelling place.

TEARING HEAVEN OPEN

As Jesus was coming up out of the water, he saw heaven being torn open and the Spirit descending on him like a dove. Mark 1:10, NIV.

*A*s our small group prayed while we studied the first few verses of Mark, Denise was very impressed that heaven actually had appeared to have been torn open so that the gentle Dove could appear. "Tearing sounds violent to me," Denise said as some of us in the group began to think about this for the first time. It was as if the Dove had finally broken through a barrier, just as a chick bursts forth from its eggshell.

"Let's think of some other times when this tearing takes place in the beginning of the Christian church," I suggested.

Another group member remembered that there was tearing right at the close of Jesus' ministry. "Then the veil of the temple was torn in two from top to bottom" (Mark 15:38, NKJV). Someone else thought of the results of the ministry of the Holy Spirit that often tore apart whole cities. "But the multitude of the city was divided [torn apart]: part sided with the Jews, and part with the apostles" (Acts 14:4, NKJV).

The next week when our group met, Denise could not wait to share what she had discovered in her Bible study at home. "I was reading in Revelation 6:14," she explained, "and I discovered that heaven is again torn open at the second coming of Jesus. Listen to what it says: 'Then the sky receded [split apart] as a scroll when it is rolled up and every island was moved out of its place' [NKJV]. The ministry of Jesus has 'tearing apart' at the beginning, middle, and end."

"What lesson is there in this for us today?" I asked.

Joe was always ready with a quick answer. "When the Holy Spirit brings Jesus into our lives, we are torn apart from selfishness and sin. Sometimes, unfortunately, it can cause division in churches, families, and friendships. There is a tearing apart from the complacency of Laodiceanism and spiritual lethargy. We are torn apart from failure and the control of Satan and are introduced to victory in Jesus. Praise the Lord!"

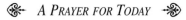

❦ *A PRAYER FOR TODAY* ❧

Thank You, Lord, for not only having a ministry of tearing but also healing and binding up the brokenhearted.

WINNING OVER WILD BEASTS

Immediately the Holy Spirit urged Jesus into the desert.
There, for forty days, alone except for desert animals, he was subjected
to Satan's temptations to sin. And afterwards the angels came
and cared for him. Mark 1:12, 13, TLB.

*I*n the wilderness of temptation wild beasts are always waiting to hurt and destroy. One of the wildest beasts is lust, because lust always results in dejection. As Oswald Chambers says: "Dejection springs from one of two sources—I have either satisfied a lust or I have not. Lust means—I must have it at once. Spiritual lust makes me demand an answer from God, instead of seeking God Who gives the answer" *(My Utmost for His Highest,* Feb. 7).

Other wild beasts of the wilderness include low self-esteem, perfectionism, and lack of trust. In this desert place people feel inferior, unloved, and unwanted. These emotions often lead to suicidal feelings and an inclination toward self-destructive behavior.

Sometimes people are driven into the wilderness by memories of incest, childhood abuse, demonic or cultic activity, legalistic religion, immorality, or addictive behavior. Depression always characterizes the wilderness, because in depression there appears to be no living water of hope, no trees of shade from the burning sun of total despair. The wild beasts in the wilderness can often take the form of other people: an unbelieving or unfaithful spouse, abusive parents, disobedient children, persecuting work or school associates, disruptive neighbors, false religious shepherds, or unfaithful friends.

Impossible as it may seem, the wilderness can "rejoice, and blossom as the rose" (Isa. 35:1). The rose that we know today (probably not the same flower mentioned in Scripture) is a thorn bush, but it grows what many consider to be the most beautiful flowers in the world. The way out of the wilderness is made possible only by the Holy Spirit, who enables us to grasp the reality that we are God's children. We are important to God. Jesus would have gone through the wilderness and on to Calvary for any one of us—even for you alone. What a rose in the wilderness that certainty is! In Jesus there is the absolute assurance of salvation that turns the wilderness into a basket of fragrant flowers and luscious fruit for those who accept the gospel.

❧ A PRAYER FOR TODAY ❧

Lord, dispel depression and dejection by an awareness of the ministration
of bread and water from Your holy angels.

BY WHOSE POWER?

But he who blasphemes against the Holy Spirit never has forgiveness,
but is subject to eternal condemnation. Mark 3:29, NKJV.

*M*y wife thinks I'm crazy," Edwin said as he talked about the wonderful way God was working in his life now that he was aware of the Holy Spirit filling him each day.

"The things those so-called Holy Spirit denominations are doing is of the devil," a retired pastor exclaimed as he discussed with a young pastor supernatural spiritual gifts that were evident within other churches in the city.

"That 'faith healer' is filled with an unholy spirit and is doing this for his own profit," Jean warned as she tried to convince her friend Paula not to attend a special prayer meeting in her local Adventist church.

Jesus faced these same three degrees of accusation. His family said that He was out of His mind (Mark 3:21). Religious leaders said that He was working by the power of Satan (verse 22). They also stated authoritatively that He had an unclean spirit, meaning that His outward actions were a cloak for control by an inner, corrupt, self-gratifying power (verse 30).

When Mark's letter went out to the early Christians, they were facing the same accusations by Jewish and Roman authorities as Jesus had faced when He had worked mightily in the Holy Spirit's power. It was important for those Christians, and all in succeeding ages, to know that Jesus had given the most severe warning about this attitude of rejection of the Holy Spirit.

A few months further into Jesus' ministry the disciples revealed that they had a similar problem. They came across a man who was casting out demons in the name of Jesus, and they had forbidden him to carry on because he was not part of their system. But Jesus informed them: "Do not stop him. . . . Whoever is not against us is for us" (Mark 9:39, 40).

God has chosen to work through imperfect instruments, but if a work needs to be stopped, He can do it in His own time and way. Until then we can always apply the test that says, "By their fruits [not rumors] ye shall know them" (Matt. 7:20).

❧ *A PRAYER FOR TODAY* ❧

Father, help me always to be willing to do Your work,
even if it is misjudged and opposed by well-meaning people.

April 28

ENEMIES UNDERFOOT

For David himself said by the Holy Spirit: "The Lord said to my Lord,
'Sit at My right hand, till I make Your enemies Your footstool.'"
Mark 12:36, NKJV.

Sonna had been troubled at her place of employment by a manager who seemed determined to make her workdays as difficult as possible. One evening in our small group we talked about Satan's methods of attack and concluded that he tries in many ways to make the life of a Christian as difficult as possible. "I'm certainly getting a lot of harassment," Sonna told us. "It's making me angry and discouraged, and I feel like resigning my position."

"Affirming the lordship of Jesus in the face of the enemy is one of the secrets of success," I suggested, reminding her that the real enemy that she was dealing with was not her office manager but evil forces. "When this attack comes, instead of reacting with anger and tears, go to a private place where you can repeat out loud a declaration of your belief in God, especially centering on Jesus Christ."

Apparently this was a purpose of the creeds of the early Christian church. One of the earliest, the Apostles' Creed, says: "I believe in God the Father Almighty, Maker of heaven and earth, and in Jesus Christ, His only Son, our Lord, who was conceived by the Holy Ghost, born of the virgin Mary, suffered under Pontius Pilate, was crucified, died, and was buried: . . . the third day He rose again from the dead. He ascended into heaven. And sitteth on the right hand of God the Father Almighty: from thence He shall come to judge the quick and the dead. I believe in the Holy Ghost, the holy . . . church: the Communion of saints, the forgiveness of sins; the resurrection of the body, and the life everlasting."

When trouble at work came again, Sonna followed the suggestion and was excited about the results. "I felt a peace and calmness come into my heart. It was not dramatic, but rather like a gentle warmth and confidence. My testimony of faith in the lordship of Jesus strengthened me and certainly defeated the enemy's attack. Now I can carry on with my job, knowing that I'm doing it in the power of the Holy Spirit."

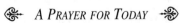

❧ *A PRAYER FOR TODAY* ❧

In the face of all enemies,
I gladly and firmly acknowledge You as my Lord and my God.

130

ALL CHRISTIANS UNDER ARREST

But when you are arrested and stand trial, don't worry about what to say in your defense. Just say what God tells you to. Then you will not be speaking, but the Holy Spirit will. Mark 13:11, TLB.

*A*lthough, tragically, reliable statistics indicate that almost a half million Christians each year are being put to death for their faith, most of the world's one billion plus Christians may never have to speak for Jesus before a hostile court.

Before we settle back into the comfort of our armchairs, though, it would be well to remember that the enemy of souls is unlikely to let us off that easily. All Christians have, in fact, been accosted by the arresting armies of evil. Those Christians who did not allow the Holy Spirit to speak words of rebuke to temptation and of affirmation of faith in Jesus have found themselves locked in the prison house of sin and spiritual darkness.

Quin Sherrer and Ruthanne Garlock tell of Pauline, who was constantly caving in to a shopping addiction. The bondage to this compulsive behavior was finally broken, however, when she allowed the Holy Spirit to speak through her.

After confessing her sin, Pauline declared aloud: "Satan, you will no longer have a foothold in my life by making me greedy for things I don't need. I renounce this idol and declare the stronghold broken by the authority of Jesus Christ. Addiction to shopping will no longer control me. I recognize this bondage of generational weakness, and by the blood of Jesus I sever it." Then she prayed, "Heavenly Father, I yield to You in this area, trusting You that this bondage is removed from my life. Thank You that by the power of the Holy Spirit and according to Your Word I can and will walk in obedience to You and in victory. I make You, and You only, the Lord of my life. In Jesus' name. Amen" *(A Woman's Guide to Spiritual Warfare,* p. 108).

Praise God! This evil was no longer able to imprison this child of God.

&ampersand; *A PRAYER FOR TODAY* &ampersand;

Lord, I will rely on You again today to give the words to speak in the face of the persuasive pressures of temptation.

WELCOME, SIGNS THAT FOLLOW

*And these signs will follow those who believe: In My name they will
cast out demons; they will speak with new tongues; they will
take up serpents; and if they drink anything deadly,
it will by no means hurt them; they will lay hands on the sick,
and they will recover. Mark 16:17, 18, NKJV.*

*A*s long as there are believers these signs will be evident in the
Christian church. This seems to be the essence of Jesus' promise.
Some have contested this belief, stating that these verses of Mark are
not included in the most reliable manuscripts of the New Testament. While it
is true that the early historian Eusebius and the Latin biblical scholar Jerome
doubted this passage—and it is not in Codex Vacticanus or Codex
Sinaiticus—most other important manuscripts and early Christian writers accepted it as authentic. As one scholar today says: "This passage certainly represents the experience and expectation of the early church" (John Rea, *The
Holy Spirit in the Bible,* p. 131).

Others, like Augustine, the North African bishop who lived from A.D. 354
to 430, have stated that supernatural signs of the Spirit did not continue after
the first-century establishment of the church. History reveals how inaccurate
that assumption is. In fact, Augustine himself had to change his opinion when
in a space of two years more than 70 signs took place in his own parish. All
these miraculous events were carefully documented and included healings of
paralysis, breast cancer, hernias, blindness, and demon possession.

Adventist pioneer Ellen White, who had seen mighty signs take place
under the power of the Holy Spirit, quoted Mark 16:17, 18 and said: "The
promise is as far-reaching as the commission. Not that all the gifts are im-
parted to each believer. The Spirit divides 'to every man severally as He will.'
. . . The gospel still possesses the same power, and why should we not today
witness the same results?" *(The Desire of Ages,* p. 823).

As a true believer in Jesus, there is no reason you cannot also see the fulfillment of promise of Mark 6:17, 18 in your ministry today. There is no
doubt that we are living in an age when God will again surprise us with
mighty miracles.

❧ *A PRAYER FOR TODAY* ❧

*Thank You, Father, for the signs that follow the gospel, not as a cheap display
but as a confirmation of Your unfailing power.*

EVEN FROM THE WOMB

*For he will be one of the Lord's great men. He must never touch wine
or hard liquor—and he will be filled with the Holy Spirit,
even from before his birth! Luke 1:15, TLB.*

W hat would it be like to have a Spirit-filled baby? Would the little one ever cry or need to have a change of diapers? As the child grew would he or she fall over and get hurt while learning to walk? Would this little girl or boy ever need to be disciplined, or would he or she be the perfect child?

Questions like these indicate some of the misconceptions that we have about the Holy Spirit. Listen to some that I heard recently. "The Holy Spirit fills only perfect people." "If people are filled with the Holy Spirit, they will not fall into sin or make any bad mistakes." "People who are filled with the Holy Spirit are always strong and never get discouraged."

If you have been tempted to think this way, please examine again the Spirit-filled lives of Moses, Elijah, and David. Look at the heated disagreements between Paul and Barnabas, or between Paul and Peter. Study the history of the conflicts between the great Spirit-filled preachers John Wesley and George Whitefield, or between Adventist pioneers James and Ellen White. John the Baptist himself ended up in some doubt about Jesus and sent some of his disciples to check Jesus out (Luke 7:19).

We do not look at the faults of Spirit-filled people in order to excuse sin or to blame the Holy Spirit, but rather to gain courage from the fact that He can use imperfect instruments in a very powerful way if they are surrendered to Him. Elizabeth no doubt saw much of the humanness of little John, but she could always rejoice in Gabriel's promise that her son was filled with the Spirit.

Parents today, even as they struggle with the difficult tendencies of their children's human nature, can also believe that these little ones who have been dedicated to God can be filled with the Holy Spirit even from their mother's womb.

❧ *A PRAYER FOR TODAY* ❧

*Father, help me see in each little child the powerful potential of
a Spirit-filled life and realize that this is why the enemy
concentrates so much of his effort on children.*

THE MYSTERIOUS CONCEPTION

The angel answered, "The Holy Spirit will come upon you, and the power of the Most High will overshadow you. So the holy one to be born will be called the Son of God." Luke 1:35, NIV.

Whom would you have chosen to be your mother? For centuries young women in Israel had prayed that they would be the mother of the Messiah. Now Jesus, in His preincarnation position as the second person of the Trinity, had made the stunning choice of who would carry Him as a tiny fertilized ovum, nurture Him as a growing embryo and fetus, give birth to Him in Bethlehem, and guide His growth for two or three decades. Mary was the blessed girl who was selected, and the Holy Spirit initiated and superintended the whole process.

Both Mary and Jesus suffered from constant suspicion and taunting for the circumstances of His birth. Jesus, the Holy One of God, chose to know what it means to be ridiculed for illegitimacy in a society that considered this to be a terrible disgrace.

Circumstances of birth can make a big difference in life. It was said of one of the recent presidents of the United States that he "was born on third base and thought that he had hit a triple." Other people start life as if they have been struck out before they even begin. Remember, however, that wherever birth has placed you on the socioeconomic ladder, that at the cross and at the grave all humanity is on the same level.

Count Nicolaus Ludwig Graf von Zinzendorf was a rich young ruler, while Christian David was a humble journeyman carpenter. Yet when the power of the Highest overshadowed them and initiated and superintended their new birth experience in eighteenth-century Saxony, they became brothers in heart and in mighty ministry for the Lord. Their faith and miraculous spiritual birth was ridiculed by many, including church leaders, but the overshadowing of the Holy Spirit enabled them to give birth to the Moravian missionary movement that changed the lives and destinies of millions.

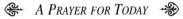

⊰ A PRAYER FOR TODAY ⊱

As at Creation and the Incarnation, Holy Spirit, overshadow my life with Your supernatural power so that I may continue in the assurance that I'm a child of God.

LEAPING FOR JOY

At the sound of Mary's greeting, Elizabeth's child leaped within her and she was filled with the Holy Spirit. Luke 1:41, TLB.

Have you ever felt like jumping for joy? That can be the effect of Jesus' ministry through the power of the Holy Spirit. It's hard to keep your feet on the ground when Jesus begins to work in your life. In fact, as we read in Luke 1:41-44, John even had a prenatal joy ministry. Jesus specifically tells His followers to leap for joy in the midst of persecution. When the Spirit of Jesus enabled Peter and John to heal the crippled man in Jerusalem, he not only leaped up but also went into the Temple "walking, and leaping, and praising God" (Acts 3:8).

Jonathan Edwards in his *Faithful Narrative of a Surprising Work of God* tells of some of the unexpected results of George Whitefield's preaching in the American colonies during the mid-1700s: "Since that time there has often been . . . an unavoidable leaping for joy" (cited in John White, *When the Spirit Comes With Power,* p. 94).

Even some who would think it undignified to leap in church know what it is to feel their hearts leap for joy when they witness the Holy Spirit's mighty working. On May 25, 1895, Ellen White was speaking at a worship service in North Fitzroy, Australia. Two brothers had become interested in the Adventist message and attended a recent camp meeting, but their wives showed little interest. In fact, one "had been brought up in the Presbyterian Church, and had been educated to think that it was very improper for women to speak in meeting, and that for a woman to preach was altogether beyond the bounds of propriety."

At the end of her sermon Ellen White felt deeply impressed to make a call. She reported: "The Holy Spirit was in the meeting, and many were stirred by its deep movings." Then a great miracle happened. The two wives went forward when the call was made, responding to the strong impression of the Spirit of the Lord. "When brethren A. saw their wives going forward, they said they felt like leaping and praising God. They could hardly believe their own eyes" *(Review and Herald,* July 30, 1895).

❧ *A PRAYER FOR TODAY* ❧

Gracious Father, may I never lose Your joy that makes me feel like walking and leaping and praising Your holy name.

May 4

SPEAKING BY THE SPIRIT

Then his father Zacharias was filled with the Holy Spirit and gave this prophecy: "Praise the Lord, the God of Israel, for he has come to visit his people and has redeemed them." Luke 1:67, 68, TLB.

As Sabbath, May 25, 1895, approached, Ellen White, because of a severe cold and hoarseness, wondered if she would be able to speak as scheduled for the worship serivce in North Fitzroy, Australia. She decided, however, to bring an earnest petition to the Lord and began to claim the promises of Luke 11: "Ask, and it shall be given you. . . . How much more shall your heavenly Father give the Holy Spirit to them that ask him?" (Luke 11:9-13).

She believed that God would fulfill His promises, so she selected a passage of Scripture for her sermon, but as she rose to speak, the portion of Scripture was taken from her mind, and instead the Holy Spirit led her to prophesy from 2 Peter 1 concerning God's grace. She testified: "I was enabled by the aid of the Holy Spirit to speak with clearness and power. At the close of my discourse, I felt impressed by the Spirit of God to extend an invitation for all those to come forward who desired to give themselves fully to the Lord" (*Review and Herald,* July 30, 1895).

Among the 30 or so who came forward were the wives of the two A brothers. These ladies had been resisting the Spirit, but now they made their full surrender to God.

Ellen White's son was surprised that she should make this unexpected call, because no other ministers were present to help pray for the people who came forward. The Spirit now moved with prophetic power on Willie, leading his mother to testify: "I never heard him speak with greater power or deeper feeling than at that time. He called on brethren Faulkhead and Salisbury to come forward, and we knelt in prayer. My son took the lead, and the Lord surely indited his petition; for he seemed to pray as though in the presence of God" (*ibid.*).

Do not be surprised if the same Spirit who chose to speak through Zacharias, the Whites, and the two Australian brothers, chooses to speak through you today.

✺ A PRAYER FOR TODAY ✺

Lord, I bless You today as You enable me to pray and speak in the mighty power of Your Spirit.

WAITING AND WATCHING

Now there was a man in Jerusalem called Simeon, who was righteous and devout. He was waiting for the consolation of Israel, and the Holy Spirit was upon him. Luke 2:25, NIV.

*A*s Simeon waited for the Consoler, or *Paraklētos,* of Israel, another Consoler, the Holy Spirit, was already with him, giving him the strength and faithfulness to keep watching and praying.

The Welsh revival of 1904, which many scholars believe was the last great revival to influence large numbers of people of all ages and classes, was sparked by young Evan Roberts, who waited and prayed for the outpouring of the Holy Spirit. We are not told how long Simeon had waited and watched for Jesus, but we do know that Roberts prayed for years that he would be present at the meeting when the Holy Spirit came in the fullness of revival power.

" 'For thirteen years,' writes Evan Roberts, 'I prayed for the Spirit; and this is the way I was led to pray. William Davies, the deacon, said one night in the society [small group]: "Remember to be faithful. What if the Spirit descended and you were absent? Remember Thomas! What a loss he had" ' " (Stephen Olford, *Heart-Cry for Revival,* p. 113).

Roberts then recalled his faithfulness right through his teenage years until the fire of revival began when he was 26. "I said to myself: 'I will have the Spirit'; and through every kind of weather and in spite of all difficulties, I went to the meetings. Many times, on seeing other boys with the boats on the tide, I was tempted to turn back and join them. But, no. I said to myself: 'Remember your resolve,' and on I went. I went faithfully to the meetings for prayer throughout the ten or eleven years I prayed for a Revival. It was the Spirit that moved me thus to think" *(ibid.).*

Just as the Spirit led Simeon to wait for the coming of the Messiah and led the disciples to tarry in Jerusalem for the baptism of the Spirit at Pentecost, so He leads sincere Christians in all ages to wait earnestly for and expect, like Evan Roberts, the special outpourings of the Spirit. "I have a vision of all Wales being lifted up to heaven," Roberts told his brother-in-law. "We are going to see the mightiest revival that Wales has ever known—and the Holy Spirit is coming soon, so we must be ready."

❧ *A PRAYER FOR TODAY* ❧

*Help me choose to be in the gatherings of Your people, Lord,
where You will pour out Your Spirit in early and latter rain power.*

A VISION OF CERTAINTY

It had been revealed to him by the Holy Spirit that he would not die before he had seen the Lord's Christ. Luke 2:26, NIV.

When the Spirit gives a vision of future possibilities, God's faithful people see the vision as reality. Simeon did. There was no doubt in his mind that he would hold the Messiah in his arms.

Dee Dee, wife of Pastor Walter Nelson, believed that God had impressed her that a certain house in Kaneohe, Hawaii, was the home that He was going to make available for this family with three growing boys. Although they did not have sufficient funds to make the purchase, Dee Dee was convinced that God would provide, and she saw the house as it could be renovated to suit their needs. Miraculously that vision came true, as I discovered when enjoying the delightful hospitality of this gifted "Martha" and her family.

Young Welshman Evan Roberts had a vision, not of holding the Messiah like Simeon or of a house for a pastor's family as seen by Dee Dee Nelson, but of the fire of revival. In his book, *Heart-Cry for Revival,* Stephen Olford tells the story of what happened as Roberts' vision became a reality: "At a certain morning meeting which Evan Roberts attended, the evangelist in one of his petitions besought that the Lord would 'bend us.' The Spirit seemed to say to Roberts, 'That's what you need, to be bent.'

"And thus he describes his experience: 'I felt a living force coming into my bosom. This grew and grew, and I was almost bursting. My bosom was boiling. What boiled in me was that verse: "God commending His love." I fell on my knees . . . and perspiration flowed freely. I thought blood was gushing forth.' . . . Meanwhile he was crying out, 'O Lord, bend me! Bend me!' Then suddenly the glory broke" (p. 113).

The Holy Spirit is as comfortable giving you a vision of people and houses as He is of great spiritual events. He will help you see the powerful potential beyond what seems possible in human strength and wisdom. Simeon knew that before he died he would see the Saviour. Perhaps some scoffed at his certainty, but with God the vision became reality.

❦ A PRAYER FOR TODAY ❧

My Lord and God, I thank You that You can again open my eyes to all the wonderful things that can be made possible today by Your Spirit.

MOVED BY THE SPIRIT

Moved by the Spirit, he went into the temple courts. Luke 2:27, NIV.

The Holy Spirit moves people not only spiritually but also geographically if necessary. Simeon was moved to the Temple area so that he could be there when the baby Jesus arrived. Philip was moved to a new location after he had baptized the Ethiopian leader. Elijah was moved to glory in a chariot of fire.

After Evan Roberts was anointed so powerfully by the Holy Spirit at Blaenanerch, Wales, in 1904, the Spirit moved him without delay into ministry. "Henceforth," he said, "the salvation of souls became the burden of my heart. From that time I was on fire with a desire to go through all Wales" (Stephen Olford, *Heart-Cry for Revival,* p. 113). Immediately the Spirit moved Roberts back to his home in Loughor, where he began to hold prayer meetings, "which in a matter of days drew larger and larger crowds as revival swept the whole region" *(ibid.)*.

The Holy Spirit moved Evan Roberts from meeting to meeting across Wales. "The chapels were thronged, with hundreds more outside. His appearance at these gatherings often caused much religious fervor and excitement, and a few words of exhortation or a brief prayer sufficed to set the congregation ablaze. The people would burst into singing and then testimony, followed by prayer, and then into singing again" *(ibid.,* p. 114).

Joseph Kemp, the pastor of Charlotte Chapel in Edinburgh, was moved by the Holy Spirit to visit the revival meetings in Wales. Listen to what happened: "I spent two weeks watching, experiencing, drinking in, having my own heart searched, comparing my methods with those of the Holy Ghost; and then I returned to my people in Edinburgh to tell what I had seen" *(ibid.,* pp. 114, 115). Immediately the revival began to sweep across Scotland. The results were miraculous. Not only did the churches become full but, as Kemp testified: "It has given to both young and old a new love for the Bible. Time would fail to tell of the purified lives, changed homes, and the brightened outlook for hundreds" *(ibid.,* p. 116).

This is the movement of the Spirit that God has for us as we pray today.

❦ *A PRAYER FOR TODAY* ❧

Lord of love, I ask today that You will enable me to be in exactly the place where You would have me to be at the center of revival and reformation.

THE BLOOD AND THE FIRE

John answered, saying to them all, "I indeed baptize you with water;
but One mightier than I is coming, whose sandal strap
I am not worthy to loose. He will baptize you with
the Holy Spirit and with fire." Luke 3:16, NKJV.

*I*f you have sung "Onward, Christian Soldiers" recently, you may have
thought of the Salvation Army, which began its mighty ministry for the poor
and needy more than 100 years ago. Ringing a bell beside one of the more
than 15,000 Christmas kettles in the United States may not seem much like warfare, but "Blood and Fire," the motto of the Salvation Army, characterizes the revival and social welfare dynamics of the Army's founder, William Booth.

Booth was converted in a Methodist chapel in Nottingham, England, when he
was 15 and was filled with the Holy Spirit at the revival meetings of visiting
American preacher James Caughey. Soon after, Booth and some young friends
set out to evangelize the poor in open air and small-group cottage meetings. After
his marriage to Catherine Mumford in 1855, their unique team ministry moved
ahead in the Holy Spirit's mighty fire. In fact, it was said that Booth's methods
were based on common sense, the Holy Spirit, and the Word of God.

Soon this Spirit-filled couple would leave the security of employment
with their denomination and rely wholly on the Spirit of the Lord. Later he
recalled: "I resigned my position and went out, from home and salary, with a
delicate wife and four little children under five years of age" (John
Woodbridge, editor, *More Than Conquerors,* p. 261). What a great harvest of
souls has resulted from that step of faith!

General and Mrs. Booth always acknowledged that their Army was the
creation of the Holy Spirit, and he exhorted his officers in 1892: "Cast yourselves upon God. Keep on watching and praying and believing and expecting
for me, for yourselves, for the whole Army at home and abroad, for the
mighty baptism of burning fire" *(Christian History,* issue 26, p. 28). Today in
more than 90 countries around the world 3 million Salvation Army soldiers
and officers have accepted "Blood and Fire" as the motto of their Spirit-filled
practical Christian ministry.

❧ *A PRAYER FOR TODAY* ☙

Baptize me again, Lord, with the Spirit and fire so that I can serve You
according to the spiritual gifts that You will choose to use through me.

A DOVE IN THE STORM

And the Holy Spirit descended in bodily form like a dove upon Him, and a voice came from heaven which said, "You are My beloved Son; in You I am well pleased." Luke 3:22, NKJV.

*D*avid Livingstone had gone back to Africa in 1858, but William Booth was convicted that the gentle Dove, the Holy Spirit, must be given the opportunity to bring the gospel to "the heathen living close at hand in darkest England" *(Christian History,* issue 26, p. 34). Millions living in abject poverty, in the squalor of terrible slums, working often more than 90 hours each week, without true religion or faith in God, would hear from General Booth and his Salvation Army that they were indeed God's beloved sons and daughters.

The darkness of satanic forces has always tried to obliterate the light of Jesus' love and truth. England in the nineteenth century was no exception, and even though the Army's motto was "Blood and Fire," these courageous, Spirit-filled soldiers for Jesus showed the gentleness of the Dove amid vicious storms of opposition.

Cyril Barnes tells of the Army under siege. "When William and Catherine Booth visited Sheffield in January 1882, the success of their Sunday meetings so angered the Army's enemies that a local gang known as the 'Blades' decided to assault them. . . . Later that day, as William Booth reviewed his troops covered with blood, mud, and egg yolk, their brass instruments battered beyond repair, he suggested, 'Now is the time to have your photographs taken!' In that one year in Great Britain alone nearly seven hundred Army personnel were brutally assaulted on the streets, simply for preaching the gospel" *(ibid.,* p. 16). A number of Salvationists in great Britain and America were killed as they shared the love of Jesus.

Being filled with the Holy Spirit like a gentle Dove does not mean freedom from opposition or persecution. It does mean, however, that there is strength of purpose, strong faith and trust in God, assurance of salvation, and a calmness and peace within that even the worst forces of hell cannot shake.

 *A PRAYER FOR TODAY*

Father, help me not be intimidated by those who are negative to the working of Your Spirit but give me an ever-growing certainty that I'm Your beloved child.

A No-Surprise Attack

And Jesus being full of the Holy Ghost returned from Jordan,
and was led by the Spirit into the wilderness. Luke 4:1.

*A*s a guest in the lovely home of Dr. Kazuo and Rose Teruya, I enjoyed the beautiful view across the Haiku Valley to Kaneohe on the Hawaiian island of Oahu. In the distance I could see the Marine Corps Air Station, and as I listened to the movement of the planes, I thought of the surprise attack that had hit this air base along with Pearl Harbor on the morning of December 7, 1941.

Rose had been living in Honolulu at the time of the attack and remembered seeing some of the 353 Japanese planes flying overhead as she heard on the radio news of what was happening. In about two hours the attack was over, and more than 2,400 Americans were dead. America was thrown violently into World War II. More than 50 years later, survivors still remember the terror of that morning.

It was not a surprise attack that rocketed Jesus into three and a half years of conflict with the enemy. As the Holy Spirit filled Jesus, He was ready for the battle. From Jesus' earliest years on His mother's knee the Spirit had fortified His mind with the Scriptures, and now as He entered the wilderness He was ready with the Word in exactly the same way that we can be ready today. Filled with the Holy Spirit, we will not be sleeping at dawn, nor will we leave for breakfast as did the two army operators at the Opana Radar Station 10 minutes before the attack on Pearl Harbor. The Spirit prepares us for victory against Satan's deceptions.

Following our seminar in the Kaneohe church, I was able to visit Pearl Harbor with Pastors Richard Among and Walter Nelson. "Were there no earlier warnings of this attack?" I asked.

"Authorities in Washington had many indications that trouble was coming, but they believed that negotiations could solve the problem," Richard explained. "They did not take into account how deceptive the enemy can be."

Today we make no negotiations with the enemy and take no chances. Through the Spirit of God we are ready for conflict at all times.

❧ *A Prayer for Today* ❧

Keep me awake, Father. Let me hide Your Word in my heart that I will not sin
against You when temptation suddenly comes.

WELCOME, MISSIONARY SPIRIT

And Jesus returned in the power of the Spirit into Galilee: and there went out a fame of him through all the region round about. Luke 4:14.

*A*dventist pioneer Ellen White had seen many visions of heaven, so on her trip to the South Pacific she was surprised to see the beautiful view of the windward side of the Hawaiian island of Oahu. Looking out from Nuunau Pali Pass over Kailua and Kaneohe to the bright blue Pacific, she exclaimed that this was more like heaven than any place she had seen on earth. I reminded my Hawaiian friends, who had shared this statement with me, that she had not yet visited New Zealand!

Mrs. White's visit to Hawaii in 1891 was about 70 years after the arrival of the first missionaries, many of whom had been converted and filled with the Spirit through the fiery, revival preaching of Charles G. Finney. When the missionaries reached Hawaii after a six-month, 16,000-mile, boat trip from Boston, they found unbelievable conditions of "destitution, degradation, and barbarism, among the almost naked savages." Although the missionaries supplied clothes to converts, it was not unusual for people to turn up naked to church. The first Adventist missionary in Hawaii was Abram La Rue, who was a Spirit-energized former gold miner. He arrived in Honolulu in 1883 and soon, with another literature evangelist, sowed sufficient gospel seed to result eventually in the baptism of the first nine believers in God's three angels' messages.

When Jesus began His Spirit-empowered missionary ministry in Galilee, He faced spiritual degradation and nakedness that hurt His heart of love more than the sight of the primitiveness of native Hawaiians in their beautiful tropical paradise. He saw not only sickness and poverty but the suffering caused by false and ineffective religion. In the sophistication of our modern, technological society, missionary ministry is as urgent as it was in Galilee or the Hawaiian Islands. Hurting humanity today can be helped by seeing the gospel at work in the lives of Spirit-filled Christians who open homes and hearts to those in need of love, acceptance, and forgiveness.

❧ *A PRAYER FOR TODAY* ❧

Holy Spirit, please fill me with a missionary spirit that will motivate me to cross oceans of social, ethnic, cultural, and religious barriers for You.

WELCOME, HEALING MINISTRY

The Spirit of the Lord is upon me, because he hath anointed me to preach the gospel to the poor; he hath sent me to heal the brokenhearted, to preach deliverance to the captives, and recovering of sight to the blind, to set at liberty them that are bruised, to preach the acceptable year of the Lord. Luke 4:18, 19.

*I*n fulfillment of this incredible prophecy from Isaiah, Jesus was involved in a total healing ministry. If you pray about this passage and analyze it carefully, you will discover that it encompasses spiritual healing, emotional healing, healing of distorted vision, healing from circumstances of bondage such as memories and addictions, healing from spiritualistic oppression, and healing of false expectations regarding the future.

Every person often needs Jesus' healing power in one or more of those areas. Some healing comes as the Holy Spirit leads hurting souls into the Word of truth. Others find healing as they communicate with their heavenly Father in prayer. Most often, though, the Spirit works through Christians who are themselves healed healers.

Attorney Tom Hamilton, who has himself known the healing power of Jesus, was used by the Lord in Arizona to free Jessie from the influence of Satan. In the same way the Lord used Pastor Richard Among to pray for a man who was subsequently healed of cancer on the Hawaiian island of Oahu.

On the island of Maui I met with a small group in the home of Jeannette Coon. Donovan and Jacque Kay had been present in the Lahaina church six months earlier, when Pastor Barry, Norma Crabtree, and a number of other church members had joined me in special prayer for the sick. We had all experienced the healing power of God in one way or another, and on the last evening Jacque Kay testified to the small group how she had been healed from Addison's disease when we had prayed for her six months earlier. Everyone in the group exclaimed what a tremendous change there had been in the life of our hostess, Jeannette, in the six months since she had had herself prayed for and gained the victory over the caffeine capsules to which she had been addicted for 30 years.

❦ *A PRAYER FOR TODAY* ❧

Lord, please continue to anoint me with Your Spirit so that I can be an agent of Your all-encompassing healing ministry.

REAL REJOICING

"Nevertheless do not rejoice in this, that the spirits are subject to you,
but rather rejoice because your names are written in heaven."
In that hour Jesus rejoiced in the Spirit. Luke 10:20, 21, NKJV.

Christians who love the Lord center their rejoicing not in what they have done, but rather in Jesus, who has made certain their place in heaven. The Holy Spirit even led Jesus to rejoice as He saw His disciples beginning to grasp the certainty of who He really is.

After the Scottish preacher Joseph Kemp had caught the fire of the Welsh revival, he returned to his home church and in 1905 led his people in a prayer movement that resulted in a mighty outpouring of the Holy Spirit in Edinburgh. Listen to Kemp tell some of the dramatic results: "The people poured out their hearts in importunate prayer. I have yet to witness a movement that has produced more permanent results in the lives of men, women, and children. There were irregularities, no doubt; some commotion, yes. There was that which shot itself through all prescribed forms and shattered all conventionality. But such a movement with all its irregularities is to be preferred far above the dull, dreary, monotonous decorum of many churches. Under these influences the crowds thronged the chapel, which only three years before maintained a 'somber vacuum.' After the first year of this work we had personally dealt with no fewer than one thousand souls, who had been brought to God during the prayer meetings" *(Heart-Cry for Revival,* p. 116).

Now the people of Edinburgh could, like Jesus, rejoice in the Spirit. "People tell us our religion is joyless," Kemp said. "Well, if the saints of the living God have no joy, who has? Jesus Christ has given us to see that joy is one of the qualities He imparts to the saints of God. The world knows nothing of it. Do not tell me that the sporting clubs, the dance halls, the movies, and operas can give you joy. They can for the moment give you some fun, but that is not joy. Joy is the gift of God. When a revival from God visits a congregation, it brings with it joy" *(ibid.,* p. 115).

&-- *A PRAYER FOR TODAY* --&

Father, the world offers empty hilarity, but today I accept again Your true
rejoicing, which brings inner laughter and eternal happiness.

A HAPPY GIVER

*And if even sinful persons like yourselves give children what they need,
don't you realize that your heavenly Father will do at least as much,
and give the Holy Spirit to those who ask for him? Luke 11:13, TLB.*

Around Christmas is the worst time of the year to work in retail sales," my middle daughter, Lyndell, informed me as she was in the midst of that time of the year at the store she managed in a large Portland shopping center. "Many people seem to be all uptight about having to give gifts."

Not so with God. He delights in giving His children the wonderful gift of the Holy Spirit.

At conversion, when a sinner invites Jesus to be his or her Saviour, the gift of the Holy Spirit is first given to dwell in that person's life (Rom. 8:9-11; Eph. 1:13; Eze. 36:26, 27). Most Christians, however, are not conscious of the Spirit's coming at conversion and know very little about Him. When they actually become aware of the Holy Spirit and consciously receive Him, this gift brings such joy that they want to repeat the experience again and again.

The Holy Spirit works with great power only when He receives the invitation to do so. This is actually a daily surrender to total control by the Spirit of every part of the body temple in which He already dwells (1 Cor. 6:19, 20). Jesus ends His most concentrated teaching on prayer by giving instruction on the repeated reception of the Holy Spirit. First, He teaches us to ask "day by day" for "our daily bread" (Luke 11:3, NKJV). Second, He tells the story of the man who persistently asked with positive expectation for three loaves at midnight. Finally, the Greek present tense in verses 9, 10, 13 suggests that Jesus was saying, "Keep on asking, seeking, knocking, and you will keep on receiving."

Did you ask yesterday? Then ask again today and tomorrow. Sometimes when children ask for a lot, their parents say, "Don't bother me." But God is the opposite of that. He says, "Keep on asking Me again and again. I just want to keep giving you more and more of the Holy Spirit every day."

❦ A PRAYER FOR TODAY ❧

*Yes, Lord, I'm asking again today for Your fabulous gift of my friend,
comforter, and empowerer—the Holy Spirit.
Thanks for hearing and answering my prayer.*

SPECIFIC CONFESSION

*And everyone who speaks a word against the Son of Man will be
forgiven, but anyone who blasphemes against the Holy Spirit
will not be forgiven. Luke 12:10, NIV.*

*A*t the cross Jesus forgave all the sins of humanity as He paid the price
for "not our sins only but the sins of all the world" (1 John 2:2,
NEB). To appropriate that forgiveness I must confess my sin as the
Holy Spirit brings conviction to my heart (1 John 1:9; John 16:8). The sin
against the Holy Spirit cannot be forgiven because conviction and confession
are rejected, and the Spirit's loving entreaties are resisted and repulsed. A person rejecting the Holy Spirit has an I-couldn't-care-less attitude.

"Confess" is an interesting word that is important to understand. It means
"to admit or acknowledge" or "to agree." So when the Holy Spirit convicts
me of sin, it is important that my confession specifically acknowledges the
exact realization of sin that the Spirit has placed upon my heart.

I like the way that Neil T. Anderson illustrates the importance of specific
confession. "Suppose a father catches his son throwing a rock at a car. Dad
says, 'You threw a rock at a car, and that was wrong.' If the boy responds,
'I'm sorry, Dad,' has he confessed? Not really. He may also say, 'Please forgive me, Dad,' but has he actually confessed yet? No. He hasn't confessed
until he agrees with his dad, 'I threw a rock at a car; I was wrong'" *(The
Bondage Breaker,* p. 81).

"When you sin, you may feel sorry, but feeling sorry or even telling God
you're sorry isn't confession. You confess your sin when you say what God
says about it: 'I entertained a lustful thought, and that's a sin'; 'I treated my
spouse unkindly this morning, and that was wrong'; 'Pride motivated me to
seek that board position, and pride doesn't belong in my life'" *(ibid.,* p. 81).

Specific confession breaks strongholds that Satan has in our lives and allows the Holy Spirit to glorify Jesus in and through us anew each day.

☙ *A PRAYER FOR TODAY* ❧

*As I confess to You the sins that Your Spirit is revealing to me today, Lord,
I rejoice in the total love, acceptance, and forgiveness
that You always give me in Jesus.*

RIGHT WORDS AT THE RIGHT TIME

**For the Holy Spirit will teach you in that very hour
what you ought to say. Luke 12:12, NKJV.**

*H*ave you ever had the experience of having the right answer at the very time you needed it? Later you may have said, "I don't know how that text came to my mind." It seems that the Holy Spirit gives us the right words just when we need them the most.

There are many reports of the Holy Spirit working mightily in Southeast Asia. In Communist Vietnam, government officials have been baffled by what God is doing. A 1992 article translated from a Vietnamese newspaper concluded: "We don't know what is happening [in the highlands], but it is something called the 'Good News' religion."

About the time of the article featuring the Good News religion the Communists began an intensive "reeducation campaign" in a village where an evangelist had been preaching. After a six-hour session, one of the officials wrote two headings on a blackboard: "Against Christ" and "For Christ." He then asked the villagers to sign their names in the appropriate column. No one responded until finally an elderly woman addressed the group. "For the past 20 years I have followed Marxism. I have followed the party line and served as your leader. But a few months ago I came to realize that Jesus Christ offers a better way."

In the moment of test and crisis the Holy Spirit not only gave this new Christian the right words to speak but also the courage to follow through with positive action. She signed her name as one who was "For Christ," and to the frustration of the Communist leaders the entire village followed suit. Those villagers' lives were on the line. For you it may be your employment, your place on the team, your popularity with your peers, your position on an important committee, or your grade in school that is at stake. Whatever the situation, you can be certain that the Spirit will give you the best words to speak and the courage to stand for Jesus and the great truths of His Word.

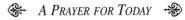

A PRAYER FOR TODAY

*Heavenly Father, I hide Scripture and evidences of Your faithfulness in my
heart and mind to be activated when they are most needed.*

THE WELCOME PROMISE

Behold, I send the Promise of My Father upon you;
but tarry in the city of Jerusalem until you are endued
with power from on high. Luke 24:49, NKJV.

*F*our words need clarification if we are going to discover the meaning of this often-quoted Holy Spirit verse. "We are having a tarrying meeting," a Pentecostal friend informed me. I was not sure what "tarrying" meant. "We are going to be endued with power," the friend explained. I was also unsure about "endued" and "power." On top of all this I had read in John 14 to 16 about 30 promises that Jesus had made to His disciples, so I was not sure which promise He was referring to as He departed from His disciples.

It is not difficult to discover the identity of the Promise that is personified in today's verse. Luke makes it very clear in his first chapter of Acts. After waiting in Jerusalem the disciples would receive the promised Holy Spirit (Acts 1:4-8). He was the One who would endue, or clothe, them with miracle-working *dynamis* (power) that would radically change lives as the disciples witnessed concerning "repentance and remission of sins" through Jesus' death and resurrection (Luke 24:46-48).

Now, what about "tarrying"? How do you tarry? The original word for "tarry" is translated "sit down" in most other passages of Scripture. But it is not a passive sitting, as the modern term "couch potato" describes a person whose main activity is relaxing at great length in front of a television set. The New Testament "sitting down" was active like an executive sitting at a desk, a jury sitting in judgment, or a national leader sitting in the seat of authority.

The disciples were to actively wait and prepare their hearts with prayer and Scripture for the coming of the Promise. In fact, during their tarrying time they had "great joy" and "were continually in the temple, praising and blessing God" (Luke 24:52, 53).

Although most of us are not living in the city of Jerusalem, we do need to "tarry" each day with a prayerful attitude of positive expectancy for a fresh outpouring of the Holy Spirit.

❦ *A PRAYER FOR TODAY* ❧

Thank You, Lord, for Your special Promise. Today I ask again
to be clothed and filled with Power from on high.

A SIGN FOR JOHN

And John bore witness, saying, "I saw the Spirit descending from heaven like a dove, and He remained upon Him." John 1:32, NKJV.

Why is it that the descent of the dove is one of the few details concerning Jesus that is mentioned in all four Gospels? At the beginning of John's record of the life of Jesus we discover the reason. The dove was a visible, supernatural sign of the Holy Spirit by which John the Baptist could recognize Jesus.

Jesus and John had grown up far apart in two different provinces of Palestine and, it seems, had never met each other. They were drawn together by the Holy Spirit to the place where John, having seen the sign of the dove, would introduce Jesus to lost humanity as "the Lamb of God who takes away the sin of the world" (John 1:29, NKJV).

Although there is no record of the Spirit descending again like a dove, He has certainly continued His ministry of identifying, proclaiming, and glorifying Jesus as our wonderful Saviour. For most people Jesus is identified by the Holy Spirit in the Word of God or in the life of another Christian. For a few, like Sundar Singh of India, the Holy Spirit reveals the living Jesus in person.

Sundar Singh was born in 1889 to a Hindu Sikh family and at a young age was deeply committed to finding spiritual truth. At 14 he became very opposed to Christianity and publicly burned a Bible page by page. Amid deep discouragement concerning religion, he prayed that God would reveal Himself to him, and he remained for hours in prayer, expecting to see perhaps Krishna or Buddha. To his amazement a great light appeared in his room, and in the light the Holy Spirit revealed "not the form I expected," Singh reported, "but the living Christ whom I had counted as dead."

The assurance of the certainty of Jesus remained on this 15-year-old as he served the Lord in India and around the world in the Holy Spirit's mighty power until he vanished almost 25 years later while on a Christian mission to the closed country of Tibet.

❧ *A PRAYER FOR TODAY* ❧

Father, in Your Word and in Spirit-filled Christians I look for signs of the Spirit that will again glorify Jesus in my heart and understanding.

WHEN JESUS BAPTIZES

I did not know Him, but He who sent me to baptize with water said to me, "Upon whom you see the Spirit descending, and remaining on Him, this is He who baptizes with the Holy Spirit." John 1:33, NKJV.

*I*f you have been baptized by immersion, you will remember that a gospel minister or some other Christian was with you in the water, baptizing you in the name of the Father, Son, and Holy Spirit. No human being, however, can baptize you with the Holy Spirit. Only Jesus does this.

Just as water baptism is an outward witness of the new-birth experience, so the baptism of the Holy Spirit is the dynamic testimony of the fullness of the presence of the Spirit who has come to dwell in the life of a Christian at conversion. Christians who are baptized with the Holy Spirit will know that it has happened, and so will those who see the new fruit and gifts in the Spirit-filled Christian's life.

Theologians have often debated whether the baptism of the Holy Spirit is a onetime event or whether it can happen many times in the life of each Christian. The Bible certainly teaches that you can be filled with the Spirit of God repeatedly, and you can sing with assurance W. A. Ogden's hymn:

"Baptize us anew
With power from on high,
With love, O refresh us!
Dear Savior, draw nigh.
We humbly beseech Thee, Lord Jesus, we pray,
With love and the Spirit baptize us today."

I like the way R. A. Torrey, former superintendent of the Moody Bible Institute, explained this when he said, "However, if we confine the expression 'baptism with the Holy Spirit' to our first experience, we shall be more exactly biblical, and it would be well to speak of one baptism but many fillings. But I would a great deal rather that one should speak about new or fresh baptisms with the Holy Spirit, standing for the all-important truth that we need repeated fillings with the Holy Spirit, than that he should so insist on exact phraseology that he would lose sight of the truth that repeated fillings are needed" (R. A. Torry, *The Person and Work of the Holy Spirit,* p. 181).

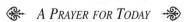

❦ *A PRAYER FOR TODAY* ❧

*As a Christian, Lord, I begin this day praising You
for completely submerging me in Your Spirit and love.*

BORN OF WATER AND SPIRIT

Jesus replied, "What I am telling you so earnestly is this:
Unless one is born of water and the Spirit, he cannot enter
the Kingdom of God." John 3:5, TLB.

People often boast about their family lineage. If we go back far enough, most of us are related to some famous—or infamous—character, the most significant, naturally, being the original Adam. From Adam we all have a heritage as part of lost humanity (Rom. 3:23; 5:15-19). But Jesus lived and died on earth so that every person may be part of a new lineage—that of eternal life in the family of God (Rom. 6:23; 8:9-16).

To be counted as a child of God it is necessary, Jesus said, to be born again. This new birth is "not of blood," that is, not of physical descent from Adam. It is not because of "the will of the flesh," which is sexual impulse; nor of "the will of man," that is, a person's desire to have descendants. It is totally the work of the Spirit of God (John 1:13; 6:63).

Charles W. Colson, former special assistant to the president of the United States, was known as Richard Nixon's hatchet man. Because of his central role in the Watergate scandal Colson served about seven months in prison and after his release began the Prison Fellowship ministry.

Listen to Colson tell of the beginning of his experience of being born of water and the Spirit: "With my face cupped in my hands, head leaning forward against the wheel, I forgot about machismo, about pretenses, about fears of being weak. And as I did, I began to experience a wonderful feeling of being released.

"Then came the strange sensation that water was not only running down my cheeks, but surging through my whole body as well, cleansing and cooling as it went. . . . And then I prayed my first real prayer. 'God, I don't know how to find You, but I'm going to try! I'm not much the way I am now, but somehow I want to give myself to You.' I didn't know how to say more, so I repeated over and over the words: *Take me"* (Charles Colson, *Born Again,* pp. 116, 117).

If you haven't already, give God the opportunity today to delight you with the born-again experience.

⚘ A PRAYER FOR TODAY ⚘

Father, I praise You today that through Jesus I have the full assurance
of new life in Your wonderful family.

WELCOME, NEW BIRTH

That which is born of the flesh is flesh;
and that which is born of the Spirit is spirit. John 3:6.

*I*f I receive a phone call in the middle of the night, please wake me," I requested my Californian hosts, Dr. Jim and Kim Cady. "My daughter Sharon, in Australia, is having a baby, and she has promised to call and personally inform me when she makes me a grandfather for the first time."

Yes, even in this overpopulated world, most births still bring rejoicing and excitement; at least it seemed so to me when I finally received the news that my "little" 10-pound-2-ounce granddaughter, Megan, had been born.

The new birth is even more exciting. Being born of "water" represents the complete cleansing aspect of regeneration, which the Holy Spirit works in us through the Word (John 15:3; 1 Peter 1:23). Being born of the "Spirit" represents the renewing aspect of the Holy Spirit's regenerating ministry as He creates in us a new heart and spirit that loves good and hates evil (Eze. 36:25-27; Titus 3:4-7).

I have enjoyed reading about the excitement of new birth in the story of Henrietta Grant, daughter of an African-American slave family. This graphic description comes from the transcript of an interview that now is located in the archives of Northwestern State University of Louisiana.

"Well, when the Spirit really got on me, it was between half past three an' quarter to four in the mornin'. Ah got up at twelve o'clock an' prayed, an' Ah said to God, 'Convert me.' At four o'clock, the minister of the Baptist Church in the country on Bayou Lafourche, came to my door with the Late Mole, the deacon of the church. . . . Ah screamed so, 'til Ah woke up the whole place. Ah woke up everybody in the quarters, even my husband. They didn't do nothing to me, they jest said, 'She's got religion.'. . . When that Spirit hit me, Ah jest saw a light lit. You talk about shoutin'—when Ah told my conversion, that church really shouted for me. An' when they dipped me in that water, there was plenty more shouting" (Hugh T. Kerr and John T. Mulder, eds., *Conversions,* p. 157).

Hallelujah!

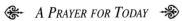

❦ *A Prayer for Today* ❧

Create in me a new heart and new spirit again today, Lord,
so that I can continue to shout and sing Your praises.

Welcome, Blowing of the Wind

The wind blows wherever it pleases. You hear its sound,
but you cannot tell where it comes from or where it is going.
So it is with everyone born of the Spirit. John 3:8, NIV.

The capital city of New Zealand is often called Windy Wellington. Its beautiful location at the southernmost part of the North Island exposes it to winds that have been known to blow people to the ground and turn vehicles over. In this city you can certainly say goodbye to your hat unless you have it firmly anchored.

Wind or breath was a common symbol of the Holy Spirit throughout biblical times. When the dry bones came together into lifeless bodies in Ezekiel 37, only the wind or breath, or Spirit, of God could make them live. There is a strong connection between the Spirit's creative work and God's wind or breath. Job's friend Elihu recognized that the breath of the Almighty had given him life (Job 33:4). When Jesus first gave the Holy Spirit to the disciples, "he breathed upon them" (John 20:22), and on the day of Pentecost the Spirit came as "a rushing mighty wind" (Acts 2:2). As with the wind in Wellington, lives were overturned by God's great power.

Jesus adds another dimension to the wind symbolism. With human birth there is always a mother who can usually be easily identified, and of course, human development and maturity can be measured and observed. But the origin of the new-birth experience cannot be clinically discovered, nor can growth in the Holy Spirit be explained in terms of weight or height. In other words, your conversion and growth as a Christian are absolute mysteries to those who have no spiritual understanding.

"What in the world has happened to you?" Randy had just become a new Christian, and his friends at the office were amazed at the remarkable transformation in his life. None of them were Christians themselves, and in fact, they thought of religion as a joke, but Randy's experience was the beginning of a new search for truth for a number of these young people.

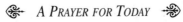

❦ *A Prayer for Today* ❧

Father, help me not demand a logical explanation for everything
but delight in the mysteries of Your saving grace.

THE SPIRIT WITHOUT MEASURE

For He whom God has sent speaks the words of God,
for God does not give the Spirit by measure.
John 3:34, NKJV.

*I*t would be tempting to believe that anyone who is full of the Holy Spirit has the Spirit without measure. From the word translated "measure" we have the English verb "meter," which means to supply in a specifically limited amount. Can God give any person the totally limitless presence and power of the Holy Spirit? It is like asking if any bucket can hold all the water in the Pacific Ocean. A million buckets could be full of ocean, but there would be still far more water than could be held in buckets covering the whole surface of the continents and islands of Planet Earth.

The context of John 3:34 clearly shows that these verses are speaking about Jesus. He is the only One who has received the Spirit without measure, for only in Him dwelt "all the fulness of the Godhead bodily" (Col. 2:9). He alone is the brightness of the glory of God "and the express image of his person." Only Jesus upholds all things in the universe "by the word of his power" (Heb. 1:3).

In view of this, it is important that each Spirit-filled Christian remember Paul's counsel to the Roman believers. Before he spoke to them of the wonderful ministry gifts that they had received from the Holy Spirit, he reminded them that they had received only a "measure of faith" and that they ought not think of themselves more highly than they ought (Rom. 12:3). It is sad to see Spirit-filled Christians sometimes acting like spiritual elite.

Paul in no way belittled the anointing of the Spirit in the lives of believers. In fact, he admonished us to "be filled with the Spirit" (Eph. 5:18). But he did want us to remember that although God has made available to us mighty Holy Spirit power, He has an eternity of limitless resources for us beyond anything that we can possibly experience at this time. The important question is Have we given ourselves to God "without measure"? If so, then God will fill us again to the absolute fullness of our capacity.

A PRAYER FOR TODAY

Lord, in full surrender I open my life to You so that I can be today
totally in the control of Your Holy Spirit.

TRUE SPIRIT OF WORSHIP

God is a Spirit: and they that worship him must worship him in spirit and in truth. John 4:24.

I do not get anything out of the worship services," the young college student explained to me as he complained about the compulsory attendance at church and chapel services that was required by the Christian college where I was teaching.

Worship, like love, cannot be legislated or forced. Worship is a spontaneous adoration of God in a heart that is drawn in love to the heavenly Father.

A blind person can never sit in reverent awe to watch the glory of the sunset over a tropical lagoon. One who is totally deaf cannot be absorbed in the music of a great symphonic orchestra. Similarly, it is not possible to worship God truly unless the Holy Spirit has opened spiritual eyes and ears to the truth of God's beauty and love.

I explained to the student that it was not worship that the college required, only attendance. The fervent hope of the college directors was, however, that students would somehow be open to the Holy Spirit during the church service so that for each of them it could become indeed a time of worship.

"It hasn't worked for me," the student said, so we prayed together, asking that this young man would open his life to the wonderful love of Jesus and the glorious joy of true worship.

It is easy to suppose that outward rituals and ceremonies are the basis of true worship. People's personal worship preferences and cultural biases are often imposed upon others. Places of worship have been considered more important than worship itself. Times of worship are scheduled as though love and adoration for God can be compartmentalized from the rest of life.

Toward the end of the semester the college student spoke to me once more. "Those worship services have certainly become a real blessing to me," he stated with obvious sincerity.

"What made the difference?" I asked.

It was a joy to hear him tell of his new personal relationship with God and of how the Spirit had led him to spend time alone, praying and growing to know his Lord through the Scriptures.

☙ *A PRAYER FOR TODAY* ❧

Thank You, Father, for the earnest desire that Your Spirit creates in my heart to enjoy worshiping You.

LIFE OR DEATH IN CHURCH

It is the Spirit who gives life; the flesh profits nothing. The words that I speak to you are spirit, and they are life. John 6:63, NKJV.

Before he understood what it meant to be filled with the Holy Spirit, famous Boston preacher A. J. Gordon struggled with spiritual deadness in his ministry and church. Can you relate to his frustration as he explained in his autobiography how he tried to bring life to his congregation by the works of the flesh?

"Well do we remember those days when drudgery was pushed to the point of desperation. The hearers must be moved to repentance and confession of Christ; therefore more effort must be devoted to the sermon, . . . more pungency put into its sentences, more study bestowed on its delivery. And then came the disappointment that few, if any, were converted by all this which had cost a week of solid toil. And now attention was turned to the prayer meeting as the possible seat of the difficulty—so few attending it and so little readiness to participate in its services.

"A pulpit scourging must be laid on next Sunday, and the sharpest sting which words can effect put into the lash. Alas, there is no increase in the attendance, and instead of spontaneity in prayer and witnessing there is a silence which seems almost like sullenness! Then the administration goes wrong and opposition is encountered among officials, so that caucusing must be undertaken to get the members to vote as they should" *(How Christ Came to Church,* p. 36). The inevitable result for A. J. Gordon was complete burnout.

Amid his turmoil Dr. Gordon looked through his study window and saw the trolley cars connected by slender lines to the power cables above. At that moment he realized that he could connect to the Holy Spirit's mighty power as his source of spiritual life. Now, instead of trying to use the Holy Spirit to supplement his works of the flesh, he became completely surrendered to the Spirit's using him. The results were dramatic, not only in his Boston church but also in an extended ministry with great soul winners such as D. L. Moody.

✦ A PRAYER FOR TODAY ✦

Father, I recognize today that there is no life in my most zealous works unless they are connected to the current of Your spiritual power.

FROM THIRST TO FLOWING RIVERS

*On the last day, the climax of the holidays, Jesus shouted to the crowds,
"If anyone is thirsty, let him come to me and drink. For the Scriptures
declare that rivers of living water shall flow from the inmost being of
anyone who believes in me." John 7:37, 38, TLB.*

The first step to becoming filled with the Holy Spirit is to recognize
in your innermost being a deep desire, thirsting, and earnestness
for God's wonderful gift. The persistent asking for the Holy Spirit
that comes from a recognition of great need has been illustrated by Jesus'
story of the man seeking bread from his friend (Luke 11:5-13). Now, as the
people saw the priests pouring out water from the Pool of Siloam, Jesus
promised them living water—that is, pure water which flows from an inex-
haustible source. The thought of this water, rather than the polluted, stagnant,
uncertain water of the world, creates in God's people a thirsting to be filled
with the Holy Spirit again and again.

The next step in becoming a beautiful waterway for the flowing of the
Spirit is to make the transition from full surrender to accepting by faith and
beginning to praise God that He has heard your prayer and given you an overflowing supply of the Spirit for this day or for an extra-special need. Now the
next part of the promise will be fulfilled, and in whatever way God chooses,
you will become a source not of one tiny stream but of multiple rivers of ministry prompted by the Holy Spirit.

The rivers of waters that flow out from you will be primarily words that
you will speak. Healing words, comforting words, edifying words, teaching
words, loving words, will all flow out in a way that will bring the ministry of
Jesus to other needy souls. The wise man said: "The words of a man's mouth
are as deep waters; a flowing brook, a fountain of wisdom" (Prov. 18:4, MT).

Those who are filled with the Holy Spirit speak to one another in psalms,
hymns, and spiritual songs (Eph. 5:18, 19). They speak words filled with
hope and joy that catch the attention of unbelievers and minister to those who
are part of the body of Jesus (1 Cor. 14:26).

❦ *A PRAYER FOR TODAY* ❧

*Lord, let my life flow with the words that are Spirit and Truth
so that others may be refreshed and invigorated.*

THE OPEN SPRING

By this he meant the Spirit, whom those who believed in him were later to receive. Up to that time the Spirit had not been given, since Jesus had not yet been glorified. John 7:39, NIV.

*A*s I travel around the world teaching seminars on the Holy Spirit's ministry, people will often offer to lend me a car so that I can drive to the meeting location or visit places of interest. I certainly don't own any of these cars, but I can remind myself that I do own a car back at my home. I don't have to return my own car to someone else after a period of temporary usage—it is mine.

It seems that throughout the time of the Old Testament the Holy Spirit was on loan to those who received the benefit of His power. He was there as a temporary possession—like a borrowed car. But Jesus promised that the time was nearing when the Spirit would be given to His followers as a permanent asset. As Peter said on the day of Pentecost, the gift of the Holy Spirit is for all who accept the call of the Lord and become part of the family of God (Acts 2:38, 39). Just as my car can remain my property as long as I live, so the Holy Spirit continues always as part of my life as long as I choose to remain alive as a child of God (Rom. 8:9). The Holy Spirit never needs to be traded in on a new design. He is always more up-to-date than next year's model.

When Jesus is glorified, the Spirit is given as a wonderful friend to dwell in each Christian's life. Historically this happened when Jesus ascended to the Father's throne and received His former glorious position as a member of the Godhead (John 17:5; Acts 2:33-36). Personally, the glorification of Jesus takes place in our lives when we receive Jesus as our Saviour. Jesus prayed that He would be glorified in those who will believe in Him, and this glorification of Jesus is the work of the Holy Spirit in believers (John 17:9, 10; 16:14).

Sometimes people lend me a car that is far more expensive than I could ever own. Others are so defective that I'm glad I do not own them. But the Holy Spirit is exactly right, reliable, and sufficient for every need in my life and ministry.

❧ *A PRAYER FOR TODAY* ❧

Thank You, Lord, for the wonderful gift of the Spirit that enables me today to move and work for You.

GREATER WORKS THAN JESUS

I tell you the truth, anyone who has faith in me will do what I have been doing. He will do even greater things than these, because I am going to the Father. John 14:12, NIV.

This is a stunning and puzzling promise. Jesus implies that all believers may do the same works that He did—even greater. The possibility of surpassing the quality and scope of Jesus' works seems unlikely. What greater works can be done than curing many people of their infirmities, afflictions, and evil spirits? Not only did Jesus give sight to the blind, hearing to the deaf, walking ability to the crippled, cleansing to the lepers, but also He raised the dead and preached the gospel to the poor (Luke 7:21, 22).

Most Bible scholars agree that the "greater things" must refer to the quantity and geographical extent of the works that would take place at the hands of believers as the gospel spread all over the world. In fulfillment of Jesus' promise, the gospel has reached you. But please remember that it is a miracle-working gospel. All the works that Jesus did are still available as part of the Holy Spirit's package of power for your life and ministry.

Soon after her return to the United States from Australia, Ellen White told of a vision that the Lord had given her of a great fulfillment of Jesus' prophetic words in John 14:12. At the beginning of the twentieth century there were only 55,000 Adventist members, but today there are nearly 8 million around the world to whom these words apply: "In visions of the night, representations passed before me of a great reformatory movement among God's people. Many were praising God. The sick were healed, and other miracles were wrought. A spirit of intercession was seen, even as was manifested before the great Day of Pentecost. Hundreds and thousands were seen visiting families and opening before them the word of God. Hearts were convicted by the power of the Holy Spirit, and a spirit of genuine conversion was manifest" (*Testimonies,* vol. 9, p. 126). What a joy it is today to be part of this greater-works-than-Jesus prophecy.

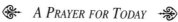 *A PRAYER FOR TODAY*

Father, may the greatest work of all be completed in me by the power of Your gracious Spirit.

WELCOME, HELPER

And I will pray the Father, and He will give you another Helper,
that He may abide with you forever. John 14:16, NKJV.

T he Greek word for "helper," *paraklētos,* is one of those words that is very difficult to translate into English. Some versions of the Bible translate it as "Comforter," while others use "Counselor" or "Advocate." *The Amplified Bible* adds "Intercessor," "Strengthener," and "Standby." He is even called the "Paraclete" in some Christian literature. Whatever you call Him, though, He is in reality your friend the Holy Spirit, and He certainly has all the attributes encompassed in this special name that Jesus gave to Him.

Although the Helper works directly *in* us as Christians, He also works *for* us through other Christians. Especially in the small group "households of faith" as we find them in the New Testament, the Holy Spirit brings comfort, strength, counsel, admonition, and edification. If you are following the biblical pattern of ministry and belong to a spiritual small group, you will agree that the Holy Spirit fulfills His role as the Paraclete, especially through the prayers and support of your friends in the group.

Following a Saturday evening revival meeting in southern California, one of the prayer partners of Trinity Power Ministries discerned that another in the group was struggling with some personal problems that were making her doubt her full acceptance with God and the fact that it is possible to enjoy real joy and happiness in the Lord. Soon the prayer team gathered around this prayer warrior and began to be used in a mighty way to bring the comfort, counsel, and positive help of the Holy Spirit. Finally, near midnight, it was time to rejoice in faith at the healing ministry revealed in the care and concern of this small group of Spirit-filled Christians.

Do you have a group of friends like this? Are you yourself an instrument of the Holy Spirit's ministry? If the answer to either question is no, then pray that God will open the way for you to become part of the richness of small group fellowship of *Paraklētos* ministry.

✙ A PRAYER FOR TODAY ✙

Lord, thank You for giving me the very best Helper a person can ever have
and also for the assurance that He will live with me forever.

WHS-6

WITH YOU OR IN YOU

Even the Spirit of truth, whom the world cannot receive, because it neither sees Him nor knows Him; but you know Him, for He dwells with you and will be in you. John 14:17, NKJV.

*I*n many ways the Holy Spirit is with all people, surrounding them with the influence of God's love. Those who have not yet accepted Jesus as their personal Saviour, no matter who they are, are recipients of the Holy Spirit's special attention. He is with them, opening up the possibility that they will be led to read the Bible or some other Christian literature or will come in contact with a Spirit-filled person who can introduce them to Jesus. Are you praying for a friend or loved one? Remember that the Holy Spirit is already working on that person's heart.

When a non-Christian accepts the Bible as the Word of God and finds in it the gospel, the Holy Spirit leads this person to accept Jesus as a Saviour. Of course, the Holy Spirit will never force or treat a person with insensitivity but will always honor each individual's free will by giving the freedom to choose to take the step of faith or to turn away at this time. If the step of faith is taken, then at that moment the new Christian becomes the Holy Spirit's dwelling place (see Eph. 1:13; Eze. 36:26, 27; Rom. 8:9; 1 Cor. 6:19, 20; 2 Cor. 1:21, 22; Acts 2:38, 39).

Let us personalize this today because you are involved in these words of Jesus. I have seen real joy in the faces of many people around the world as they have realized for the first time that they actually have the Holy Spirit living in them from the moment of conversion. Are you sure about that yourself? Is it a reality for you now? If not, open your Bible to the texts that I have given and pray through them, asking the Holy Spirit to be with you and lead you into the wonderful assurance of this truth.

The world will not understand what has happened when you celebrate the joyful certainty that the Holy Spirit is now in you as part of your Christian life, but you will know and rejoice that you are actually the dwelling place of the Spirit of the living God.

❦ *A PRAYER FOR TODAY* ❦

I praise You, Jesus, because You have given me this wonderful gift of the Holy Spirit to be a friend who is at the center of my life every day.

WELCOME, TEACHER

But the Helper, the Holy Spirit, whom the Father will send in My name,
He will teach you all things, and bring to your remembrance
all things that I said to you. John 14:26, NKJV.

A good teacher understands the varieties of learning styles by which different personalities can best discover and internalize truth. One learning style inventory has defined four basic ways that the Holy Spirit reaches hearts and minds as He teaches all things. Where do you see yourself in this inventory today?

First, He works with *concrete experiencers,* who need real, down-to-earth examples to help them understand spiritual principles. Jesus effectively used parables to reach these people. As they heard stories that encompassed familiar scenes, they could identify with and personalize the teaching. The Holy Spirit teaches people-oriented learners today with real-life stories from Scripture and modern life. The emphasis is not theoretical.

Next, there are *active experimenters,* who learn easiest by doing. Just as Jesus sent out the 72 evangelists to have some practical experience (Luke 10:1-17), so the Holy Spirit often teaches the active experimenter by having them prepare to lead a Bible study group, do door-to-door surveys, or engage in some other hands-on experience, such as prayer partner ministry.

Third, the Spirit delights to teach *abstract conceptualizers.* These people like authority-directed, systematic study of the Word, which will involve verse-by-verse analysis of a passage and will result in firm opinions concerning propositional truth. These people will often journal their prayers so that even the spiritual experience of communion with God can be documented and analyzed.

Finally, there are the *reflective observers,* who do not give immediate responses to truth but listen carefully to lectures and discussions and then take time to think about what they have heard. They may listen a number of times to tapes of meetings and like to do homework in preparation for a small-group study or meeting (see *Discipleship Journal,* March/April 1993, pp. 19-21).

Not only does the Holy Spirit want you to enjoy your learning style, but in a small group He will teach you to identify with and relate to people who enjoy learning in other ways.

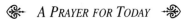

A PRAYER FOR TODAY

Lord, I thank You for understanding me and working with me as I am.

LET ME INTRODUCE YOU TO JESUS

But when the Helper comes, whom I shall send to you from the Father,
the Spirit of truth who proceeds from the Father,
He will testify of Me. John 15:26, NKJV.

*I*f I introduce you to a friend whom I really want you to come to know and like, I will try to find a point of common interest that can provide some immediate bonding. Perhaps a church or religious affiliation, sport or hobby, national or family background, occupational or educational similarity, will be the basis for rapid rapport. The more important it is to me that you become friends, the more diligently I will do the homework necessary to uncover your commonalities.

The Holy Spirit excels in introducing people to Jesus, and He does it in a way that is progressively revealing. The more we get to know Jesus, the greater the Holy Spirit's ability to show us attributes of Jesus' character that stimulate new levels of friendship and love in our hearts.

Colin, the *concrete experiencer,* meets Jesus as a very personable friend and empathetic Saviour in stories, relational Bible study, and actual events of daily life. Annette, the *active experimenter,* develops a friendship with Jesus as she helps others who need practical nurture and spiritual growth. The Holy Spirit doesn't say to Annette, "You must sit down and listen to 20 sermon tapes if you're going to know Jesus." Rather He says, "Here's some ministry for you to prepare for and do."

The Holy Spirit introduces Arthur, the *abstract conceptualizer,* to Jesus and develops their friendship by deep exploration of the Word. This may involve inductive Bible study, sermons, seminars, and systematic research. Rhonda, the *reflective observer,* grows slowly into a relationship with Jesus by quietly contemplating what she has learned in small groups or from sermon tapes and numerous books about the Christian life.

Perhaps someone has tried to lead you to develop a deep friendship with Jesus in a way that has not appealed to you, and you have allowed that to turn you off from Jesus. Please remember that the Holy Spirit does not make that mistake, but has a way that is the very best for you.

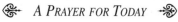

A PRAYER FOR TODAY

Holy Spirit, paint a fresh, bright picture of Jesus in me today.

WELCOME, ADVANTAGE

Nevertheless I tell you the truth. It is to your advantage that I go away;
for if I do not go away, the Helper will not come to you; but if I depart,
I will send Him to you. John 16:7, NKJV.

I t must have been hard to convince the disciples that Jesus' departure from them would be an advantage. They were all together as a group with a wonderful Person. His love was unfailing. His teaching was inspiring. His healing was better than any medical insurance plan. He could provide food in times of emergency. Who would want a Person like that to leave?

But one problem the disciples did not fully comprehend. Jesus had chosen voluntarily to surrender His omnipresence so that when they were scattered abroad He would not be present bodily with them all at the same time. Distance from Jesus would have disturbed the disciples, so they would have been inclined to cluster their lives around Him rather than move out to the distant places of earth.

The disciples' advantage in receiving the Holy Spirit is our advantage also. Wherever we live or minister, the Holy Spirit is with us as fully and completely as if there were no other person on earth. What an advantage!

All this is easier to comprehend if we think of a simple illustration that I often use. Television is available in most parts of the world today. So television images are most likely running through the room where you are now. To prove this you could turn on a portable TV and discover that you can receive the whole picture right "out of the air" without being connected to any outside source. If 100 people with portable TVs were in your meeting room, or in the next house, or suburb, they could all receive the full picture, not just one hundredth part each.

Jesus' offer of the Holy Spirit's advantage is available to you right now. If you haven't already done so today, tune in your antenna of prayer and receive the fullness of God's Spirit. As you do, you will see the full picture of Jesus' love and truth coming into focus.

 *A PRAYER FOR TODAY*

Father, help me take Your picture of love and truth out to the world
in the omnipresent power of the Holy Spirit.

CONVICTION, NOT ACCUSATION

And when He has come, He will convict the world of sin,
and of righteousness, and of judgment. John 16:8, NKJV.

Tony was a married man who found himself in a close friendship with a lady whom he greatly respected as a leader in his church.

As they prayed and studied the Bible together, an attachment began to develop that they suddenly realized was becoming potentially dangerous. Although no immorality was involved, Tony and Samona began to feel distressed and guilty, but the Lord in love enabled them to work through the situation so that they could rejoice in His victory.

Satan was quick to attack this sorrowful pair with vicious accusations, making them feel that they were eternally lost and that they would be better off dead, out of the church, or fully involved in sin. The Holy Spirit did not work that way, however. He helped Tony and Samona see Jesus as their wonderful Saviour, who forgave their weakness and loved them unconditionally.

As a Christian who desires to be right with God, how can you distinguish Satan's accusations from the conviction of the Holy Spirit? Neil Anderson writes, "Do you feel guilty, worthless, stupid, or inept? That's a sorrow provoked by accusation, because those feelings don't reflect truth. Judicially, you are no longer guilty; you have been justified through your faith in Christ, and there is no condemnation for those who are in Christ. You are not worthless; Jesus gave His life for you. You are not stupid or inept; you can do all things through Christ. . . . But if you are sorrowful because your behavior doesn't reflect your true identity in Christ, that's the sorrow according to the will of God, which is designed to produce repentance. It's the Holy Spirit calling you to admit on the basis of 1 John 1:9, 'Dear Lord, I was wrong.' As soon as you confess and repent, God says, 'I'm glad you shared that with Me. You're cleansed; now get on with life.' And you walk away from that confrontation free. The sorrow is gone, and you have a positive new resolve to obey God in the area of your failure" (*The Bondage Breaker,* pp. 146, 147).

❦ A PRAYER FOR TODAY ❦

Please continue to convict me of sin, Holy Spirit,
so that I can always know that I am right with You.

June 4

SPEAKING ABOUT HIMSELF

However, when He, the Spirit of truth, has come, He will guide you into all truth; for He will not speak on His own authority, but whatever He hears He will speak; and He will tell you things to come. John 16:13, NKJV.

*F*or the third time Jesus calls the Holy Spirit the Spirit of truth. Our understanding of truth is progressive, because He gradually enlightens our minds. This is why it is extremely important that we do not judge others by where we are in our perception of truth. We are all at different places in our learning experience with the Lord.

The Holy Spirit had to lead me into a new understanding of truth regarding this very verse. For many years of my ministry I used a version of the Bible that said, "He shall not speak of himself." Taking these words literally and neglecting to check the original meaning, I found myself telling people that the Holy Spirit will have nothing to say about Himself but rather will speak only of Jesus. If fact, I taught that if people were talking a lot about the Holy Spirit, this was an indication that they did not have the true Spirit at all.

I became puzzled, though, when I discovered more than 200 references to the Holy Spirit in the New Testament—17 or 18 in one chapter alone (Romans 8). Then the Holy Spirit led me to see that the verse is saying that He does not teach on His own authority, independently of the Father and Son, but rather teaches truth as a mouthpiece for Them. Now as I lead seminars about the Holy Spirit I have to apologize for the error that I had been teaching in ignorance.

As you pray for the leading of the Spirit of truth today you may find that He will begin to open your mind and heart to some new understandings. Just yesterday a friend said to me, "I've had to reevaluate recently what is at the center of my whole belief system."

Some teaching that you have dogmatically defended may have to be seen in a different light. But remember that in Jesus the truth will set you free.

A PRAYER FOR TODAY

Father, give me the courage to accept the new and fresh beauty of Your truths for me today.

WELCOME, GLORIFICATION OF JESUS

He will glorify Me, for He will take of what is Mine
and declare it to you. John 16:14, NKJV.

*I*t has been said that no book apart from the Bible has influenced Christianity as much as John Bunyan's *Pilgrim's Progress.* This classic allegory was written, along with many of his other 60 books, during his 12 years in Bedford jail, where Bunyan found himself following his arrest in 1660 for leading a small-group spiritual meeting of more than five people.

John Bunyan had grown up "godless, careless and so greatly given to blasphemy that he was a source of terror to others" *(They Found the Secret,* p. 17). But in his famous autobiography, *Grace Abounding to the Chief of Sinners,* this once-illiterate tinker tells how the Holy Spirit glorified Jesus at his conversion and throughout his life.

"Oh, methought, Christ! Christ! there was nothing but Christ that was before my eyes." Bunyan continued, "I was not now (only) for looking upon this and the other benefits of Christ apart, as of his blood, burial, or resurrection, but considering him as a whole Christ; as he in whom all these, and all other his virtues, relations, offices, and operations met together, and that he sat on the right hand of God in heaven.

"'Twas glorious to me to see his exaltation, and the worth and prevalency of all his benefits. . . .

"Further, the Lord did also lead me into the mystery of union with the Son of God. . . . By this also was my faith in him, as my righteousness, the more confirmed in me; for if he and I were one, then his righteousness was mine, his merits mine, his victory also mine. Now I could see myself in heaven and earth at once; in heaven by my Christ, by my head, by my righteousness and life, though on earth in my body or person" (pp. 101, 102).

The apostle Paul and John Bunyan agree on the wonderful glorifying ministry of the Holy Spirit: "But we all, with unveiled face, beholding as in a mirror the glory of the Lord, are being transformed into the same image from glory to glory, just as by the Spirit of the Lord" (2 Cor. 3:18, NKJV).

❦ A PRAYER FOR TODAY ❧

Holy Spirit, please glorify Jesus in my transformed life today so that,
like John Bunyan, I can see myself in heaven and earth at once.

WELCOME, BREATH OF GOD

Then he breathed on them and told them, "Receive the Holy Spirit."
John 20:22, TLB.

*I*n 1644, at the age of 16, John Bunyan was drafted to serve as a soldier in the British parliamentary army. A few years later, however, the breath of Jesus' Spirit of life came into him, and he became a great Christian warrior of the spoken and written word.

John Bunyan tells how the Lord used "three or four poor women sitting at a door, in the sun, talking about the things of God," to create within him a desire to come to know the Saviour *(Grace Abounding to the Chief of Sinners,* p. 26). These women certainly knew what it meant to have the Spirit of God breathed into them, as Bunyan later testified. "And, methought, they spake as if joy did make them speak; thay [sic] spake with such pleasantness of scripture language, and with such appearance of grace in all they said, that they were to me as if they had found a new world" *(ibid.,* p. 27).

Jesus' disciples found a new world as they were fully converted and received the Spirit, whom Jesus symbolically breathed upon them. In the same way, the Holy Spirit became a mighty force in Bunyan's life. Martin Luther's *Commentary of the Epistle of St. Paul to the Galatians,* with its beautiful teachings on the ministry and fruit of the Spirit, became Bunyan's most valued book apart from the Bible. In fact, as he found the fruit of joy and service in Galatians, he claimed the right to preach "on the basis of the Spirit's work within him and the church's recognition of his calling" (Richard L. Greaves, *Christian History,* vol. 5, No. 3, p. 10).

Like most of the disciples, John Bunyan did not have a formal education. However, for this special servant of God "the inner workings of the Holy Spirit were fully sufficient to plumb the deepest mysteries of God, secrets which were hidden from even the greatest intellects unless their minds were enlightened by the Spirit" *(ibid.,* p. 9).

In the same way the Holy Spirit will equip you again today for a joyful Christian ministry suited exactly to who you are, and with the Spirit's leading, you will continually discover new depth of meaning in the Word.

❧ *A PRAYER FOR TODAY* ❧

"Breathe on me, Breath of God, fill me with life anew, that I may love what Thou dost love, and do what Thou wouldst do."

THE ACTS OF THE HOLY SPIRIT

In the first book, Theophilus, I wrote about all that Jesus did and taught from the beginning until the day when he was taken up to heaven, after giving instructions through the Holy Spirit to the apostles whom he had chosen. Acts 1:1, 2, NRSV.

The book of Acts, with more than 50 references to the mighty Spirit of the Lord, shows what extraordinary things ordinary men and women can do when filled with the presence of the third person of the Godhead. Before the 28 chapters of Acts are completed, the new religion of Christianity has become an unstoppable force, even in the face of the most severe opposition and persecution.

Today we are still writing the twenty-ninth chapter of the Acts of the Holy Spirit. And the same Person and power that exploded Christianity onto the world scene is moving with vigorous effectiveness to bring us to the great climax of history when Jesus will return again.

Notice how gracefully Luke begins the transition between the ministry of Jesus and that of the Holy Spirit. Apparently Jesus for 40 days had been introducing the Holy Spirit to the disciples and had been using the Spirit as His Instructor to lead the Beginning a New Religion seminar. The syllabus had concentrated on all the details of the spiritual kingdom of grace and glory, the mighty kingdom of God, excepting classified information on the final times and seasons (verses 3, 6, 7). Now that the disciples knew the Holy Spirit so well, they would recognize Him instantly when He came to fill them a short time after Jesus' departure. He did not come as a stranger but as a special friend.

In preparation for the Holy Spirit to fill you with even more spiritual power for life and ministry than you ever experienced before, you may need to give Jesus the opportunity to use His Spirit to instruct you in a time of concentrated and extended study and prayer. Read every Bible verse on the Holy Spirit, and ask the Spirit to reveal Himself to you in the Word, showing you especially those things relating to the kingdom of God. Then as He comes in latter-rain power, you will recognize Him and receive Him with joy.

 *A PRAYER FOR TODAY*

Lord, I thank You for giving me the privilege of living in what appear to be the final, climactic years of Your Spirit's power.

WELCOME, PROMISE

And being assembled together with them, He commanded them not to depart from Jerusalem, but to wait for the Promise of the Father, "which," He said, "you have heard from Me." Acts 1:4, NKJV.

"Make promises sparingly, and keep them faithfully," I was advised many years ago. In Jesus' last meeting with His disciples before the crucifixion He made promises lavishly. In fact, in John 14-16 we read more than 30 wonderful promises, all of which Jesus has not only kept faithfully but made possible through the most amazing Promise of all—the Person of your friend and mine, the Holy Spirit.

Jesus called the Holy Spirit the "Promise of My Father" (Luke 24:49, NKJV), and Paul calls Him "the Holy Spirit of promise" (Eph. 1:13, NKJV). Peter promised the Promise to all people, of all ages, who accept Jesus as their Saviour (Acts 2:38, 39), and Paul says that this Promise is received by faith (Gal. 3:14). You can be absolutely certain that this promise will be fulfilled for you today as you open your heart and life to Jesus.

In the seventeenth century John Wilmot, Earl of Rochester, wrote on the bedchamber door of Charles II, "Here lies our sovereign lord the king, whose promise none relies on." It seems that the promises of political leaders have not become any more reliable with the passing of three or four centuries. As Benjamin Franklin said when he wrote of the fact that not even the promise of the endurance of the U.S. Constitution can be ultimately relied on: "In this world nothing can be said to be certain except death and taxes" (Letter to Jean-Baptiste Le Roy, Nov. 13, 1789).

Not so with God. All His promises are as totally trustworthy as His perfect character.

Classical economist John Stuart Mill once wrote that there is no such thing as absolute certainty, but 2,000 years of history have proved the complete confidence that we can have in the presence and power of the Holy Spirit in the lives of all who have taken Jesus at His word and claimed the Spirit as their special Friend. This promise is not like a rope of sand but is as totally dependable as the sun, moon, and stars.

❧ *A PRAYER FOR TODAY* ❧

Father, in the certainty that Your Promise is unfailing,
I claim again today Your wonderful presence in my life, knowing that
Your Holy Spirit will fill me with complete confidence, hope, and joy.

HOLY SPIRIT BAPTISM

"John baptized you with water," he reminded them, "but you shall be baptized with the Holy Spirit in just a few days." Acts 1:5, TLB.

*A*ll four Gospels record John's prediction that Jesus would baptize His followers with the Holy Spirit. This new baptism would not eliminate water baptism but would be an added, separate dimension that would enable Christians to go forward, not only knowing that they were saved and forgiven by the sacrifice of Jesus but also that they were mightily empowered for victory and ministry.

Joseph Harvey Waggoner attended school for only six months, but was self-educated so effectively that he became a prolific writer. As a young editor of a political paper in Wisconsin, he became an Adventist in 1852 and was so baptized and filled with the Holy Spirit that he would walk more than 50 miles to share the great truths of God's Word. "J.H." was one of the committee of three that recommended the name Seventh-day Adventist for the denomination. He also wrote and edited many of the books and magazines that enabled this young church to move ahead in the power of the Holy Spirit.

In 1877 Waggoner wrote an interesting little book on the office and manifestations of the Holy Spirit. In it he voiced his concern that his church not be confused on the baptism of the Spirit. Some, apparently, were saying that water baptism was the fulfillment of the promise of Holy Spirit baptism. "This position is specious," Waggoner warned, "and may become, and often is, the foundation of a very sad delusion. . . . In all cases where [water] baptism is taken as the evidence of the gift of the Spirit, the professing penitent is lulled into carnal security, trusting solely to his baptism as the evidence of his favor with God" *(The Spirit of God*, p. 35).

Waggoner quoted a number of passages from the book of Acts concerning those who were baptized with the Holy Spirit and then concluded that this experience is always a matter of "personal conscious experience" *(ibid.,* p. 36).

Have you been baptized with the Holy Spirit? If so, you will know, just as surely as you know whether or not you have been baptized by immersion in water.

❧ A PRAYER FOR TODAY ❧

Dear Lord, I praise You for the mighty power of Your Spirit that floods into my life again today.

WELCOME, WITNESSING POWER

But when the Holy Spirit has come upon you, you will receive power to testify about me with great effect, to the people in Jerusalem, throughout Judea, in Samaria, and to the ends of the earth. Acts 1:8, TLB.

*I*s the Holy Spirit given primarily so that Christians can witness about Jesus? The answer can be yes or no. It is no if we believe that the development of the fruit of the Spirit, Christian sanctification, and prayer power have no part in our witness for Jesus. The answer is yes if we believe that all we do and are testifies to others in some way for or against Jesus.

In the eighteenth century John Wesley taught the baptism of the Spirit is a postconversion "second work of grace" which brings entire sanctification into a Christian's life so that the sinful nature can be eradicated and the life perfected. Nineteenth-century Methodists called this the "second blessing." Although the early Adventists came from a Methodist background, they opposed the teaching of the holiness of human flesh and emphasized rather the biblical truth of victory over sin and the development of a Christlike character by the Holy Spirit's power.

During the nineteenth century, through evangelical authors and preachers such as A. J. Gordon, F. B. Meyer, Andrew Murray, Dwight L. Moody, and R. A. Torrey, a new understanding of the baptism of the Spirit was emphasized. Perhaps you have read some of their inspiring books on this topic and discovered their teaching that the power of the Spirit comes upon Christians so that they can be powerful in witness and service for their Lord.

These writers and the Adventist pioneers taught that at regeneration the Holy Spirit imparts life, and if you receive this, you are saved by Jesus' blood. The baptism of the Holy Spirit gives you power and fits you for service. The work of the Holy Spirit within you brings constant cleansing from sin and victory over the world, the flesh, and the devil. The baptism of the Spirit does not make you more saved but gifts you and makes you useful for God's service.

❧ A PRAYER FOR TODAY ❧

Father, by the power of the Holy Spirit make my Christian witness effective all the way from the "Jerusalem" of my home to the farthest part of my sphere of influence.

NOT REALLY A RELIGION

Brothers, the Scripture had to be fulfilled which the Holy Spirit spoke long ago through the mouth of David concerning Judas, who served as guide for those who arrested Jesus. Acts 1:16, NIV.

Look at how carefully in the book of Acts Luke builds the foundation for the Holy Spirit's mighty ministry. First he recounts how Jesus used the Spirit as His instructor in the How to Start a New Religion course (Acts 1:2). Next Luke records how Jesus informed the disciples that the source of the power that would explode His little sect into a world religion would be the Holy Spirit (verse 8). Finally Luke reminds his readers that the textbook Jesus' followers would use is actually the result of the Holy Spirit's reaching down to humanity for more than 1,000 years.

Although Christianity is listed as one of the world's great religions, it is not a religion at all if "religion" is defined as a way in which people seek God, with the emphasis on human effort. In contrast, Christianity is the good news of God seeking people—calling Where are you? as He did to Adam and Eve in the Garden of Eden. In the power of the Holy Spirit, Christianity 101 teaches that Jesus came looking for lost humanity and made possible our eternal salvation by His sinless life and His sacrificial death on the cross.

I did not know much about God until I became part of an Adventist congregation as a young teenager. Intellectually I accepted the teachings of the church but was using them to find and work my way up to God. Like the other young people I met in the church, I was certainly not at all successful, although we had all been baptized to be part of the religious culture.

One night I was standing outside a movie theater and smoking a cigarette during the intermission when I finally listened to the Holy Spirit, who was convicting me with the very words of Scripture that I had learned in the youth class. Within a few days I gave my life fully to the God who had found me, forgiven me, and saved me by the blood of Jesus.

Why not let Him find you today?

❦ *A PRAYER FOR TODAY* ❦

Thank You, Lord, for reaching down to me by Your Spirit-inspired Word.

WELCOME, PENTECOST

Now when the Day of Pentecost had fully come, they were all
with one accord in one place. And suddenly there came a sound
from heaven, as of a rushing mighty wind,
and it filled the whole house where they were sitting. Acts 2:1, 2, NKJV.

*B*efore the days when you could visit an airport and watch and listen to the huge jumbo jets taking off and landing, the most earth-shattering event (for a young boy, anyway) was to stand at a country train station and feel everything shake as the great thundering steam express sped past.

The 120 men and women who had been joining together in earnest prayer for 10 days in old Jerusalem apparently did not know that the day of the feast of Pentecost was to be the day when the Spirit would roar down upon them with the combined force of a Boeing 747 and the Flying Scotsman Express. It was a sudden or unexpected event. Luke uses words that mean loud noise and violent wind to describe the sound effects.

The Holy Spirit in the Old Testament had come like a gentle breath of wind. Now He came like a holy hurricane, like a tornado of supernatural intensity.

I was about 18 years old when I first knew what it meant to be filled with the Holy Spirit. I had known about Jesus and the doctrines of the church for some time but had only recently accepted Jesus as my personal Saviour. After enjoying the assurance of salvation and the expectancy of the return of Jesus for some time, I found two great desires filling my heart. The first was to be like Jesus, and the second was to be able to work in some special way for Him. As I studied and prayed, it became clear that these two desires could become reality only through the Holy Spirit's power.

I had stood on the platform of our little New Zealand train station many times as the express to Rotorua had thundered through, but when the Spirit came and filled my life in answer to earnest prayer, it was as if the day of Pentecost had come again with mighty power.

❦ *A PRAYER FOR TODAY* ❧

Lord, bring me, along with Your people whom I know, into earnest prayer
for the great hurricane or gentle breeze of Holy Spirit power.

TONGUES OF FIRE IN THE TEMPLE

*They saw what seemed to be tongues of fire that separated
and came to rest on each of them. Acts 2:3, NIV.*

*H*ave you ever felt as if the fire has gone out in your local church congregation? Does it seem as though every Sabbath worship service is just the old routine, just business as usual? Many people, it appears, come primarily for the purpose of leaving. Their whole focus is on When will this be over so that we can get out of here? Thousands leave annually, never to return.

On the day of Pentecost in Jerusalem the Holy Spirit started a fire in the Temple that blazed with burning intensity in contrast to the boring ceremonialism and routine ritualism that had made a farce of the word "festival" in the Jewish religion. There is no doubt that the Holy Spirit desires to do the same to our empty forms of worship today.

You may have thought that the disciples were in the upper room when the tongues of fire appeared, but there is good evidence that they were actually at the Temple. The Gospel writers often referred to the Temple by the term *house,* and it is unlikely that any ordinary Jewish home or rooftop room was large enough to handle 120 people. As well as this, the followers of Jesus were daily in the Temple area and would be there especially for the conclusion of the Feast of Weeks. As soon as the Holy Spirit filled the disciples, a large crowd gathered to hear them speak, which could take place only in the broad open area of the Temple courtyard and not in the narrow, winding streets of the old city.

God wants the tongues of fire to burn in congregations and Christian gatherings today. At Pentecost the flame was divided so that a portion rested on each of the 120 who were in one accord in one place. So the Spirit enables the fire of God's Word (Jer. 20:9; 23:29) to burn with intensity in the lives of true disciples today, consuming the selfish pride and cold formalism that grips many churches. As a result, multitudes right in your community will be drawn to hear with amazement the Spirit-filled proclamation of the everlasting gospel.

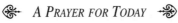

A PRAYER FOR TODAY

*Father, help me be a blazing torch of Your love and grace
in my congregation and neighborhood.*

June 14

SPEAKING BY THE SPIRIT

And they were all filled with the Holy Ghost, and began to speak with other tongues, as the Spirit gave them utterance. Acts 2:4.

*M*any times as I have taught and preached in countries around the world I have prayed for this ability to speak in foreign languages rather than having to use an interpreter. On more than one occasion I have been informed that an interpreter was giving his own message rather than what I was saying. In Brazil the Lord blessed me many times with a wonderful interpreter, Daniel Perria dos Santos. One day his lovely little daughter, Daniella, said to her mother in Portuguese, "Poor Willamese [as she called me] cannot talk properly, so my daddy has to tell the people what he is saying."

On the day of Pentecost the disciples did not have a communication problem. Apparently all the speakers who drew the crowd together in the Temple courtyard were Galileans (verse 7), who suddenly began to speak in the diverse and complex languages of the nations surrounding the Mediterranean. I can imagine them calling out, "All right, now, will everyone who speaks Arabic gather in this area here?" As 16 groups of "devout men" (verse 5) began milling about, trying to sort themselves out at the direction of some uneducated Galileans, others (verse 13) who saw the confusion but apparently had not heard the miracle of the languages made the rash judgment that the disciples were all drunk.

In San Luis Obispo I was privileged to stay in the home of Ron and Marla Rasmussen while holding revival meetings in the church they pastored. One evening I listened to their two delightful little daughters, Laurita and Danita, talking. One informed a friend, "Pastor Williams speaks with a British accident!" Fortunately their mother quickly made the correction and said that I spoke with a New Zealand accent. Whatever it was, it was sometimes hard for the children to understand. Not so when the Holy Spirit gives us the opportunity to share God's message of love. Even within your own language He will enable you to speak with a intelligibility that all who are open to the Spirit of the Lord will understand.

❦ *A PRAYER FOR TODAY* ❦

Holy Spirit, please give me words to speak today that will communicate Jesus clearly to all who are ready to listen.

NINE O'CLOCK IN THE MORNING

Some of you are saying these men are drunk! It isn't true! It's much too early for that! People don't get drunk by 9 A.M.! Acts 2:15, TLB.

When God does the unexpected, unbelievers always seem to find something to be skeptical about. As Peter reminded the crowd, it was unreasonable even to think that at this time of the day a large group of devout people would be under the influence of alcohol. Actually they were possessed by another kind of Spirit—a Power who would send shock waves throughout the whole Roman Empire.

When Episcopalian pastor Dennis J. Bennett received the baptism of the Holy Spirit in the 1960s, it sent a shock wave through his whole denomination. Many, even in his own California congregation, thought that he was drunk, and eventually he was forced to resign and take another pastorate in the Seattle area. Bennett's book, *Nine O'clock in the Morning,* in which he describes the misunderstandings that can arise when the Holy Spirit falls on members of a conservative, traditional congregation, is still a best-seller.

I like the way Pastor Bennett describes what happened at the time when the disciples were accused of being drunk. "[The Spirit of God] overwhelmed them—this is what the Scripture means when it says He 'fell upon them,' or 'came upon them'—baptizing their souls and bodies in the power and glory that was already dwelling in their spirits. . . . He overflowed from them out into the world around, inspiring them to praise and glorify God, not only in their own tongues, but in new languages, and in so doing, tamed their tongues to His use, freed their spirits, renewed their minds, refreshed their bodies, and brought power to witness" *(The Holy Spirit and You,* pp. 28, 29).

Like the disciples, we too can be set apart in body, soul, and spirit by the Holy Spirit (1 Thess. 5:23; 2 Thess. 2:13). The Holy Spirit, who came to dwell in us at conversion, can be given access to every part of our bodies, minds, and personalities so that we can be part of a dramatically new witness for Jesus. When this happens, don't be surprised if some skeptics suggest that you are drunk.

A PRAYER FOR TODAY

Father, help me not be intimidated by the unbelief of others but be strong and confident in my witness for You.

YOUTH WELCOME THE SPIRIT

And it shall come to pass in the last days, says God, that I will pour out
of My Spirit on all flesh; your sons and your daughters shall prophesy,
your young men shall see visions, your old men shall dream dreams.
Acts 2:17, NKJV.

*A*t the age of 18, as a young carpentry apprentice, I was filled with the
Holy Spirit in answer to my earnest prayers. As the Spirit came upon
me, I fell before the Lord and opened my heart fully to serve Him.
Although I had not informed anyone of my experience, my pastor soon approached me with the request that I preach at a series of evangelistic meetings. When I reminded the pastor that I was very nervous about public
speaking and that I had not even preached a sermon, he promised to help me
prepare a talk for the worship service on the next Sabbath. He showed me
how the sermon must have an introduction, a main body with a number of
clear points, and a conclusion that would summarize what I had tried to say.
Finally, he helped me find suitable illustrations.

As soon as I began to preach I was again filled with the Holy Spirit. He revealed that I had received a spiritual speaking gift that was to stay with me
through more than 25 years of preaching to large and small gatherings of people around the world. Although I knew very little about the methods of public
evangelism when I preached my first sermons, people were converted.

If you are a person of many years' experience in the church, are you open
to the possibility of God using the young people in some special way? Are
you helping young people know that they are born again and that they are
filled with the Holy Spirit? Are there teenagers in your local congregation
who can be encouraged to prophesy by sharing with large or small groups
words of "edification, exhortation, and comfort" (1 Cor. 14:3)?

The pastor and church board members who asked me to begin to preach
were older people who "dreamed dreams" of seeing the church move ahead
in the power of the Holy Spirit. They saw that the energy and enthusiasm of
a Spirit-filled youth would help make that possible, and they were not disappointed. Neither will you be when you facilitate the way for young people to
serve the Lord.

❦ *A Prayer for Today* ❦

My Lord and my God, please minister to me today
through one of Your young sons or daughters.

AN EXCITED YOUNG SERVANT

And on My menservants and on My maidservants I will pour out My Spirit in those days; and they shall prophesy. Acts 2:18, NKJV.

*I*f Peter could claim that the outpouring of the Holy Spirit on the day of Pentecost was the fulfillment of Joel's prophecy, how much more can we claim this, living near to the day when "the sun will be turned to darkness and the moon to blood" (verse 20, NIV)? Yes, even as we approach the twenty-first century, God's servants are being filled with the Holy Spirit for service, for ministry. Both male and female servants pray that they will be able to prophesy, and as they do, God will use them to speak "edification, exhortation, and comfort" (1 Cor. 14:3).

I sometimes look back on the notes of the first sermons that I preached as an 18-year-old carpentry apprentice and realize that it was a miracle that God could use them at all. The evangelistic meetings had been advertised in the newspaper, without the name of the speaker being included. Some people from the construction company where I was employed attended the opening meeting and were surprised to find one of their work associates preaching.

I spoke on the prophecy of Daniel 2 and explained that the return of Jesus was as certain as the rise and fall of Babylon, Medo-Persia, Greece, and Rome. The Lord gave strong prophetic words to the audience, stating that the only way any person present could be ready to meet Jesus was to come to know Him as their personal Saviour now. That night, as a small group of people accepted Jesus, my work associates were surprised that a young carpenter could be used so effectively as a servant of God.

I was still excited about the meetings when I arrived back at the building site on Monday morning. But the word had already spread to the worldly tradesmen, who began to make a mockery of the "Bible basher" in their midst. Some tried to pour beer over me so that I would appear to have been drinking. Others cursed and swore and made my work as difficult as possible, but nothing could detract from the joy of being a Spirit-filled young servant of the Lord.

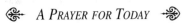

❦ *A PRAYER FOR TODAY* ❧

Lord, I thank You for the ways You are going to use me as Your servant during the next 24 hours.

THE WELCOME SIGNAL

*Exalted to the right hand of God, he has received from the Father
the promised Holy Spirit and has poured out what
you now see and hear. Acts 2:33, NIV.*

*W*e were waiting for Queen Elizabeth II to arrive for the big celebration at the historic Maori village of Waitangi in the beautiful Bay of Islands in North New Zealand. We could not see the location where she would leave her car and begin to walk, but we did know that the flag would be raised and the guns would give their salute to signal that the great event had taken place.

Although the disciples could not see what was happening in heaven, the outpouring of the Holy Spirit on the day of Pentecost was the dramatic signal to them that Jesus had been fully received back into His position of glory and power on God's throne.

In John 14, in the limitations of His humanity Jesus had prayed to the Father that He—the Father—would give the Holy Spirit to His disciples (verse 16). Jesus promised that the Father would send the Holy Spirit in Jesus' name (verse 26). In John 15 Jesus now promised that He would send the Holy Spirit, but that the Spirit would proceed from (come out from, or be discharged from) the Father (verse 26). Finally, in John 16 Jesus again stated that He would be the One who would send the Spirit to His followers (verse 7).

Predictably, theologians since the early centuries of Christianity have had heated discussions about whether the Holy Spirit comes from the Father or the Son, and the Eastern Orthodox and Roman Catholic churches split over this and other issues. But Peter in his Pentecostal sermon, which was inspired by the Holy Spirit Himself, said that Jesus received the Holy Spirit from the Father and then poured Him out like a mighty waterfall of witnessing power and love upon His waiting disciples. Pentecost was not a day for theological controversy but rather a moment of great triumph for the gospel. The flag was flying, and the salute sounded out. Brand-new Christianity celebrated the glorification of the Lord Jesus Christ.

A PRAYER FOR TODAY

*Lord, from Your glorious heavenly throne keep pouring Your Spirit upon me as
I await Your witnessing power for this new day.*

WELCOME, THE BEST GIFT

*And Peter replied, "Each one of you must turn from sin, return to God,
and be baptized in the name of Jesus Christ for the forgiveness
of your sins; then you also shall receive this gift,
the Holy Spirit." Acts 2:38, TLB.*

What a gift! The Holy Spirit has often been called the greatest gift, because without Him Jesus' death on the cross would have been no more than a historical event. The Spirit makes it possible for sinners to learn of Jesus and accept Him as their Saviour. On top of all of this blessing provided by the Holy Spirit, the Spirit Himself is actually an incredible gift that comes right into a person's life when he or she becomes a born-again Christian (Eze. 37:26, 27; Rom. 8:9; 2 Cor. 1:21, 22).

Peter linked water baptism with the initial gift of the Holy Spirit coming to dwell in one's life because in New Testament times the born-again experience, true repentance, and water baptism apparently all took place within the same context. This was the experience of at least 3,000 people on the day of Pentecost (Acts 2:41). As soon as the Ethiopian confessed faith in Jesus, he was baptized (Acts 8:37, 38). Lydia, the businesswoman from Thyatira, was baptized with her household as soon as she opened her heart to the things that Paul taught (Acts 16:14, 15). The Philippian jailer and his household were baptized the same night that they believed on the Lord Jesus Christ (Acts 16:31-33). Today, because conversion and water baptism are often separated by months or more, there is sometimes confusion regarding the role of the Holy Spirit in these wonderful events.

If you have been baptized by immersion, you will remember what happened. The spirit of self-centeredness that was on the throne of your life was represented as dying and being buried under the water, and you rose up with a new Spirit on the throne—the Holy Spirit of life in Jesus Christ.

Some young people who were baptized recently in Los Angeles were so excited about their new life in Jesus that they came up out of the water shouting "Hallelujah!" as the gift of the Holy Spirit filled their lives. Praise God for His wonderful Power Gift today. Why not allow the Holy Spirit to energize you again for fellowship and ministry?

❧ A PRAYER FOR TODAY ❧

*Lord, as the old hymn says, "Baptize us anew with power from on high."
Yes, "with love and the Spirit baptize us today."*

THE HOLY SPIRIT FOR THOSE AFAR OFF

For the promise is to you and to your children, and to all who are afar off, as many as the Lord our God will call. Acts 2:39, NKJV.

San Luis Obispo on the central Californian coast is a long way from old Jerusalem, but as Peter said, the Holy Spirit is available to all whom God will call in any place or era of earth's history. As the church family came together for a Holy Spirit seminar and revival, I warned the people that in answer to many prayers this would be a life-changing experience. When revival comes, it is always a dramatic, transforming event. The Holy Spirit certainly did not disappoint the people who gathered from the San Luis Obispo/Arroyo Grande area. In fact, a single mother became known as the "miracle lady" after only one day of meetings.

Rosie had spent 17 years in church schools but had wandered away from God after her college graduation. She soon became an agnostic and lived a godless lifestyle for many years. Now, for the past year Rosie had attended church occasionally but had some very important areas in her life that she was unwilling to surrender to God, including her desire to continue smoking. During the first meeting the Holy Spirit convicted Rosie that she could be totally surrendered to God and have full assurance of salvation and victory power. On Sabbath morning the Holy Spirit continued to speak to Rosie's heart. And when the call was made, she came forward to indicate her desire to be filled with the Spirit. Finally, at a special gathering for prayer and anointing on Sabbath afternoon, Rosie surrendered totally to God and experienced the miracle of complete healing.

During the following week of meetings the whole group rejoiced many times as Rosie shared her testimony: "To be so lost and then to be found is such a miracle! Praise God for His peace and His love and grace!" Yes, the Holy Spirit had once again come to one who was far off. And Rosie's witness to the victory power of God over her unwilling heart and smoking habit inspired many others to allow the Holy Spirit to work great miracles in their lives.

❧ *A PRAYER FOR TODAY* ❧

Sometimes I seem to be far off from You, Father, but I thank You that even then You are always calling me back and offering me the wonderful gift of Your Spirit.

FILLED AGAIN

Then Peter, filled with the Holy Spirit, said to them,
"Honorable leaders and elders of our nation . . ." Acts 4:8, TLB.

*P*astor, I feel that it's not possible for the Holy Spirit to use me in any special way."

When I asked Marvin the reason for his strong statement, he replied, "Two years ago I fell into sin and ended up denying Jesus. I think it could be many years before God trusts me to serve Him again."

I was happy to remind Marvin of the experience of Peter, whom God had filled with the Holy Spirit on the day of Pentecost. "Marvin, it was only 50 days after Peter had denied Jesus with cursing and swearing that God chose to minister through him in a mighty way."

A short time after Pentecost the Lord chose to fill Peter again. It was necessary now, in the crisis at the Temple following the healing of the crippled man, for the Holy Spirit again to wholly take possession of Peter's mind. As Luke wrote this in the original language of the text he implied that this was a sudden, temporary action that gave Peter power at that time beyond usual human capacity. Luke differentiates between this experience and the fullness of the Spirit that seems to characterize the whole life of a person who is thoroughly saturated in the Spirit and who reveals His fruit and gifts.

Marvin was facing a number of situations in which he would need an extra measure of the Holy Spirit if he was to minister to people who were struggling with evil, deep depression, family crises, and severe health problems. A small group gathered around this earnest young man and prayed that God would fill him again with the Holy Spirit. As we anointed Marvin with oil he began to weep and praise God. "Lord, I believe that You have done for me what You did for Peter," he prayed. "And I know that You will not only continue to fill me for Your service but that You will fill any person who comes in meekness and submission to Your will."

Marvin has been asked to preach and share his testimony in a number of churches. Through his lay ministry the Holy Spirit has brought hope and healing to many lives.

&- *A Prayer for Today* -&

Lord, when I feel like a Peter or Marvin, who has hurt a best friend, help me
remember how wonderfully You used these men when they were again
surrendered and filled with Your Spirit.

BOLDNESS IN THE FACE
OF A DEATH DECREE

After they prayed, the place where they were meeting was shaken.
And they were all filled with the Holy Spirit
and spoke the word of God boldly. Acts 4:31, NIV.

*D*o you have a praying group of friends with whom you meet regularly and to whom you can turn in a crisis just as Peter and John were able to do? Here is another interesting question: If you and your prayer group were facing a death decree and your meeting place was surrounded by armed enemies, what would you be praying about?

I think I would pray, "Lord, please get me out of here safely. Get me away to a place where I can have freedom to proclaim Your Word."

The prayer team in Acts 4 prayed a radically different prayer. They asked for boldness to speak God's word in the very place where their lives were being threatened. They asked that signs and wonders would reveal the power of Jesus' name. Are we willing to do that now in the relative peace of our neighborhood, office, school, or home? Will we do it in the face of danger from gangs, crime, peer pressure, jealous associates, family disunity? Despite the possibility of unemployment or material failure?

The Holy Spirit did not disappoint those Christians in old Jerusalem. The place where they prayed was shaken, and they were able to speak with boldness. The Holy Spirit no doubt also gave these faithful witnesses wisdom and tact so that their boldness did not become bluntness and their earnest sincerity did not become insensitivity.

An elderly grandmother in the Los Angeles area was meeting with her prayer group when bullets began to fly through the house. She was the only one who did not dive for cover on the floor. After 14 bullet holes were found in the house, some of the group began to discuss moving from the area.

"They aren't going to frighten me," I heard the grandmother testify. "I'm going to stay right here and witness to my community. We're going to shake up this whole place for Jesus."

☙ *A PRAYER FOR TODAY* ❧

Thank You, Lord, for the inner strength to not be intimidated by
the pressures of those who would silence my witness for You.

GREAT AMAZING GRACE

With great power the apostles continued to testify to the resurrection of the Lord Jesus, and much grace was upon them all. Acts 4:33, NIV.

*M*uch grace," representing the power of the Holy Spirit, is mighty beyond measure. If you could ask a man who had sunk to the lowest level of humanity, who had been flogged for desertion by the British Navy, who had become the captain of a slave trading vessel, who had beaten, tortured, and raped his human cargo, he would tell you that "much grace" is the amazing grace that saved one who was lost and blinded by sin.

When John Newton was 23 years old, the Holy Spirit led him to give his life fully to the Lord Jesus, and the change was so dramatic that Christians more than 200 years later are still being impacted by it. If you are wondering if Newton's experience with "much grace" has affected you, just remember that one of the best-known Christian songs today is Newton's "Amazing grace! how sweet the sound, That saved a wretch like me! I once was lost, but now am found, Was blind, but now I see."

Thousands were converted as they heard Newton preach in the little church he eventually pastored in Olney, England. Many of the 300 hymns he wrote are still popular today. Newton, together with Alexander Hamilton and Thomas Jefferson, received in 1792 an honorary degree from what is now Princeton University, but nothing ever meant as much to him as God's amazing grace. The power of the Holy Spirit had lifted him up from spiritual death to resurrection life in Jesus.

As Newton's friend John Wesley said in his famous twelfth sermon: "By the 'grace of God' is sometimes to be understood that free love, that unmerited mercy, by which I, a sinner, through the merits of Christ, am now reconciled to God. But in this place it rather means that power of God the Holy Ghost which 'worketh in us both to will and do of his good pleasure'" (Wesley, *Sermons,* vol. 1, p. 105).

Yes, that amazing grace, the power of the Holy Spirit, is still available and mighty for you today!

❧ *A PRAYER FOR TODAY* ❧

Thank You, Lord, that Your Spirit can still lift a sinner from the "guttermost" of wretchedness to the uttermost of victory with You.

DON'T LIE TO THE HOLY SPIRIT

Then Peter said, "Ananias, how is it that Satan has so filled your heart that you have lied to the Holy Spirit and have kept for yourself some of the money you received for the land?" Acts 5:3, NIV.

I surrender all," the old hymn says. And sometimes we sing it, although in reality we are not even surrendering half to God. Evangelist Luis Palau tells the story of a respected millionaire who stood up at a luncheon and testified, "I owe it all to the Lord. When I was a young fellow, a call was made for me to surrender all. Young as I was, and poor as I was, everything I had I surrendered to Christ. I didn't have much money, but I put it on the table, along with all my possessions, and said, 'Christ, I give everything back to you.' It was after that God began to bless me, and now I'm a wealthy man."

At that point, a voice from the back of the room shouted, "I challenge you to do it again."

Luis Palau concludes: "Ever wonder why most of those who respond to the call to 'surrender all' are young? They don't have that much to surrender—maybe three T-shirts, two pairs of jeans, and their dad's car keys. But when you get to middle age and you own a house and two cars and a condo on the beach, it's a different story" *(Say Yes!* p. 110).

We do not know how old Ananias and Sapphira were or how much they possessed, but when they sang "I Surrender All" and yet gave only a portion to the Lord's work, they were deceiving not just their fellow Christians but, as Peter said, they were lying to the Holy Spirit.

Then the worst blow to this deceptive couple came when Peter reminded them that the Holy Spirit is actually God, along with the Father and the Son. They had lied to God. God had not required them to give all their land value—that had been their own decision. Their deceptive attitude, however, revealed hearts that were in reality far from being willing to be completely honest with God and man.

We may possibly fool ourselves and others when we sing "I Surrender All," but we certainly can't fool God.

❧ *A PRAYER FOR TODAY* ❧

Father, I ask You to help me consider prayerfully and honor faithfully the pledges that I make to You.

RUINED BY UNRESOLVED GUILT

Peter said to her, "How could you agree to test the Spirit of the Lord? Look! The feet of the men who buried your husband are at the door, and they will carry you out also." Acts 5:9, NIV.

Could Ananias and Sapphira have been forgiven? There is no doubt about that. Jesus had died for their sins, along with the sins of the whole world. But they had rejected the Spirit's promptings to repentance and had decided to put His genuineness and power to the test. And, as the title of the book by television speaker George Vandeman says, *Guilt Can Be Lethal.*

Because of conservative Christianity's high behavioral and attitudinal standards, it can produce more guilt than any other system of philosophy or religion. It also has the most effective solution for guilt—the sacrifice of Jesus for the sins of all humanity. But if Christians do not totally believe and accept the forgiveness they have in Jesus, their unresolved—and often unreasonable—guilt will destroy their peace of mind and lead them into deep depression, discouragement, and despair. It may even destroy them, as it did Ananias and Sapphira.

Christian psychologist and professor Roy W. Fairchild says: "Much depression is caused by pathological and neurotic guilt, where the distressed person feels much more guilt than appears to be warranted by the circumstances. For example, people in their fifties and sixties who exaggerate their teenage misdemeanors, which now become the center of their thinking and convince them of their unredeemable 'sinfulness' are experiencing neurotic depression. When they come to the pastor, they often want to be chastened, saying in affect, 'I am no good. I don't deserve happiness. I must be made to pay for my sins'" *(Finding Hope Again, pp. 30, 31).*

You can be absolutely sure that guilt need never be lethal. The Holy Spirit is certainly not a killer who took life from the deceptive couple in old Jerusalem. In fact, the ministry of God's Spirit is to bring, even to the chief of sinners, the assurance of peace of mind and eternal life in Jesus Christ.

A PRAYER FOR TODAY

*Thank You, Lord, for unfailing forgiveness and grace
even in the face of the worst sins.*

WHICH COMES FIRST?

*And we are His witnesses to these things, and so also is the Holy Spirit
whom God has given to those who obey Him. Acts 5:32, NKJV.*

*D*o we obey so that we can receive the Holy Spirit or do we receive
the Holy Spirit so that we can obey?

For many years, on the basis of today's text, I taught that it
was necessary first to obey God, and then the Holy Spirit would be given to
the person who was keeping all God's commandments. This erroneous teaching enabled me to judge those who professed to be filled with the Spirit. If
they were not obeying everything in God's Word, as I saw it, then I would say
that they must be filled with an unholy spirit.

To my embarrassment a few years ago, I discovered that this was one of
a number of texts about the Holy Spirit that I was misusing. Kevin Wilfley
helped me understand this. "The word translated 'obey' in this verse is not the
same as the word translated in the verse that says, 'Children, obey your parents' [Ephesians 6:1]," Kevin explained. "The word Peter used in Acts 5:32
means to willingly submit to an authority as to a good friend."

Now, this is good news, because it means that the Holy Spirit is given to
people who are not following every commandment, rule, or standard of
Christian behavior but who are open to God's leading. Praise the Lord that
the Holy Spirit gives us the power to obey!

Recently a minister shared with a good friend a dilemma he faced: "I've
been convicted of my need to overcome a certain character weakness that I've
detected in my life, but I'm not sure that I actually want to do anything about
it."

The Holy Spirit enabled the minister's friend to give a very good answer:
"Just tell the Lord that you're willing to be made willing. If you'll do that
much, the Holy Spirit will help you do the rest."

Yes, you can be sure that the Holy Spirit is always given to every person
who is willing to be made willing.

✿ *A PRAYER FOR TODAY* ✿

*Father, help me be always conscious that I am living within Your will for my
life at this time and that Your Spirit makes this possible.*

THE SPECIAL SEVEN

*Now look around among yourselves, dear brothers, and select
seven men, wise and full of the Holy Spirit, who are well thought of by
everyone; and we will put them in charge of this business. Then we
can spend our time in prayer, preaching, and teaching. Acts 6:3, 4, TLB.*

*L*et's make Arnold a deacon," the church board decided. "He'll do an
excellent job of keeping the church grounds tidy." Where this jani-
torial, groundsman, offering-plate-distributor concept of deaconing
came from we do not know, but it is certainly not biblical. When Paul wrote
to Timothy, he could testify that the deacons he knew had "great boldness in
the faith" (1 Tim. 3:13). They had no buildings to care for. Their ministry was
practical and powerful in the Holy Spirit.

The 12 apostles felt a responsibility to be servants, or deacons, of spiritual
ministry to the multitudes who were sweeping into the new religion. The seven
Spirit-filled men were chosen to be servants, or deacons, of practical ministry
to the large number of new converts who needed nurture and tender loving
care. Some needed financial aid; others needed counseling; all needed positive
information for spiritual growth. For this reason it was imperative that the
seven be of good reputation, and full of the Holy Spirit and wisdom.

Years ago the state schools in New Zealand had compulsory Bible classes
each week for the students. I attended the Anglican class and remember sitting in the back of the room, listening to old Archdeacon Hodgson try to explain some abstract Christian teaching to 50 or 60 restless youth. I had never
heard of a deacon, let alone an archdeacon, and wondered if the term applied
in some way to building construction. Actually I was quite close to the mark.
The true, Holy Spirit-filled deacon will oversee all the practical ministry of
the household of faith. He will see that the believers are built up, bound together, cared for, and comforted. And if the church has a building, he will involve all the members in its maintenance.

If your congregation has deacons like the first seven, it will indeed be
blessed in Holy Spirit ministry.

❧ *A PRAYER FOR TODAY* ❧

*Help me, Lord, to appreciate the men and women You use so effectively
in practical Christian ministry. I praise You for their faithfulness
and true witness for Jesus.*

EMPHASIZING ETHNIC EQUALITY

This proposal pleased the whole group. They chose Stephen,
a man full of faith and of the Holy Spirit; also Philip, Procorus,
Nicanor, Timon, Parmenas, and Nicolas from Antioch, a convert to
Judaism. They presented these men to the apostles, who prayed and laid
their hands on them. Acts 6:5, 6, NIV.

The constituency meeting in a large North American conference was divided over ethnic representation on the executive committee. Should Asians, African-Americans, Caucasians, and Hispanics all have subgroups on the committee, or should the committee be formed on the basis of the popular vote for each person?

Political wrangling had not yet entered the church when it became necessary in old Jerusalem to choose seven men as practical Christianity "vice presidents." But there had been some ethnic concerns. It was perceived that the Greek-speaking widows were not receiving fair treatment. By this time there were already thousands of Christians, mainly Hebrew-speaking Jews, but when they met and made their selection of the men to fill this important position for the whole church, they chose seven men with Hellenistic names, indicating that they were from the Greek-speaking minority.

After the apostles prayed and laid hands on the seven, the deacons moved into ministry for the whole body of believers, not just their minority ethnic group. The fruitage became immediately obvious, as it will today when ethnic representation and recognition are connected to the consciousness of ethnic equality. The mighty power of the Holy Spirit in these deacon ministers enabled them to play a most significant part in spreading the Word of God so that "the number of the disciples multiplied greatly in Jerusalem, and a great many of the priests were obedient to the faith" (verse 7, NKJV).

After the conference constituency meeting was over and the ethnic groups were all fairly represented, one delegate testified to me that the moving of the Holy Spirit in the meeting was obvious and that a spirit of unity and love indicated that the fruitage for the kingdom of Jesus in that part of the country will be great.

❦ *A PRAYER FOR TODAY* ❦

Although we are all one through the blood of Jesus, Father, help me recognize
that races, sexes, and cultures all have unique characteristics
and differences that make them special.

June 29

ANGEL FACE

And they were not able to resist the wisdom and the Spirit by which he spoke. . . . And all who sat in the council, looking steadfastly at him, saw his face as the face of an angel. Acts 6:10-15, NKJV.

*H*ave you ever seen a face that impressed you as being like an angel? Perhaps it was the delightfully innocent face of a pretty child or that of a strikingly beautiful woman or handsome man. At one of the first Adventist camp meetings I attended, when I saw the black face, shining eyes, and brilliant white smile of Solomon Island pastor Kata Rangoso, it seemed to me that I had seen an angel.

Like Stephen, Kata Rangoso was a man of good report, full of the Holy Spirit and wisdom. His father was a cannibalistic tribal chief and headhunter who was one of the first, under the influence of the missionaries, to ban the human sacrifice of young children. At the age of 12 Kata Rangoso began his education with pioneer Adventist missionary Captain G. F. Jones and soon showed the keen mind and total dedication to the Lord Jesus that would enable him to become a great Christian leader.

At the beginning of World War II Kata Rangoso was left in charge of the Adventist work in the Solomon Islands, and before long his strong religious convictions led him into conflict with the British commanding officer. After severe mistreatment, Rangoso and his assistant, Londi, were thrown into prison and left to die. All across the island the Adventist people gathered for prayer. And in answer to those prayers it appears that the two prisoners that night saw an angel.

About 10:00 p.m. a man with a bunch of keys walked past the armed guards and opened the gates. Calling Rangoso and Londi, he led them through the gates and down the path to the beach, where he directed them to the empty canoe that would take them home. When they turned to thank him, he was gone, although they could see the moonlit path for more than 100 yards. Later they discovered that the only keys that could be used to open the gates had been on their peg beside the officer all night.

 *A PRAYER FOR TODAY*

Lord, I praise You that Your hedge of angels will always protect the faith of Your trusting child.

REJECTING THE RESCUER

You stiff-necked people, with uncircumcised hearts and ears! You are just like your fathers: You always resist the Holy Spirit! Acts 7:51, NIV.

I t is popular today to blame most of our problems on our parents. Sometimes this blame is valid, but on the other hand, it can be merely an excuse for our own difficulties today. It seems, however, that Stephen recognized that the Jewish leaders of his day had been programmed into rejection of the Holy Spirit by their hard-hearted ancestors. They apparently had emotions that were damaged by centuries of pious pride, and now, as their religious system was drowning in a sea of traditionalism and animosity, they once again rejected their rescuer—the Holy Spirit.

As we have joined together for seminars on the Hawaiian island of Maui I have often listened to Barry and Norma Crabtree tell of the wonderful experiences that the Lord has given them through their lifetime of ministry and mission service. The Holy Spirit has worked many miracles in their lives, and Norma's life itself is a miracle. Norma's parents, the Ferrises, were longtime missionaries in the Pacific Islands. When they first arrived in the Solomon Islands, the Ferrises were transported to their new location on the little mission vessel *Kima,* whose captain was the young teacher Kata Rangoso. Rangoso was a very experienced sailor and knew all the safe passages through the coral reefs, but somehow in the night the boat hit a rock, and little 3-year-old Norma was thrown into the dark water.

One of the crew dived into the lagoon to try and rescue Norma, but he couldn't find her. As soon as Rangoso realized the situation, he dived deep into the water and searched in the darkness amongst the treacherous branches of the coral. After coming to the surface for a breath Kata Rangoso, praying desperately for the little girl, plunged under the water again. Suddenly his hand touched her clothing and hair, and Norma was saved.

As the Jewish leaders listened to Stephen they also could have been saved, but they resisted their rescuer, the Holy Spirit, who would have led them into the safety of Jesus' kingdom of love.

❧ A PRAYER FOR TODAY ❧

As I'm submissive to Your Spirit, Lord, I know that You will lift me up even if I seem to be struggling today with failure.

July 1

DYING FOR JESUS

But Stephen, full of the Holy Spirit, looked up to heaven and saw the
glory of God, and Jesus standing at the right hand of God.
Acts 7:55, NIV.

Kata Rangoso faced death in the Solomon Islands because in the power of the Holy Spirit he insisted on obeying God rather than the British military officer controlling the area as Japanese forces moved in to attack. Like Stephen, Pastor Rangoso had prayed earnestly to his God: "Jehovah, I am Your servant. This is an awful time, for the blood of men is being spilled. If You know my work here or in some other place is not finished, You save me, Jehovah. . . . Please take away the sins of the men who are doing wrong. But I put myself in Your hands to do what You like with me. Amen" *(No Devil Strings,* pp. 75, 76).

If you can pray Rangoso's prayer, you too can be released from the fear of what the enemy may do.

Rangoso was thrown across a 40-gallon gasoline drum and beaten until the blood flowed from his back. Then, as he stood up, the officer smashed the pastor's face with the butt of his revolver. An island girl who was present started to cry. "Oh, master!" she said in pidgin English, "stop—no killim Rangoso. Him good pastor belong Seven-day. Stop, no killim more."

Reuben E. Hare tells the story of what happened next to this Spirit-filled pastor as he again refused to disobey God. "The firing squad was drawn up. Kata Rangoso was placed in position, and quietly he waited for the fatal order to be given. The officer instructed the firing party to shoot when he counted up to three. In a dramatic silence he started to count: 'ONE! TWO! ——' Somehow the word would not come; he could not say 'three.' He started again: 'ONE! TWO! ——' Still his tongue refused to speak the fatal word. In a towering rage he shouted: 'You watch 'im this time, ONE! TWO! ——' For the third time speech failed. In fact, the officer was dumb, and did not speak at all for nearly three days" *(Fuzzy-Wuzzy Tales,* p. 43).

Yes, long ago Stephen died because of his witness for his beloved Jesus, but in 1943 on a beautiful island in the South Pacific God chose to spare the life of one of His modern-day servants.

A PRAYER FOR TODAY

Father, my life is in Your hands. Please use me as long
as You see that I can serve you effectively.

THE LEADERS MAKE CERTAIN

*When they arrived, they prayed for them that they might
receive the Holy Spirit. Acts 8:15, NIV.*

Jerusalem was fast becoming a Christian ghetto as thousands of new believers crowded around the places and people at the nerve center of the new religion. Saul soon changed all that. Not only did he gladly consent to the assassination of Stephen, but also he entered every house-church he could locate, violently arresting every Christian he could lay hands on. To the dismay of the enemy, however, God, as usual, brought good out of evil as the scattered believers turned the tragedy into a missionary triumph. In the power of the Holy Spirit they "went every where preaching the word" (Acts 8:4).

Philip, another Spirit-filled deacon, spearheaded the thrust of Christianity into the territory of Samaria. Jesus had sown some seed here, and now as Philip ministered with a blazing display of signs and wonders, multitudes were convicted "concerning the kingdom of God, and the name of Jesus" (verses 6, 12). There was great joy in the city, and large numbers were baptized in Jesus' name. The fruitage of bitter persecution was indeed sweet.

Meanwhile, back at headquarters there was concern that the Samaritan Christians might not have received the Holy Spirit experience that the Jerusalem believers had enjoyed since Pentecost. Immediately Peter and John were commissioned to take the two-day, 40-mile walk and to pray for a mighty outpouring of the Holy Spirit among these new converts. The Holy Spirit was such a special friend and dynamic power in the apostles' lives that they were anxious that no Christian miss the blessing.

What would happen today if Spirit-filled leaders personally made certain that every newly baptized person was fully aware that he or she was a Spirit-filled member of the body of Christ? The power released by connecting Spirit and truth would amaze the world and enable us as born-again Christians to participate in the true signs and wonders that will precede Jesus' second coming.

❧ A PRAYER FOR TODAY ❧

*I ask You, Lord, to fill me anew this day with the strength
and love that comes from the certainty of being completely controlled
by the indwelling Holy Spirit.*

ONLY IN JESUS' NAME

*For as yet the Spirit had not come upon any of them; they had only
been baptized in the name of the Lord Jesus. Acts 8:16, NRSV.*

*D*id Philip make a mistake when he baptized in the name of Jesus,
or was this a valid form of baptism? Although, according to
Matthew, Jesus had instructed His disciples to baptize in the
name of the Father, Son, and Holy Spirit (Matt. 28:19), the early Christian
church apparently baptized new converts in Jesus' name and considered the
complete filling of the new Christian with the Holy Spirit as a separate and
distinct event.

On the day of Pentecost Peter had admonished his listeners to be baptized
in Jesus' name for the forgiveness of sins and for the reception of the initial
gift of the Holy Spirit (Acts 2:38). But this was not the equivalent of the
mighty infilling of the Holy Spirit that Peter and John came to bring the
Samaritans who had already been baptized by immersion.

Later, as Peter witnessed to the household of Cornelius, the new converts
received the baptism of the Holy Spirit (Acts 11:16) before they received
water baptism in the name of Jesus (Acts 10:44-48). Paul received the Holy
Spirit and was baptized in water, calling on the name of Jesus (Acts 9:17;
22:16). When Paul ministered to the disciples at Ephesus, they were baptized
in Jesus' name and then, after special prayer, received the outpouring of the
Holy Spirit (Acts 19:5, 6).

Perhaps you, like the Samaritans in Acts 8, have been baptized only in the
name of the Lord Jesus. I was in this position for a number of years as a
teenager. I had been converted and was the dwelling place of the Holy Spirit
but did not realize the fullness of His mighty power. If this is your situation,
request a few Spirit-filled friends and church leaders to meet with you to worship, study the Word, and pray. Together, ask God to pour out His Spirit upon
you in the way He chooses to reveal Himself at this time. As you take the step
of faith, believing that He has filled you, you will praise Him with an assurance that you have never enjoyed before.

❧ *A PRAYER FOR TODAY* ☙

*Dear God, help me not be satisfied with less than the fullness
of all You have for me today.*

PLACE YOUR HAND ON MY HEAD

Then laid they their hands on them,
and they received the Holy Ghost. Acts 8:17.

*P*astor, will you please place your hand on my head and pray that I will receive the baptism of the Holy Spirit?" The young man who made this request was very earnest and sincere.

"Andrew," I replied, "I'll certainly be happy to pray for you in this way, but first of all let's talk about some Bible facts concerning the laying on of hands."

I explained to Andrew that in the New Testament the act of laying hands on a person was used in three different ways. Often Jesus and the early Christians laid hands on the sick while they prayed for their healing. This gesture was also used at the time of consecration or ordination for specific ministry. Then, as Andrew had discovered, the laying on of hands often accompanied special prayer for the filling of a life with the Spirit's mighty power. Even in Old Testament times the touch of a human hand symbolized the transferring of powers or qualities from one individual to another. Fathers conveyed blessings to their children in this way, and the penitent sinner laid his hand on the head of the animal to be sacrificed.

"While the laying on of hands was one of the foundational doctrines of the early church (Heb. 6:1, 2), that has been forgotten by many Christians today. It is only symbolic and doesn't contain any mystical or magical qualities," I reminded Andrew. "In fact, there are a number of instances when the Holy Spirit was poured out in a powerful way without any reference to the laying on of hands [for example, Acts 2; 10], so it's not absolutely essential."

Following our little discussion, Andrew and I, together with a number of others, knelt in prayer as we all placed our hands on this young man and specifically asked the Lord to pour out His Spirit upon him. Tears of joy and songs of praise followed as Andrew testified that he had indeed received the blessing for which we had prayed.

❦ *A PRAYER FOR TODAY* ❧

Father, help me reach out and touch those who need indications of fellowship
and strength from those who are filled with Your Spirit.

BUYING SPIRITUAL POWER

When Simon saw this—that the Holy Spirit was given when the apostles placed their hands upon people's heads—he offered money to buy this power. Acts 8:18, TLB.

hurch history tells the tragic story of thousands of ambitious individuals who thought they could, like Simon, buy spiritual power. Even today the wealth of some Christians places them in positions of authority in local congregations and conferences. As a result, true spirituality is sometimes sacrificed on the altar of materialistic religion, and "like a corporation, moves the church of God."

Simon's business was religious trickery, and as a magician he was able to exert control and enjoy great prestige among the people. As a successful entrepreneur, Simon's wealth had enabled him to import new tricks, most involving sleight of hand, from distant parts of the Roman empire. Now, it seemed, one had arrived at his own back door, and Simon wanted the laying-on-of-hands act at any price.

But he was mistaken. First, the Holy Spirit is not transferred through human hands but is Jesus' gift to each heart fully surrendered to God. Second, the Holy Spirit cannot be bought by money, position, or popularity. He is free to all who are saved by Jesus' sacrifice. The Holy Spirit is not a business proposition but a Person of power and love.

Bible commentator Adam Clarke, writing at the beginning of the nineteenth century, gathered from the apostolic fathers a humorous but tragic—and unsubstantiated—story of the fate of Simon. It is said in ancient Christian tradition that Simon did not repent but went to Rome, where he boasted before Emperor Claudius that he could fly. During his flying exhibition, Peter and Paul, who supposedly were present, prayed that Simon's deception would fail, at which time he came tumbling down and "died soon after of his bruises" *(Clarke's Commentary,* vol. 5, p. 742).

Likewise, any system of religion that professes to control the distribution of the Holy Spirit will surely crash. Let us remind ourselves again that the Spirit is God's free gift directly available to all people today.

❧ *A PRAYER FOR TODAY* ❧

Dear Lord, please free me completely from thinking that any of my works or worthiness can earn me even one of Your precious gifts.

July 6

THE SIGN THAT TRIGGERED SIMONY

And [Simon] said, "Give me also this ability so that everyone on whom I lay my hands may receive the Holy Spirit." Acts 8:19, NIV.

*A*pparently there was clear evidence that the Samaritan believers had been filled with the Holy Spirit. Simon had seen that evidence and wanted to acquire the spiritual ability with money, hence giving the name "simony" to the corrupt religious practice of trying to purchase spiritual power or position.

What was the convincing sign that Simon had seen? His reaction indicates that something supernatural was immediately evident, and Peter gives us a clue as to what the evidence was when he says to Simon, "You have neither part nor portion in this matter" (verse 21, NKJV). The word translated "matter" is *logos,* which means "word," "kind of speaking," or "speaking" as it is translated in 1 Corinthians 1:5, NIV. Evangelical scholar F. F. Bruce concludes that "the context leaves us in no doubt that their reception of the Spirit was attended by external manifestations such as had marked His descent on the earliest disciples at Pentecost" *(The Book of Acts,* p. 181).

Although the gift of tongues can still be an instant evidence of the baptism of the Holy Spirit, it is important to heed the warning of respected Pentecostal scholar John Rea when he says: "People may desire or be encouraged by others to seek for a manifestation of tongues. If they speak a few unintelligible syllables, they are told that they have been baptized in the Holy Spirit. But it may be a Pentecost without repentance, a Pentecost without Christ. If they bypass obedience to Christ and His cross, if there is no repentance and remission of sins, the experience they receive may well be a counterfeit" *(The Holy Spirit in the Bible,* p. 193).

Simon wanted the gift without a true relationship with the Giver. Some still have the same problem 20 centuries later. On the other hand, we can be sure that even today all the gifts of the Spirit are readily available to every person who comes in true surrender to God's mighty power.

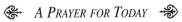

A PRAYER FOR TODAY

Help me be comfortable, Lord, with every indication
of Your presence in my life.

July 7

THE SPIRIT SAYS GO

The Holy Spirit said to Philip,
"Go over and walk along beside the chariot." Acts 8:29, TLB.

The call of the Holy Spirit leading men and women into mission service has many times been as clear as Philip's call to meet the government official from Ethiopia. As Harold Lindsell states in *Missionary Principles and Practice,* the story of John G. Paton, pioneer missionary to the South Pacific, illustrates the impelling power of the Holy Spirit's working.

Last century a synod of the Reformed Presbyterian Church of Scotland was looking for a missionary for the cannibal islands of the New Hebrides (now Vanuatu). They took a poll of the synod members, but when the votes were counted the results were inconclusive. As a cloud of sadness began to fall over the synod, John G. Paton says, "The Lord kept saying to me, 'Since none better qualified can be got, rise and offer yourself!' Almost overpowering was the impulse to answer aloud, 'Here am I, send me.' But I was dreadfully afraid . . . and yet I felt a growing assurance that this was the call of God to His servant and . . . the voice within me sounded like the voice from God" (p. 66). Lindsell concludes: "Indeed the Holy Spirit was speaking to John G. Paton's heart, calling him, and at the same time granting him heart assurance that this was the will of God for his life" *(ibid.).*

Although hundreds of people groups around the world have not yet heard the gospel, some of the neediest areas are the vast cities of Planet Earth, where by the year 2010 more than three of every four people will live. Some large population areas of the world's 42 supercities have no Christian evangelization bringing hope and healing to the masses of hurting and lost humanity.

Are we listening for the call of the Holy Spirit today? Are we as willing as Philip, John G. Paton, and thousands of others to go when the Spirit says go? God may not call you to cross salt water to be a missionary today. He may be calling you to cross socioeconomic, cultural, ethnic, or pride barriers to open small-group ministry centers in communities and neighborhoods within 100 miles of your home.

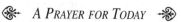

A PRAYER FOR TODAY

Holy Spirit, let me be sensitive to Your voice
as it calls in love and assurance today.

July 8

CAUGHT AWAY BY THE HOLY SPIRIT

*And when they came up out of the water, the Spirit of the Lord
caught away Philip, and the eunuch never saw him again,
but went on his way rejoicing. Acts 8:39, TLB.*

On June 13, 1793, the Spirit of the Lord caught William Carey away from his Baptist ministry in Moulton, near Northampton, England, and took him to more than 40 years of nation-changing, life-changing missionary service in the crowded country of India.

William Carey inspired the modern missionary movement by his vision of continents for Christ. He had supported his Baptist ministry by working as the village cobbler and teacher, but as Carey became an expert in biblical languages he also carefully studied the leather and brown paper world map on his wall. The burning conviction could never leave his mind that "God so loved the world."

At a conference of ministers Carey stood up and urged the beginning of a missionary movement that would take the gospel to a world dying without Jesus. The old chairman of the conference became annoyed at William Carey and said, "Sit down, young man, you are a miserable enthusiast. When God wants to convert the heathen, He can do it without your help."

But the Holy Spirit was speaking strongly to Carey's heart, and soon his positive response to the Spirit would catch Carey away so that those who tried to quench the Spirit would see Carey no more.

On May 31, 1792, Carey preached his now-famous sermon at Nottingham. F. W. Boreham sums up Carey's message: "We dare not separate without doing something! Lengthen the cords! Strengthen the stakes! Expect great things from God! Attempt great things for God! Here am I; send me, send me!" *(A Bunch of Everlastings, p. 165).*

The same Holy Spirit is speaking to God's people about the 42 super-cities around the world today. Vast numbers are living and dying without Jesus. It is time to attempt great things for God in the power of the Holy Spirit. Right now God may be preparing you to work with one or more of a million new house-churches that could open as gospel centers in the slums, apartments, and suburbs of the world's cities this year.

❧ A PRAYER FOR TODAY ❧

*Father, move me in my attitudes and values so that I can have a part
in the urgent mission of Your church.*

201

BAPTIZED BY A LAY EVANGELIST

And Ananias went his way and entered the house; and laying his hands on him he said, "Brother Saul, the Lord Jesus, who appeared to you on the road as you came, has sent me that you may receive your sight and be filled with the Holy Spirit." Acts 9:17, NKJV.

On October 1 each year the Greek Orthodox Church celebrates the martyrdom of Ananias, whom they believe was one of the 70 disciples sent out by Jesus during the time of His ministry. But why did God use a person who was most likely an obscure layman and not one of the most prominent apostles to baptize Saul? Certainly some unusual circumstances surround the rebirth of early Christianity's most prestigious convert.

A number of times I have walked along the street called Straight in old Damascus, enjoying the sights and smells that make an Arab city so fascinating for a Westerner. This is the oldest continually inhabited city in the world, and Straight Street follows the same route that it did when Paul, the now blind leader of the Christian Extermination Party, was brought here following his dramatic encounter with Christ somewhere on his 150-mile trip from Jerusalem.

Saul was filled with the Holy Spirit at the hands of a layman only three or four days after his transition from being a leading Pharisee who was filled with the intent of murder. When there is true conversion, God does not impose long probationary time before baptizing a new convert with His Holy Spirit. God's affirmation is as rapid as His salvation through the blood of Jesus. A new Christian can be one of the mightiest witnesses for the kingdom of God.

Another surprising fact that surfaces in Saul's experience is that the official leaders of the Christian church most likely would not have accepted him, laid hands on him, or baptized him as did Ananias. In fact, weeks later—even after Paul had risked his life for Jesus in Jerusalem—the apostles were unwilling to believe that he was really a true disciple. But Ananias had been open to God's voice and as a result had the privilege of baptizing the man who became the most powerful and productive of all the apostles.

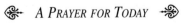

❦ *A PRAYER FOR TODAY* ❧

Thank You for the assurance today, Father, that Your Spirit can fill and use any person who is willing to obey You.

WELCOME, COMFORT

Then the churches throughout all Judea, Galilee, and Samaria had peace and were edified. And walking in the fear of the Lord and in the comfort of the Holy Spirit, they were multiplied. Acts 9:31, NKJV.

*W*hat does it mean to be a comfortable Christian? Sometimes in motels I have tried to sleep on mattresses that certainly were not comfortable. They were either as hard as the floor, felt like a bag of tennis balls, or sagged like a loose hammock. Morning took a long time to arrive, and when it did, it was accompanied by multiplied aches and pains. Yes, I am definitely in favor of comfort. But comfortable Christians sometimes sleep their spiritual life away.

"Brother Ashbury, would you be willing to help with a large contribution to our new church building fund?" I asked the 70-something retired builder.

"Pastor, I'm sorry to disappoint you, but I have only about $1 million left, and I need it for a comfortable and secure retirement."

"Across the city there's a community of more than 100,000 people without even one small group house-church that is a home of hope or center of tender loving care in the name of the Lord Jesus. Will someone move into an apartment or house in that area and pioneer a ministry of love?" the pastor of a large city church challenged his congregation.

"Sorry, Pastor," came the unanimous reply, "we're all very comfortable where we are. It would be inconvenient for us to move."

Livingstone, Carey, Judson, Paton, Taylor, and a hundred others left the comfort of nineteenth-century England to bring the gospel to millions around the world. Jesus left the comfort of heaven to die a most uncomfortable death on the cross. So what is the comfort of the Holy Spirit that filled the early Christian churches? It is the assurance of love, the sweet knowledge that someone understands and cares in the most difficult circumstances of life. It is the certainty that even in the hardest tribulations and battles of spiritual warfare and ministry we have a faithful Friend whose affection for us is not dependent on our performance or success (2 Cor. 1:3-7, NIV).

❦ A PRAYER FOR TODAY ❧

I praise You, Lord, for the unconditional love of those people You use to bring to Your children the comfort of the Holy Spirit.

WELCOME, VOICE

Meanwhile, as Peter was puzzling over the vision, the Holy Spirit said to him, "Three men have come to see you." Acts 10:19, TLB.

Some days seem to homogenize into each other so that soon they cannot be remembered as anything more than part of the old routine. Other days are so extraordinary that years later we can remember with exact precision everything that happened on them.

The day recorded in Acts 10 certainly was unique and unforgettable for Peter. First, he was exceptionally hungry as he waited for his noon meal. Second, he received an amazing vision of an upside-down parachute full of wild beasts, reptiles, and birds. Third, as the aerial zoo went up and down three times, Peter received the invitation to slaughter the creatures and turn them into a barbecued lunch. On top of all of this, three Gentiles arrived at the gate and asked to see Peter, who was still entrenched in ethnic prejudice. Have you ever had a day like that?

In the midst of the confusion Peter heard the Holy Spirit speak, bringing meaning to all the day's strange events.

In Simi Valley I listened to Anna tell of some days that she will never forget. Her daughter had gone through a painful divorce and had been alienated from her church and from her mother. Now, after three months, Anna had no idea of the whereabouts of her daughter. In final desperation Anna prayed, "Lord, I have no way to get in touch with my daughter, but wherever she is right now, please call her name and let her know I love her."

Two days later Anna's daughter called and said, "You'll probably think that I'm out of my mind, but two days ago I was alone in the house and I distinctly heard your voice calling my name. I've thought about the meaning of this and feel that God wants me to talk to you again."

In answer to the Holy Spirit's call, Anna's daughter is back home. In the same way, in response to the Spirit's voice on one of Peter's most memorable days, the Gentiles in Cornelius' house came home to the family of God.

In the midst of a day of mundane or multitudinous events you too can hear God's voice.

✦ *A PRAYER FOR TODAY* ✦

*As I listen for Your voice, Lord, help me hear distinctly
the homecoming steps that You want me to take today.*

July 12

KNOWING THE RIGHT ADDRESS

*God anointed Jesus of Nazareth with the Holy Spirit and with power,
who went about doing good and healing all who were oppressed by the
devil, for God was with Him. Acts 10:38, NKJV.*

*H*as God ever given anyone your address? Notice that the Holy Spirit revealed His knowledge of addresses in Joppa (near modern Tel Aviv). The commander of a Roman army regiment received in a vision the exact address of Peter, who journeyed to the Gentile's home in the Mediterranean city of Caesarea, where he shared the good news about Jesus in a crowded house meeting.

If Peter had not listened to the Holy Spirit's voice, he would have not recognized the three Romans at his door as a remarkable opportunity to spread the gospel to the Gentiles. Perhaps God has given someone your address at home or at your work or school, and some subtle form of prejudice has robbed you of the willingness to tell of Jesus' mighty works in the power of the Holy Spirit. The person who came by "coincidentally" was too young (or old), too rich (or poor), too educated (or uneducated), or a different color, race, ethnic group, or culture. It wasn't that you rejected him or her—you just didn't recognize that individual as an opportunity. *Why would he or she listen to me?* you probably thought.

The Holy Spirit knows the right address for the preaching of the gospel. It is the address of every person on Planet Earth. As the Holy Spirit revealed to Peter, "God shows no partiality" (verse 34). In fact, Peter explained that Jesus "went about doing good and healing all who were oppressed by the devil" (verse 38).

Often the address that God has given to someone so that he or she can meet me and hear of Jesus' great ministry has been on a bus, plane, or train. God brings us together and then, while honoring our free will, provides opportunities for witness. The Holy Spirit makes it easy. He doesn't expect me—or want me—to force information on any person. He just asks me to wait and listen for any sign that this is the time and place that He has chosen for this soul to hear that Jesus' power can still break the oppression of sin and evil.

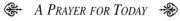 *A PRAYER FOR TODAY*

*Lord, please give me Your words to speak as I come in contact with people
You have chosen for me to minister to today.*

205

A GENTILE PENTECOST

While Peter was still speaking these words, the Holy Spirit fell upon
all those who heard the word. Acts 10:44, NKJV.

*H*ave you ever seen crowds fall down and worship a man? I have
seen it happen a number of times as people enter into the presence of the pope. Even on the street they would bow down as
they cried out "Papa, Papa!" When Cornelius fell down and worshiped Peter,
the apostle immediately lifted him up and said, "Don't do it. I'm also a man."
The news of Peter's miracles may have reached Cornelius, but Peter knew
that if Cornelius would only fall down before the Lord Jesus, then the Holy
Spirit could fall down upon Cornelius and fill him to overflowing with God's
mighty power.

Just as the ready acceptance of the gospel even by members of the KGB
in the former Soviet Union indicated that some were already secret believers,
so it is possible that Cornelius was a believer in Jesus even before he met
Peter and his six friends. Peter, in his preliminary talk to Cornelius, following the falling-down incident, realized that Cornelius and his family and associates already knew the word about Jesus (Acts 10:37). And the Holy Spirit
soon confirmed that by gripping them and taking possession of them, as
Luke's word for "fell" suggests.

The outpouring of the Holy Spirit upon the Gentiles came about six years
after Pentecost. Apparently the disciples had taken the gospel commission to
mean "Go into all the world and preach to *Jews in every nation* where they
have been dispersed." Now God showed them conclusively that *"whoever* believes in Him will receive remission of sins" (verse 43) means *every person
in the world.* Even the Gentiles! If you are not Jewish, you can be glad that
the early Christian church finally got the message.

There is no set formula for the corporate outpouring of the Holy Spirit. In
Acts 2 and 4 it happened after extended periods of prayer. In Acts 8 it took
place after the laying on of hands. Here in Acts 10 the Spirit was poured out
in the middle of the sermon. Whatever method God chooses to use today, rejoice in it and worship Him in the praise of adoration and thanksgiving.

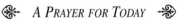

A PRAYER FOR TODAY

*Father, I bow down before You, opening my life again today
to the infilling of Your Holy Spirit.*

A BIG SURPRISE

And those of the circumcision who believed were astonished, as many as came with Peter, because the gift of the Holy Spirit had been poured out on the Gentiles also. Acts 10:45, NKJV.

*E*ven the most devout Christians are sometimes amazed to discover that God can work outside their own denomination or religious belief system. People place God in a box with various doctrinal statements and creeds as solid walls and believe that it is impossible for Him to function beyond the exterior of those boundaries. The Jewish Christians who came to the Gentile house with Peter were astonished that God gave the gift of the Holy Spirit to the people whom their race and religion despised. But God has many surprises for Christians—even today.

"I had not planned to be here this Sabbath," Lena told me during a Holy Spirit seminar I was teaching at the new Penticton church in beautiful British Columbia. "I know that the Lord led me here today, because I enjoy learning more about the Holy Spirit." Then I watched the amazement on the faces of the Adventists in her small group as Lena told of her first experience with the Holy Spirit.

"I was formerly a Roman Catholic and first became filled with the Holy Spirit at the beginning of the charismatic movement in the Catholic Church," Lena explained. "We spent a lot of time in prayer and were deeply earnest about our relationship with the Lord. When I was baptized with the Holy Spirit I began to speak in tongues and greatly enjoyed praising and blessing God. We were very earnest about our study of the Bible and often met in small groups to study and pray. Sincere searching of the Scriptures, asking for the enlightenment of the Holy Spirit, eventually led me to see more of God's truth, and today I'm a Seventh-day Adventist Christian."

Doubtless, countless other people are at various stages of the same path that Lena traveled. God's Spirit is leading them and filling them, and we must not be surprised or judgmental when they surface as sincere seekers of truth and righteousness.

A PRAYER FOR TODAY

Lord, help me be freed from the narrow thinking that would confine Your work to the restrictions that my preconceived ideas place upon it.

AN INDISPUTABLE SIGN

For they heard them speaking in tongues and praising God.
Then Peter said, "Can anyone keep these people from being baptized
with water? They have received the Holy Spirit just as we have."
Acts 10:46, 47, NIV.

O nce again the gift of tongues turned up as the sign that the Holy Spirit had been poured out. It had happened in Jerusalem, Samaria, and now with the Gentiles in Caesarea. Obviously there was no other immediate proof that God could give to the skeptical Jewish Christians that His acceptance of these non-Jews was as complete as His approval of the disciples on the day of Pentecost. The Jewish Christians perceived that the Gentiles in the house of Cornelius suddenly began speaking fluently languages that they had never learned, and in these languages they heard them praising and magnifying God. The evidence was indisputable even to the skeptical Jewish minds.

The important question now is What about today? Are tongues still the sign? Most Pentecostals will say yes, although Paul seems to say that not all Spirit-filled Christians will receive the gift of tongues (1 Cor. 12:10, 30). Charismatics will say that any one of the supernatural spiritual gifts, including tongues, can be the sign, although Paul emphasizes that the gifts are for building up the church, rather than for an external evidence of Spirit filling (1 Cor. 14:12).

Many evangelicals will say that all supernatural spiritual gifts, including tongues, ceased at the end of the first century and that the evidence that people are filled with the Spirit is that they will come into obedience to God's Word. Once again, however, we notice that Paul says that those who wait for the coming of Jesus will not miss out on any of the spiritual gifts (1 Cor. 1:7). Obedience, on the other hand, is a fruitage that will develop throughout a lifetime and is made possible by the indwelling of the Holy Spirit.

Today, as always, it is important not to look for or demand a sign but rather to allow God to indicate in whatever way He chooses that He is still filling His people with His Spirit.

❧ *A PRAYER FOR TODAY* ☙

Come, Holy Spirit, and fill my life again today, giving any spiritual gift
You choose to enrich my life and ministry for You.

A MESSAGE FROM THE SPIRIT

The Spirit told me to have no hesitation about going with them.
These six brothers also went with me, and we entered the man's house.
Acts 11:12, NIV.

*E*arly one week intercessory prayer warrior Anna Withers felt strongly impressed that her pastor, Jere Wallack, should lead the congregation in prayer the next Sabbath with a special emphasis on God's message to Moses at the burning bush. During the week the urgency of her impression increased until she decided to call Pastor Wallack on Friday and tell him that the Lord was speaking to her. The pastor was not home when Anna called, so rather than leave a message on his answering machine, she decided to let the Lord deliver the message.

Unknown to Anna or to the pastor, Laura, the church music director, had chosen "We Are Standing on Holy Ground" as the final song before the pastoral prayer, and the church secretary had listed Pastor Jere as the one who would lead the prayer that Sabbath morning at Simi Valley just before I preached the sermon on the inner witness of the Holy Spirit.

"My heart was suddenly filled with the message of the conversation between God and Moses at the burning bush, surrounded by 'holy ground,'" the pastor told me later. As he invited the congregation to come forward and share with him in the prayer time, he spoke the words that the Holy Spirit was impressing upon his mind. As the Lord had also told Anna earlier in the week, it was the message of God to Moses at the burning bush. "Trust God," the pastor told his congregation. "He will surely be with you and set you free from the bondage and oppression of sin. Receive His message. Don't argue. Listen! Accept! And follow!"

I noticed as the call was made that there was a tremendous response from the people. In the midst of the crowd Anna came and knelt before the Lord. She was so overwhelmed with the awesomeness of God's delivery of the burning-bush message to the pastor at just the right time that she had taken off her shoes before walking to the front of the church.

❦ *A Prayer for Today* ❧

Thank You, Lord, that just as You spoke to Moses, Peter, and Cornelius, so
You can still speak to Your faithful servants today.

A SOMETIMES DIFFERENT FALL

*As I began to speak, the Holy Spirit came on them
as he had come on us at the beginning. Acts 11:15, NIV.*

Catherine Marshall, widow of Dr. Peter Marshall, the Scottish Presbyterian pastor who became chaplain of the United States Senate, tells of the understanding she came to in preparation for the time when the Holy Spirit would fall upon her and have a profound effect on her life.

"There are definite steps to be taken if we are to receive the baptism of the Spirit," Catherine writes in her book *The Helper.* "There must be a real thirst resulting in specifically asking Jesus Himself for this gift. There must be repentance, forgiveness, and a break with one's old life. There must be the set of the will to obedience, and the desire and intention to use one's life . . . for ministry to others" (p. 67).

"As I searched out the experience of other Christians on this . . . ," she says, "I learned that some had had manifestations of the Helper's presence—such as feelings like a series of electric shocks, waves of liquid love pouring through one's body, feelings of impossible joy, speaking a heavenly language—while others had not" *(ibid., p. 69).*

Her research into the lives of some who were undoubtedly filled with the Spirit, such as Dwight L. Moody, John Wesley, Evan Roberts, and others in her own time during the 1940s, showed Catherine that there is no one right way for the Holy Spirit to reveal Himself. Certainly the Holy Spirit does not play games of empty exhibitionism.

"So I knew," she concludes, "that although I should not deny their validity, I should guard against demanding a highly emotional or dramatic experience as initial proof of my baptism in the Spirit. Our triumphant Lord does not need to prove anything. If Jesus wanted to grant me some dramatic evidence, fine. But I would wait for *His* timing on any manifestation at all of the Helper's presence" *(ibid.).*

As Peter testified to the other leaders of the early Christian church, the Holy Spirit came upon the Gentile believers not in a way that they demanded but as He saw best for their needs at that time.

❧ A PRAYER FOR TODAY ❧

*Lord, give me the faith to remember that You always do
what can bring the most good in all circumstances.*

WELCOME, GENTLE SPIRIT

Then I remembered what the Lord had said: "John baptized with water, but you will be baptized with the Holy Spirit." So if God gave them the same gift as he gave us, who believed in the Lord Jesus Christ, who was I to think that I could oppose God? Acts 11:16, 17, NIV.

C atherine Marshall was very earnest in her desire to be filled with the Holy Spirit and spent a whole summer studying all that Scripture has to say about the Helper. Eventually, though, the day came when she knew that she wanted her own personal experience.

"Since at that time I had no group to lay hands on me, very quietly and undramatically I asked for the gift of the Spirit," she explains. "The setting was my bedroom with no other human being present. . . . Nothing overt happened that first day. I experienced no waves of liquid love or ecstatic joy. But then in the next few days, quietly but surely, the heavenly Guest made known His presence in my heart" *(The Helper,* pp. 68, 69).

Catherine Marshall goes on to tell of the growing evidence in her life that the Holy Spirit was actually filling her. The words she spoke were different. She sensed a guidance in the decisions of her life. He became a major creative agent in her writing and ministry.

What about the dramatic manifestations such as Peter found irrefutable in the experience of the Gentiles in Caesarea? "Some of these were to come later," Catherine Marshall tells in her book *(ibid.,* p. 70). "Some I have never yet experienced." When people asked her about tongues, she would tell them, "Everything Paul has to say about tongues reflects a common-sense, balanced view. On the one hand, he refuses to give this one gift undue emphasis or importance; on the other, he will not reject it" *(ibid.,* p. 153).

The Holy Spirit understands what is necessary in every situation. In the house of Cornelius an immediate tangible sign was necessary. In the house of Catherine Marshall the Spirit could come and be recognized in a quiet, gentle way. Likewise, He will always know the best way to reveal Himself to you. He may come like a mighty rushing wind or like a gentle dove.

❧ A PRAYER FOR TODAY ❧

Thank You, Lord, for dealing so understandably with me, even in the most important spiritual areas of my life.

BEGINNING A BARNABAS MINISTRY

For he was a good man, and full of the Holy Ghost and of faith: and much people was added unto the Lord. Acts 11:24.

A Barnabas ministry is extremely important for your survival as a spiritually strong member of the body of Christ. If your church or community does not have a Barnabas ministry, it is possible that the Lord may be leading you to initiate this vital part of Christianity right where you live.

Barnabas was a nurturer, an encourager, who is mentioned about 30 times in the New Testament. We first meet him in Acts 4:36, where he is introduced as a "son of encouragement" or a "son of prophecy." In the New Testament setting a person with the gift of prophecy spoke "edification, exhortation, and comfort" (1 Cor. 14:3), and it appears that the apostles immediately recognized this special nurturing ability in Joseph from Cyprus. He was a model of one of the most important yet most neglected ingredients of true Christianity—genuine, sustaining, caring love that ministers without ulterior motives.

When the apostles in Jerusalem heard of the great number of conversions in Antioch, they sent Barnabas to consolidate the new groups of believers. He was full of the Holy Spirit and also had the spiritual gift of great faith. When he saw what the hand of the Lord had done in Antioch, he immediately initiated a concert of praise and "encouraged them all that with purpose of heart they should continue with the Lord" (Acts 11:23, NKJV). This display of love and Christian caring was so powerful that "a great many people were added to the Lord" (verse 24).

A Barnabas-like ministry should be a vital part of every church today when loneliness and depression grip our society like an epidemic. Barnabas ministers will reach out in the church and community, bringing people into small groups where friends will listen, pray, and care. They also will be involved in one-to-one caring for those who cannot join a group. Even a regular telephone call can be enough to save a life by words of "edification and exhortation and comfort" (1 Cor. 14:3, NKJV).

⇝ A PRAYER FOR TODAY ⇜

Father, lead me today to those whom I can minister to in love and affirmation. Also give me friends like that.

A PROPHET WHO NEED NOT APOLOGIZE

Then one of them [the prophets in Antioch], named Agabus, stood up and showed by the Spirit that there was going to be a great famine throughout all the world, which also happened in the days of Claudius Caesar. Acts 11:28, NKJV.

Once again God surprises us as His Spirit inspires the first predictive prophecy recorded after Pentecost. Agabus was one of the preaching-teaching prophets who were a vital part of the early Christian ministry. These men and women taught the Word in a way that brought great edification to the church. Occasionally God would use one of these prophets to speak concerning the future.

In March 25, 1993, for 45 seconds an earthquake of 5.7 on the Richter scale jolted Oregon and much of the Pacific Northwest. The epicenter was only 12 miles from our house, so everything here was well shaken. Soon people began to wonder about the aftershocks, and a Christian minister circulated a prophecy, supposedly from God, that on May 3 an earthquake of 8 or 9 on the Richter scale would devastate Portland, Oregon, as a punishment for being a center for satanism. The media gave the prediction headline attention, but when his prophecy failed to come to pass, the "prophet" disappeared into Montana, returning later to apologize on TV.

Agabus did not need to apologize for his prophecy. As he predicted, the second of four disastrous famines during the reign of Claudius Caesar soon followed, confirming the accuracy of the Holy Spirit's foreknowledge.

But why predict a famine and not some dramatic religious event? Why not a prophecy like John's Apocalypse? There are a number of important reasons. The rapid fulfillment of the prophecy confirmed again God's supernatural leading of His church. A famine of this proportion was a natural event over which there could be no allegation of human control or manipulation. The fact of the famine was and is an occurrence verifiable in the historical records of the Roman Empire. And, beyond all this, it gave the Christians opportunity to prepare practical help in advance for those who would be the worst affected.

❦ *A PRAYER FOR TODAY* ❧

Give me the calmness, Lord, to remember that even the calamities of nature can be used to Your glory as I'm prepared to help those in desperate need.

POWER, PRAYER, AND SERVICE

While they were worshiping the Lord and fasting, the Holy Spirit said,
"Set apart for me Barnabas and Saul for the work
to which I have called them." Acts 13:2, NIV.

*W*hat is the liturgy of your church?" the Episcopalian pastor asked me. In Adventist terms, he was inquiring about the order of service we follow. In today's verse Luke uses a Greek word translated "ministered" in the King James Version, from which we get the English term "liturgy." Its primary meaning is not a formal order of ceremonial worship but spontaneous prayer and praise. This ministry of prayer and praise blesses God and brings His blessings to His people in return.

I have discovered that growing churches always have a significant emphasis on prayer and praise. Listen to a pastor from one of the fastest-growing churches today: "As staff evangelist I am in charge of the evangelistic and missions outreaches of the church. So I am often asked, 'What is the evangelism program of the church?' My answer often startles pastors and lay leaders. The evangelistic program of our church is the daily prayer meeting! . . . Each morning Monday through Friday we meet at 5:00 and 6:00 for prayer. We agree in united prayer that the Holy Spirit will do His blessed work of drawing people to Christ. We set ourselves to see the harvest come in. We prepare for it by being sure that counselors and follow-up teams are ready to minister to the harvest the Lord will bring. . . . Also, the first Friday night of each month is given to an all-night prayer meeting" (David Shibley, *Let's Pray in the Harvest,* pp.14-16).

The church in ancient Antioch was certainly blessed with a prayer and praise liturgy, and as a result, the Holy Spirit spoke through one of the prophets, giving directions for the church to recognize especially the sowing and harvest ministry team of Barnabas and Paul. A concentration on prayer and praise in your church community will have the same effect. The Holy Spirit will reveal His will concerning your ministry and the spiritual gifts of each person in your small group or congregation. As a result, the harvest will be bountiful.

✎ A PRAYER FOR TODAY ✎

Father, I praise You for giving me the privilege
of being able to bless You in true worship and service.

July 22

SENT OUT BY THE SPIRIT

*The two of them, sent on their way by the Holy Spirit, went down to
Seleucia and sailed from there to Cyprus. Acts 13:4, NIV.*

Like the Christians in Antioch, the Adventist pioneers needed and received directions from the Holy Spirit. At the end of 1873 James and Ellen White again crossed the American continent and once more were involved in ministry in California. But the work was slow, and funding for special needs was very hard to find.

The group of earnest missionaries from the East Coast knew the secret of spiritual power. "How we wrestled! How we prayed with earnest desire for the Lord to open ways whereby we could advance the work in California, for we saw the ideas of the workers were narrow and restricted," Ellen White later wrote (cited by A. L. White, *Ellen G. White: The Progressive Years,* p. 419).

Then the direction of the Holy Spirit came as it had to Barnabas and Paul. "We held a meeting in an upper room of a house in Oakland, while prayer was wont to be made. We knelt down to pray, and while we were praying, the Spirit of God like a tidal wave filled the room, and it seemed that an angel was pointing across the Rocky Mountains to churches in this [the eastern] part of America.

"Brother [John I.] Tay, who is now sleeping in Jesus, rose from his knees, his face as white as death, and said, 'I saw an angel pointing across the Rocky Mountains'" *(ibid.).*

In obedience to the Spirit's direction Ellen White returned to the East, where the Lord used her in a mighty way in camp meetings, temperance rallies, and fund-raising for the Californian ministry. When John Tay saw the vision of the angel, he had been an Adventist for about only one year. Twelve years later the Holy Spirit also sent out this 54-year-old, who worked his passage on six ships to the remote South Pacific island of Pitcairn. Five years later he pioneered the ministry of the three angels in the beautiful Fijian Islands.

Who is listening today as the Holy Spirit seeks to send out missionaries to the vast masses of population in the great cities of Planet Earth?

❦ *A PRAYER FOR TODAY* ❧

*In the midst of the busyness of life help me to be sensitive,
Lord, to Your suggestions and directions.*

A LOOK THAT CONVICTS

*Then Saul, who also is called Paul, filled with the Holy Spirit,
looked intently at him. Acts 13:9, NKJV.*

*I*n 1759 Howell Harris, the Spirit-filled Welsh Methodist revivalist, was asked to join the Beaconshire Militia in preparation for a possible invasion of Britain by French Roman Catholic armies. Twenty-four young men came with him from his Christian community at Trevecka, and Harris became a commissioned officer who preached whenever the Lord provided the opportunity.

When his regiment arrived in Great Yarmouth, Harris was told that a Methodist preacher had been cruelly mistreated when he had tried to hold an open-air meeting in this town. Harris was stirred into action and asked the town crier to announce that another Methodist would preach in the marketplace. A large crowd gathered, armed with stones, brickbats, clods of earth, and other missiles, determined to severely injure or even kill the audacious preacher.

When Harris and his soldiers joined the angry, threatening crowd, he was told that the preacher had not arrived. "Then a sermon you will have from a soldier," Howell Harris replied. At first the crowd thought it a joke as this army officer and his soldiers began to sing hymns of praise. Then, like Paul on the Island of Paphos, Harris looked intently at the crowd and, in the Spirit's mighty power, preached to them the gospel of Jesus Christ. Soon the hostile mob became calm and listened quietly as the influence of the Spirit was felt in many hearts.

Some, like the proconsul at Paphos, believed and were converted that day in Great Yarmouth, and this was the first of many religious services Harris led in that city. In fact, in this English coastal town, filled with prejudice and hatred against the new revival movement of the Christian faith, small groups of believers were soon organized, and a Methodist chapel was built to the glory of God.

Almost 20 centuries after Paul and two centuries after Howell Harris, the Holy Spirit can still give His witnesses the look of intense conviction and deep sincerity.

✤ *A PRAYER FOR TODAY* ✤

*Lord, may the certainty of my faith shine out from my face wherever I share
Your great message of truth, forgiveness, and love in Jesus.*

THE JOY OF THE LORD

And the disciples were continually filled with joy
and with the Holy Spirit. Acts 13:52, NASB.

*I*t appears that a lot of modern Christianity suffers from a severe allergy to joy. Outside a church building many Christians seem fairly happy, but when some get together for a meeting it's as if they suddenly have to impress God that they believe He is a humorless, mournful, frightening Deity who must be appeased at any cost. Martin Luther's view of God was certainly different. He emphatically declared, "It is pleasing to the dear God whenever thou rejoicest or laughest from the bottom of your heart" (cited by Donald E. Demaray, *Laughter, Joy, and Healing,* p. 67).

When the great revival began in the time of Ezra and Nehemiah, the people had to be told to stop weeping and mourning and to be happy. "The joy of the Lord is your strength," the revivalists exhorted, and as a result, the people did what humanity was really made for—they rejoiced greatly (Neh. 8:10, 12).

Jesus came to give "the oil of joy for mourning, the garment of praise for the spirit of heaviness" (Isa. 61:3). His disciples were full of joy even in the worst circumstances (Luke 24:52; 1 Thess. 1:6), and the ministry of the Holy Spirit brought the fruitage of joy wherever His power moved hearts and minds.

The disciples, filled with the Holy Spirit, were also continually filled with joy. This means that being in a church meeting with them would have been a happy experience. Although there would be no empty levity, there would be joyful praise and delightful laughter, as well as tears of true repentance and solemn consecration. As James S. Stewart, famous Scottish minister and professor at the University of Edinburgh, once said: "When Christian worship is dull and joyless, Jesus Christ has been left outside—that is the only explanation" *(ibid.,* p. 68). God intends that His people be joyful in His "house of prayer" (Isa. 56:7).

A young, Spirit-filled Christian wrote from her personal experience with the Lord: "Faith is ours to exercise, but joyful feeling and the blessing are God's to give" (Ellen G. White, *Early Writings,* p. 72).

If you haven't already, let the Holy Spirit fill you with His fruit of joy today.

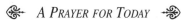

A PRAYER FOR TODAY

Let me smile at the storms of life, Lord, because of the core of joy
You have placed in my heart.

DEALING WITH LEGALISTS

*And God who knows the heart bore witness to them, giving them the
Holy Spirit just as he did to us; and he made no distinction between us
and them, but cleansed their hearts by faith. Acts 15:8, 9, RSV.*

*H*ave you ever met a legalist? Legalists are quite easy to recognize
because they believe that people are saved by Jesus plus something else. Some legalists have multiple "pluses."

"Pastor, I can tell you who will be saved in this church," an earnest young
legalist informed me.

I was intrigued, so I asked, "How can you be so sure?"

His answer stunned me as outright legalism. "I watch to see who eats
cheese at the potluck!"

Although I believe in practicing the principles of healthful living, I am
sure that the truth Peter explained at the first Jerusalem council still applies—
we are saved only through the grace of our Lord Jesus (Acts 15:11).

The Holy Spirit led the early Christian church to deal with its legalists in
a very diplomatic way. The Spirit could have given an apostle the answer to
the pharisaical legalists, and their dissent could have been stifled without discussion. But the Lord led the church leaders to call a "General Conference"
session. Representatives of all the churches arrived, and time was given for
"much disputing" (verse 7).

When the multitude came to see that no human reasoning could bring a
solution, Peter, Paul, and Barnabas testified of the Holy Spirit's mighty power
among the uncircumcised Gentiles. The Gentile Christians had received the
witness of the Spirit just as had the circumcised Jewish Christians (Rom.
8:16). The Holy Spirit had also worked miracles and wonders for the Gentile
Christians (Acts 15:12). God knows the heart.

"You say that God is pouring out His Spirit on those cheese-eating
Adventists, pastor. I just can't believe it," the young man emphatically exclaimed to me. Years later he apologized for his judgmental and critical spirit,
but unfortunately some sensitive souls had been offended and never returned
to our church family again.

❦ *A PRAYER FOR TODAY* ❧

*Thank You, Lord, for Your free gift of salvation. May I never, for myself or
others, add or subtract from any of the essentials of the true Christian life.*

THE HOLY SPIRIT AND US

For it seemed good to the Holy Spirit, and to us, to lay upon you no greater burden than these necessary things. Acts 15:28, NKJV.

O ne of the most successful preachers to graduate from Charles H. Spurgeon's world-famous pastor's college in London was Archibald Brown. The Holy Spirit richly blessed Brown's ministry, and thousands packed his London church to hear his powerful preaching of God's Word. After Archibald Brown's death the secret of his great spiritual power was found in the well-worn Bible that he had used for many years. In the margin beside Acts 15:28 he had written: "Ah, how important is a partnership with the senior partner, the Holy Spirit! Without His partnership, no life of faith or evangelical work has value."

You do not have to be an official denominational pastor to have a partnership with the Holy Spirit. If you ask Him, the Holy Spirit will be your senior partner in your office, school, home, business, profession, or trade. Your secular life will find true strength in your awareness of spiritual certainty at the very core of your being. Even the mundane will be transformed into ministry, and there will be a new sense of purpose in all that you do. Jesus will be glorified and exalted.

Of course, if a preacher does not have this sense of partnership with the Holy Spirit, the result will be devastating to his or her ability to communicate powerful Christianity. G. Campbell Morgan, renowned pastor of Westminster chapel in London, said in his commentary on Acts: "If those who preach the gospel are not empowered with this invisible power and the church does not reflect to the world this eternal and mysterious light it has received, both of them will always be lacking, good for nothing and as cold as death, though their outward appearance seems to be spotlessly perfect and just fine.

"If we really want to fill London with the Holy Spirit, we should by all means do our business in partnership with the Holy Spirit" (*The Acts of the Apostles,* commentary on Acts 5:30, 32).

Morgan's words apply also to your city or community. It is time that Christianity moved from being just part of the culture to giving evidence that it is a powerful partnership with God.

❧ *A PRAYER FOR TODAY* ❧

Holy Spirit, I am glad today to come under Your direction and leadership in every area of my life.

WHEN THE SPIRIT SAYS NO

Now when they had gone through Phrygia and the region of Galatia,
they were forbidden by the Holy Spirit to preach the word in Asia.
Acts 16:6, NKJV.

*I*f anyone had told me six months ago that I would not only be in the church today but actually leading a prayer group, I would have laughed at them."

How often I have heard words like these from people whom God is now using in a wonderful way.

"What happened?" I usually ask, and the explanation always shows the Spirit's unfailing wisdom.

"God had someone share His love with me at the very right time. Even a few weeks earlier I would not have listened and might have asked the person to leave."

Joe Aldrich, president of Multnomah School of the Bible and author of *Life-Style Evangelism,* talks about crossing traditional boundaries to reach the unbelieving world. We must be sensitive to the Holy Spirit's timing for each life and not rush off to "Asia" before the Spirit is ready to lead us there. Listen to this practical example Aldrich gives.

"When your neighbors are over for dinner, don't feel compelled to 'say' something spiritual. Many seem to feel that if they have not shared their 'witness' before the evening is over, they have failed. Not so. One couple we saw trust Christ took three years of careful cultivation. For most of that period, spiritual things were off limits. It soon became obvious we were not free to discuss such matters. During this time we probably ate together at least thirty times. I wish you could meet this couple today! Patience does pay off" (pp. 206, 207).

It may seem hard to believe, but we need to be as sensitive to the Holy Spirit saying no to some of our cherished witnessing plans as we are to the Spirit saying yes. If He closes doors today and makes it clear that this is not the right time to share some gospel truth, do not smash the door down or feel defeated. Remember, as Paul and his mission team discovered, when one door closes, God always opens another.

❦ *A Prayer for Today* ❧

Lead me by Your Spirit today, Father, so that I may not be discouraged
by the closed doors in hearts and minds around me.

SORRY—NO VISA

When they came to the border of Mysia, they tried to enter Bithynia,
but the Spirit of Jesus would not allow them to. So they passed by
Mysia and went down to Troas. During the night Paul had a vision
of a man of Macedonia standing and begging him,
"Come over to Macedonia and help us." Acts 16:7-9, NIV.

*I*f you are an experienced international traveler, you will know the importance of two vital documents. Your passport identifies who you are and where you come from, and a visa, stamped in your passport, gives you permission to enter your country of destination. During a world tour that took me to speaking and study appointments in about 30 countries, I discovered that I did not have a visa for Iran. Without the Lord's miraculous intervention I would have been stranded in Iraq for a long time.

When Paul and his team reached the Bithynian border the Holy Spirit said, "Sorry, no visa." Fortunately the group was not stranded in a foreign airport. They simply turned and walked down the road to Troas. Perhaps God is turning you toward Troas today, and you are feeling disappointed. The thought of Bithynia is exciting: the book you wanted to write; the friend you wanted to visit; the family member you wanted to share your faith with; the house you wanted to buy; the new job you looked forward to so much. "Sorry, no visa," the Lord seems to say.

Paul's night of disappointment was suddenly illuminated by an incredible vision, and the whole situation took on a new meaning. The call to Macedonia exploded the gospel into one of the most cultured and important areas of the Roman Empire.

Your Macedonian call may not come immediately after the Spirit of Jesus closes the way to some cherished aspiration, but you can be sure that the Holy Spirit never closes one door without opening another.

In 1834 David Livingstone was accepted by the London Missionary Society as a medical missionary to China, but the door was closed by the Opium War. "Sorry, no visa." However, the Lord was opening another door. Robert Moffat inspired Livingstone with a vision of Africa, and you know the rest of the story.

❧ *A PRAYER FOR TODAY* ☙

Open my eyes, Lord, to see reality as You see it, knowing the end from the
beginning. Give me a consciousness of walking with Jesus today.

I AM WITH YOU

When Silas and Timothy came from Macedonia,
Paul devoted himself exclusively to preaching, testifying to the Jews
that Jesus was the Christ. Acts 18:5, NIV.

*I*n the midst of terrible trouble a consciousness of Jesus' presence can sustain your life. That is one of the most important ministries of the Holy Spirit.

Violent opposition to the proclamation of the gospel greeted Paul and his team in Corinth, but he was motivated by the Holy Spirit to preach the Word. This was a turning point for Paul, who said: "From now on I go to the Gentiles" (Acts 18:6, NIV).

As Paul faced the prospect of a new and somewhat frightening direction in his ministry, the Lord spoke to him in a vision and said: "I am with you" (verse 10, NIV). Jesus, who has chosen to retain His humanity, passed on to the Holy Spirit the joy of representing Him with, and in, all His people (John 15:26; 16:7, 14; Ps. 139:7-10). The awareness that Jesus is with His people, through His Spirit, has enabled them to take His Word into the scariest situations of life.

David Livingstone understood the certainty of Jesus' presence, as we discover in his diary entry for January 14, 1856: "Evening. Felt much turmoil of spirit in prospect of having all my efforts for the welfare of this great region and this teeming population knocked on the head by savages to-morrow. But I read that Jesus said: 'All power is given unto me in heaven and in earth. Lo, I am with you always, even unto the end of the world.' It is the word of a gentleman of the most strict and sacred honour, so there's an end of it!" (Seaver, *David Livingstone, His Life and Letters,* p. 256).

Livingstone went on to bring the gospel to the indigenous settlements represented by the smoke of a thousand campfires, and as he later testified at the University of Glasgow: "On those words [that Jesus would always be present] I staked everything, and they never failed!" (cited in F. N. Boreham, *A Bunch of Everlastings,* p. 131).

Neither will they fail today as God's people meet the challenge of the 42 megacities of the world and thousands of yet unreached people groups.

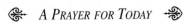

✦ A PRAYER FOR TODAY ✦

Father, may I never take the presence of Your Spirit for granted
but always delight that Jesus is with me.

July 30

Do You Know the Answer?

*He said to them, "Did you receive the Holy Spirit when you believed?"
And they said to him, "We have not so much as heard whether
there is a Holy Spirit." Acts 19:2, NKJV.*

*I*f Paul asked you that question, could you give a positive reply? I hope
so, because it is an important question for all Christians. The disciples
at Ephesus were men who "believed"—a term that is used about 20
times in Acts to mean those who accept Jesus for salvation. This is the same
word Paul used when he later wrote to the church at Ephesus and said,
"Having believed, you were sealed with the Holy Spirit of promise" (Eph.
1:13, NKJV).

Have you accepted Jesus as your personal Saviour? If so, you have received
the Holy Spirit to dwell in your heart (Eze. 36:25-27; Rom. 8:9; 2 Cor. 1:21,
22). Paul's discussion with the 12 Ephesian disciples came about 20 years after
the outpouring of the Holy Spirit on the day of Pentecost, but these men, like
Apollos (Acts 18:24-28), had a pre-Pentecost experience. They had been baptized by John and had accepted Jesus as Saviour but had not received the baptism of the Holy Spirit. Many Christians 2,000 years later are in the same
situation, knowing only a pre-Pentecost relationship with the Lord.

There is no doubt that these 12 men at Ephesus would have heard about
the Holy Spirit. John had preached about the Spirit, used Old Testament references to the Spirit, and had prophesied that Jesus would baptize His followers with the Spirit. But the problem is revealed in their reply, as given in
the margin of the New American Standard Bible: "No, we have not even
heard whether the Holy Spirit has been given." They had not heard of
Pentecost.

I assume that you have heard of Pentecost. Most Christians have, but is it
more than a historical event for you? An intellectual understanding of
Pentecost will be about as helpful for you as learning information pertaining
to the invention of electricity. When electricity is not just a theory but instead
the current comes into your house and the appliances are connected and
turned on, mighty power is available. So it will be as you have a post-
Pentecost experience with the Spirit.

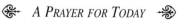

A Prayer for Today

Turn on the power, Lord. Let it flow through my life today.

223

AN EPHESIAN PENTECOST

And when Paul had laid his hands upon them, the Holy Ghost came on them; and they spake with tongues, and prophesied. Acts 19:6.

*P*aul had received his "visa" for Asia, and now the Holy Spirit, in an immediately visible way, confirmed His willingness to fill the people of this ethnic origin. Just as tongues were used in Jerusalem at Pentecost, in Samaria, and with the Gentiles at Caesarea, they are used once again at Ephesus as undeniable proof of the outpouring of the Holy Spirit.

Many Christians believe that the same initial sign is used by God today, but Pentecostal preacher Mario Murillo issues a timely warning: "Some early Pentecostals reduced tarrying [for the Holy Spirit] to legalistic torture. They believed you had to suffer to earn Holy Ghost power. On the other hand, many charismatics have cheapened the act of waiting, and the results are equally disastrous.

"One extreme frustrates the seeker and adds unwarranted pain to waiting on God. The Spirit is hindered because He is ready to give us the gift but we are too preoccupied with self-abasement to receive it. The other extreme is instantism. The seeker is instructed to babble a few syllables and is excitedly told that they've 'got it.' This has aborted many from truly getting the Holy Spirit baptism. The convert is sent home with a synthetic experience without truly encountering the power of God" *(Fresh Fire,* p. 131).

Although tongues appear extremely easy for Satan to counterfeit, the early Christians fully accepted this sign as an authentic communication from God. Connected to the fruit of the Spirit and the truths of God's Word, true tongues have been used by God many times throughout recorded church history. In fact, as Jaroslav Pelikan, one of the leading church historians today, has said: "The history of the church has never been altogether without the spontaneous gifts of the Holy Spirit."

Whatever way God chooses to reveal Himself now, you can be certain that you will know, as surely as did the Ephesians, that you are filled with the Holy Spirit.

✎ *A PRAYER FOR TODAY* ✎

Help me, Father, avoid seeking some dramatic external sign of Your power and to concentrate instead on the reflection of the character of Jesus.

August 1

AIMED BY THE SPIRIT FOR CHINA

When these things were accomplished, Paul purposed in the Spirit,
when he had passed through Macedonia and Achaia, to go to
Jerusalem, saying, "After I have been there, I must also see Rome."
Acts 19:21, NKJV.

*I*f I had a thousand lives, I would give them all for the women of China."
Lottie Moon, who spoke those determined words, was converted when
she was 18. Charlotte Diggs Moon had grown up as part of the aristoc-
racy of antebellum Virginia and excelled as a student who spoke French,
Latin, Italian, and Spanish. She was also proficient in Greek and Hebrew. As
an early teen she had resisted all religious influences but finally professed
faith in Jesus Christ at a revival meeting in the Charlottesville Baptist Church,
December 22, 1858.

Lottie, as she was called, graduated with an M.A. from the Albemarle
Female Institute, because only men were admitted to the University of
Virginia. There at Albemarle, in the midst of her studies, she heard the Spirit's
voice aiming her for ministry to the women of China. After 10 years of teach-
ing, Lottie finally set sail for China, supported by dedicated women in five
Richmond, Virginia, churches.

In China Lottie's courage became legendary. Taunted as a "devil woman,"
struggling with disease, feeding and caring for hungry and destitute women,
she ministered to the people in the power of the Holy Spirit. "We must go out
and live among them, manifesting the gentle, loving spirit of our Lord,"
Lottie said. "We need to make friends before we can hope to make converts"
(John Woodbridge, editor, *More Than Conquerors,* p. 62).

Shortly before she died from the results of starvation and sickness,
Charlotte Moon spoke those now-famous words, "If I had a thousand lives, I
would give them all for the women of China."

Are there any modern Lotties willing to be aimed by the Holy Spirit to
help millions of hurting women in the supercities of today? I have met a few
who care—a few dedicated and self-sacrificing women who are friends to
women in need. They have Barnabas-like ministries, showing in the power of
the Holy Spirit, the "gentle, loving spirit of our Lord."

❦ *A PRAYER FOR TODAY* ❧

Heavenly Father, forgive me for being dominated by plans for my own comfort
while thousands do not know what basic happiness means.

CAPTIVATED BY THE SPIRIT

And now, compelled by the Spirit, I am going to Jerusalem,
not knowing what will happen to me there. Acts 20:22, NIV.

Sadhu Sundar Singh was known as "the apostle with the bleeding feet." Following his conversion in 1903, at the age of 16, he began to walk from village to village in northern India, captivated, like Paul, by the Holy Spirit. Stoning, arrest, exposure to extreme weather, and lack of food could not stop this young man who believed that Jesus belonged to India and was not some foreign God. (See the May 18 reading.)

Just as the Spirit led Paul to Jerusalem, so He beckoned Sundar to Tibet, a closed country that was dominated by Buddhism and devil worship. The filth and degradation of the people appalled Sundar. They stoned him as he bathed in some cold water, because they believed that holy men never washed. But amid hostility Sundar Singh, in the power of the Holy Spirit, brought the knowledge of the washing of regeneration through Jesus Christ.

During a time of training for ministry in Lahore, Singh's denomination told him that he must never again enter Tibet. However, he felt compelled by the Spirit, and he told his church leaders that it would be unthinkable for him to reject God's call. During his subsequent visits to Tibet, he was sewn into a wet yak skin and left to be crushed to death as it shrank in the hot sun, tied in cloths laced with scorpions and leaches to sting him and suck his blood, and roped in a tree as bait for wild animals. Always, though, faithful secret Christians rescued him so that his ministry could continue a little longer.

Twice the Holy Spirit took Sundar Singh to preach Jesus to large crowds in Britain, Europe, the United States, and Australia. He was amazed at the materialism in these countries and their deep need of the gospel despite their traditional Christian denominations. But still India and Tibet were calling, and finally, in 1929, he reached Kalka, a small town below Simla in Tibet, but he was never seen or heard of again. While he was only in his early forties, Sadhu Singh's work for the Lord was completed.

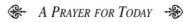

❦ *A PRAYER FOR TODAY* ❧

My Lord and God, help me be certain about the work
You have called me to do and never deviate from it.

RUNNING INTO TROUBLE

Except that the Holy Spirit testifies in every city, saying that chains and tribulations await me. Acts 20:23, NKJV.

While Christians in Western nations, following a basic instinct of humanity, seem to look for the easiest and most popular ways to preach the gospel, Spirit-filled believers in many other parts of the world are still willing to proclaim the everlasting gospel in the face of personal hardship and danger.

Northern India, 66 years after Sadhu Sundar Singh, is still one of the greatest global mission challenges in the world. Robert Folkenberg, president of the Seventh-day Adventist Church, reports that the Rajasthan and Madhya Pradesh states are among the most difficult areas. "It was in this area, at the conclusion of evangelistic meetings where four people had been baptized [in 1993], that a political leader filed a complaint with the government that mass conversions were taking place. As a result, the police were ordered to jail Mr. Masih, the Adventist evangelist.

"Mr. Masih and the four new members were called before the council and asked if the charges were true. When he testified that he was commissioned by Jesus Christ to preach, teach, and baptize, he was slapped on the face.

"During the interrogation the new members were asked if they had been bribed to be baptized, a charge which they vigorously denied. In fact, they testified, they had pledged to pay one tenth of their income to support the church. The local press wrote blazing articles against Christianity, and the situation was dangerous" (Robert Folkenberg, Newsletter, June 14, 1993).

As God's people prayed for Paul 2,000 years ago, so there were many in 1993 praying for northern India and the situation with Mr. Masih. On his release from prison the Spirit-filled evangelist was again called to the police station, where, much to his surprise, the magistrate treated him kindly and simply requested that he fill out an application to proceed with the meetings.

Praise God that He still has people who will not be intimidated by personal risk and threat of danger! Even in their own neighborhoods Spirit-filled believers are not comfort-zone Christians, but people who hazard confronting Christ's enemies.

❧ *A PRAYER FOR TODAY* ❧

Until my work for You is finished, Lord, I know nothing can destroy me.

FEEDING OR FLEECING THE FLOCK

*So keep watch over yourselves and over all the flock which the Holy
Spirit has placed in your care. Be shepherds of the church of God,
which he made his own through the sacrificial death of his Son.*
Acts 20:28, TEV.

Seventy million sheep and 3 million people—that's about the usual statistics of the population of New Zealand. White sheep grazing on green, golf course-like pastures help make New Zealand one of the most beautiful countries in the world. But every sheep must be cared for in one way or another, and although the sheep farmers of New Zealand do not lead their huge flocks around like the shepherds of the Middle East, they do constantly oversee their well-being.

The sheep are cared for, though, not so that they can reach a ripe and happy old age, but so that they can end up as food or fleece for millions of people around the world who must be fed and clothed. Jesus, however, did not die for His flock so that it could be exploited for the greed of others but for the purpose of it sharing His eternal joy.

The church in the first centuries of Christianity was divided into small group fellowships or flocks. For each flock there was apparently a shepherd, who was known as an elder, pastor, or bishop. The Holy Spirit placed the flock in the care of these spiritual leaders, who were not over the church but were part of it. They were what we would call today lay leaders of small groups. They did not fleece the flock to build a big organization or structures that could rival pagan temples, but instead they fed the flock so that it could be strong in the face of the enemy.

Every Christian today needs the fellowship of a flock and the care of a shepherd. Although a large gathering of multiple small flocks can provide a wonderful opportunity for a weekly festival of worship and praise, it cannot meet the need for close fellowship and shepherding care. This is why still today the Holy Spirit is appointing small-group leaders who care and share.

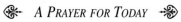 *A PRAYER FOR TODAY*

*Father, are You calling me to be a shepherd? If so please help me
gather the flock that You would like me to pastor for You.*

DID PAUL DISOBEY THE SPIRIT?

We went ashore, found the local believers and stayed with them a week.
These disciples warned Paul—the Holy Spirit prophesying through
them—not to go on to Jerusalem. Acts 21:4, TLB.

*D*id the disciples misunderstand the messages that they received from the Holy Spirit, or did Paul disobey the direction of God at this time? Scholars are divided over this question, notwithstanding the fact that Paul himself seems clear that he was to go to Jerusalem. Although others may give advice and convey messages that they believe are from God, ultimately each person must make decisions on the basis of his or her own convictions and the weight of evidence that he or she personally concludes is a revelation of God's will.

Fortunately, Paul did not need to make a political decision. He was not running for office, so he did not need to calculate how many votes he would lose by not following the desires of the outspoken people. The "Stay With Us" party were sincere and loved Paul, but had interpreted God's prophetic warnings of danger ahead to mean that Paul should not go to Jerusalem. Rather, they should have seen them to be warnings for the need of much prayer and spiritual preparation.

Let's think about some of the decisions that you may be facing at this time. Perhaps you are wondering whom to marry or where to retire. You may have to decide about a school or midlife career change. Perhaps you are thinking about buying or selling a house or car. Yes, life is full of decisions. It is wise to ask for a lot of advice. Ask your small-group members to keep you in prayer so that you may know God's will. But do not end up making the decision on the basis of the people you want to please or because of obligations you have to family or friends. It is your decision, and you must live with the results.

Paul firmly believed that the Holy Spirit was leading him back to Jerusalem. Although it is possible that Paul did make the wrong decision at that time, as we all sometimes do, God can bring good out of evil and turn the worst circumstances to His glory. Plus, Paul could go on to his death, not blaming others but rejoicing that he had finished his race with joy (Acts 20:24).

❧ A PRAYER FOR TODAY ❧
Give me confidence, Lord, so that I can walk the path that is best for my life.

A PROPHECY OF MARTYRDOM

*He took Paul's belt, bound his own feet and hands with it and said,
"The Holy Spirit declares, 'So shall the owner of this belt be bound by
the Jews in Jerusalem and turned over to the Romans.'"*
Acts 21:11, TLB.

Name the first Holy Spirit revival movement in the early Christian church," I asked a large group of Oregon pastors. "Its name is similar to one of the states of the U.S."

We were all surprised when evangelist's wife, Mary Walter, was the only one to know the answer, Montana. The New Prophecy movement, as it was originally called, was eventually known by the name of its founder, Montanus—hence, Montanism.

You may not have heard of the New Prophecy movement, or Montanism, but it is possible that you have read of one of its most heroic martyrs. She was only in her 20s—a young mother with a nursing son—but as she prepared for baptism, Perpetua was captured by Roman solders and condemned to death.

The New Prophecy movement had begun in Phrygia around A.D. 170 and soon spread throughout the Christian church. At first it was tolerated, but eventually—mainly because of false accusations by a hyperconservative named Praxeas—it was rejected by the bishop of Rome. Nevertheless, the witness of this new movement in the power of the Holy Spirit led many people to Jesus, including the famous North African lawyer Tertullian and Perpetua, a young, cultured noblewoman.

Some Montanists, including many women, claimed to have the gift of prophecy. This was a threat to the established church leaders, who had already become entrenched in traditionalism, but to these fervent Christians it was the voice of God. Like Paul, in the face of the male and female prophets at Ceasarea, Perpetua counted it an honor to suffer and die for the name of the Lord Jesus. In the great amphitheater in Carthage, on March 7, 205, she was tossed and injured by wild animals and finally killed by a gladiator's sword. Even Perpetua's unbelieving father had begged her to recant, but she had said, "I cannot deny what I am, and I am a Christian."

☞ A PRAYER FOR TODAY ☜
*Lord, I ask for a determination like Paul's and Perpetua's
to be what You would have me be no matter the consequences.*

THE ACTS CONTINUE

So when they did not agree among themselves, they departed after Paul had said one word: "The Holy Spirit spoke rightly through Isaiah the prophet to our fathers." Acts 28:25, NKJV.

*A*fter more than 60 references to the Holy Spirit, Luke gives no real conclusion to the book of Acts of the Spirit. Indeed, he even leaves us wondering about the "rest of the story" of Christian superstars Paul and Peter. Eusebius, bishop of Caesarea at the beginning of the fourth century, wrote a history of the Christian church. This Christian historian states that Paul was beheaded and Peter crucified upside down and that their tombs and inscriptions were still visible in his day.

But Acts 28 is not the end of the ministry and power of the Holy Spirit. At the end of the first century, John was filled with the Spirit on Patmos. Justin Martyr wrote about A.D. 135 that Christian believers in his day possessed the supernatural "gifts of the Spirit of God." Irenaeus, bishop of Lyons (c. 130-200), wrote: "We have heard of many of the brethren who have foreknowledge of the future, visions and prophetic utterances; others, by laying hands on the sick, heal the sick and restore them to health. . . . We hear of many members of the church who have prophetic gifts, and, by the Spirit speak with all kinds of tongues, and bring men's secret thoughts to light for their own good, and expound the mysteries of God."

Every century between the beginning of Christianity to the present has had witnesses who tell of the supernatural works of the Holy Spirit in their day as the book of Acts continues to be written. These accounts are not anonymous fiction produced by fringe groups, but carefully documented firsthand evidence of God's mighty power. The testimony can be summed up by Severus, who wrote of prophecy and miracles during the time of Martin of Tours in the fourth century: "I have written nothing of which I have not certain knowledge and evidence. I should, in fact, have preferred to be silent rather than to narrate things which are false."

Where you live today the book of Acts continues to be written, and God gives you the privilege to be part of it.

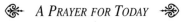

✥ *A PRAYER FOR TODAY* ✥

Father, forgive me for settling for a form of Christianity but denying its power to work miracles and change lives.

WELCOME, SPIRIT OF HOLINESS

*And who through the Spirit of holiness was declared with power
to be the Son of God by his resurrection from the dead:
Jesus Christ our Lord. Rom. 1:4, NIV.*

The New Prophecy movement, later called Montanism, emphasized not only the gifts of the Holy Spirit, including prophecy, but also personal and corporate holiness in second- and third-century Christianity. "Writing from the perspective of the Methodist renewal in eighteenth-century England, John Wesley declared that Montanus was 'one of the best men then upon earth' who, 'under the character of a Prophet, as an order established in the church, appeared (without bringing any new doctrine) for reviving what was decaying, and reforming what might be amiss'" (Howard A. Snyder, *Signs of the Spirit,* p. 23).

The Holy Spirit is indeed the Spirit of Holiness, as the first Christian revival movement declared, and He will not only bless the people of God with miracle-working power but also with victory power over sin and worldliness. Tertullian, the great North African lawyer who became a leader of the New Prophecy movement, stated that the holiness of the church was simply the holiness of its members. And the *Schaff-Herzog Encyclopedia of Religious Knowledge* concludes that "Montanism was simply a reaction of the old, primitive church against the obvious tendency of the church of the day—to strike a bargain with the world, and arrange herself comfortably in it" (Vol. III, p. 1562).

The church still faces the same problem because of a lack of Holy Spirit power in its members.

It is important to remember, however, as did the early Christians and revivalists, that the Spirit of holiness is also the Spirit of grace. No person is saved by private holiness or by the corporate holiness of the church, but by Jesus' perfect holiness, which is credited to every sinner who personally accepts Jesus' sacrifice. The Holy Spirit draws each sinner to Jesus and reveals the grace that can only make salvation possible. Then, as the New Prophecy movement proclaimed, holiness of the church or individual is the fruit of the Holy Spirit in the life of each saved person who is eagerly awaiting the return of Jesus.

❧ *A PRAYER FOR TODAY* ❧

*Spirit of Holiness, thank You for reminding me of the forgiveness that
Jesus offers and the overcoming power that is always available.*

August 9

A True Jew in the Spirit

But he is a Jew who is one inwardly, and circumcision
is that of the heart, in the Spirit, and not in the letter;
whose praise is not from men but from God. Rom. 2:29, NKJV.

*I*t's so good to see you, sweetie," Richard greeted Debbie after not having been with her for a few days.

"I love you, sweet man," she replied. "I've missed you so much."

Words like "sweet" and "honey," according to the English dictionary, are often used as terms of endearment. They obviously are not describing external taste but a special relationship between two hearts. Without the relationship the words are meaningless.

Paul used a similar play on words when he spoke about the Jews and the Spirit. The Jews understood that their name meant praise, and in fact, they believed that they were God's praise on earth. But pride had led them to glory in praise from people rather than have the true heart relationship with God. That relationship would be the source of an outpouring of praise from the Lord.

Strangely, the external rite of circumcision became a major source of Jewish pride. Eventually, conflict with Christianity brought Jewish thinkers to the same conclusion that Paul expressed to the Romans. Jewish writer, Rabbi Dipman, explained it this way: "A certain Christian mocked us saying, 'Women, who cannot be circumcised, cannot be reckoned among the Jews.' Such persons are ignorant that faith does not consist in circumcision, but in the heart. He who does not have genuine faith is not a partaker of the Jewish circumcision; but he who has genuine faith is a Jew, although not circumcised" *(Nizzachon,* Num. 21, p. 19).

Richard liked to call Debbie "Sweetie," not because of her clothes or perfume, but because of her character, personality, and love for him. So God's people are His praise and joy when the Spirit within enables them to transcend reliance on externals such as Sabbathkeeping, tithing, or healthful living. Instead, the Holy Spirit creates in people's hearts a bond of love with God. It is a realization that God is bigger than any box in which organized religion with its rules and rites may try to enclose Him.

✣ A Prayer for Today ✣

Father, forgive me for relying on my works to earn Your favor
and let me remember that Your love is unconditional.

WELCOME, A WATERFALL OF LOVE

*Now hope does not disappoint, because the love of God has been
poured out in our hearts by the Holy Spirit who was given to us.
Rom. 5:5, NKJV.*

When people fall in love for the first time, they are often surprised by the incredible power of this indescribable emotion, desire, and concern for another person. "I don't intend ever to marry," an attractive young woman informed her parents. "I want to concentrate on my career without having to be concerned about looking after a man."

Connie was surprised how that all changed when she met Peter. To be with Peter and to share her life with him became as important to Connie as anything else she had planned to do. Love certainly made the difference.

Like a mighty waterfall, the Holy Spirit pours God's love into every heart He fills. It is a comforting love, an assuring love, a love that is secure and constant. God's love is part of Himself, because "God is love." The human heart does not have the capacity to hold a fraction of God's love, so it overflows onto all who come in contact with a Spirit-filled person.

Hanging under the eaves of the back porch of our house are flowering pot plants that must be watered every day. On the deck, directly under the hanging pots, are more containers of geraniums, which always benefit as my wife waters the plants above. The overflow pours down upon them so that they receive double liquid blessings to keep them alive and green. In the same way Jesus' love overflows from a Spirit-filled life and blesses others with freshness and joy.

Lottie Moon, the brilliant young Virginian who gave her life for the women of nineteenth-century China, was known by her amazing love for the people to whom she ministered. "How she loved us," the P'ingtu church members wrote after her death. Confucian Li Show-ting had been deeply impressed with Lottie's love and the beautiful picture of her God that he found in the New Testament. After his conversion he became a Christian evangelist whom the Lord used to baptize more than 10,000 converts in northern China.

✽ *A PRAYER FOR TODAY* ✽

*Pour Your love into my heart today, dear Lord,
so that it may bring refreshing to some parched soul.*

A NEW MOTIVE AND POWER

But now we have been delivered from the law, having died to what we
were held by, so that we should serve in the newness of the Spirit and
not in the oldness of the letter. Rom. 7:6, NKJV.

Billy Graham tells of an experience that his friend Allan Emery had while growing up as part of a wealthy Christian family in the city of Boston. One day his father received a call saying that a well-known Christian had been found drunk on the sidewalk. Immediately the father sent his chauffeured limousine to pick up the man, while his mother prepared the best guest room.

Allan watched wide-eyed as the beautiful coverlets were turned down on the exquisite old four-poster bed, revealing the monogrammed sheets. "But Mother," he protested, "he's drunk. He might even get sick."

"I know," his mother replied kindly, "but this man has slipped and fallen. When he comes to, he'll be so ashamed. He'll need all the loving encouragement we can give him."

The Emerys had been delivered from the bondage of the law that demanded that the drunk Christian be punished for his sin. They could have scorned him or made him an example to teach others about the dangers of alcohol. They could have thought of their own reputation or standing in the community. Instead they revealed the love of a God who treats sinners as the most important people in the world. They are—Jesus died for them!

The newness of the Spirit in the life of a born-again Christian does not mean that sin is excused or indulged as if it no longer matters how a person behaves. Instead, the Holy Spirit creates the desire to serve God from the motivation of love and a heart overflowing with gratitude for forgiveness and victory power in each life that He fills.

Christians like the Emerys, serving in the newness of the Spirit, treat others as they know God has treated them. Rather than legalistically imposing on others works that they believe must be performed to merit salvation, those who serve in the newness of the Spirit reveal God's compassion and grace.

✒ A PRAYER FOR TODAY ✒

Thank You, Lord, for deliverance from legalistic religion that would crush my
spirit and lead me to treat others differently than You have treated me.

August 12

WELCOME TO THE MOUNTAINTOP

*There is therefore now no condemnation to those who are
in Christ Jesus, who do not walk according to the flesh,
but according to the Spirit. Rom. 8:1, NKJV.*

Often at Holy Spirit seminars I have asked the question "Which chapter in the Bible mentions the Holy Spirit more than any other?" What would your answer be? Until I had studied about the Holy Spirit for some time, I would have guessed John 14, John 16, Acts 2, or 1 Corinthians 12. The correct answer, I discovered, is Romans 8, in which Paul mentions the Spirit at least 19 times.

There are many titles given to the Holy Spirit in Romans 8, including "the Spirit of life in Jesus Christ," "the Spirit of God," "the Spirit of Christ," "the Spirit of Him who raised Jesus from the dead," and "the Spirit of adoption." In Romans 8 Christians "walk . . . according to the Spirit," "live according to the Spirit," "are led by the Spirit," "have the firstfruits of the Spirit," and by the Spirit "cry out, 'Abba, Father.'"

Years ago Australian evangelist George Burnside preached an outstanding sermon on Romans 8 at a General Conference session. He proclaimed that, to him, this is the greatest chapter in the Bible. It begins with "no condemnation," and ends with no separation, and in between, "all things work together for good to those who love God." The Holy Spirit, Paul tells us, makes all this possible through our Lord Jesus Christ.

Begin today to "walk . . . according to the Spirit" along the entire pathway of Romans 8. Pray a number of times through the whole chapter, and ask the Holy Spirit to lead you into all truth concerning the revelation of Himself and the Father and Son found in these 39 verses. Also request that the Spirit help you see where you are personally in Romans 8, and write down your response to each new discovery that you make about yourself and your relationship with God.

When asked why they would risk their lives to climb mountains, mountaineers have been known to reply, "Just because they are there." But when you reach the mountaintop in Romans 8 you are rewarded with a breathtaking panorama of truth and joy.

⚜ A PRAYER FOR TODAY ⚜

*Help me, Father, find time to be alone with You in prayer and to study today so
that I may enjoy each moment with You.*

THREE LAWS IN ROMANS 8

Through Christ Jesus the law of the Spirit of life set me free
from the law of sin and death. Rom. 8:2, NIV.

*A*fter driving for 25 years on the left-hand side of the road, I found that driving on the "right" side in America required concentration. One or two narrow escapes made three laws quickly become obvious. The laws of the 50 states are consistent and strictly enforced: "All traffic must drive on the right-hand side." The second law naturally followed the first: "If you drive on the left side of the road, you will most likely be involved in an accident. If the police catch you before you are killed, you will be arrested and convicted according to the first law."

With my family in the car one morning, I drove out of a gas station in Spokane and proceeded up the wrong side of the road. Suddenly three lanes of traffic were approaching us head-on, and only a violent swerve over the median strip saved our lives. Then a third law came into effect. My family watched constantly that I did not make the same mistake again. Wouldn't you? They became helpers to save my life—and theirs.

Look at the three laws in Romans 8, and notice some similarities and differences to my driving situation. First, there is the law of God, with its righteous requirements (verses 7 and 4).

Second, there is the law of sin and death. Puritan pastor Thomas Jacomb, in his sermons preached in 1672 on Romans 8, described this law as a metaphor for the way in which sin [breaking the first law] "assumes a strange kind of authority" over the sinner. The grip of this sin, if not repented of and forsaken, inevitably leads to death.

Unlike road rules, all the "will" power, "won't" power, and concentration in the world cannot enable me to obey perfectly the law of God, so Paul's third law comes into effect. The law of the Spirit of life in Christ Jesus not only negates the claims that the law of sin and death have upon me, but provides the power to fulfill the requirements of the first law, the law of God.

❦ *A PRAYER FOR TODAY* ❧

Lord, I praise You for the freedom I have in Jesus
from the consequences of the law of sin and death.

In Him and in You—By the Spirit

*That the righteous requirement of the law might be fulfilled
in us who do not walk according to the flesh but according
to the Spirit. Rom. 8:4, NKJV.*

I can never live right, do right, or be right," the young man said in a
rather discouraged voice.

"Dean, let me tell you what Paul would say if he were here today,"
I replied. "No matter how you think or feel at the moment, the Holy Spirit can
enable the righteous requirements of the law to be fulfilled in you."

It seemed impossible to Dean until he began to understand what Paul was
teaching in Romans 8.

Paul began by saying that there is no condemnation to those who are in
Christ. Then he stated that *in* Christ a person can be free from the law of sin
and death. What does it mean to be "in Christ," where more than 160 times
the New Testament places the Christian? As I have listened a number of times
to Pastor Jack Sequeira expound the gospel from the book of Romans, I have
appreciated his "in Christ" illustration.

"If I place this church bulletin *in* my Bible," Jack explains, "then whatever happens to the Bible happens to the bulletin. For instance, if I send this
Bible to my son in China and the Communists discover it, and they confis-
cate and burn it, then the bulletin is also burned because it is *in* the Bible. In
the same way, when Jesus came and took humanity, I was counted as being
in Him. When He died on the cross, it was as if I died, because I was *in* Him.
When He lived a sinless life, I was also *in* Him. As I accept Him as my
Saviour, His doing and dying is counted as my forgiveness and complete obedience to the righteous requirements of the law."

"Dean," I concluded, "as A. J. Gordon, famous Boston pastor from the
past century, said, a true Christian walk is a reproducing in our lives of the
righteousness which is already ours in Christ *[In Christ,* p. 21]. The Holy
Spirit makes this possible not to save us, but because we are already saved in
Jesus."

❧ *A Prayer for Today* ❧

*Lord Jesus, I praise You for dealing a death blow
to the controlling power of sin in my life.*

WHAT IS ON YOUR MIND?

For those who live according to the flesh set their minds on the things of the flesh, but those who live according to the Spirit, the things of the Spirit. Rom. 8:5, NKJV.

*M*y father promised me a computer game for Christmas," a neighborhood boy informed me with tears in his eyes. "I saw the one I wanted at the store and thought about it all weekend. I imagined having so much fun with it. But when my father went back to the store to buy it today, it had been sold, and there are no more available."

That is what it means to set your mind on something. Have you ever done it? No doubt we all have. The thought of a person, position, possession, or pleasure has so dominated our thinking that all life begins to revolve around it. It is not a casual good or bad thought that indicates the controlling power of our life but that which is the preoccupation or "set" of the mind.

When a person is born again, the mind naturally becomes set on Jesus. The indwelling presence of the Holy Spirit turns the thoughts and affections to Jesus. But the Christian soon finds that the "flesh," or lustful part of his or her nature, still has some strong attractions to things that can again dominate the mind. This is why being constantly filled with the Holy Spirit is so important. God's Spirit renews our minds and uses spiritual music, Scripture, prayer, and association with Christian friends to focus our thinking on things of eternal value.

"Steve," I said to our neighborhood boy, "have you thought about another new computer game that is out now and is a lot of fun but also helps you learn many interesting things?"

"Tell me about it. Is it boring?"

I gave him all the information I could remember, and he ran away excitedly to talk to his father. Telling him to forget the game that had gripped his mind for the weekend would not have worked, but the thought of something new and better had replaced the old obsession. So the Holy Spirit works to direct our preoccupations to things that are most important.

&- *A PRAYER FOR TODAY* -&

Fill my mind, Father, with the things that will stimulate positive spiritual thinking and affections.

CHOOSING A DESTINATION

For the mind set on the flesh is death, but the mind set on the Spirit is life and peace. Rom. 8:6, NASB.

To be preoccupied with the things of the flesh, that is, the lustful desires of the self-centered sinful nature, is like being soaked in a flammable substance and playing with matches. The mind "set on the flesh" plays with the potential of death, not because God arbitrarily condemns it but because it loses its desire to be with Him.

Arnold Wallenkampf tells a parable of a neighbor who has spilled the contents of a five-gallon can of gasoline over his clothes. You see him all wet and advise him to go change as quickly as possible. "Your neighbor dutifully listens to your admonition. Then he casually explains to you that he surely plans to change coveralls, but first he intends to burn some rubbish on a bonfire in his backyard. You become still more insistent in your appeal that he change clothes at once. He must not come close to the fire in his gasoline-saturated clothes.

"But all your kind and well-meaning counsel is of no avail. Your neighbor picks up a pile of leaves and other rakings. But as he approaches the fire, a capricious wind blows a tongue of flame in his direction. The next moment your neighbor is aflame from head to foot. Nothing can save him. He is in a gasoline-fed inferno" *(Justified,* p. 28).

While the mind set on the things of the flesh is never at rest but is constantly worried and suspicious, the life that is filled with the Holy Spirit finds that it has an inner peace and joy in spite of external circumstances. The reason for this peace and joy is a certainty that the Holy Spirit brings of eternal life in Jesus Christ. People filled with the Spirit know that they are saved by Jesus' blood, that they are God's children, and that their destiny of eternity with their Lord is absolutely certain.

❧ A PRAYER FOR TODAY ❧

I praise You, Lord, for the indescribable joy of knowing You and the life and peace that You have made freely available through Jesus' sacrifice for me.

NO OPTIONAL EXTRA

*But you are not in the flesh but in the Spirit, if indeed the Spirit of God
dwells in you. Now if anyone does not have the Spirit of Christ,
he is not His. Rom. 8:9, NKJV.*

*A*s a pastor I had often preached to my congregations as if they were
Christians but were lacking the Holy Spirit. "If only you had the
Spirit, you would become involved in all my pet programs," I implied. Not only was I trying to use the Spirit instead of letting Him use me,
but also I was mistaken in what I was telling the people. It is impossible to be
a born-again Christian and not have the Holy Spirit.

Paul is very definite in Romans 8:9. Either one has the Holy Spirit
dwelling within or else that person is not a Christian. This is not a threat but
a reality. The reason is clear—at conversion the Holy Spirit makes the transition from being "with" to being "in" a person. This was the promise of the
new covenant outlined in the Old Testament and brought to reality in the New
(Eze. 36:25-27; John 14:16, 17; 2 Cor. 1:21, 22).

A few years ago I bought a house through the Veterans' Administration.
The exterior needed painting so, because I was on vacation, I asked the authorities if I could go ahead and paint the house, even though all the purchase
formalities were not yet completed. They readily agreed, with the stipulation
that I could not occupy the house until all the papers were signed. A couple
of weeks later, when all the legal requirements were finalized, we received
our key and moved into the house.

At Calvary we were "bought with a price" by Jesus' sacrifice. But when
we personally accept Jesus as our Saviour and put our lives willingly into His
hands, the Holy Spirit receives the key to our body temple and comes to dwell
within us (1 Cor. 6:19, 20).

Now I share the good news with Christians everywhere, "You already
have the Holy Spirit dwelling [living, abiding] in you. Make the most of this
mighty Person of power and invite Him to have total control of every part of
your life."

❦ *A PRAYER FOR TODAY* ❦

*I praise You, Holy Spirit, for coming into my life from the moment of
my conversion. I give You permission to fill me totally today.
Use me to serve You in the way that will best glorify Jesus.*

WELCOME, LIFE IN CHRIST

And if Christ is in you, the body is dead because of sin, but the Spirit is life because of righteousness. Rom. 8:10, NKJV.

*J*esus promised that the Holy Spirit would be sent in His name (John 14:26), so Paul calls the Holy Spirit the "Spirit of Christ." Through the Holy Spirit, Jesus, who is enthroned in heaven, is counted as being in His people. With His Spirit in the "inner man" Christ dwells in the heart of each born-again Christian by faith (Eph. 3:16, 17).

Now we can see why the enemy of souls does not want Christians to know what it means to be filled with the Holy Spirit. The powers of darkness understand that they are defeated in the life of a person who is fully aware that he or she has Jesus living within. Although that person's body is "dead because of sin" and is destined to return to the dust, there is a principle of life in every born-again Christian that can never be destroyed.

Within your being, if you have accepted Jesus as your Saviour, is an eternal life force, namely the Holy Spirit. He does not give life or manufacture life. He *is* life. He who has the Spirit has life because, "he who has the Son has life" (1 John 5:12). Thus Paul states that the Spirit in us is life "because of righteousness." This is not our righteousness, nor the righteousness of the law, but the righteousness of Jesus Christ, which at conversion is counted as righteousness for even the worst sinner.

The idea that a Christian must work to earn eternal life is a blatant trick of the enemy. First, why would a person need to work for something he or she already possesses as a gift? The Holy Spirit is a gift (Acts 2:38; 10:45), and so is eternal life (Rom. 6:23). Second, working to merit eternal life always leads a person back into the hands of the enemy because of discouragement or pride. Put your name in Romans 8:10 and say, "Praise God! Jesus is in me today, and even though my body is destined to die because of sin, the Holy Spirit is filling me with eternal life because Jesus' righteousness is counted as if it is my own."

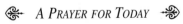

❧ *A Prayer for Today* ☙

*Lord of love, let me always honor the life of Jesus within me
and live to glorify His name.*

RAISED FROM THE DEAD

And if the Spirit of him who raised Jesus from the dead is living in you, he who raised Christ from the dead will also give life to your mortal bodies through his Spirit, who lives in you. Rom. 8:11, NIV.

Occasionally men, and sometimes even women, engage in a sport known as arm wrestling. Usually two people face each other head to head, place their right elbows together, and grip hands. Then, with a lot of straining of muscles, they see who can force the other's hand to the table.

While it would trivialize the terrible conflict between the Holy Spirit and the forces of evil to compare it with arm wrestling, nevertheless it is true that the Holy Spirit can flatten the "arm" of sin in every confrontation with evil. Sin's greatest claim to victory is the universality of death. This fruitage of sin reigns supreme across all humanity, but the Holy Spirit dealt death a fatal blow when He raised Jesus from the dead (Eph. 1:19, 20; 1 Peter 3:18).

None of humanity's most noble achievements have been able to conquer the grave. No one has received a Nobel Prize for raising the dead. But Jesus showed His total superiority over sin and its bold claims. On top of all that Jesus demonstrated at His resurrection is the fact that now the body that is "dead because of sin," the mortal body of a born-again Christian, has been wrestled out of Satan's hand. It has life by the Holy Spirit—spiritual life now and physical life on the resurrection morning when this mortal shall put on immortality (1 Cor. 15:53).

Years ago a group of senior theology students who were with me for a field school of evangelism I was teaching challenged me to an arm-wrestling contest. Perhaps they felt that they could relieve some of their classroom frustrations in this way! My years as a builder had given me a fairly strong arm, so I readily agreed. With some students I won, while with others I lost. However, my arm soon became tired, and I was forced to give up. But please remember and rejoice that the Holy Spirit never tires and will always have life enough for you.

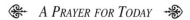

A PRAYER FOR TODAY

Father, I celebrate the destiny of life that Jesus has made possible for me.

FROM TERRORIST TO EVANGELIST

For if you live according to the sinful nature, you will die; but if by the Spirit you put to death the misdeeds of the body, you will live.
Rom. 8:13, NIV.

Shortly before the downfall of Communism, when the Soviet-controlled nations of Eastern Europe brought together more than 3,500 government officials, social workers, and medical personnel for a drug abuse conference in Budapest, they invited Nicky Cruz to be their main speaker. Nicky had been a leader in the dreaded Mau Mau gang in New York City and had terrorized whole neighborhoods, but through the power of the Holy Spirit, this Puerto Rican youth had become a mighty witness to God's saving grace.

It seemed that Nicky was destined to an early death, just as he had beaten and killed others on the streets. After one of his many arrests he was told by a court psychiatrist that unless he changed, he was on a "one-way street to jail, the electric chair, and hell." Nicky, who was 18 at the time, only laughed (*One Who Believed,* p. 72).

In his autobiography, *Run Baby, Run,* Nicky Cruz tells of his feelings before the Holy Spirit came into his life. "The rumbles in the streets were exceeded only by the nightmare of the violence that seethed in my own heart. I was an animal without conscience, morals, reason, or any sense of right or wrong" (p. 92).

Spirit-filled preacher David Wilkerson was absolutely amazed when Nicky gave his life to Jesus. "The conversion hardest for me to believe was Nicky's," David writes in *The Cross and the Switchblade.* "There he stood, a great grin on his face, saying in his strained, stammering way, 'I am giving my heart to God, Davie'" (p. 82).

Nicky Cruz allowed the Holy Spirit to "put to death the misdeeds of the body" and to bring him a new life of victory in Jesus. At the Communist conference in Budapest 30 years after his conversion Nicky not only told of the great power of the Holy Spirit but gave the invitation for others to accept Jesus that day. Now it was his turn to be surprised as more than a thousand people responded favorably.

❦ *A PRAYER FOR TODAY* ❧

Father, help me never to consider even the worst sinner as a hopeless case for Your Spirit.

LED BY THE SPIRIT INTO FORT GREENE

For all who are led by the Spirit of God are sons of God.
Rom. 8:14, TLB.

*A*fter David Wilkerson sold his television set, he began to spend time in prayer instead of watching the programs that had fascinated him until midnight many evenings. Immediately the Holy Spirit began to lead him in many remarkable ways. He was especially drawn to a copy of *Life* magazine that showed the faces of seven young New York gang members who had stabbed to death a 15-year-old polio victim. He could not forget those faces and knew that the Spirit was leading him to New York City, 350 miles away.

After months of taking the eight-hour drive to New York at least once a week and meeting many young gang members in the most dangerous situations, David Wilkerson began to realize that he could reach them in no ordinary human way. "If these boys were going to change dramatically, the transformation would have to come about in their hearts," David writes in *The Cross and the Switchblade* (p. 56). "I knew I could never bring this about: it would have to be the work of the Holy Spirit. But perhaps I could act as a channel through which the Holy Spirit would reach these boys" *(ibid.)*.

Some people are led by materialism, hedonism, or egotism, but only those who are led by the Spirit really know who they are and where they are going. David Wilkerson knew who he was in Jesus Christ, but the Holy Spirit gave him a vision of young people coming to this same assurance in one of the world's largest housing developments, Fort Greene. This was the home of two of the most vicious gangs in New York, the Black Chaplains and the Hispanic Mau Maus, who had declared war not only on other groups but also on the police.

After the miraculous conversion of many of these violent gang members, the Holy Spirit led them to the police headquarters, where they requested the amazed police officers to autograph their Bibles. The Spirit led these former drug addicts and terrorists, victims of poverty and abuse, to have complete assurance that they were God's children.

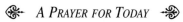

A PRAYER FOR TODAY

Lead me, Lord, in the absolute assurance that I'm Your child.

WELCOME TO THE FAMILY

For you did not receive the spirit of bondage again to fear, but you
received the Spirit of adoption by whom we cry out, "Abba, Father."
Rom. 8:15, NKJV.

A family is a unit of people who are bound together not only by blood relationship but also by love and respect. In fact, while people who are closely related and even married or born into a family may have no true family ties, others may be "family" who are bonded together only in spirit and by their common love for the Father in heaven. It is a delightful ministry of the Holy Spirit to unite all who accept Jesus as their Saviour into the family of God and into fellowship with each other.

When David Wilkerson first met gang leader Nicky Cruz on the streets of New York, Nicky said, "Go to hell, preacher. . . . You come near me, preacher, and I'll kill you" *(Run Baby, Run,* p. 122). Nicky was one of 18 children born to a family in Puerto Rico. At 15 he had moved to New York and was soon living on the streets, where he proved his toughness with an endless cycle of drugs and brutal violence. His only family was the dreaded Mau Mau gang until the Holy Spirit introduced him to Jesus Christ.

Discussing the meeting where he was converted, Nicky says, "He [Wilkerson] started talking and it was all about the Holy Spirit. The preacher said the Holy Spirit could get inside people and make them clean. He said it didn't matter what they'd done, the Holy Spirit could make them start new, like babies" *(The Cross and the Switchblade,* p. 93). Although he found it hard to believe that he could be loved by God and born into a new family, Nicky went forward and accepted Jesus. The Spirit of adoption worked another miracle of saving grace and now, in joy, Nicky could pray to his new Father in heaven.

Since his conversion Nicky Cruz has never stopped leading young people into God's family. After three years of Bible training in California, he returned to his former New York ghetto to direct the Teen Challenge ministry. Six years later he was back in California to start Outreach for Youth Ministries, and since then he has spoken to more than 21 million people around the world, introducing them through the Spirit to "Abba, Father."

❧ *A PRAYER FOR TODAY* ❧
Father, may I know You with the respectful and
comfortable familiarity of a true "Daddy."

WELCOME, INNER WITNESS

For his Holy Spirit speaks to us deep in our hearts, and tells us that we really are God's children. Rom. 8:16, TLB.

When John Wesley landed in Georgia after a very rough crossing of the Atlantic, he was directed to Moravian bishop Spangenberg for spiritual counsel. One of the first questions Spangenberg asked him was "Have you the witness within yourself? Does the Spirit of God bear witness with your spirit that you are a child of God?" *(The John Wesley Treasury,* p. 65).

Wesley, who later became the founder of the Methodist Church, did not know what to answer. Would you? For many years, even as a church pastor, I would also have been puzzled about the question.

The Bible makes it clear that the witness of the Spirit is an assurance of salvation that the Holy Spirit communicates to the spiritual consciousness or understanding of every person whom He fills (1 John 5:6, 10-13). No person, though, is saved on the basis of having a feeling that he or she is a child of God. Salvation comes by faith in Jesus Christ, and a fruitage of that salvation is the indwelling presence of the Holy Spirit. The Holy Spirit creates within the people He fills a "spiritual perceptivity which is an intuitive ability to recognize God." They know that there is no doubt that they are part of His family through the life and death of Jesus.

A *Signs of the Times* article in 1893 stated: " 'Now the Spirit itself beareth witness with our spirit, that we are the children of God,' is the language of Paul in Romans 8:16. . . . God would not have His people depend on a guess or a wish or a faint hope that they might be His children; He desires them to have sure evidence, evidence absolutely unimpeachable. The Christian need not grope in blindness or doubt. God will give him such plain evidence that it will not be presumptuous to make the claim or to rest upon the assurance that he is a child of God" (Feb. 6, 1893).

What a powerful statement of certainty! Don't be ashamed today to say, "I am God's child."

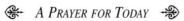

✎ *A PRAYER FOR TODAY* ✎

I praise You, Lord, that I can sing "Blessed assurance, Jesus is mine!" with the confidence of the inner witness of the Spirit.

A CHRISTIAN'S SWEET HOPE

And not only they, but we also who have the firstfruits of the Spirit,
even we ourselves groan within ourselves, eagerly waiting
for the adoption, the redemption of our body. Rom. 8:23, NKJV.

*A*s I drove through the heavy traffic on a Los Angeles freeway I listened to a tape of Pastor Jack Sequeira explaining the gospel in Romans. "When you talk about heaven," Jack explained, "you can tell the difference between a carnal Christian and one who understands the gospel and is filled with the Holy Spirit. The carnal Christian thinks about heaven in terms of mansions and streets of gold, while the Spirit-filled Christian looks forward to getting rid of a body that keeps causing him or her to let Jesus down."

For the apostle Paul the joy of heaven, apart from being with Jesus, was that he would have a new body—a new nature—that would never hinder him from always doing God's prefect will.

When Pastor Sequeira and his family first moved to Ethiopia, their house at the college had an orange tree growing in the back yard. When the first orange ripened, however, the family was disappointed to discover that the fruit was too sour to eat. Jack's young daughter had a brilliant idea to solve the problem—feed the tree with sugar. So in preparation for the next season, the family fertilized around the tree with sugar, making sure that it was well watered into the ground. But when the new fruit came, it was just as sour as the old. The sugar had not changed the nature of the tree. Only a new tree could bear sweet fruit.

Within the born-again Christian the Holy Spirit produces the sweet fruit of love, joy, peace, longsuffering, kindness, goodness, faithfulness, gentleness, and self-control. What a delight this fruit is, but it seems that the selfish and sinful tendencies of the flesh are always striving for the supremacy. All the culture, education, or political programs in the world cannot make sweet the sourness of rebellious human nature. So, like Paul, we eagerly wait for the wonderful resurrection day when we will have new bodies to enjoy for eternity.

❧ A PRAYER FOR TODAY ❧

Thank You, Lord, for the sweet firstfruits in my life and the joyful hope
of a new nature that will always delight in You.

WELCOME, STRONG SPIRIT OF PRAYER

And in the same way the Spirit also helps our weakness; for we do not know how to pray as we should, but the Spirit Himself intercedes for us with groanings too deep for words. Rom. 8:26, NASB.

*H*ave you ever needed help to lift a heavy object? Paul tells us that this is the ministry of the Holy Spirit, especially as He works through the prayers of God's people. The Holy Spirit never makes the excuse, as do some of our friends, of having a bad back and so not being able to help lift the load.

Adam Clarke, the Methodist preacher, scholar, and commentator, writing almost 200 years ago, explained the word that Paul uses for "helps" in this verse. "[This word] signifies such assistance as is afforded by any two persons to each other, who mutually bear the same load or carry it between them. He who prays, receives help from the Spirit of God; but he who prays not receives no such help. Whatever our strength may be, we must put it forth, even while most implicitly depending on the strength of God Himself" *(Clarke's Commentary,* Vol. VI, p. 100).

Years ago we owned a heavy piano, which always caused some concern as we moved from house to house in our evangelistic ministry in Australia. Usually the piano was a struggle for four or five men to lift, so we were surprised on one occasion when only two men arrived to carry the piano to the waiting truck. One man was very large and muscular, while the other was very small, so we wondered what would happen. To our amazement, the large man placed a huge leather strap around his shoulders and back and around the piano and then, with a lot of bellowing and grunting, lifted the piano and began to move it endwise out of the house. The strong man could lift the piano but could not see where he was going, so the small man guided and moved the front end of the piano in the right direction until, without one scratch, the piano was safely on the truck.

In the same way, Paul tells us that the Holy Spirit helps us in every situation of our lives. But He cannot help our prayers if we do not pray. Paul uses a word that signifies a team effort, no matter how small our part may be.

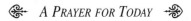

☙ *A PRAYER FOR TODAY* ❧

I praise You, Holy Spirit, for being willing to team up with me in prayer so that I can benefit from Your great strength.

August 26

TOO HURT TO PRAY IN WORDS

And he who searches our hearts knows the mind of the Spirit, because the Spirit intercedes for the saints in accordance with God's will.
Rom. 8:27, NIV.

*H*ave you ever happened on someone who needed help? Perhaps her car had broken down or he had fallen on a mountain trail and fractured a leg. Maybe it was a homeless man or woman who had been beaten and robbed. The person was too worried or in too much pain to know what to say or do, but you were able to give the desperately needed assistance.

When Paul, in Romans 8:26, 27, discusses the Holy Spirit's ministry, he twice uses a word that is translated "intercede" in some versions. As A. T. Robertson wrote: "It is a picturesque word of rescue by one who 'happens on' . . . one who is in trouble and 'in his behalf' . . . pleads 'with unuttered groanings' . . . or with 'sighs that baffle words'" *(Word Pictures in the New Testament,* Vol. IV, p. 377).

The Spirit does not intercede for God's children before the Father as Jesus is pictured as doing in Hebrews. Rather, the Holy Spirit creates within the heart of each person He fills a deep desire to deal with the situations of life according to God's will.

Often in the crises of life the Holy Spirit discovers that we cannot even speak in prayer. Like the man in Jesus' story, who was robbed on his way down to Jericho, we lie bruised and bleeding on the side of life's road. Our groans and sighs indicate our desperate need, and as the "good Samaritan" Holy Spirit comes by He binds up our wounds and negotiates for our care at the inn of Jesus' unfailing love.

Take time to talk to your friend the Holy Spirit, and ask Him to help you pray. You can do it at any time. Just say, "Dear Helper, I am not sure what is best for me in these circumstances. I do not even know what to pray. There are hurts and hopes in my life that I don't really understand. So I ask You to create within me an earnest desire to be totally submissive to Your will and to be fully willing to follow Your leading. I praise You and thank You in the name of Jesus.

❧ *A PRAYER FOR TODAY* ❧

Father, please lead me to a small group of friends where I can give and receive true help and unconditional love.

Conscience Confirmed by the Spirit

I am speaking the truth in Christ—I am not lying; my conscience confirms it by the Holy Spirit. Rom. 9:1, NRSV.

I will swear on a stack of Bibles that what I say is true." If you have heard a person speak in this way, you will know that he or she is rather definite about giving the impression of not lying. "My conscience is crystal clear," someone else will say. Is the conscience "the guardian in the individual of the rules which the community has evolved for its own preservation" as Somerset Maugham once wrote, or is it the voice of God?

Paul was so stirred about the subject he would discuss next with the Romans that he began chapter 9 with a triple oath that answers some questions concerning the Holy Spirit and the human conscience. First Paul gives his oath that he is telling "the truth in Christ." Next is Paul's negative oath: "I am not lying." Third is the cowitness oath: "The witness of my conscience and the witness of the Holy Spirit in me agree."

In Romans 2:15 Paul says that the heathen have a cowitness, or side-by-side witness, between the law and their conscience. In Romans 9:1 Paul, like all born-again, Spirit-filled Christians, has the cowitness between the Holy Spirit and his conscience. Normal people know what they have done or thought, and their conscience, educated by cultural environment, family upbringing, and religious standards, approves or disapproves of their actions. The final questions, then, for the Spirit-filled Christian are What does the Holy Spirit tell me about this action? How does this measure up to principles the Spirit has inspired in God's Word? This we can call the "Law of the Cowitness."

In 1885 James Russell Lowell wrote:

> "In vain we call old notions fudge,
> And bend our conscience to our dealing;
> The Ten Commandments will not budge
> And stealing *will* continue stealing."

Beyond the good and bad feelings of conscience is the witness of the Holy Spirit. A conscience may be bent and God's law broken, but the Holy Spirit always remains straight and true.

 *A Prayer for Today*

Lord, because of the union between my life and the Holy Spirit, may I have a conscience without offense to God and other people.

WHEN THE SPIRITUAL TEMPERATURE IS HIGH

Never flag in zeal, be aglow with the Spirit, serve the Lord.
Rom. 12:11, RSV.

Your face is glowing," I said to a friend recently.

A glowing face usually means that the eyes are sparkling, the lips are smiling, and there is a general look of satisfaction and joy on the countenance. My friend's glow came from within as love found expression in actions and words. So it is when a life is filled with the Holy Spirit. Like a radiant golden crown, the glow of the Spirit attracts the attention of all who see its beauty.

Journalist and lay preacher Sherwood E. Wirt spent 15 years writing for Billy Graham's *Decision* magazine. In his book *Afterglow* Wirt tells of the radiance of love that came into his life after being filled with the Holy Spirit on January 9, 1972. Two Canadians who had been part of a revival in Winnipeg had come to Sherwood Wirt's church in Minneapolis and after the service had invited people to join them for an afterglow meeting in the basement. Twenty-five men and women gathered to pray and minister to one another.

In the meeting Sherwood opened up and expressed the feeling that something was really missing in his life—and it seemed to be the most important piece. Soon people gathered around him to pray, and as they laid their hands on him, he asked the Lord to fill him with the Holy Spirit. There wasn't a big outburst of excitement, but rather the quiet working of the Spirit. Later Sherwood wrote that one of the Canadians, Evelyn, smiled in his direction when the prayer time was finished. " 'You probably don't have much of a sensation of blessing now,' she said. 'Don't worry. The feeling will come later—and how!' She was right. It came. And it has never left" (p. 15).

There is no doubt that the glow of the Spirit is the glow of love. As Wirt says: "The flame of the Spirit is the flame of love. The unction of the Spirit is the unction of love. The baptism of the Spirit is the baptism of love. The filling of the Spirit is the filling of love" (*ibid.,* p. 93).

❦ *A PRAYER FOR TODAY* ❧

Shine out of my life, Holy Spirit, so that others may recognize
the true simplicity and beauty of Jesus' love.

August 29

Characterizing
the Kingdom of God

For the kingdom of God is not food and drink, but righteousness and peace and joy in the Holy Spirit. Rom. 14:17, NKJV.

*H*ave you ever struggled with a concept of God's kingdom that is based on externals? A religion, church, or individual formulates a kingdom criteria list and then makes that the basis judging whether or not a person is part of God's family. The result can be devastating. Paul was concerned that Christians "edify one another" (Rom. 14:19). Instead, by judgmentalism they were hurting each other (verse 4).

As Joe Aldrich says in *Life-Style Evangelism:* "The legalist carefully builds his own pattern of living and then tries to make it normative for the entire Christian community" (p. 45).

Paul illustrates this problem with food and drink. Whether it be religious food laws or principles of healthful living that are misused, the results are the same—people are offended as the criteria for belonging to the kingdom center on externals.

Good food and drink are important for maximum physical and mental well-being and can affect spiritual sensibilities, but ultimately the kingdom of God is not a matter of what a person eats or drinks but is "righteousness and peace and joy in the Holy Spirit."

The Spirit continually witnesses to those He fills that they are saved because Jesus' righteousness is counted as theirs. Although this righteousness is translated into right living by the power of the Holy Spirit, the saved know that right works are not the basis of their salvation but the fruitage of it. As a result of this assurance, the Holy Spirit makes certain that the saved have peace with God through the Lord Jesus Christ. And assurance and peace naturally translate into an inner core of unshakable joy.

If you have accepted Jesus as your Saviour, welcome the joy of the Holy Spirit into your life again today. Don't be discouraged by the standards of others, but allow the Spirit to lead you into all truth. As He reveals what is best for you at this time, resist the temptation to impose this on others. Let the Holy Spirit lead them also in the path of righteousness, peace, and joy.

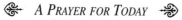 *A Prayer for Today*

Joyfully, Lord, I walk in the way that You have chosen for my life.

WELCOME, HOLY SPIRIT OF HOPE

May the God of hope fill you with all joy and peace as you trust in him,
so that you may overflow with hope by the power of the Holy Spirit.
Rom. 15:13, NIV.

*F*amous English poet Alexander Pope in his most celebrated work, "An Essay on Man," wrote in 1733: "Hope springs eternal in the human breast." But at the end of the eighties in America, an average of more than 500,000 teenagers attempt suicide each year. Hope had finally failed to spring alive in their hearts.

The Spirit pours so much hope into the lives of those who trust in God's saving grace that they overflow with joy and peace. Just a few hours before well-known Portland doctor Louis Machlin died, his wife, Becky, said to him, "I will see you in the morning."

Louis' affirmation of hope was strong and certain. In fact, his hope had grown through his last years as he had come really to understand the gospel and baptism of the Holy Spirit. And hope had overflowed from his life to all he met.

Why, in a society so amply supplied with churches, would a half million teenagers attempt suicide each year? Often churches have majored in programs rather than personal nurture. They have exalted rules and standards rather than love, acceptance, and forgiveness. President Lyndon Johnson said in his first State of the Union message: "Unfortunately many Americans live on the outskirts of hope—some because of poverty, some because of their color, and all too many because of both." But these people make up a very small percentage of those who attempt to take their own lives. More often the "haves" rather than the "have nots" lose hope in a materialistic society.

As Dr. Roy W. Fairchild, professor of spiritual life and psychology at San Francisco Theological Seminary, says: "Hope is not merely a longing for what we are presently missing, but rather a desire to experience more fully what we have already received" *(Finding Hope Again*, p. 52).

What we have received through Jesus' life and death can be experienced fully in true hope and joy by the power of the Holy Spirit. Praise the Lord!

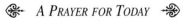

☙ *A PRAYER FOR TODAY* ❧

God of Hope, I rejoice in the consciousness that with You
life is always worth living.

THE JOYFUL SEQUENCE OF SALVATION

To be a minister of Christ Jesus to the Gentiles with the priestly duty
of proclaiming the gospel of God, so that the Gentiles might become an
offering acceptable to God, sanctified by the Holy Spirit.
Rom. 15:16, NIV.

*A*s a young evangelist I reversed the sequence of salvation as we find it in Romans 15. First I would teach people truth and line up before them what I considered to be all the requirements that God expected of those He would save. I would then wait to see if they were willing to be obedient, and if they began to keep the Sabbath, pay tithe, practice health reform, etc., I would indicate that they had hope of salvation.

Finally, I said, if they performed all these requirements well enough, it demonstrated some progress in sanctification. Therefore, they could rejoice a little—but not much—because they were unsure whether they would make it through the time of trouble!

Praise God for the joy of discovering the wonderful approach Paul used as he ministered to the Gentiles in the power of the Spirit. First, the moment the Gentiles heard of Jesus and accepted Him as their Saviour they could rejoice and praise the Lord (Rom. 15:7-11). As Jesus became the Lord of their lives they had full hope in Him by the Spirit's power (verses 12, 13). Now, because of the gospel, the Gentiles were counted as sanctified before God, even although they obviously still had much to learn and many victories to gain (verse 16). Finally, because they were saved by Jesus and rejoiced in Him, they now became obedient to the truths that the Holy Spirit progressively revealed. They did this happily, not to be saved but because they knew they were saved (verse 18).

Which sequence are you following in your own life and witness to others? If you haven't already made the transition, I know that you are in for a wonderful surprise as you move from the legalistic sequence to the gospel sequence of joy and hope in Jesus. This is the ministry of the Holy Spirit. Sing praises to God as you remember that the Spirit presents you always as a holy person to God.

☙ *A PRAYER FOR TODAY* ❧

Lord, I rejoice again today in the absolute assurance of salvation
I have as a "Gentile" in Jesus.

September 1

MIGHTY SIGNS AND WONDERS

In mighty signs and wonders, by the power of the Spirit of God, so that from Jerusalem and round about to Illyricum I have fully preached the gospel of Christ. Rom. 15:19, NKJV.

*A*t least 10 kinds of signs and wonders were connected to the preaching of the gospel in the book of Acts. Not only were the unsaved stirred by witnessing the gift of tongues, but also they saw healings, visions, raising the dead, and other miracles. Fourteen times in Acts signs and wonders are mentioned in combination with the preaching of the gospel, and the effect on church growth was explosive.

By the middle of the nineteenth century most churches had drawn up creeds that excluded signs and wonders. When miraculous gifts such as healings and prophecy began to occur in the early Adventist Church, the mainline denominations ridiculed these as dangerous and deceptive. In answer, young Adventist preacher James White wrote a strong reply that in 1864 was included as the preface to *Spiritual Gifts,* volumes 3 and 4. "The gifts have been superseded in the popular churches by human creeds. . . . We, too, would exalt the Bible, and would say to those who would represent us as taking the gifts instead of the Bible, that we are not satisfied with a part of the Sacred volume, but claim as ours the Bible, the whole Bible, gifts and all. . . . It is evident that if the gifts were received, they would destroy human creeds, and if creeds be received, they shut out the gifts" (pp. 29, 30).

Some evangelical Christians, basing their belief on the notes in the Scofield Bible, say that signs and wonders terminated at the end of the first century. James's wife, Ellen, certainly corrected this misconception when the Holy Spirit led her to write about our present time: "In visions of the night, representations passed before me of a great reformatory movement among God's people. Many were praising God. The sick were healed, and other miracles were wrought" *(Testimonies,* vol. 9, p. 126). But then, warning of the danger of deception, she wrote: "God's people are not the only ones who will have miracle-working power in the last days" *(Manuscript Releases,* vol. 19, p. 54).

Don't let the dangers stop you from expecting a miracle today.

❦ A PRAYER FOR TODAY ❦

Lord, I'm open to Your signs and wonders, especially as they relate to changed lives and spiritual victories.

THE PRAYERS OF THOSE WE LOVE

I urge you, brothers, by our Lord Jesus Christ and by the love that the
Spirit gives: join me in praying fervently to God for me.
Rom. 15:30, TEV.

Some time shortly before A.D. 60 Paul verbalized his earnest desire that the people in Rome, who were filled with love by the Holy Spirit, agonize on his behalf in prayer. At the beginning of the twentieth century James D. Vaughan felt the same urgent need as expressed in his beautiful hymn:

> "I want my friends to pray for me,
> To bear my tempted soul above,
> And intercede with God for me;
> I need the prayers of those I love."

As the twenty-first century begins, our need for intercessory prayer warriors is imperative. We need to know that people are genuinely praying for us and with us. In cultural Christianity a polite expression of concern is "I'll be praying for you" or "I'll remember you in my prayers." But how often does it happen? Only in Spirit-filled Christianity, where the love of God is poured into a person's life (Rom. 5:5), are these prayer promises a reality.

On June 12, 1993, more than a million Christians in 40 nations marched through the streets of more than 850 cities, towns, and villages. Their emphasis was on intercessory prayer not only for the unsaved millions in the vast cities of earth but also for spiritual missionary workers and national leaders. They had concentrated prayer that the powers of evil lose their control over individuals and geographical areas and that in a supernatural way Jesus' saving power and truth would be revealed.

If the Lord leads you into an intercessory prayer ministry, begin today to pray for leaders, nations, cities, and individuals whom the Holy Spirit brings to your attention. Ask the Lord to introduce you to others with this same conviction, and join together with them regularly for prayer. As your group increases in size, make certain that every intercessor has a prayer partner for his or her own personal strength. Yes, like even the great apostle Paul, we all need the prayers of those we love.

A PRAYER FOR TODAY

Father, I praise You for the people whose prayers
have made a difference in my life.

POWER EVANGELISM

My message and my preaching were not with wise and persuasive
words, but with a demonstration of the Spirit's power. 1 Cor. 2:4, NIV.

*J*ohn Wimber was a jazz musician when he was converted in 1962.
Eventually he joined a Friends church in California, where he
served the Lord as a member and pastor for more than 13 years.
After moving for a short time into seminary teaching, he began in 1977 a
home prayer meeting that grew into the Vineyard Fellowship. In 10 years it
mushroomed to more than 140 congregations with more than 40,000 members. The Vineyard emphasizes the gifts of the Spirit.

Although evangelicals may not agree with all Wimber's methods or theology, his definition of power evangelism sounds very similar to that of the
apostle Paul. "Power evangelism is a spontaneous, Spirit-inspired, empowered presentation of the gospel. Power evangelism is evangelism that is preceded and undergirded by supernatural demonstrations of God's presence"
(Power Evangelism, p. 35).

Paul not only preached the great message of salvation through Jesus' life
and death but also exhibited God's omnipotence by the signs and wonders
that the Holy Spirit chose to work through him. Paul deeply desired that converts base their faith not in his remarkable reasoning and debating ability but
in God's miracle-working power.

The Western mind, with its emphasis on rationalism and the scientific
method, has been confronted mainly by programmatic evangelism, which majors in logical message-centered communication, with organization and technique taking high priority. The results have been predictably disappointing. On
the other hand, non-Western societies, and especially developing countries,
have seen tremendous church growth as Paul's pattern of power evangelism
has been followed. Spiritual gifts have been used to God's glory.

One way you can follow Paul's outreach method is by seeking opportunities to pray for the healing of sick people in your community. You need not
give the impression that you are a healer but that you have an all-powerful
God. At the same time, you can teach the simple principles of healthful living, which will also demonstrate the great power of the Creator God.

❦ A PRAYER FOR TODAY ❧

Lord, help me not be satisfied with a merely theoretical faith,
but enable me to practice the practical Christianity of Jesus.

September 4

THE SPIRIT'S REVELATION TO A LAWYER

But God has revealed it to us by his Spirit. The Spirit searches all things, even the deep things of God. 1 Cor. 2:10, NIV.

Back in 1821 Charles Finney was a very successful New York lawyer who had little interest in the things of God. God, however, had deep things to reveal to Finney through the Holy Spirit. These great truths would not only change his life but also set a pattern for revival and evangelism that would still be influencing Christianity at the end of the twentieth century.

Finney had no religious upbringing and found sermons "dull, uninteresting, and listless" whenever he attended church. Although he had a number of discussions with a well-educated preacher, he felt that many questions were left unanswered and terms undefined. "What did he mean by repentance?" Finney wrote. "Was it a mere feeling of sorrow for sin? Was it altogether a passive state of mind, or did it involve a voluntary element? . . . What did he mean by faith? . . . Was it merely a conviction, or persuasion, that the things stated in the gospel were true?" *(Memoirs of Rev. Charles G. Finney,* p. 8).

The 29-year-old lawyer was in the place Paul describes where his eye could not see nor his ear hear the things that God has prepared for those who love Him. Perhaps you know someone in the same position as Charles Finney. If so, never give up hoping and praying for this individual's conversion, because at the most surprising moment the Holy Spirit can reveal deep things to a mind that suddenly becomes open to God.

Paul's words in 1 Corinthians 2:9, 10 relate primarily not to heaven but to the gospel. When Finney began to see and hear, through the working of the Holy Spirit in his life, the change was dramatic. "Just at this point the whole question of gospel salvation opened to my mind in a manner most marvelous to me at the time. I think I then saw, as clearly as I ever have in my life, the reality and fullness of the atonement of Christ. I saw that His work was a finished work; and that instead of having, or needing, any righteousness of my own to recommend me to God, I had to submit myself to the righteousness of God through Christ" *(ibid.,* p. 14).

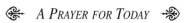

A PRAYER FOR TODAY

Father, reveal Your deep things to me again today all to the glory of Your gospel in Jesus Christ.

September 5

THE SPIRIT BAPTIZES A LAWYER

For what man knows the things of a man except the spirit of the man which is in him? Even so no one knows the things of God except the Spirit of God. 1 Cor. 2:11, NKJV.

hat are you thinking?" I asked a friend.

Have you ever wondered what was going on in someone else's mind? Only the person himself or herself can know all the words, pictures, and feelings that are filling his or her thoughts. In the same way, only the Holy Spirit knows what is in God's mind.

"What does God want me to do? Where does God want me to go? What does God think of me when I am ashamed of being seen on my knees before Him?"

The Holy Spirit, who knows exactly what God thinks, brought young attorney Charles Finney the answers to his urgent questions. In response to Finney's confessions, tears, and fervent prayers, he received what he calls "a mighty baptism of the Holy Ghost" *(Memoirs of Rev. Charles G. Finney,* p. 20).

"Without any expectation of it, without ever having the thought in my mind that there was any such thing for me, without any recollection that I had ever heard the thing mentioned by any person in the world, the Holy Spirit descended upon me in a manner that seemed to go through me, body and soul. I could feel the impression, like a wave of electricity, going through and through me. Indeed it seemed to come in waves and waves of liquid love; for I could not express it in any other way. It seemed like the very breath of God" *(ibid.).*

In that moment of overwhelming power, the Holy Spirit communicated to Finney what was in God's mind for him. He immediately recognized the "doctrine of justification by faith, as a present experience" *(ibid.,* p. 23). His sense of condemnation was gone. He knew that God was calling him to preach. He learned that "obedience to the revealed will of God must be immediate, implicit, and irrevocable" (V. Raymond Edman, *Finney Lives On,* p. 46).

What God has in mind for you may differ in some ways from what He had in mind for Finney, but as you are filled with the Holy Spirit, you will surely know.

❧ A PRAYER FOR TODAY ❧

Give me Your grace, dear Lord, to remember that Your thoughts for me are always good and best and that I can do Your will in Your power.

LISTING GOD'S GIFTS

Now we have received, not the spirit of the world,
but the Spirit who is from God, that we might know the things
that have been freely given to us by God. 1 Cor. 2:12, NKJV.

*A*s happened to New York lawyer Charles Finney, at conversion and our subsequent filling with the Holy Spirit we come to recognize the things that God has freely given us. Finney knew that he had received the gift of eternal life (Rom. 6:23) and also the gift of the Holy Spirit (Acts 2:38). He rejoiced that righteousness is a gift (Rom. 5:17), as was his calling and ability to minister (Eph. 3:7).

Perhaps, from the Scriptures, you can add to the list of "things that have been freely given to us by God."

Primarily, however, Paul is discussing our source of spiritual wisdom. It does not come from a school, college, or university as is often the case with intellectual knowledge, but it depends on the illumination provided by the Holy Spirit. Scripture itself is a gift that was "freely given" by inspiration of God (2 Tim. 3:16), and it is the Spirit of truth (John 14:17) who enlightens the human mind to discern the "deep things of God."

As Charles Finney was opening his heart to God in earnestness and sincerity, the Spirit began to illuminate his mind. "Just at that point this passage of Scripture seemed to drop into my mind with a flood of light," Finney testifies. " 'Then shall ye go and pray unto me, and I will hearken unto you. Then ye shall seek me and find me, when ye shall search for me with all your heart.' I instantly seized hold of this with my heart.

"I had intellectually believed the Bible before; but never had the truth been in my mind. . . . I knew that it was God's word, and God's voice, as it were, that spoke to me" *(Memoirs of Rev. Charles G. Finney,* p. 16).

Later Finney again wrote: "The whole Scripture seemed to be all ablaze with light, and not only light, but it seemed as if God's Word was [alive] with the very life of God" (cited in V. Raymond Edman, *Finney Lives On,* p. 58).

Don't rely on secondhand sources for your understanding of the "deep things of God," but pray through the Scriptures, asking the Spirit to illuminate your mind with true spiritual wisdom.

❦ *A PRAYER FOR TODAY* ❧

Lord, I claim again all the great gifts You've freely given.
Help me to see Jesus and His truth clearly in His Word.

SHARING SPIRITUAL TRUTH

And we impart this in words not taught by human wisdom but taught
by the Spirit, interpreting spiritual truths to those who possess
the Spirit. 1 Cor. 2:13, RSV.

Following his conversion in 1821, Charles Finney went to his law office and met his partner, Judge Wright. Immediately the Holy Spirit led Finney to impart words that were beyond human wisdom. As the judge heard the truth of God's gift of salvation through Jesus and the baptism of the Spirit, he came under deep conviction and left the office to spend time in prayer. When he returned a few days later, Judge Wright fell on his knees in thanksgiving to God and told how "the Spirit of God came upon him and filled him with . . . unspeakable joy" *(Memoirs of Rev. Charles G. Finney,* p. 33).

Soon after the judge's dramatic experience Finney was able to speak in his local Presbyterian church. The building was packed to capacity, and as Finney spoke, a fellow lawyer loudly expressed his belief that Finney was deranged. But the vast majority of the crowd was deeply moved by Finney's unaffected and Spirit-filled testimony. A few days later when he preached at Evans Mills, Finney testified that "the Spirit of God came upon me with such power, that it was like opening a battery upon them. For more than an hour, and perhaps for an hour and a half, the Word of God came through me to them in a manner that I could see was carrying all before it" (cited by V. Raymond Edman, *Finney Lives On,* pp. 41-43).

The Holy Spirit used Charles Finney in a mighty way to bring revival to the spiritually dead churches of his day—not only in America but throughout Great Britain. On one occasion, when Finney spoke at a joint service of Baptists and Congregationalists, "the Spirit of God came in such power into that service that for a long time none could arise from his knees, but only weep, confess, and melt down before the Lord" *(ibid.,* p. 43).

Let us pray that once again the Holy Spirit will be able to impart "spiritual truths to those who possess the Spirit" so that we can be part of the last great revival—the latter-rain revival.

❧ A PRAYER FOR TODAY ❧

Father, may I listen as Your Spirit interprets spiritual truth to me
in a way that will bring great revival in my life.

RESISTING REVIVAL

But the natural man does not receive the things of the Spirit of God, for they are foolishness to him; nor can he know them, because they are spiritually discerned. 1 Cor. 2:14, NKJV.

Cultural Christians often resist revival as "foolishness" because human nature alone is incapable of discerning the significance of spiritual things. The word Paul used for "discerning" means a sifting process to get at truth, as a judge would investigate facts. Only those who are filled with the Holy Spirit can know and understand the spiritual facts of revival.

When lawyer Charles Finney was filled with the Holy Spirit and began to be used by the Lord in mighty revival meetings, he expected some opposition from the unsaved, whose economic or social interests were affected by the preaching of the gospel. He was saddened, however, as V. Raymond Edman writes, by the "subtle and dangerous opposition that came from professing Christians. At the very outset of his witnessing for Christ in his own community Finney proposed to the young people that they join in a concert of prayer for revival, and that each should pray at sunrise, at noon, and at sunset. Afterward he organized a daily prayer meeting that met before the breaking of the day, with the result that revival power began to sweep the community.

"Then he began to learn to his sorrow that the older members of the church found fault with him and this new movement among the new converts" *(Finney Lives On,* p. 50).

He also faced opposition to revival in one denomination by members of another, and leading preachers of the day branded the revival as religious excitement.

Dr. Lyman Beecher, the famous Boston preacher who had initially opposed Finney's revival meetings, later testified: "That was the greatest work of God and the greatest revival of religion that the world has ever seen in so short a time. One hundred thousand [in one year] were reported as having connected themselves with churches as a result of that great revival" *(ibid.,* p. 69).

Do not be surprised to the resistance that may arise to revival in your own community and congregation. Pray for the Spirit, and allow Him to prepare your heart so that when the revival comes you will be an active participant in it.

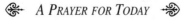

❧ *A PRAYER FOR TODAY* ❧
Lord, as I discern Your truth, begin Your great revival with me.

September 9

BUILDING OR WRECKING THE TEMPLE?

Don't you realize that all of you together are the house of God, and that the Spirit of God lives among you in his house? If anyone defiles and spoils God's home, God will destroy him. For God's home is holy and clean, and you are that home. 1 Cor. 3:16, 17, TLB.

*A*s the Holy Spirit leads individual Christians together to form His body or church, He counts that group of believers as His house or home. The Jewish religious leaders in the first century ridiculed Christians because they did not have a temple or even synagogues. Paul, therefore, reminded the followers of Jesus that God's focus was not on material buildings but on spiritual fellowship and unity among those who love the Lord.

The ministry of the Holy Spirit is to bind Christians together in love and purity, so He does not appreciate any person who would corrupt or wreck the church. As the Greek scholar A. T. Robertson said: "There is warning enough here to make every pastor [or member] pause before he tears a church to pieces in order to vindicate himself" *(Word Pictures in the New Testament,* Vol. IV, p. 99). God warns that church wreckers will be destroyed.

Charles Finney was deeply concerned about those who were wrecking the church in the middle of the nineteenth century. Adventist pioneer Ellen White, who also had the same concern, quoted Finney as saying: "We have also another corroborated fact: the almost universal absence of revival influence in the churches. . . . Suffice it that the evidence thickens and rolls heavily upon us, to show that the churches *generally are becoming sadly degenerate.* They have gone very far from the Lord, and He has withdrawn Himself from them" *(The Great Controversy,* p. 377).

The agency for church purification is not destructive or judgmental attacks on leadership, doctrine, or standards, but the power of the Holy Spirit in the lives of the individuals who unitedly make up the body of Christ. Prayer and revival will do the work of "housecleaning" in "God's building." As the Holy Spirit convicts church members of the things that need correcting in their lives, so the church is convicted, reconverted, revived, and reconstructed on its foundation of Jesus Christ.

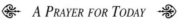

❧ *A PRAYER FOR TODAY* ☙

Thank You, Lord, for calling me to be part of the house where You dwell. May I always be a builder of the body of Jesus.

WELCOME TO THE SAINTS

And that is what some of you were. But you were washed, you were sanctified, you were justified in the name of the Lord Jesus Christ and by the Spirit of our God. 1 Cor. 6:11, NIV.

Years ago I read the story of a small boy who visited a beautiful English cathedral with his father. The young lad was intrigued with the stained-glass windows, and when he asked about the people pictured there, he was told that they were saints. Sometime later, when telling about his visit to the cathedral, the boy was excited that he had seen the saints and explained that "they are the people whom the light shines through."

Although the people Paul wrote to in Corinth were struggling with many personal problems, Paul said they were called to be saints and said that they were sanctified (1 Cor. 1:2). Today, using Reformation theological terminology, we would say that they were believers, or Christians, and that they were in the process of being sanctified.

Arnold Wallenkampf differentiates between theological sanctification and biblical sanctification and says: "Biblical sanctification, therefore, usually denotes the sinner's affirmative response to God's pleading through the Holy Spirit, and his acceptance of Jesus as his Saviour. This is in contradistinction to God's acceptance of the sinner, which is denoted by justification" (*Justified,* p. 97). God counts the persons who turn to Him as holy or invests them with holiness so that they can be called saints.

The Seventh-day Adventist Bible Commentary has an interesting note about biblical sanctification: "The Greek emphasizes the thought that we were sanctified and now stand in a state of sanctification. Sanctification is here viewed, not from the aspect of a continual process . . . but in terms of the original change from sin to holiness, and as a continuation in that state" (vol. 7, p. 460).

As the little boy said, saints are the people the light shines through. You can be one of those people, because by Jesus' blood and the Spirit's power you have been washed, sanctified, and justified. In God's sight you are as clean and transparent as a stained-glass window.

☙ *A Prayer for Today* ❧

In Your strength, Lord, help me be as clean and clear of sin as You count me as being through the blood of Jesus.

HOLY SPIRIT TEMPLE TWO

Do you not know that your body is a temple of the Holy Spirit, who is in you, whom you have received from God? You are not your own.
1 Cor. 6:19, NIV.

Watchman Nee tells the story of a Chinese brother who was traveling by train and found himself in a coach with three non-Christians. In order to pass the time the three men decided to play cards but needed another person to make up a group of four. When they asked the Christian to join them, he replied, "I'm sorry to disappoint you, but I cannot join your game for I have not brought *my* hands with me."

"Whatever do you mean?" they asked in blank astonishment.

"This pair of hands does not belong me," he explained as he told of the transfer of ownership that had taken place in his life when he accepted Jesus as his Saviour. This Chinese brother was able to experience many wonderful victories because he "regarded the members of his body as belonging entirely to the Lord."

Holy Spirit Temple One, Paul explained to the Corinthians, is the corporate body of believers, which he also calls "the church." God warns that anyone who corrupts or defiles the church will be destroyed, because the church is the body that Jesus has purchased with His own blood (1 Cor. 3:16, 17; Acts 20:28). Now, in 1 Corinthians 6:19, 20 Paul introduces the Corinthians to Holy Spirit Temple Two. This temple is the whole person who at conversion becomes the dwelling place of the Holy Spirit.

The Holy Spirit is not in a compartment in the mind or spiritually sensitive segment of an individual, but it inhabits the total being. He is either Lord of all or He is not Lord at all. The Chinese Christian on the train recognized that it was not just his heart but also his hands that belonged to the Lord. He could apply the same principle to any part of his body.

Paul does not threaten us in this verse with the dangers of defiling Temple Two, but rather he tells us of our great potential in the power of the Holy Spirit. Yes, it is possible—even in our bodies—to glorify God.

✥ A PRAYER FOR TODAY ✥

Father, may I glorify You today as Lord of every part of my life and every member of my body.

September 12

PERSONAL OPINION OR INFALLIBLE TRUTH?

But she is happier if she remains as she is, according to my judgment— and I think I also have the Spirit of God. 1 Cor. 7:40, NKJV.

What do you mean, Paul?" There are a number of times in Paul's writings when we would like to ask him that question. Even Peter had the same problem with his fellow apostle and said that Paul wrote "some things hard to understand" (2 Peter 3:16).

Dr. Stanley M. Horton, commenting on 1 Corinthians 7:40, suggests a couple of alternatives. "After giving his judgment on certain questions concerning marriage, Paul says, (literally), 'I think I also have the Spirit of God' (7:40). He has already stated He has the Spirit. Some take it that he does not have an actual saying of Jesus about this matter, but that he indeed has the Spirit of God. Others take it as irony, with Paul saying that he too could say he had the Spirit just as much as (and more than) any of his enemies who oppose his teaching" (*What the Bible Says About the Holy Spirit,* p. 206).

We can be certain from many references in Paul's writings that he is sure that he is filled with the Holy Spirit. But even Spirit-filled people can be fallible in their opinions and can misunderstand some details of revelations that come to them from the Holy Spirit. Paul himself faced this situation when prophetic interpretations were given about his arrest in Jerusalem (Acts 21:4-14). This is why he warns Christians not to despise prophecies but to test all things and hold fast to that which is good (1 Thess. 5:20, 21).

There is no uncertainty, however, with the conviction of sin and the knowledge of truth that the Holy Spirit brings to those who surrender to Him. American Methodist evangelist Sam P. Jones tells of a woman who came forward in one of his meetings. "Dr. Jones," she said, "God is speaking to me about sin in my life, but I don't know exactly which one or what."

Sam Jones replied, "Kneel down and guess at it."

And, as Dr. Jones testified, "The moment she knelt down, she hit it right on the head."

❧ A PRAYER FOR TODAY ❧

Lord, I'll listen carefully to Your Spirit as He convicts me of those things that are essential for my salvation and witness to others.

CURSE JESUS OR CLAIM HIM AS LORD

*No one speaking by the power of the Spirit of God can curse Jesus, and
no one can say, "Jesus is Lord," and really mean it, unless the Holy
Spirit is helping him. 1 Cor. 12:3, TLB.*

*A*s I made my way through the Turkish city of Izmir to the traditional
site of Polycarp's grave, I marveled again of the great faith of this
fearless old Christian martyr. Polycarp was born about A.D. 70 and
knew eyewitnesses of Jesus, possibly including the apostle John. Sometime
before 110 he became a faithful bishop of Smyrna, as Izmir was then known.
When Polycarp was 86 years old, he was arrested after an urban mob of Jews
and heathen blamed him for natural disasters that had come upon that area of
Asia.

In the authentic account of Polycarp's martyrdom, written by the
Christians of Smyrna, we have the famous testimony of this great man of
God. He was commanded to say, "Lord Caesar," but each time he would
reply, "Lord Jesus." Finally the proconsul urged Polycarp, "Swear, and I will
release thee; curse the Christ."

Polycarp replied in the power of the Holy Spirit, "Eighty and six years
have I served him, and he did me no wrong; how can I blaspheme my king,
who saved me?" Like millions of others through the centuries, Polycarp tri-
umphantly died for his faith as a Christian.

The Jewish religious leaders in the first century, including possibly Paul
before his conversion, professed to be inspired by the Spirit of God when they
denounced and cursed Jesus. Paul told the Corinthians that the Jewish claim
was an impossibility. So were the heathen claims that their gods had denounced Jesus. Any supernatural power that professed to be from the Holy
Spirit and resulted in the belittling of Jesus was obviously not from God.

Paul declared that the true gifts of the Spirit, distributed as the Spirit sees
best, will result in the glorification of Jesus as Lord. God, through a prophetic
gift, had shown Polycarp how he would die. That vision was confirmed as he
finally proclaimed Jesus Christ as Lord in the power of the Holy Spirit.

❧ *A PRAYER FOR TODAY* ☙

*Give me a witness strong and true, dear Lord, so that Your name
will be exalted through each of the spiritual gifts You choose to use.*

September 14

SEEKING SPIRITUAL GIFTS

There are different kinds of gifts, but the same Spirit. 1 Cor. 12:4, NIV.

Ray and Susan had just completed a "spiritual gifts inventory" and, after checking dozens of little boxes, had come to a remarkable conclusion. Ray discovered, he said, that his gift was martyrdom, whereas Susan scored high on celibacy. Now they were facing a marital crisis, and as I talked with them in the early eighties, they confirmed my initial skepticism of spiritual gift inventories.

Little was written about spiritual gifts prior to 1970. Then it became popular, by listing all your strong and weak points, likes and dislikes, abilities and disabilities, to try to work out the special place that God had for you in His work. Often this information was misused. For instance, those who did not have a generous nature excused themselves from sacrificial giving, saying this was not their spiritual gift. Today, however, some helpful instruments have been developed to give people the opportunity to discover how they can minister most effectively for the Lord.

There are three biblical lists of spiritual gifts that you can pray through. Two lists contain supernatural service or supportive ministry gifts and the other, supernatural power ministry gifts. All the gifts exalt the Lordship of Jesus and not the recipient or even the Holy Spirit. Look at the "gifts of God" in Romans 12, and you will discover special capacities that are given for serving the Lord. In Ephesians 4:1-16 you will find the gifts of Christ, which are primarily capacities given for ministry offices.

You will notice a distinct difference when you read about the gifts of the Holy Spirit in 1 Corinthians 12. These are nine supernatural gifts that are available to all Christians at any time according to the need that arises before them as they serve the Lord. (You may want to read what Spirit-filled Adventist pioneer Ellen G. White wrote about this in *The Desire of Ages*, p. 823.)

As J. Rodman Williams has said in reference to the gifts in 1 Corinthians 12: "Spiritual gifts are not latent talents or trained abilities brought to heightened expression. The pneumatic charismata aren't simply more of what is already present, no matter how elevated. They are endowments, not enhancements" *(Charisma,* November 1992, p. 26). These endowments are available for you today.

* A PRAYER FOR TODAY *

Help me, Lord, to know and use every gift You give me for service.

269

GIFTS FOR THE GOOD OF ALL

The Holy Spirit displays God's power through each of us as a means of helping the entire church. 1 Cor. 12:7, TLB.

The Roman emperor Constantine modified the religion of Christianity from a ministry movement involving every member to a spectator sport. William McRae in his book *Dynamics of Spiritual Gifts* tells of a question asked of Bud Wilkinson, football coach of Oklahoma University before he joined the President's Physical Fitness Program. "What contribution does professional sport make to the physical fitness of Americans?"

He answered with his now-famous statement: "Very little. A professional football game is a happening where 50,000 spectators, desperately needing exercise, sit in stands watching 22 men on the field desperately needing rest" (p. 11).

Where the church consists of an audience watching a few talented—and often burned out—up-front performers, there is much evidence of a lack of spiritual fitness. God's will is that every Christian reveal the Spirit's power through spiritual gifts so that the whole church be blessed. Where this does not happen, because of Constantine's model of the church, then it fails to fulfill its ministry in nurture, outreach, and corporate worship.

For most of the first 300 years of its existence, Christianity was a small group house-church movement. As circumstances permitted, the small groups would come together for a combined festival of prayer and praise, but it was only in the small group setting that every member of the body was able to use his or her spiritual gifts for the common good of the church. If the church consisted of 10 members in a house, then at each meeting every member had an opportunity to minister with a song, message from the Word, a special revelation, or tongue and interpretation (1 Cor. 14:26). There were no spectators. All were participants.

The first reformation of the church was a battle over theology. The second is a struggle over methodology. The first reformation released the church from error of belief. The second releases it from error of function. In the power of the Holy Spirit you can be part of the return of Christianity to its roots of spiritual gift involvement by every member.

❧ *A PRAYER FOR TODAY* ❧

Lord, help me become involved in the ministry of Your church.

WORDS OF WISDOM AND KNOWLEDGE

For to one is given the word of wisdom through the Spirit, to another the word of knowledge through the same Spirit. 1 Cor. 12:8, NKJV.

There is a man in this congregation tonight who has pain in his back from two crushed vertebrae. God is healing his condition right now." The sincere preacher who spoke these words had no human foreknowledge of the injured visitor in his evening meeting, so some would say that the pastor had a "word of knowledge."

Although the Holy Spirit can, if necessary, give to His servants a revelation of specific details of the lives of others, this ability comes most often in the category of the spiritual gift of prophecy. This, for instance, was the case countless times in the ministry of Ellen G. White.

The spiritual gifts of wisdom and knowledge are both "speaking" gifts, gifts that involve words. Paul mentions "wisdom" or "wise" 20 times in the first two chapters of 1 Corinthians, while he mentions "knowledge" or "know" 20 times in the first eight chapters. He says that the message of the gospel did not depend on human wisdom or knowledge but on words that demonstrated the mighty power of the Holy Spirit (1 Cor. 2:1-5).

The spiritual gift of the word of wisdom, according to one definition, enables a Christian to declare divine truth in a way that transcends his or her own natural capacity. The gift of the word of knowledge is a supernatural ability to teach the things of God so that the practical outworking of the plan of redemption is clearly seen.

Although these "word" gifts are inspired messages that have a great impact on the hearers, they do not add anything to the Scriptures or contradict them in any way. Rather they provide a fuller apprehension of the personal application of Scriptural truth.

In your small group setting, which was the pattern of the early Christian church, people whom God chooses to use with these gifts will be surprised at the way in which they can comprehend and articulate divine truth. They will recognize that they are operating beyond their own natural capacity, and others will say, "I can't believe how clearly you explained that to me!"

❧ *A PRAYER FOR TODAY* ☙

Lord, help me hear the words of wisdom or knowledge that You may want a friend to share with me or have me communicate to others.

SUPER FAITH AND DIVINE HEALING

To another faith by the same Spirit, to another gifts of healings by the same Spirit. 1 Cor. 12:9, NKJV.

*A*t the end of a seminar on the Holy Spirit at Lahaina, on the island of Maui, a small group remained for a special healing service. Pastor Barry and Norma Crabtree assisted, along with prominent Oregon physician Dr. Louis Machlin and his wife, Becky, and the Holy Spirit chose to work some wonderful miracles in that meeting through the spiritual gifts of faith and healing.

When our time of prayer and anointing came to a close, a dentist and three other people came into the church and asked if we could wait until an elderly lady was brought in. On her arrival the doctor examined her extremely painful and badly swollen arthritic knee, which she had been unable to bend or move for a number of weeks. We prayed and sang together and put the healing of the knee into God's hands, knowing for sure that He would release her from the symptoms at the time He saw best.

As I anointed her, Aunty Pat suddenly cried out "O God, thank You!" and to our amazement we immediately saw the swelling subside and the knee return to normal. In a few minutes she was completely free of pain and able to walk out of the church. When I visited the church six months later, I found that her symptoms had not returned.

Scripture tells of three kinds of faith. One is essential for salvation (Eph. 2:8), whereas another is part of our character developed by the Holy Spirit (Gal. 5:22). The third is a miraculous trust in God's power to work miracles and victories in the most difficult circumstances. This is the spiritual gift of faith and is illustrated in Hebrews 11:33-35.

It is interesting also to notice that healing is the only gift listed plurally. There are gifts of healings because God can work healing miracles in a number of ways. But while He works through giving an understanding of natural health principles and medical science, He wants especially to empower His people to enjoy the miracles of divine healing in answer to the prayers of faith.

❦ *A PRAYER FOR TODAY* ❧

Lord, I don't claim to have a gift of healing or great faith,
but use me to pray earnestly for those with special needs.

September 18

ENERGIZED FOR MIGHTY MINISTRY

It is the same and only Holy Spirit who gives all these gifts and powers, deciding which each one of us should have. 1 Cor. 12:11, TLB.

Which of the nine supernatural gifts of the Spirit could you use most effectively at this time? The answer depends not upon your desire, but on the decision of the Holy Spirit, who decides on the basis of the needs that you will meet today. Although the Spirit apparently designs that some people be especially effective with certain gifts, He can energize any person He fills to meet the necessity of the moment.

If there is need of a miracle, we do not say, "Sorry, the one with *dynamis* power is not here." If there is need for healing prayer, we do not excuse ourselves by saying, "Unfortunately the one with the gift of healing is on vacation." Whatever the circumstances, we can pray earnestly for the supernatural gift to meet it. In fact, Christians are told to "desire" and be "eager" for spiritual gifts, especially the gift of prophecy (1 Cor. 14:1, 12, 39).

In a small group we prayed for the gift of healing so that a man who was having a severe health problem might recuperate. Instead, the Lord provided a special gift of faith, which gave the sick person exceptional courage. Someone else in the group was given a gift of the discerning of spirits and began to recognize the source of the circumstances that were causing the health problem. Another group member was given a gift of prophecy and was used in an extraordinary way to bring "edification, and exhortation, and comfort" (verse 3).

This is an example of true gospel ministry in the Spirit's power. It involves people caring for people rather than the impersonal, formal gatherings that have come to characterize much of cultural Christianity. Spiritual gifts, whether they involve supernatural powers, practical Christian service, outreach, nurture, or leadership are all part of a team ministry. They center in small groups and extend into individual, midsize, and large group activities. If you are not already a small group member and want to see spiritual gifts flourish as they did in Bible times, now is the time to become involved in this part of real Christianity.

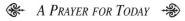

❦ *A PRAYER FOR TODAY* ❧

Lord, I thank You that each day is a new beginning, a new opportunity to serve You and bless others.

273

BAPTIZED INTO ONE BODY

For indeed we were all brought into one body by baptism, in the one
Spirit, whether we are Jews or Greeks, whether we are slaves or free
men, and that one Holy Spirit was poured out for all of us to drink.
1 Cor. 12:13, NEB.

*A*t conversion we become part of the body of Jesus, and this is con-firmed by water baptism. There is evidence that in New Testament times conversion and water baptism followed closely together (see the June 19 reading). But the baptism in or with the Spirit enables us to function powerfully as spiritually gifted members of the body (Acts 1:5, 8). Although opinions differ, apparently Paul is emphasizing Spirit baptism in 1 Corinthians 12:13 as he talks about body-life ministry.

The pouring out of the Holy Spirit so that He completely fills, or baptizes, a Christian should not, as the Adventist pioneers emphasized, be confused with water baptism (see the June 9 reading). Sometimes it may take place before water baptism, as in Acts 10:44-48. Most often it happens some time after water baptism, as in Acts 8:12-17. Ideally it would happen on the same occasion as water baptism, but be distinct from it, as at the baptism of Jesus.

A Christian knows that he or she has "drunk of," been "filled with," or "baptized in" the Spirit because it is a "personal, conscious experience," as J. H. Waggoner wrote in 1877. It is also confirmed by the "witness with our Spirit" (Rom. 8:16). That person recognizes immediately the lifeblood of spiritual gifts beginning to flow through him or her to some need, as part of the body of Jesus.

Graham accepted Jesus as his Saviour and was born again while he was an academy student. After he was immersed in water by his pastor, Graham continued as a member of his youth group but soon found himself in the routine of cultural Christianity. One evening at a meeting about the Holy Spirit he became aware that the Spirit had filled his life in a very definite way. Immediately the Spirit gave him a gift of exceptional faith, and he began to minister effectively to other young people in the group. He was now part of the life of the body.

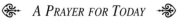

❧ A PRAYER FOR TODAY ❧

Pour into my life, Holy Spirit, so that I will overflow
with spiritual blessings for others.

A Trick or a Treat?

For those who speak in a tongue do not speak to other people but to God; for nobody understands them, since they are speaking mysteries in the Spirit. 1 Cor. 14:2, NRSV.

No subject concerning the Holy Spirit has stirred up more controversy than that of the gift of tongues. Is it a trick or a treat for Christians? Some say that tongues are known languages. Others suggest that they are the language of heaven. Because of their fear of tongues, some Christians have resisted any emphasis at all on the Spirit.

Although Paul was writing to a church where some members had misused tongues, he did not oppose this gift. "He who speaks in a tongue edifies himself" (1 Cor. 14:4, NKJV). "I wish you all spoke with tongues" (verse 5). "If I pray in a tongue, my spirit prays" (verse 14). "I thank my God I speak with tongues" (verse 18). "Do not forbid to speak with tongues" (verse 39).

Sometimes people who have received this gift have faced opposition from those who reject Paul's statements. Consequently, the gift is kept in the closet rather than being used as God intended. (See readings for July 6 and 15.)

Because tongues were to be expected at the regular gatherings of the church (verse 26), Paul gave careful guidelines given to control their public use. The number of messages in tongues was not to exceed three (verse 27). If there was no interpretation, the message should not be given (verse 28). The exercise of this gift was not to cause confusion but to be part of the beauty and order of the gathering (verses 33, 40).

Tongues are also a sign to unbelievers (verse 22). As a young pastor I heard veteran missionary Raymond Mitchell tell an interesting experience that happened as he began his ministry in Fiji. Many of the residents in Fiji were from India, and in preparation for his work among them Pastor Mitchell had tried to study their very difficult language. At a large civic meeting a government official stood and addressed the crowd, "We have asked SDA Pastor Mitchell to open our meeting with prayer. He has been in our country only a few days but can already pray in the Indian language. The Pentecostal pastor has been here for many years but still cannot speak our dialect." Raymond Mitchell testified that the Lord had indeed given him the true gift of tongues.

❧ *A Prayer for Today* ☙

Lord, may I never resist Your Spirit as He enables me to serve You and glorify Jesus.

EXCEL IN BODY BUILDING

So with yourselves; since you are eager for manifestations of the Spirit, strive to excel in building up the church. 1 Cor. 14:12, RSV.

*H*ave you detected the deep concern that Paul had for the body building of the church? Of course, he was not talking about constructing a fancy stone edifice with ornate decorations and comfortable pews. "We have a beautiful new building in this city," a church leader informed me. He was disappointed, however, to admit that there was little spiritual life in the congregation.

Each time Paul uses the words "edify" or "edification" in his discussion about the church he is talking about spiritual growth. Church members are to pray especially that they may prophesy so that the church can be edified (1 Cor. 14:1-4), and for the same reason tongues must be interpreted (verse 5). Members of the body are to excel in spiritual gifts so that the body can be built up (verse 12). When the members of the body come together, it is important that all things be done in a way that will result in edification (verse 26). When the church is spiritually edified, then there will be growth in outreach that will result in extensive missionary and evangelistic ministry.

Prophecy is the primary body-building exercise of the church. Often this gift has been neglected because of the idea that it is given to only a few unique individuals with apocalyptic vision. Paul, on the other hand, taught that all Christians are to pray that they may prophesy (verse 1).

If you are given this gift, what will happen? Will you see visions of beasts rising out of the sea? That is unlikely. Will you receive the role of resident prophet in the church like Daniel, John, or Ellen White? That is not the intent of this New Testament spiritual gift. But you will be given a special ability to bring "edification, and exhortation, and comfort" (verse 3) to individuals and group meetings of the church. Don't be hesitant. Go ahead and ask God to use you in a prophetic pastoral ministry. It is possible for all the church to be gifted in this way (verses 22-25), and even unbelievers will recognize God's mighty power.

❧ A PRAYER FOR TODAY ❧

Even in the small things of life, help me, Lord, to bring spiritual uplifting and strength to the members of Your church.

September 22

ESTABLISHED, ANOINTED, SEALED, AND SECURED

Now it is God who makes both us and you stand firm in Christ. He anointed us, set his seal of ownership on us, and put his Spirit in our hearts as a deposit, guaranteeing what is to come. 2 Cor. 1:21, 22, NIV.

I have often wondered about lifetime guarantees. "This microwave oven has a lifetime guarantee," the advertisement stated. *Whose lifetime?* I wondered. Is it my lifetime or the lifetime of the product? I can imagine, when the microwave becomes defective, returning it to the store only to be informed, "Sorry, its lifetime is over!"

When Paul wrote to Corinth, he was writing to a city that was involved in business, commerce, and trade. Everyone wanted a guarantee. So Paul informed the Christians that they had the best security that any person could ever receive—they had received the Holy Spirit. He is "the earnest" (KJV), "pledge" (NASB), "guarantee" (RSV), "first installment" (TLB and NRSV), and "deposit" (NIV) of all that God has for His people. God does not give a lifetime guarantee; He gives an eternal guarantee of total security.

On top of all the assurance of the guarantee of the Spirit, Paul uses two other words that were very significant. To "establish" was a business term that meant to make a firm, commercial transaction that was legally certain to endure. In this way, through the sacrifice of Jesus, Christians are bound to God and to each other. The bond is strong and dependable.

At conversion born-again Christians are not only established in Jesus and given the Holy Spirit in their hearts as a guarantee of eternity, but also they are anointed and sealed by the Spirit. The Corinthians understood sealing because it was a regular part of their trade practices. Sealing placed the name of the owner or manufacturer on an article and also gave validity to official documents. In the same way, at conversion God willingly places His name upon those who accept Jesus as their Saviour. The newly born-again person, without any time of probation, can say, "I'm a Christian. I'm a child of God." No wonder Christians who understand the meaning of "establish," "seal," and "guarantee" have complete assurance of their salvation in Jesus.

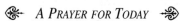 *A PRAYER FOR TODAY*

Lord, I praise You for being so generous in the way You confirm how special I am to You.

A Letter Written on the Heart

They can see that you are a letter from Christ, written by us. It is not a letter written with pen and ink, but by the Spirit of the living God; not one carved on stone, but in human hearts. 2 Cor. 3:3, TLB.

Elizabeth Pilenko grew up in a wealthy, aristocratic Russian home at the beginning of the twentieth century. Her church had taught her about Jesus, but she could not reconcile the riches of the church with the thousands of people who died of starvation and exposure each winter.

At 18, as a student of the University of St. Petersburg, she learned of plans for the Communist revolution, but after the overthrow of the czar, she became disillusioned and fled to France.

In the midst of poverty and sorrow in Paris, Elizabeth turned to God, and the Holy Spirit began to write a beautiful letter of love on her heart. Soon she returned to the religion of her childhood and became a nun of the Russian Orthodox Church, changing her name to Mother Maria. Mother Maria was eventually able to raise enough money to open a small hospital in Paris, where she cared for orphans and the critically ill.

After the Nazis occupied France during World War II, Mother Maria began hiding Jews in her hospital and was eventually discovered and arrested by the Gestapo. Sentenced to Ravensbrück women's concentration camp, Mother Maria was given many opportunities to minister in the mighty power of the Holy Spirit. Very few women lived through the fearfully inhumane conditions at Ravensbrück, where reportedly more than 95,000 women, including Corrie ten Boom's sister, Betsie, died (see February 12-14).

"One day in 1945, when women prisoners were being lined up outside the gas chamber for the fate they had come to know, a young girl began screaming with fear. As two guards moved threateningly toward her, Mother Maria ran forward and put her arms around the girl's shoulders. Then she said 'Don't be afraid. Look, I shall come with you'" *(One Who Believed,* p. 14). While Mother Maria's captors said her death was a mistake, we read with wonder the letter of love that the Holy Spirit wrote on a Russian nun's heart.

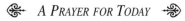

A Prayer for Today

Whatever letter You chose to write on my heart, Lord,
may I allow it to bring the fullness of praise to Jesus.

September 24

WELCOME, MINISTRY OF SPIRIT-LIFE

*[Christ] also made us sufficient as ministers of the new covenant, not
of the letter but of the Spirit; for the letter kills, but the Spirit gives life.
2 Cor. 3:6, NKJV.*

Surprising as it may seem, the letter of the gospel can kill just as
surely as can the letter of the law. In fact, as Methodist commentator Adam Clarke wrote: "It may be safely asserted that the *Jews,* in
no period of their history, ever rested more in the letter of their *law* than the
vast majority of Christians are doing in the *letter* of the Gospel" *(Clarke's
Commentary,* Vol. VI, p. 324).

The letter of the gospel can include such wonderful truths as water baptism, the Lord's Supper, ministry, gathering together for worship, victory over
sin, etc. But without the atoning sacrifice of Jesus, all these are insufficient to
save. To believe that I am saved by, for example, being baptized or involved in
ministry rather than by faith in Jesus will be the "letter that kills."

On the other hand, a new covenant ministry will proclaim not the legalism of the letter but life in the Holy Spirit through Jesus' blood. This will not
diminish in any way the importance of the letter of the gospel but will place
it in its right relationship to the spirit of the gospel.

Paul illustrated the difference between letter and spirit by discussing the
Ten Commandments. As long as they are viewed as a means of salvation, they
are a letter that kills. They cannot save anyone, because "all have sinned and
come short of the glory of God" (Rom. 3:23). They are a "ministry of death"
(verse 7) in that they confirm the authority and justice of the "wages of sin."
The new covenant, however, is an agreement of life in the Spirit. The Ten
Commandments are not changed or destroyed but are written by the Spirit in
the minds and hearts of those who have been saved by Jesus' life and death
(Jer. 31:33; Eze. 36:25-27).

Every denomination has its letter and its spirit. If you are willing to live
by the spirit, then the letter of the standards and doctrines of your denomination, if biblical, can be proclaimed and enjoyed in the setting of the new
covenant.

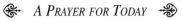

❧ *A PRAYER FOR TODAY* ☙

*Father, help me never to proclaim a list of rules
as the basis of any person's salvation.*

september 25

A BRIGHTER FACE THAN MOSES'

Shall we not expect far greater glory in these days when the Holy Spirit is giving life? 2 Cor. 3:8, TLB.

Brother R, one who had opposed the working of the Holy Spirit in the life of 17-year-old Ellen Harmon, was completely changed as the Spirit prostrated him in a small group prayer meeting in Portland, Maine, (see readings for January 25 and 26). Later Ellen White wrote: "His face was lighted with the glory of heaven. . . . In a prayer meeting soon after, H.P., the brother who had confessed that he was wrong in his opposition, experienced the power of God in so great a degree that his countenance shone with a heavenly light, and he fell helpless to the floor. . . . Cold formality began to melt before the mighty influence of the Most High" *(Signs of the Times,* Mar. 16, 1876).

An evidence of the power of God in people's lives, according to the Jewish leaders in Paul's day, was that their faces shone as the face of Moses. A shining face was looked upon as being the face of an angel. Rabbi Gedalia said that "when Moses and Aaron came before Pharaoh, they appeared like those angels which minister before the face of the Lord; for their stature appeared greater, and the splendor of their faces was like the sun" *(Clarke's Commentary,* Vol. V, p. 727). When Moses came down from Mount Sinai, his face shone so brightly that the people could not look at him (verse 7). No wonder the Jewish leaders were so amazed at the trial of Stephen when, through the mighty power of the Holy Spirit, his face shone like that of Moses—like the face of an angel.

Although it was almost impossible for even the Jewish Christians to understand, the ministry of the Holy Spirit as He exalted Jesus in the lives of all He filled would be much more glorious than Moses' Sinai experience.

In an age before sunglasses it was blinding to look at Moses' face. Today born-again believers with the assurance of salvation and the fullness of the Holy Spirit shine with a glow that is incomprehensible to the unsaved. Like Brethren R and H.P., God's people today are radiant with the love of Jesus. You may not recognize it in yourself, but you will certainly see it in a group of Spirit-filled Christians.

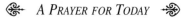

❧ *A PRAYER FOR TODAY* ☙

Even when I'm under pressure, Lord, help me reflect the brightness of Jesus' love, joy, and peace.

WELCOME, SPIRIT OF LIBERTY

Now the Lord is the Spirit, and where the Spirit of the Lord is,
there is freedom. 2 Cor. 3:17, NIV.

*A*s I drove through the beautiful Oregon countryside I listened a number of times to a tape of Darlene and the Set Free music group singing their theme song, which proclaimed freedom in Jesus. The release from physical, emotional, or spiritual bondage is as liberating as coming out of a maximum-security prison after living for years behind bars. It's a time to shout and sing for joy.

Primarily, however, Paul is writing about the liberty that a Spirit-filled Christian has to enter freely into God's presence. The Spirit is God, just as the Father is God and the Son is God. He is called the "Spirit of God" and the "Spirit of Christ" (Rom. 8:9). This in no way diminishes the personal identity of the Holy Spirit any more than Jesus' individual personality was destroyed by saying, "I and My Father are one" (John 10:30, NKJV). As part of the Tri-unity, or Trinity, the Holy Spirit takes away the veil that keeps the human mind from comprehending closeness and communication with God.

As the Holy Spirit leads a surrendered sinner to Jesus the veil begins to open up, and at the moment of conversion it is drawn completely aside by Jesus (2 Cor. 3:14). Now in prayer the new Christian feels a freedom of access to God that is uninhibited by guilt or fear. The more the Holy Spirit fills a life, the freer that person feels to rejoice in God's presence. Baptized in the Spirit, Christians have been known to feel so close to God that they will, like the early Adventists, shout and sing praises for hours.

Is there a prison that is keeping you from the liberty that the Holy Spirit has for you? Perhaps it is pride: "What will others think of me?" Perhaps it is fear: "What will happen if the Spirit takes over in my life?" Perhaps it is sin: "Will I have to give up some of the things I really enjoy doing?"

Whatever the bondage, allow the Holy Spirit to cut you loose from it. True freedom is the most valuable asset of all. As Jesus said, those who are free in Him are free indeed.

    A PRAYER FOR TODAY

Holy Spirit, I rejoice in the release from all that would hinder
my awareness of God's presence in my life.

September 27

Mirror, Mirror on the Wall . . .

But we all, with unveiled face, beholding as in a mirror the glory of the Lord, are being transformed into the same image from glory to glory, just as by the Spirit of the Lord. 2 Cor. 3:18, NKJV.

*J*erome, who in Bethlehem first translated the Bible into Latin, said in about A.D. 400: "The face is the mirror of the mind, and eyes without speaking confess the secrets to the heart." Mirrors in ancient times were made of highly polished metal, usually brass, and in the bright sunlight they gave the face a glorious golden glow.

Did Jesus sound egotistical when He promised that the Holy Spirit would glorify Him? At a General Conference session the delegates and visitors saw a brilliant display of laser lights depicting the glories of Jesus' second coming. Was this the glorification that He was eagerly anticipating? Certainly Jesus was anticipating His return to glory with the Father on His throne, but His great hope and joy was to be glorified in His followers here on earth (John 17:10, 21, 22).

Although the transformation, or metamorphosis, of a Christian into the image of Jesus is not physical, the face, as Jerome stated, is the mirror of the mind. When a Spirit-filled Christian looks into a mirror, the face that looks back is his or her own—wrinkles and all. But there will be a difference when the face reflects the character of one who has the "mind of Christ" (1 Cor. 2:16). That face will display an openness—a freedom from the oppressed look of one who is grappling with guilt and fear. It will show the gentle radiance of one who has the inner assurance of salvation.

One day I sat in a cave near the Church of the Nativity in Bethlehem and thought of Jerome, who spent many years here translating the Bible into the language of his people. Already in his day there was much evidence of corrupt Christian leaders. In fact, he wrote: "Avoid, as you would the plague, a clergyman who is also a man of business." On the other hand Jerome himself, and some of the other Christians around him, were by the power of the Holy Spirit reflecting in their own way the image of Jesus.

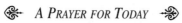

❧ *A Prayer for Today* ❧

Thank You, Lord, for being willing to keep working on the transformation process in my life.

September 28

PREPARED FOR REVIVAL

Now He who has prepared us for this very thing is God, who also has given us the Spirit as a guarantee. 2 Cor. 5:5, NKJV.

The great Scottish preacher James A. Stewart in *Drops From the Honeycomb* tells of a remarkable revival that took place in a European city prior to World War II. Usually as he had come to preach in other cities it had taken weeks or months of prayer and spiritual preparation before the revival came. But in this city, where the meetings had begun with only seven people at a Friday-evening prayer service, in five days thousands were filling the auditorium, and large numbers were converted.

"One evening the Lord very kindly allowed me to discover the secret of the blessing," Dr. Stewart wrote. "Being afraid that I would not have sufficient power of the Spirit to proclaim the Evangel to the thousands who had gathered, I made my way to the basement of the auditorium in order to have a few minutes in prayer. I began to pray in the darkness, but it was not long before I felt an overwhelming sense of the majesty of God. I knew right away there was someone else in the large basement praying.

"I quietly put on the light, and there I saw at the extreme end of the basement some twelve sisters, flat on their faces before God! They were totally unaware of my presence. They were 'inside the veil,' touching the Throne, by the power of the Spirit, while upstairs God was working mightily among the unsaved" (cited in *Herald of His Coming,* June 1993, p. 9).

As Charles E. Bradford has said, "revivals are not worked up, but prayed down." It is not that prayer earns revival, but it is a matter of hearts opened fully to the Holy Spirit and having the "guarantee" of the Spirit within so that He can have clear channels through which to flow.

When Paul wrote to the Corinthians, he reminded them that the Holy Spirit within is the guarantee of the resurrection of their bodies. In the same way He is the guarantee of the resurrection, or revival, of a "dead bones" (Eze. 37) Christianity in our lives and churches.

❦ *A PRAYER FOR TODAY* ❦

Father, move with Your Spirit upon my church so that we may experience the new life and joy that we can experience by Your Spirit.

NO LUXURY CRUISE

But in all things we commend ourselves as ministers of God:
in much patience, in tribulations, in needs, in distresses, in stripes,
in imprisonments, in tumults, in labors, in sleeplessness, in fastings;
by purity, by knowledge, by longsuffering, by kindness, by the Holy Spirit,
by sincere love. 2 Cor. 6:4-6, NKJV.

A Christian newsletter recently told the story of two Chinese girls who went to share the gospel in Inner Mongolia. They were not well received, so they worked alongside farmers and as the opportunity arose told them about Jesus' love. After a few months some families became Christians, and a church was established. The Communist police soon moved in, and the girls were shot at, arrested, and badly beaten. Eventually they were fined, released, and—praise God—through a series of miraculous events were able to carry on with their ministry.

I saw a luxury cruise advertised for Christians who wanted to know more about the Holy Spirit and how to use spiritual gifts in their ministry. Unless the boat sinks or the passengers become seasick, luxury cruises can be fun and full of refreshing relaxation. But, as Paul well knew, the Holy Spirit never promised a luxury cruise for those who move ahead in Christian service. He has promised, however, unfailing strength and an inner core of joy that cannot be shaken.

The Voice of the Martyrs, Inc., newsletter tells about an evangelist in the Philippines who preached at great risk in a territory occupied by Communist terrorists. The evangelist was accompanied on one visit by his 8-year-old nephew, who loved to be involved in ministry for other children. Some soldiers were saved and left the Communist groups, which so angered the terrorist leaders that they abducted the boy and tortured him for several hours before killing him.

Although the evangelist recognizes that his ministry among the terrorist soldiers and their families is no luxury cruise, he continues his dangerous mission for Jesus in the power of the Holy Spirit. If he doesn't, who will? Perhaps someone from the luxury cruise will answer the call.

❧ *A PRAYER FOR TODAY* ❧

Your ministry, Lord, may involve some sleeplessness and suffering,
but it will never involve working without Your constant help.

WELCOME TO WONDERFUL FELLOWSHIP

May the grace of the Lord Jesus Christ, and the love of God, and the fellowship of the Holy Spirit be with you all. 2 Cor. 13:14, NIV.

When 72-year-old Charles Haines died in apparent poverty in a cockroach-infested Spokane flophouse, authorities were surprised to discover $11,000 hidden in the room. Later they found that Haines, who had lived on about $30 a month, received a veteran's monthly pension of $563 and had more than $22,000 in the bank. A neighbor said that Haines shaved his head to save paying for haircuts and "probably had the first dime he ever made and was always worried that someone was going to get it" (reported in the *Oregonian,* Dec. 12, 1990).

Most people would consider Charles Haines crazy, but unfortunately his actions picture the relationship that many Christians have with the Holy Spirit. He is dwelling in the heart of every born-again believer but remains as unused as Haines' money. The Holy Spirit is carefully hidden away in the religious literature and music that many church attenders have in their homes, while at the same time they live in spiritual poverty.

In the seventies the new buzzword in Christianity was *koinōnia.* In many places koinōnia groups and ministries began as people found exciting new fellowships and opportunities to grow together and with the Lord. This word, meaning partnership, communication, and sharing, is used about 20 times in the New Testament. Christians have koinōnia with Jesus (1 Cor. 1:9) and even with His body and blood in the Lord's Supper (1 Cor. 10:16). They have koinōnia in ministry (2 Cor. 8:4; Gal. 2:9) and in the sharing of their faith (Philemon 6). Christians have koinōnia not only with the Father and the Son but also with each other (1 John 1:3, 7).

To have koinōnia with the Holy Spirit, as Paul emphasizes in his benediction, means to talk with Him, enjoy His company, be in conscious fellowship and partnership with Him, and experience His mighty power in one's life.

We can say that Charles Haines had no "koinōnia" with his money, so neither he nor others in need were helped by it. How unfortunate it would be to have the same experience with your friend the Holy Spirit.

❧ *A PRAYER FOR TODAY* ❧

Holy Spirit, I'm sorry that I've neglected You and have not had the fellowship that You have wanted with me. Please help me change that now.

october 1

THE HOLY CLUB OR THE MIDNIGHT PRAYER MEETINGS

This only I want to learn from you: Did you receive the Spirit by the works of the law, or by the hearing of faith? Gal. 3:2, NKJV.

Speaking of John Wesley and his friends, John Mallison wrote: "Methodism actually began with a small 'koinōnia' group comprising just four students at Oxford University. They contracted with each other to study the Scriptures, live a Christian lifestyle, witness verbally, and undertake social concern both collectively and individually" *(Building Small Groups,* p. 13). These men eventually realized, however, that the Holy Spirit could not be received by the works of the "Holy Club."

On October 14, 1735, John Wesley sailed for Georgia, hoping to learn the meaning of the gospel by preaching it to the Indians. Because of his contact with the Moravian Christians from the estate of Count Zinzendorf in Saxony, he learned the value not only of small groups but of extemporaneous prayer, hymn-singing during worship, and the use of lay people in ministry.

Howard A. Snyder, in his book *The Radical Wesley,* writes: "Because of his zeal and his innovations he was accused of 'leaving the Church of England by two doors at the same time'—Roman Catholicism and Puritan Separatism. But at heart his experiments sprang from the desire to recover the spirit and form of early Christianity" (p. 21).

Although Wesley now had the right motives and the right methods, he was still trying to accomplish through the right works what could happen only as the result of true, saving faith. Back in London, on May 24, 1738, John Wesley broke what Dorothy Marshall called the "faith barrier." In the little chapel on Aldersgate Street his famous heart-warming experience took place. Later Wesley wrote in his *Journal:* "I felt I did trust in Christ, Christ alone for salvation; and assurance was given me that He had taken away my sins, even mine, and had saved me from the law of sin and death" (E. P. Rudolph, *The Wesley Treasury,* p. 68). At that moment, John Wesley received the Holy Spirit's indwelling presence, not by the works of the law but by the hearing of faith. There was little change now in Wesley's works and methods, but the results were dramatically different.

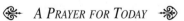 A PRAYER FOR TODAY

Thank You, Lord, for providing freely what I can never earn for myself.

october 2

LETTING THE SPIRIT CONTINUE HIS WORK

Are you so foolish? After beginning with the Spirit, are you now trying to attain your goal by human effort? Gal. 3:3, NIV.

*H*enry G. Bosch retells Isaac Page's story of a poor man in Ireland who was plodding along toward home, carrying a huge sack of potatoes. A horse and wagon came by, and the driver stopped to offer him a ride. The man accepted and climbed up on the seat alongside the driver but kept holding the bag of potatoes in his arms. When the driver suggested that he lay it down on the wagon floor, he replied warmly in his Irish brogue, "I don't like to trouble you too much, sir. You're a-givin' me a ride already, so I'll just carry the potatoes!"

Although you received the Holy Spirit to dwell in you at conversion, are you now trying to carry the potatoes of the Christian life by human effort? Paul calls the Galatians "foolish," as the result of their being "bewitched" (Gal. 3:1). That is strong language, and Paul uses it because he knows that the originator of salvation by works for Christians was certainly not God.

John Wesley, commenting on Galatians 3:3, said: "Having set out under the light and power of the Spirit by faith, do you now, when ye ought to be more spiritual, and more acquainted with the power of faith, expect to be *made perfect by the flesh?* Do you think to complete either your justification or sanctification, by giving up that faith and depending on the law?" *(Notes on the New Testament, p. 686).*

Before his Aldersgate and Fetter Lane experiences, Wesley had tried every legalistic means to attain holiness. Having now experienced the certainty of salvation and the witness of the Spirit, he could never go back.

Accepting the Spirit's power does not mean, however, that the sack of potatoes is thrown off the wagon. As Howard Snyder said concerning Wesley: "He saw that works were worthless in attaining the new birth, but he was equally persuaded of the absolute moral necessity of good works as the evidence of regeneration and the inevitable expression of holy love" *(The Radical Wesley, p. 46).*

❦ A PRAYER FOR TODAY ❦

Reveal to me, Father, any works that I'm relying on in place of full acceptance of Your Spirit's power.

WHY MIRACLES HAPPEN

Therefore He who supplies the Spirit to you and works miracles among you, does He do it by the works of the law, or by the hearing of faith?
Gal. 3:5, NKJV.

I don't know how long it took the Galatian Christians to get the message, but three times in four verses Paul repeats his point of emphasis. It is not by the works of the law but by faith that the Spirit is received. Have we allowed the Holy Spirit to impress this great certainty upon our minds today? If so, we will see wonderful miracles take place now, just as in Galatia.

Luther revolutionized Christianity by discovering the meaning of saving faith. Paul in Romans 1:17 and Galatians 3:11 quotes the very words that the Spirit 15 centuries later would impress on the mind of this Roman Catholic monk. The historian D'Aubigné tells what happened to Luther as he climbed Pilate's staircase in Rome. "But while he was performing this meritorious act, he thought he heard a voice of thunder crying from the bottom of his heart, as at Wittenburg and Bologna, 'The just shall live by faith'" *(History of the Reformation,* p. 70).

Because of his strong emphasis on "the hearing of faith," Luther was also convinced that he served a miracle-working God. This is illustrated in an experience related in *Our Daily Bread.* "In 1540, Frederick Myconius was very sick and about to die. He wrote a farewell letter to his dear friend Martin Luther, who sent back this response: 'I command you in the name of God to live because I still have need of you in the work of reforming the church. . . . The Lord will never let me hear that you are dead, but will permit you to survive me. For this I am praying, this is my will, and may my will be done because I seek only to glorify the name of God.' Myconius, who had become too weak to talk, regained his strength and outlived Luther by two months" (May 26, 1993, vol. 37, No. 12).

Are you seeing miracles in your church congregation, your small group, and your own life? If not, by faith give the Holy Spirit the opportunity to bring a great revival.

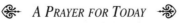

A PRAYER FOR TODAY

Lord, Your miracle of saving grace continues
to bring me rejoicing and hope.

THE WELCOMING STEP OF FAITH

He redeemed us in order that the blessing given to Abraham might come to the Gentiles through Christ Jesus, so that by faith we might receive the promise of the Spirit. Gal. 3:14, NIV.

*J*esus called the Holy Spirit the "promise of my Father" (Luke 24:49), and Paul described Him to the Ephesians as the "Holy Spirit of promise" (Eph. 1:13). Peter also confirmed that the Holy Spirit is promised to every converted person (Acts 2:38, 39). There is only one condition for receiving the promise, and that is the initial step of faith that brings a person into the family of God.

When seeking new fillings of the Holy Spirit, Christians will again take the step of faith. Faith is the basis of all that is important in the Christian life.

Until conversion the Spirit works with sinners, leading them to learn of Jesus and the plan of salvation. As soon as a sinner opens his or her heart in surrender and by faith invites Jesus to be his or her personal Saviour, the Holy Spirit takes up residence in that life and represents Jesus there. In this way, with salvation, the promise of the Spirit is received by faith.

Let me make this personal for you. If you have received Jesus as your Saviour, you can praise God right now that you are also the Holy Spirit's dwelling place. That's God's promise, and you can be absolutely certain of it.

Many times Christians pray for fresh infillings of the Spirit. This is another way of expressing the invitation for the Holy Spirit to have complete access to every part of the life. They offer deeply earnest prayers. They thirst for more of the Spirit. They surrender fully to God's will. They often shed tears of repentance. None of these things earn or merit the Holy Spirit. They only indicate a heartfelt desire to receive a new infusion of His mighty power.

But once again, in the midst of all this intensity, the step of faith must be taken. Without any emotional sign, the praying Christian thanks God in faith for coming and filling him or her with the Holy Spirit. By faith God is praised, and the resultant blessing fully enjoyed.

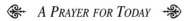

❧ *A PRAYER FOR TODAY* ❧

May the truth of Your Spirit be not a theory to me,
Lord, but a living reality of power in my life.

WHS-10

OUR FATHER UNDERSTANDS

And because you are sons, God has sent forth the Spirit of His Son into your hearts, crying out, "Abba, Father!" Gal. 4:6, NKJV.

*M*y father rarely listened to me, and even when he did, he had no idea of what I was trying to tell him." Anne's complaint about her father is one that is commonly heard. Often the relationship between parents and children gradually breaks down because of a lack of communication.

Those of us who are spiritual teenagers can also relate to what David Elkind writes in *All Grown Up and No Place to Go:* "The term 'communication' suggests that we have a specific message and our only problem is having the time, the opportunity, or the right words to get that message across. But in my experience with teenagers I have found the problem is somewhat different. The true problem is that teenagers are not really sure what it is that is bothering them. They need to talk in a rather free-wheeling way in order to discover what they want to say to us" (p. 204).

As Christians, we cry out to God even when we are not sure what we need to say. The word Paul uses for "crying out" both times he writes of Abba, Father, can be likened to the call of a raven and is similar to the inarticulate "groanings which cannot be uttered" of Romans 8:26. Through the Spirit we are assured that our free-wheeling talking to Abba, Father, is always heard and understood, and we can be sure that He does listen and respond in the best way.

Some of the most beautiful prayers in the English language are found in the old Anglican prayer book. Many of them were written by the great Reformer William Tyndale, who died for his faith in Jesus and His Word. Following each of the Ten Commandments, Anglicans and Episcopalians read the beautiful prayer: "Lord, have mercy upon us, and incline our hearts to keep this law." But many Christians learned from later Reformers such as John Wesley the joy of extemporaneous prayer. "My heart was so full," Wesley wrote in his *Journal,* "that I could not confine myself to the forms of prayer which we were accustomed to use there."

Today Spirit-filled Christians rejoice in just talking to Abba, Father.

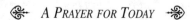

&⁓ *A PRAYER FOR TODAY* ⁓&

You know what's on my heart, Father, even when I can't express it to You in the words that I'd like to use.

October 6

WHY CHRISTIANS FIGHT

And so we who are born of the Holy Spirit are persecuted now by those who want us to keep the Jewish laws, just as Isaac the child of promise was persecuted by Ishmael the slave-wife's son. Gal. 4:29, TLB.

*I*n the foreword to his book *Great Church Fights* longtime Baptist pastor Leslie B. Flynn tells of a father who heard a commotion in his yard and looked outside to see his daughter and several playmates in a heated quarrel. At his reprimand his daughter explained, "We're just playing church!"

Unfortunately, friction in churches has been so heated that many Christian books have been written about conflict management.

Although there are many reasons for church fights, no fights are so bitter as those involving doctrines and methods of worship and ministry. Disagreement often degenerates into persecution, and eventually people leave the church, never to return. It began to happen in the time of the New Testament, and it continues almost 21 centuries later, much to the delight of the forces of evil.

Often at the basis of church fights is a misunderstanding of salvation. The Judaizing Christians of Paul's day believed that salvation came from Jesus *plus* specific works of the law. They caused continuous friction with those who believed that salvation is received only by faith in the life and death of Jesus. Tragically, church history tells us that those who have taken the most legalistic and conservative stand for truth have often been the most willing to persecute and even kill those who disagree.

In the eighties a denomination split over whether the hands should be raised over the head in worship or whether they should just be raised in front of the body. The issue was not the hands but whether salvation was jeopardized by incorrect procedures. Church fights have developed over the color of the new carpet in the sanctuary. On top of the pride of opinion was the fear that somehow the "wrong" color would affect the worship service and endanger the congregation's chances of salvation.

The Holy Spirit would have us remember the words of Luther's associate, Melanchthon: "In essentials, unity; in nonessentials, liberty; in all things, charity" (cited in *Home Book of Quotations,* p. 242).

❧ A PRAYER FOR TODAY ❧

Lord, give me the tolerance to accept the idea that people have the right to differ from me even in the things that I consider most important.

A TANTALIZING TASTE

For we through the Spirit eagerly wait for the hope of
righteousness by faith. Gal. 5:5, NKJV.

*M*any a man has visited a large supermarket with his wife for "a few minutes of shopping" only to discover that she intended to do an extended tour up and down each aisle as she examined the products as if they were interesting artifacts in the British Museum.

On one such excursion I became rather hungry and, after failing to hurry my wife out of the store, followed her suggestion to try some of the samples that were being offered. One morsel was very tasty, but to get enough to satisfy my hunger I would have had to buy a whole can of the product!

The Christian who has accepted Christ's righteousness and is filled with the Holy Spirit has tasted a little of the glory of God's presence. The taste is so good that it creates an earnest desire to meet Jesus at His second coming and to share in the wonderful glories of eternity. The hope of righteousness by faith is the redemption of the body, which means unlimited fellowship with God (Rom. 8:23). The thought of this "hope of the glory of God" is so exciting to believers that they rejoice and praise God in anticipation (Rom. 5:2).

Paul's point in Galatians 5:1-6 is that the person who is trying to be saved by the law does not have this same eager anticipation. Legalists are never certain whether they have done sufficient good works, whether their works have been good enough, or whether they will make it through the seven last plagues. They are shackled to a yoke of bondage that dampens joy and hope. In fact, as Paul says, they have "fallen from grace" and have lost the taste of "faith working through love" (verses 4, 6, NKJV).

I imagined tasting the delightful sample at the supermarket and then being told, "You must work, cleaning the building, in order to obtain a can of this product." On asking how much work I must do, I am told, "We will periodically evaluate the quality and quantity of your work and will eventually decide when you have done well enough."

I am sure that I would reject their offer and walk away disappointed. But we never have to walk away from God's saving grace.

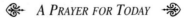

❧ A PRAYER FOR TODAY ❧

Lord, may my heart be continually excited about meeting You soon.

october 8

HELPING A PREACHER WALK

So I say, live by the Spirit, and you will not gratify the desires of the sinful nature. Gal. 5:16, NIV.

As a child, Samuel Logan Brengle had been converted one Christmas Eve in a little Methodist church near his home in Indiana. During his first years of ministry in the second half of the nineteenth century, he felt an ever-increasing hunger for the complete filling of the Holy Spirit in his life. Although he loved the Lord and had been through seminary in Boston, he knew that he had to be emptied of all that held him back from walking in the Spirit.

In a little volume later published by the Salvation Army, Brengle wrote: "I saw the humility of Jesus, and my pride; the meekness of Jesus, and my temper; the lowliness of Jesus, and my ambition; the purity of Jesus, and my unclean heart; the faithfulness of Jesus, and the deceitfulness of my heart; the unselfishness of Jesus, and my selfishness; the trust and faith of Jesus, and my doubts and unbelief; the holiness of Jesus, and my unholiness" (cited in V. Raymond Edman, *They Found the Secret,* p. 9).

A view of oneself, such as Samuel Logan Brengle received, can be a terrible shock and a great discouragement unless some important points are remembered. First, he was already saved by his acceptance of Jesus' life and sacrifice. Second, the Holy Spirit was not revealing this to make salvation more difficult but in order that Brengle might know the joy of walking in victory through the Spirit's power. Third, although Brengle's victory over these sins would not make him more saved, it would give him a mighty witness as he worked for the salvation of others.

After several weeks of prayer, Bible study, and surrender to God, Brengle became aware of the Holy Spirit filling his life. "My heart melted like wax before the fire; Jesus Christ was revealed to my spiritual consciousness, revealed in me, and my soul was filled with unutterable love," he wrote *(ibid.,* p. 11). Eventually the Lord led this Spirit-filled Methodist minister into the Salvation Army. There God used him to bring to thousands a knowledge of what it means to walk in the victory power of the Spirit.

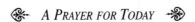

❧ *A PRAYER FOR TODAY* ❧

Lord, You've come to my rescue many times when I've fallen.
Help me hold Your hand as I walk again today.

293

DOING WHAT YOU DON'T WANT TO DO

For the sinful nature desires what is contrary to the Spirit, and the Spirit what is contrary to the sinful nature. They are in conflict with each other, so that you do not do what you want. Gal. 5:17, NIV.

A man had been bitten by a dog and had become violently ill. His doctor explained to him, "You've been bitten by a rabid dog, and you're dying of rabies. There's nothing I can do for you."

The stricken man asked for a pencil and paper and then spent several hours thinking and writing.

On a return visit the doctor remarked, "You're certainly making a long will."

To which the patient retorted, "I'm not making my will; I'm making a list of people I'm going to bite" (see *Great Church Fights,* p. 114).

As the Galatian Christians became bewitched by legalism, they began to bite and devour each other (Gal. 5:15). As a result, the church suffered from a spiritual hydrophobia that threatened to destroy it. Dr. Adam Clarke summarized Paul's warning to the Galatians in this way: "You are convinced of what is *right,* and ye wish to do it; but, having abandoned the Gospel and the grace of Christ, the law and its ordinances which ye have chosen in their place afford you no *power* to conquer your evil propensities" *(Clarke's Commentary,* Vol. VI, p. 411).

Both legalists and those who turn gospel liberty into license find themselves surrendering to the capacity to sin that remains in all Christians. Legalists may fall into the trap of hatred, contention, jealousy, outbursts of wrath, selfish ambition, dissension, and heresy as easily as those who espouse "cheap grace" may fall into any of the other "works of the flesh" that Paul lists (verses 19-21). Because they have no power to give them victory, those who do not walk in the Spirit's strength find themselves doing the things that they do not really want to do.

On the other hand, those who are filled with the Spirit and understand the full implications of freedom in the gospel are able to rejoice in obeying the truth. They do, in the power of the Spirit, what the craving of their old sinful nature does not really want to do. And they praise God for the victory.

❧ A PRAYER FOR TODAY ❧

Help me, Lord, do what is right,
even when some part of me wants to act in another way.

october 10

THE LEADING QUESTION

But if you are led by the Spirit, you are not under law. Gal. 5:18, NIV.

*P*ioneer Adventists, because of their emphasis on the Sabbath, were often accused of being "under the law" rather than "under grace." Unfortunately, this accusation was often true, as Spirit-filled Ellen White many times lamented. On one occasion she wrote: "As a people, we have preached the law until we are as dry as the hills of Gilboa that had neither dew or rain" *(Review and Herald,* Mar. 11, 1890). Later she said: "In presenting the binding claims of the law, many have failed to portray the infinite love of Christ. Those who have so great truths, so weighty reforms to present to the people, have not had a realization of the value of the atoning Sacrifice as an expression of God's great love to man" *(ibid.,* Feb. 3, 1891).

Despite their tendency toward legalism, the Spirit constantly led the early Adventists back to an understanding of grace. In fact, their message was the everlasting gospel, which was described as " 'the third angel's message in verity' " (A. G. Daniells, *Christ Our Righteousness,* p. 65).

At the Minneapolis General Conference session in 1888, some controversy erupted regarding the law in Galatians, but Ellen White again revealed her understanding of the gospel: "In this scripture [Galatians 3:24], the Holy Spirit through the apostle is speaking especially of the moral law. The law reveals sin to us, and causes us to feel our need of Christ and to flee unto Him for pardon and peace by exercising repentance toward God and faith toward our Lord Jesus Christ" *(Selected Messages,* book 1, p. 234).

The question now is Are we being led by the law or by the Spirit? If we are being led by the law, we will have no assurance of salvation, and our witness to others will consist of a list of do's and don'ts. Eventually we will find ourselves practicing, or wishing we could practice, things we have condemned in others. We will be fanatically strict in some matters of the law while justifying the breaking of others.

When we are led by the Spirit, on the other hand, we have the assurance of God's grace and the joy that sin does not have authority over us.

❧ *A PRAYER FOR TODAY* ❧

I place my hand in Yours, Lord Jesus,
knowing that You'll always lead me home.

WELCOME, TASTY FRUIT

But the fruit of the Spirit is love, joy, peace, longsuffering, kindness,
goodness, faithfulness, gentleness, self-control. Against such
there is no law. Gal. 5:22, 23, NKJV.

*E*verything I enjoy," a lady said facetiously, "is either sinful or fattening!"

Usually fruit does not fall into those categories, and Paul makes it clear that no law will condemn the person who enjoys the fruit of the Spirit. The Stoics of Paul's day listed four cardinal virtues: temperance, prudence, fortitude, and justice. But living with a Stoic could be like living with a block of ice or eating tasteless food. Paul's inspired list of Spirit-fruit is tasty, warm, friendly, and a delight to live with, even in the most difficult circumstances.

Driving through the beautiful Yakima Valley in Washington State, my family was amazed at the seemingly endless miles of apple orchards. The fruit on thousands of acres of trees was ripe and ready to pick, and even the air was filled with the scent of apples. Little fruit stands along the road sold cases of apples and bottles of apple juice. Huge packing sheds were ready to prepare the fruit for distribution around the world. In the midst of all this I was surprised to see a pickup truck carrying a box that advertised "New Zealand Apples."

Christians are to be known and recognized by the fruit of their lives, the fruit of the Spirit. Some seek to validate their Christianity by a display of spiritual gifts, miraculous answers to prayer, and eloquent expositions of biblical truth. God says that without love, which is the basic Spirit fruit, all else is meaningless (1 Cor. 13:1-3).

Just as apples are apples whether they come from Washington or New Zealand, so the fruit of the Spirit can be recognized wherever it is found. It is not conditional on belonging to a certain church, worshiping in a specific building, or espousing a predetermined creed. The fruit of the Spirit tastes good to young and old and to people of every socioeconomic strata. Just as there is no law against apple trees bearing apples, so if you are filled with the Spirit, you can have a Spirit-fruit festival without fear of God's condemnation.

✤ *A PRAYER FOR TODAY* ✤

Lord, ripen Your fruit in my life and fill me with Your sweetness.

october 12

FRUIT FROM A FACTORY

If we live in the Spirit, let us also walk in the Spirit. Gal. 5:25, NKJV.

*A*t an import store we recently bought some artificial, decorative fruit. This fake fruit, made in Taiwan, looked very attractive and realistic, but of course, as our Pomeranian discovered, was not at all suitable for food. Because in Oregon we enjoyed an abundance of fresh fruit, we were not tempted to eat the factory-made papier-mâché imitations.

Dr. Samuel Chadwick completed his years of ministry as principal of Cliff College in Sheffield, England. In his book *The Way to Pentecost* Chadwick expresses his concern about the neglect of the Holy Spirit that was evident in his church. "The church affirms its faith in the Holy Ghost every time it repeats its Creed, but does the church really believe its belief? . . . The church is the Body of Christ begotten, unified, and indwelt by the Spirit, but forgetting the Spirit, men wrangle over limbs, functions, and orders. The Christian religion is hopeless without the Holy Ghost" (p. 6).

Living as he did in the industrial city of Sheffield, Samuel Chadwick was very familiar with the noise and pollution of factories. Speaking of the great need of the living fruit of the Spirit in the lives of church members, Chadwick wrote: "Works belong to the workshop; fruit belongs to the garden. One comes from the ingenuity of the factory; the other is the silent growth of abounding life. The factory operates with dead stuff; the garden cultivates living forces to their appointed end" *(ibid.,* p. 101).

Those who live in the Spirit will not rely on the factory-made fake fruit of human works for their salvation or the validation of their Christianity. The true fruit of their lives will be seen and known. Fake fruit can last indefinitely, but Spirit-fruit can last only as long as it is connected to the source of life. Walking in the Spirit means that you are constantly connected by the Spirit to Jesus and are allowing the beautiful fruit to grow. You don't have to worry about it happening, as though you were working an artificial fruit machine in a factory. You just have to let the fruit grow in the garden of God's love.

 *A PRAYER FOR TODAY*

Lord, I rejoice today in being alive and fruitful in Your power.

Welcome, Gentle Restorer

My friends, if anyone is detected in a transgression, you who have received the Spirit should restore such a one in a spirit of gentleness. Take care that you yourselves are not tempted. Gal. 6:1, NRSV.

The Roman poet Mantuanus once wrote in *De honesto Amore:* "This is a common evil; at one time or another we have all done wrong. Either we are, or have been, or may be, as bad as he whom we condemn." Paul was very concerned that the Spirit-filled Galatian Christians deal gently with all transgressors. "Remember," we can hear Paul warning, "tomorrow you may need to be lifted up onto your feet again. Treat these people as you yourselves would like to be treated."

As a new teenage Christian I slipped into the habit of smoking and attending the theater, both of which were grounds for discipline in the church I had joined. None of the strict members knew what I was doing, otherwise my name would have come to the board for censure or disfellowshipping. Fortunately the Lord brought to our city a young Christian worker who befriended me and in deep sincerity prayed that I would respond to the Spirit's victory power.

"Garrie, what you are doing will lead you away from God," Mostyn warned me in true Christian love. "I know God has a wonderful ministry for you, so why allow the enemy to steal it away? Just put your problems into Jesus' hands. He'll give you a new start."

Mostyn was right, and I soon made the choice that turned me back to God and into an active preaching ministry for Him. I shudder to think what would have happened if I had been dealt with in a cold, disciplinary way.

Have you become aware of a Christian who has fallen into one of the "works of the flesh" that Paul mentions in Galatians 5:19-21? If so, how are you going to deal with it? Are you going to begin a network of damaging gossip? Are you going to lobby for church disciplinary action? Filled with the Holy Spirit, you will deal with the fallen in a way that reflects all the fruits of the Spirit in your life.

☙ *A Prayer for Today* ❧

Lord, help me be a protector and nurturer of those who are struggling with sin.

WELCOME, HARVEST

If he sows to please his own wrong desires, he will be planting seeds of evil and he will surely reap a harvest of spiritual decay and death; but if he plants the good things of the Spirit, he will reap the everlasting life which the Holy Spirit gives him. Gal. 6:8, TLB.

Some people sow their wild oats and then pray for a crop failure. Years ago I read about a magical rice seed on sale in Japan that would with prayer, its marketers claimed, produce any crop desired—wheat, barley, watermelon, whatever. The biblical principle, however, remains true in all ages: "Whatever a man sows, that he will also reap" (Gal. 6:7, NKJV).

Fortunately an exception has been made possible by Jesus. The Saviour sowed nothing but good and in return reaped a harvest of hell on earth. He did it so that those who deserve to reap hell can instead look forward to a harvest of eternal life. Unfortunately, every person has planted "seeds of evil," and even as Christians we find ourselves sowing seeds that will not produce an orchard full of Spirit fruit.

"I often lost my temper at home," a pastor admitted. Although he reaped damaged relationships with his family, he was able to claim God's forgiveness and begin to walk in victory through the Spirit.

As a college teacher, I often had the opportunity to talk with theology students who, before their conversion, had been heavily involved with drugs. Although they were sure that they had not been affected mentally and emotionally, there was much evidence to the contrary. Until the resurrection day they would have to live with the results of sowing the wrong seed. Spiritually, however, Jesus had broken for them the sowing-reaping law, and they rejoiced as they served God in the power of the Holy Spirit.

We live in an age of bargain hunters. People want to sow without reaping and reap without sowing. We want education without study, money without work, physical fitness without exercise, and spiritual vitality without prayer and Bible study. But, as Paul says, if we continue to plant the good things of the Spirit, we will reap a welcome harvest of spiritual blessings.

❧ *A PRAYER FOR TODAY* ❧

Help me, Lord, today to sow kindness and love, knowing that they will result in a harvest of joy in the lives of many people.

WELCOME TO THE SUPERPOWER SUMMIT

*In Him you also trusted, after you heard the word of truth, the gospel
of your salvation; in whom also, having believed, you were sealed with
the Holy Spirit of promise. Eph. 1:13, NKJV.*

*H*ave you ever been in the middle of a power struggle? It can happen anywhere—from homes and corporations to international affairs. After riding in a Turkish taxi from Izmir to Ephesus, I walked with keen anticipation down the ancient stone streets and sat on the stage of the great Ephesian amphitheater. Here Paul had addressed the crowd and found himself in a riot that engulfed the whole city (Acts 19:21-41). The followers of Diana of the Ephesians claimed mighty power, but Paul recognized that he was on the side of the Superpower of God.

When Paul later wrote to the Ephesian Christians, the Holy Spirit inspired the New Testament's most power-packed letter. Here Paul used more words and illustrations of Holy Spirit power than are grouped together in any other part of Scripture. Take time to read prayerfully through the whole letter. You will soon discover that this is God's Superpower message for you today.

Review with Paul in Ephesians 1:13 the steps that can lead to spiritual power in any life. First, the Holy Spirit guides us to the Word. It is the Bible, written or spoken, that introduces us to Jesus. This is why Scripture distribution is so important. Next, the Holy Spirit helps us discern that the Word is true, accurate, and reliable. When we come to this conclusion, we are then led to discover the gospel of our salvation, and if we are willing, we take the step of faith and accept Jesus as our personal Saviour. At that moment we become the dwelling place of the superpowerful Holy Spirit.

Every year the leaders of the world's economic superpowers meet for a summit of discussion and interaction. Sometimes they have strong disagreements. At other times statements of unity and cooperation are signed by all the presidents and prime ministers. Ephesians is Paul's spiritual superpower summit, but it resulted in no statement of agreement with evil. Rather, the Holy Spirit is shown to be the all-conquering superpower for our life.

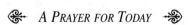

A PRAYER FOR TODAY

*Thank You, Lord, that with Jesus
I can be always on the winning side.*

A REASON FOR PRAISE

His presence within us is God's guarantee that he really will give us all that he promised; and the Spirit's seal upon us means that God has already purchased us and that he guarantees to bring us to himself. This is just one more reason for us to praise our glorious God.
Eph. 1:14, TLB.

*I*f you are looking for "one more reason . . . to praise our glorious God," go to the bank of heaven and cash a check that God has given you as He has filled you with His Holy Spirit. One of the biggest checks is the certainty of eternity in heaven. The payment of that check is guaranteed, and it is impossible to be miserable about it.

Charles Spurgeon told a story in one of his sermons about a lady who worked for more than 20 years caring for a very wealthy man. Because the man had no heirs, he decided to leave a large part of his fortune to the woman who had faithfully served him. So when he was about to die, he wrote something on a small piece of paper and handed it to the lady. The housemaid was very grateful that her employer had remembered her and pinned the paper on the wall of her shack on the outskirts of London.

"Several years later," Terry Law recounts in his book *The Power of Praise and Worship,* the woman "became very sick, and Spurgeon, the great preacher, was called to visit her. After he had prayed for her, he walked around the room and noticed this piece of paper on the wall. He turned to the woman and asked her about it, and she told him the story. He added, 'Can you read?' She said, 'No. I have never been taught how to read.' And then he said, 'Madam, this piece of paper is a check for a great deal of money. You did not have to be living in these poor circumstances. You could have been living in the finest houses in London, eating the finest food'" (pp. 85, 86).

Cash your check today, and begin to praise God in your private time with Him, in your small group meeting, and with the congregation where you rejoice in corporate worship. Your eternity with God is as certain as His Spirit's presence in you.

❧ *A PRAYER FOR TODAY* ❧

Help me be aware, Lord, of opportunities to show how happy I am about the guarantee of salvation in Jesus that Your Spirit has given me.

A WELCOME VIEW OF GOD

I keep asking that the God of our Lord Jesus Christ, the glorious
Father, may give you the Spirit of wisdom and revelation,
so that you may know him better. Eph. 1:17, NIV.

Y ou may have 20/20 vision, but unless there is light, you will see nothing. You may also have a brilliant intellect, but without the Holy Spirit of wisdom and revelation, "the eyes of your understanding" (Eph. 1:18) will never be enlightened to comprehend spiritual things. Only in the light of the Spirit can God be known and loved. That is why satanic forces are determined that Christians remain ignorant of the Holy Spirit.

When Catherine Marshall was filled with the Holy Spirit (see July 17 and 18 readings), it seemed that He made her aware of Jesus' presence in her room. "The experience that was my foretaste of immortality," Catherine writes, "occurred in the early-morning hours of that September day back in 1943 when I suddenly knew that the risen Christ was standing beside my bed. . . . This was not a vision. I saw nothing with the retina of my eyes. Yet I 'saw' every detail clearly with the eyes of the Spirit. . . . There was the total encounter of person to Person. The vividness and impact of Jesus' personality in its myriad facets broke over me like waves cresting on a shore: His kingliness (I wanted to fall down on my knees and worship), yet the down-to-earthness of His light touch, His sense of humor, and His loving 'You are taking yourself much too seriously. There's nothing here I can't handle'" *(The Helper,* p. 152).

I have not met many people who have had a similar experience to Catherine Marshall, have you? Yet I do not know anyone who has been filled with the Spirit who has not overflowed with love for Jesus. They want to talk about Him, sing about Him, read about Him, and worship Him. The eyes of their understanding have been enlightened, and they have caught a glimpse of "the riches of the glory of His inheritance" (verse 18, NKJV).

If you pray earnestly each day for the wisdom and revelation of the Holy Spirit, you will not only enjoy walking in the light yourself but also will be able to communicate the knowledge of God in a marvelous way.

❧ A PRAYER FOR TODAY ❧

I'm sorry, Lord, for the times when I haven't seen beyond
the mundane problems and possibilities of this life.

October 18

THE BIBLE'S MOST POWERFUL VERSE

*And what is the exceeding greatness of his power to us-ward
who believe, according to the working of his mighty power. Eph. 1:19.*

*D*anger. Keep out!" the sign read in large red letters on the high fence surrounding the Portland Electric Company's substation. Where there are huge concentrations of power, we always see warnings of danger. Power out of control can become a Chernobyl disaster, destroying thousands.

Although spiritual power can also be dangerous if it is not insulated by love and truth, Paul in his power-packed statement to the Ephesian Christians issues no warnings. He allows the full impact of God's superpower to burst upon his readers, showing them that, rather than destroying life, this power can actually raise the dead (verse 20). The Holy Spirit still has this explosive power available to raise people from spiritual death, give Christians victory over the enemy, and revive the church. But the forces of evil have frightened Christians away from this power by posting the warning signs: "Danger. Keep out!"

Paul combines four power words in this one verse, and with the first he uses two superlatives to create all the emphasis that is possible: "And what is the exceeding greatness of His power [*dynamis*—mighty miraculous power] toward us who believe, according to the working [*energeia*—strong, powerful, efficient] of His mighty [*ischys*—powerful force, ability] power [*kratos*—powerful strength, dominion]" (NKJV). Paul leaves no doubt he is absolutely convinced that the Holy Spirit is no wimp!

What comes to mind when you think of exceptional power? A lot of noise? Forcefulness? Bullying? Pride? Pushiness? The Holy Spirit does not use His incredible power in that way. He is gentle and kind. He honors free will. Only with demons does He use deadly force in His power encounters. You do not have to fear the Holy Spirit's power. It is dangerous only to the powers of darkness. Keep your connection to the power source, and you will always have light and life.

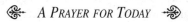 *A PRAYER FOR TODAY*

*Envelop my weakness in Your strength, Lord,
and then enable me to use that spiritual power with others
as carefully and caringly as You have with me.*

No Welcome for the Unholy Spirit

At that time you followed the world's evil way; you obeyed the ruler of spiritual powers in space, the spirit who now controls the people who disobey God. Eph. 2:2, TEV.

C. S. Lewis once wrote: "There are two equal and opposite errors into which our race can fall about the devils. One is to disbelieve their existence. The other is to believe, and to feel an unhealthy interest in them" *(The Best of C. S. Lewis,* p. 13).

Although the devil is not omnipresent, he does have many fallen angels serving as his agents. They use methods of harassment, oppression, and accusation to make life as difficult as possible for people so that God can be blamed for the suffering and hurts of society.

The ruler of these satanic powers is exposed by Paul, and in his superpower letter to the Ephesians Paul shows the weapons and armor that can safeguard a Christian from deception. In fact, prayer and truth, in the power of the Holy Spirit, can bind these evil forces.

Acts magazine, published by the World Map Organization, tells of a missionary working in the mountains of Brazil and Uruguay in South America. One day he was distributing tracts in a village where the border between the two countries ran down the center of the main street. "On the Uruguayan side of the main street, no one would accept his gospel tracts. But on the Brazilian side everyone accepted the tracts graciously and were open to hearing his testimony concerning his faith in Christ. He moved back and forth across the street with the same bewildering results. Then he noticed a woman who refused his tract on the Uruguayan side of the street cross to the Brazilian side. He followed her and again offered her a tract. She accepted it gratefully, and he was able to witness to her about the Lord" (cited in Terry Law, *The Power of Praise in Worship,* pp. 46-48).

The missionary discovered that much intercessory prayer in that area of Brazil had preceded his work, binding the evil powers who had claimed territorial authority. The same had not happened in Uruguay, and the difference was noticeable. If today you use, where you live, the mighty prayer weapons of the Spirit, you will also notice remarkable results.

❧ *A Prayer for Today* ❧

I thank You, Father, that because of Jesus
no evil force can claim to be my prince.

October 20

INTO THE BLANKET ROOM

For through Him we both have access by one Spirit to the Father.
Eph. 2:18, NKJV.

*A*fter a long climb up and down the traditional Mount Sinai, our group returned to Saint Catherine's Monastery, only to find the entrance door closed. We were exhausted and wanted to rest on our bunks, but the notice on the door stated that there would be no access until the monks had completed their prayers. It was late in the evening when we finally entered the monastery, and by now the weather was very cold.

The monks had supplied us with one blanket each, and in the unheated stone building we soon began to feel extremely cold. As the group leader, I entreated the bishop for more blankets, but he stubbornly refused, insisting that this was a monastery and it was good for us to "suffer for the Lord." In the middle of the night one of my group members from tropical New Guinea began to suffer from hypothermia. We shared clothing and blankets with him, but none of us could sleep because of the intense cold.

Eventually I woke the bishop again and spoke with righteous indignation that he could let his guests die of the cold. Reluctantly he agreed to open the blanket room to give us one extra blanket for the man from New Guinea. When we gained access to the room, which was full of warm woolen blankets, we were all suddenly from New Guinea and wrapped ourselves in two or three blankets each. The next morning the monastery was surrounded by snow—the first on the Sinai Peninsula for more than 10 years.

Have you felt spiritually cold, and have you worried that you may soon die from a lack of warmth in your Christian experience? Does access to God seem closed? This will not happen when you are conscious of the Holy Spirit's presence in your life. Through Jesus' sacrifice the key to heaven has been provided, and the Holy Spirit gives you the strength to take the key and open the door into God's wonderful blanket room. You are entitled to the warmth of heaven's love not because you are from New Guinea but because you are a child of God.

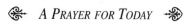 *A PRAYER FOR TODAY*

As Your Spirit takes me into Your presence, Lord,
I feel warm, secure, and comfortable today.

THE WONDER OF THE WORLD

We who believe are carefully joined together with Christ as parts of a beautiful, constantly growing temple for God. And you also are joined with him and with each other by the Spirit, and are part of this dwelling place of God. Eph. 2:21, 22, TLB.

From the top of the 24,000-seat amphitheater in Ephesus I looked east toward the site of one of the seven wonders of the ancient world. Only a few broken remains rising from some swampy land identify the location of the Temple of Diana. In ancient times it had been destroyed and rebuilt seven times—each time a little larger—until in Paul's time it was four times as large as the Parthenon in Athens. At the center of the temple was a statue of the fertility goddess Diana, or Artemis, which was believed to have fallen from heaven, as the sustainer of all life.

Paul explained to the Ephesian Christians that they were also part of a growing temple. The Christian temple was constructed not of stone, marble, and precious metals but of people who loved and served the Lord. As mainstream Christianity fell away from the simplicity of the gospel, it tried from the time of Constantine to construct buildings to rival the grandeur of pagan temples. Some Christianity even today seeks to impress the world with expensive buildings, but the Holy Spirit's temple-building method is still the same. He is joining people who have been born again into fellowships of faith that reveal by practical Christianity the glory of God, who is the only giver and sustainer of life.

Just as the basic unit of society in New Testament times was the household, where family ties held relatives together, so Christianity drew people into households of faith (Gal. 6:10), or households of God (Eph. 2:19). Here, as the family of God, believers prayed and studied together. They nurtured each other and united in the ministry of spiritual gifts. Meeting regularly in houses, without constructing any material buildings, the Christians proclaimed their God's exceeding greatness. In earth's last days the Holy Spirit is still building in the same way. He unites God's people into households of faith where true Christianity flourishes.

A PRAYER FOR TODAY

What a privilege it is, Lord, to be part of Your glorious temple, which is truly the wonder of the world.

October 22

KNOWING THE RIGHT TIME

Which was not made known to men in other generations as it has now been revealed by the Spirit to God's holy apostles and prophets.
Eph. 3:5, NIV.

*H*ave you noticed that God knows the right time to reveal further truth to us? We sometimes look back and thank the Lord that information we were not ready to receive earlier came to us just when we needed it.

John managed the spare parts department in a car dealership when he became a Christian. Not long after this the company asked him to do something that would involve breaking one of the Ten Commandments. When he refused, John lost his job and had to find his way home without the usual company car.

Was this the right time for God to bring the truths of the Bible to John? I saw John walking from work the same day that he was fired and later prayed with him, assuring him that God would honor his faith. After a short but trying time of unemployment, John received a much better job and was greatly blessed. "Even without receiving the new job, I would have been glad for the opportunity to witness as I did at the dealership," John testified. "It was the right time for a number of the people there."

Only after Jesus' death could the Holy Spirit make it known that the Gentiles could be saved without coming under the Jewish religious system. Before the beginning of Christianity such a teaching would have been impossible for the Jews to understand. In fact, it still remained a mystery to those not filled with the Spirit. The wonderful revelation of truth that the Spirit had brought to Paul and to the other apostles and prophets was a joy for him to proclaim, in God's timing.

As the Holy Spirit gives you opportunities to witness, it is important to seek the Lord's leading concerning topics you should present. Always begin by telling of Jesus and His love, and then be sensitive to the circumstances of people's lives and where they are in relationship to spiritual things. I am glad that this is how God has dealt with me.

 *A PRAYER FOR TODAY*

Lord, I thank You for the many indications that You deal with people according to their individual needs.

WHERE IS THE MINISTER?

Of which I became a minister according to the gift of the grace of God given to me by the effective working of His power. Eph. 3:7, NKJV.

*A*lthough the word "channel" has developed some negative connotations because of the New Age movement, it is still true to say that all Christians are to be channels through which God's spiritual gifts can flow. God has ordained every Christian to be a minister.

Once Constantine's methodology gripped the church in the fourth century, ministry became the profession of a few official spokesmen for God. Christians were gathered into large groups, and the laity became passive listeners rather than channels of power. In these last days we see churches breaking the grip of Constantine. Members, especially in congregations where small groups flourish, are being released for ministry.

The Holy Spirit answers, as He did to Paul in Ephesians 3:7, every question we may have about our ministry.

"I haven't had the training or education to be in ministry."

The Spirit says, "Just use the gifts I have given you."

We claim, "But I don't deserve to be in ministry. I'm not good enough."

The Spirit replies, "You have this ministry because of God's grace. Only Jesus was good enough."

We look for an excuse. "How will I have the strength to carry on this ministry?"

The Spirit confirms, "I will give you energy-effective operating power."

Then comes our final question: "What if I fail?"

The Spirit takes responsibility: "You have my *dynamis* guarantee of miracle-working potency."

In the New Testament, ministry was a team activity in households of faith. It involved people pooling their gifts for nurture and outreach. There were no superior or inferior gifts or ministries. Christians were channels for the "best gifts" (1 Cor. 12:31, NKJV), which were the gifts most needed in the present situation. Leaders were servants in the households of God, supporting and coordinating the ministry of each member.

Don't ask today, "Where is the minister?" Instead ask, "How can I minister most effectively for God in the power of the Holy Spirit?"

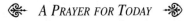 *A PRAYER FOR TODAY*

Renew my energy, Lord, so that I may work effectively for You.

SPIRITUAL LIFTING POWER

That He would grant you, according to the riches of His glory,
to be strengthened with might through His Spirit in the inner man.
Eph. 3:16, NKJV.

This is one of my favorite Bible verses. Often when people say that they will remember me in prayer, I ask them to claim for me this wonderful promise, which is found at the beginning of Paul's greatest prayer. What an amazing truth this is—the Holy Spirit can actually strengthen us with might, which is God's miraculous, *dynamis* superpower!

Years ago I read the well-documented story of a young mother who was working in her kitchen when she heard brakes squealing on the road at the front of her house. A few minutes later, remembering that her little child was playing outside, she rushed out to see what had happened. A crowd had gathered around a small car that was stopped in the middle of the road, and to the mother's distress, she learned that her boy was trapped underneath.

Some people tried to strengthen the mother with hope: "The ambulance is coming. The paramedics will rescue your boy." Others tried to strengthen her with faith: "Just trust in God. Everything will be OK. He will not let you down." Friends were anxious to strengthen the mother with love: "We care for you. We will be here for you no matter what happens." But the deep concern that the young mother had for the child strengthened her with might. In a moment that stunned the onlookers she lifted the front of the car off the ground so that her little boy could be brought out to safety.

When the Holy Spirit strengthens with might, He gives us spiritual lifting power. Every Christian, ministering to others in the power of the Spirit, can "lift the heavy burdens and set the captives free" through Jesus' mighty name. Strengthened with might in our own thoughts and emotions, we also are given supernatural strength to think positively and live victoriously. As the Holy Spirit continually leads us to Jesus the burdens of guilt and fear, which can be heavier than a car, are lifted from us, and we rejoice in the riches of His glory.

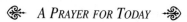 *A PRAYER FOR TODAY*

Father, I praise You for that inner strength You give as the Holy Spirit
leads me through the Word and prayer.

WELCOME, WAVES OF LOVE

That Christ may dwell in your hearts through faith; that you, being rooted and grounded in love, may be able to comprehend with all the saints what is the width and length and depth and height—to know the love of Christ which passes knowledge; that you may be filled with all the fullness of God. Eph. 3:17-19, NKJV.

*C*an you see why the forces of evil are committed to keeping you from understanding what it means to be filled with the Holy Spirit? If this is not clear to you, please pray through Ephesians 3:14-21 again. As you connect Paul's words here to Jesus' own promises concerning the Spirit in John 14-16, you will see that the Holy Spirit is the one who actually represents Jesus in us as Christians and fills us "with all the fullness of God."

Because Jesus has chosen to retain His humanity, the omnipresent Spirit enables Christ to dwell in our hearts by faith. Satan does not want us to understand this, because the more we are filled with the Holy Spirit, the more we are rooted and grounded in God's love (Rom. 5:5). We are also able to comprehend the four dimensions of that love and, as a result, will have super strength against the enemy. Those who are "rooted and grounded" are not blown away by the subtle tricks and violent attacks of the forces of the "prince of the power of the air."

When New York attorney Charles Finney was filled with the Holy Spirit, it seemed to him that "waves and waves of liquid love" flowed through him. (See September 4-9 readings.) Telling of the experience that brought him understanding of Jesus' love, he said: "No words can express the wonderful love that was shed abroad in my heart. . . . It was in fact impossible for me to doubt that the Spirit of God had taken possession of my soul. . . . Instead of feeling that I was sinning all the time, my heart was so full of love that it overflowed" *(Memoirs of Rev. Charles G. Finney,* pp. 20-23).

Now is the time in your own life, small group, and church congregation to let the Spirit raise the victory flag of Jesus' love. Demons will retreat because they drown in the waves of God's liquid love. Praise, pray, sing, talk about, and live the love that goes beyond natural human understanding.

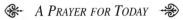

A PRAYER FOR TODAY

Lord God, fill me with all that will enable me to reflect Your character and stabilize me in Your love.

UNTHOUGHT-OF POWER

*Now to Him who is able to do exceedingly abundantly above all
that we ask or think, according to the power that works in us.
Eph. 3:20, NKJV.*

*I*t is popular in Christian literature today to list amazing answers to
prayer as evidence that God can do "exceeding abundantly above all
that we ask or think." As one who has been privileged to see God work
astounding miracles in answer to prayer, I am tempted to retell one of those
experiences now as an illustration of my belief in the Holy Spirit's wonder-
working power. I have a home, health, and ministry as the direct result of
prayer.

A famous TV evangelist, when questioned by the media for driving a very
expensive Mercedes, replied, "Do you expect me to be driving a Honda?" He
claimed to serve a God who can "do exceeding abundantly above all that we
can ask or think," even materially.

But despite the popular use of Ephesians 3:20, Paul is not here talking about
answers to prayer—material or spiritual. To the contrary, he is saying that God
can do much *more* than we can ever ask or request of Him. He can go beyond
our prayers and surprise us with spiritual blessings for which we would never
have thought of asking. I have often been involved with congregations in days,
nights, and weeks of prayer, and yet we have not even touched the fringes of
what God has for us through the mighty power of the Holy Spirit.

The magnitude of God's ability to do far beyond anything we can ask or
think must not stop us asking in faith and thinking of things, however mundane, that we can bring to God in prayer. But it is important that we do not
limit God's work in our lives by our prayers. We must give Him room to display the Holy Spirit's power working in us and through us.

For example, rather than asking that the Holy Spirit enable us to lead one
soul to Jesus each week, we can pray, "Lord, use me to the full extent of my
spiritual, emotional, physical, and intellectual capacity." Instead of just asking the Lord for help overcoming our bad temper, we can pray, "Lord, please
enable me to fully reflect Your character of love."

❧ A PRAYER FOR TODAY ❧

*Father, thank You for doing more than I have ever asked You.
May I never limit Your limitless power by my lack of vision.*

WELCOME, UNITY OF LOVE

Make every effort to keep the unity of the Spirit
through the bond of peace. Eph. 4:3, NIV.

We cannot have the fullness of the Spirit until the whole church is united. At Pentecost the disciples were of one accord in one place."

I agreed and disagreed with the brother who made this categorical statement. Individually any Christian can be filled with the Spirit, even if no other one is interested or united in this blessing. One person filled with the Holy Spirit can be a catalyst to spark interest in the Spirit within a whole congregation.

Corporately, however, unity among a group of church members is essential if a congregation is going to receive fresh revival fire. Evangelist D. L. Moody once said: "There is one thing I have noticed as I have traveled in different countries. I never yet have known the Spirit of God to work where the Lord's people were divided. . . . I think there are a good many ministers in this country who are losing their time; they have lost, some of them, months and years. They have not seen any fruit, and they will not see any fruit because they have a divided church. Such a church cannot grow in divine things. The Spirit of God does not work where there is division, and what we want today is the spirit of unity among God's people, so that the Lord may work" (Dwight L. Moody, *Secret Power,* pp. 124-126).

True unity is possible only through the Holy Spirit because it is based on the fruit of the Spirit and has its foundation in genuine Christian love. Unity that requires uniformity of beliefs, outreach methodologies, and worship style, along with cultural conformity, will always be elusive. Satan will persist in agitating divisiveness in these areas if church members continue to deal with each other in a spirit of intolerance.

When, through the power of the Spirit, believers seek to eliminate divisions, they will leave their differences in God's hands. This does not mean that they will compromise any cherished belief or personal preference, but they can look beyond these, "bearing with one another in love" (Eph. 4:2, NKJV) and joined in the bond of peace made possible by the blood of Jesus.

❧ *A PRAYER FOR TODAY* ❧

Father, on this special day that You've given me,
help me be a unifying factor among the Christians I know.

October 28

NOT ONE AND THE SAME

There is one body and one Spirit, just as you were called in one hope of your calling; one Lord, one faith, one baptism; one God and Father of all, who is above all, and through all, and in you all. Eph. 4:4-6, NKJV.

The church in Ephesus was made up of two distinct groups—Jewish and Gentile Christians. Because they were constantly in conflict, Paul reminded them of the essentials that they had in common. Would Paul need to remind you and your church of these seven "ones"? Would the agreement of your congregation on these basic points pave the way for a great revival?

Instead of using the numeral one, which can confuse the intent of Paul's remarks, read the verses using the word "same," applying them to your church. All members, no matter what their socioeconomic, racial, religious, or cultural background, may now through their conversion belong to the "same" body. They all have the "same" Spirit, the "same" hope, the "same" Lord, the "same" faith, the "same" baptism, and the "same" God, who is actually in them all and is the Father of them all.

The unifying intent of Paul's words has sometimes been missed through dissension caused by taking his "ones" numerically. Is there one body or two (the church visible and invisible)? Is there one Spirit or two (both the Father and the Holy Spirit are called "Spirit")? Are there two Lords (the Father and the Son are both given this title)? Is there one faith or three (saving faith, the spiritual gift of faith, and the Christian faith)? How many baptisms are there (the Bible lists at least six—Moses' baptism, the baptism of suffering, the baptism of fire, John's baptism, water baptism, and baptism with the Holy Spirit)? Is there one Father or two (both God the Father and Jesus are called "Father")?

Perhaps this will be a good test of the willingness of you and your church or group to be open to the unity of the Spirit. After having discussed the "ones" numerically, there will be divergences of belief. Can you now use the word "same" and say, "We may have different opinions, but we are part of the same body and all want to be filled with the same Holy Spirit"? When that happens, you will have taken a giant step toward the last great revival.

 *A PRAYER FOR TODAY*

Lord, bind me together in love and joy with my fellow Christians.

october 29

GRIEVED BY WORKS
AND NOT THE GOSPEL

And do not grieve the Holy Spirit of God, with whom you were sealed
for the day of redemption. Eph. 4:30, NIV.

No one short life affected the Christian missionary movement more than that of David Brainerd. Famous missionaries at the beginning of the nineteenth century were inspired by the Holy Spirit as they read the journal of this young man. Brainerd had a profound influence on the conversion of native Americans, and as a consequence of the hardships he endured, died in his thirtieth year at the home of Jonathan Edwards.

David's father was a member of the King's Council for the colony of Connecticut, but at 14 David was left an orphan. In 1739 he entered Yale and remained first in his class until he was unjustly expelled just before his graduation. He had supported George Whitefield and Jonathan Edwards and criticized a Yale tutor who had opposed the Great Awakening.

Soon after leaving Yale, Brainerd moved into missionary ministry for the Native Americans. Jonathan Edwards later wrote that Brainerd's conversion "was not the end of *his work,* or of the course of his diligent strivings in religion, so neither was it the end of the *work of the Spirit* of God on his heart" (Jonathan Edwards, *The Life of Rev. David Brainerd,* p. 345).

On a number of occasions, however, David Brainerd feared that he had grieved the Holy Spirit. In his journal this great missionary stated: "Hundreds of times I renounced all pretenses of any worth in my duties; . . . yet still I had a secret hope of *recommending* myself to God by my religious duties. . . . Once, I remember, a terrible pang of distress seized me; and the thought of renouncing myself, and standing naked before God, stripped of all goodness, was . . . dreadful to me" *(ibid.,* pp. 13, 14).

An understanding of the meaning of Jesus' sacrifice brought the relief that Brainerd needed. "I wondered that all the world did not see and comply with this way of salvation, entirely by the *righteousness of Christ,*" he wrote with rejoicing in his heart *(ibid.,* p. 25). The Holy Spirit, as Brainerd discovered, is grieved more by our attempts at salvation by works than by anything else.

A PRAYER FOR TODAY

God, may I remember the certainty of salvation I have by the Spirit's sealing
and not be discouraged by looking at my works.

WELCOME, GOSPEL SPIRIT

For the fruit of the light consists in all goodness, righteousness
and truth. Eph. 5:9, NIV.

*A*s a young missionary not yet 30, David Brainerd, wrapped in a bear's skin and coughing blood from his tuberculosis, would lie on the frozen ground at night and cry to God to save the Indians. Little wonder that hundreds came to know the meaning of "goodness, righteousness and truth." Sometimes as he preached, Brainerd would have to use a drunken interpreter, but even then the gospel was able to reach hearts and change lives.

Brainerd began his inspiring ministry in 1742. He worked for the Native Americans first in Massachusetts and New York, then at the forks of the Delaware River, and finally in central New Jersey. Living in shelters he had constructed, sleeping on straw, and eating a sparse diet, he soon found his health deteriorating, and in less than five years he returned to New England. There in the home of Jonathan Edwards and nursed by Edwards' daughter Jerusha, to whom he was engaged, he died on October 9, 1747—a short life of sacrifice, but one bearing the fruit of millions around the world accepting Jesus as a result of the missionaries who followed Brainerd's example.

As a student at Yale, David Brainerd had tried to endear himself to God by his prayers and piety but had found no joy. Instead, as always with those who rely on salvation by works, he suffered from feelings of self-righteousness at one extreme to total dejection and failure at the other. A dramatic change that would affect his whole ministry came to Brainerd when he was filled with the Holy Spirit. A light of "unspeakable glory" seemed to fill his soul. He had an inward apprehension of God that revealed the real meaning of goodness, righteousness, and truth.

"At this time the *way of salvation* opened to me with such infinite wisdom, suitableness, and excellency, that I wondered I should ever think of any other way of salvation; I was amazed that I had not dropped my own contrivances, and complied with this lovely, blessed, and excellent way before," Brainerd wrote (Jonathan Edwards, *The Life of Rev. David Brainerd,* p. 25).

Have you allowed the Holy Spirit to give you this wonderful fruit of His presence in your life? It will certainly make a great difference.

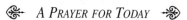

❦ *A PRAYER FOR TODAY* ❧

Father, grow the fruit in my life that will be a faithful witness
to the light of the gospel.

october 31

UNDER THE INFLUENCE

And do not be drunk with wine, in which is dissipation;
but be filled with the Spirit. Eph. 5:18, NKJV.

*A*t least eight times the New Testament speaks of people being filled with the Holy Spirit. It also states that it is possible to be filled with indignation, envy, confusion, and unrighteousness. "Filled" in this setting means to be dominated, possessed, or controlled by an emotion, attitude, or outside force. Have you ever been filled with anger or love? If so, you will know how either one can affect your thinking, actions, and even your appetite. In the same way, a person who is filled with alcohol is, unfortunately, fully under its influence.

Twice Paul has stated that the Ephesians were sealed with the Holy Spirit (Eph. 1:13; 4:30). The Spirit had come to dwell in them at conversion and was God's guarantee of their eternal inheritance (Eph. 1:14). But now Paul was concerned that they be totally surrendered to the Spirit each day so that He could be the controlling influence of their lives.

Many born-again Christians, like physician Walter L. Wilson, have testified of the great change that came in their lives when they were filled with the Spirit. Dr. Wilson's conversion gave him a love for Scripture and a diligence in serving God, but he was troubled by the ineffectiveness of his Christian experience and outreach.

Then came January 14, 1914. Dr. Wilson lay on the carpet in his study as he was deeply convicted of his need to be filled with the Spirit. Listen to the prayer that changed his life. "There in the quiet of that late hour, I said to the Holy Spirit, 'My Lord, I have mistreated You all my Christian life. I have treated You like a servant. When I wanted You I called for You; when I was about to engage in some work I beckoned You to come and help me perform my task. . . . I shall do so no more. Just now I give You this body of mine; from my head to my feet I give it to You. . . . I hand it over to You to live in it the life that You please'" *(They Found the Secret,* p. 123).

No wonder Dr. Wilson became a beloved physician whom the Holy Spirit used to win a great harvest of souls for the Saviour.

 *A PRAYER FOR TODAY*

Holy Spirit, I give You permission to take possession of every part of me
and use me as You choose.

November 1

SINGING IN THE SPIRIT

Speaking to one another in psalms and hymns and spiritual songs, singing and making melody in your heart to the Lord. Eph. 5:19, NKJV.

Great revivals of Holy Spirit power have always been accompanied by inspirational Christian music and singing. Writing of events surrounding the mighty outpouring of the Holy Spirit upon the Moravian Christians on the estate of Count Zinzendorf in August 1727, John Greenfield says: "The baptism with the Holy Spirit upon our fathers two centuries ago produced such a spiritual floodtide of sacred song as had not been experienced in the Christian Church before or since" *(Power From on High,* p. 57).

Like the mighty Mississippi overflowing its banks in the great floods of 1993, the Holy Spirit broke down the barriers of traditionalism and lifeless religion and flooded the lives of Christians with songs that glorified Jesus, the wonderful Saviour.

Paul tells us that Christians will be able to minister to each other in "psalms and hymns and spiritual songs," indicating a variety in sacred music. Commenting on this, Professor John Rea, an editor of the *Wycliffe Bible Encyclopedia,* says: "The 'psalms' were almost certainly the canonical Old Testament psalms sung to instrumental accompaniment. The 'hymns' may denote Christian compositions sung with or without music. 'Spiritual songs' were those inspired on the spot by the Holy Spirit, unpremeditated words with unrehearsed melodies sung 'in the Spirit' " *(The Holy Spirit in the Bible,* pp. 295, 296).

There is no indication that Spirit-inspired music was given to the church for performance by a few professionals. Rather, it was part of the admonition and sharing between brothers and sisters in the faith (Col. 3:16).

As you pray for the Holy Spirit to fill you, your small group, and church congregation, do not be surprised at the way a variety of Christian music will come to the forefront. You will sing the great old hymns with new meaning and fervor. Scripture songs, choruses, and psalms will be filled with a significance that will make them come alive for you. Even spontaneous music may come from your lips, as happened in the early Christian church. In all this Jesus will be glorified and ministry among believers will take place.

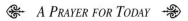

❧ *A PRAYER FOR TODAY* ❧

Father, please fill my heart with a new song of blessing and joy.

November 2

RESISTING ENEMY FORCES

For we are not fighting against people made of flesh and blood,
but against persons without bodies—the evil rulers of the unseen world,
those mighty satanic beings and great evil princes of darkness who rule
this world; and against huge numbers of wicked spirits in the
spirit world. Eph. 6:12, TLB.

Reading Paul's description of evil forces can make us overly apprehensive about them. I like the way that Neil T. Anderson, in *The Bondage Breaker,* gives this a more healthy perspective. "Some Christians are a little paranoid about evil powers, suspecting that demons lurk around every corner just waiting to possess them. That's an unfounded fear. Our relationship to demonic powers in the spiritual realm is a lot like our relationship to germs in the physical realm. We know that there are germs all around us: in the air, in the water, in our food, in other people, even in us. But do you live in constant fear of catching some disease? Not unless you're a hypochondriac! . . .

"It's the same in the spiritual realm. Demons are like little invisible germs looking for someone to infect. We are never told in Scripture to be afraid of them. You just need to be aware of their reality and commit yourself to live a righteous life in spite of them. Should you come under attack, deal with it and go on with life. Remember: the only thing big about a demon is its mouth. Demons are habitual liars. In Jesus Christ the Truth, you are equipped with all the authority and protection you need to deal with anything they throw at you" (p. 77).

The Holy Spirit enables every Christian to "be strong in the Lord, and in the power of his might" (Eph. 6:10). This involves being clothed, as Paul says twice, in the "whole armor of God." No demonic germ can penetrate the protective clothing that the Spirit has tailor-made for each Christian. The armor of God does not prevent you from being attacked and may even provoke violent assaults from evil forces. You can be certain, however, that if your armor is "whole," you will be "able to stand" victorious. Sing God's praise. You are filled with the super power of the Holy Spirit.

❧ *A PRAYER FOR TODAY* ❧

Lord, please make me aware of any gap that I've allowed to open in my armor
and forgive me for any sin into which I've fallen as a result.

WELCOME, POWER OF TRUTH
AND RIGHTEOUSNESS

Stand therefore, having girded your waist with truth, having put on the breastplate of righteousness. Eph. 6:14, NKJV.

The Holy Spirit leads us into all truth and assures us of righteousness. In this way He provides two critical elements of armor against the forces of evil who base their strategy on lies and deception. If the powers of evil use past or present circumstances to convince you that you yourself are evil or worthless, defeat that lie with the truth that you are a child of God, and that your sins are covered by the blood of your Saviour Jesus and cannot be held against you.

If you come into conflict with evil influences, remember that while they can plant lying, deceptive thoughts in your mind, they cannot read your thoughts and are not sure that they have been successful unless they hear words or see confirming actions. If you are being attacked outwardly or have indicated in any way that evil is affecting your thinking, it is important to resist Satan by affirming truth and righteousness aloud in prayer. In this way he can hear what is happening and be put to flight.

I was holding revival meetings in an area of Arizona where there is a great deal of activity by satanic cults. Usually I sleep well, but at about 3:00 a.m. each morning I would awake and begin to wrestle with overpowering negative thoughts: *Give up! You're unworthy to do these meetings. You're going to die.*

After a week of praying to the Lord for help, He brought a friend to stay in the house with me. When I shared with him what I was experiencing, he explained that this was happening at a prime time of night for spirit activity. I must pray aloud in the name of Jesus, he said, defeating these lies with the belt of truth and the breastplate of Christ's righteousness.

"Father, I thank You that I am Your child," I prayed aloud when I was awakened the next night. "I claim the righteousness of Jesus my Saviour and resist Satan's lies in the name of Jesus." Soon I was able to sleep again, and within a few nights was entirely free from this attack.

Remember, the enemy cannot stand in the presence of the truth.

⟡ *A PRAYER FOR TODAY* ⟡

I praise You, Lord, for the mighty power of the Holy Spirit as He glorifies Jesus in my life, defeating the attacks of the enemy.

November 4

BIG SHOES AND SHIELD

And having shod your feet with the preparation of the gospel of peace;
above all, taking the shield of faith with which you will be able to
quench all the fiery darts of the wicked one. Eph. 6:15, 16, NKJV.

Jodi's husband was not a Christian, so she noticed that at times the enemy used Sam to attack her and her commitment to God's service. His accusations were unreasonable and unjust and were far from the truth. Jodi determined, in the power of the Holy Spirit, that she would walk in the shoes of the gospel of peace. Because she knew who she was through the gospel of Jesus' grace and love, she did not need to retaliate to her husband's negative onslaughts. Jodi was calm and walked in peace, which also, eventually, found its way into Sam's heart.

As evil forces fire their blazing darts at God's children, the Holy Spirit enables them to move the shield of faith quickly into place. Faith means believing God's Word so that we become willing to do in the Spirit's power what it says.

Quin Sherrer and Ruthanne Garlock tell the story of Chris, who came from a dysfunctional family and suffered abuse as a child. Even after becoming a Christian she was tormented by thoughts of suicide until prayer and counseling helped free her of this oppression.

"Then I learned," Chris says, "that the enemy always tests your deliverance. Though I knew the Holy Spirit had powerfully ministered to me, I would occasionally have thoughts of suicide again. I had to use the shield of faith to deflect those fiery darts. Over and over I would say to the enemy, 'Satan, I resist you. I have been delivered in Jesus' name. I will live and not die. You are defeated, and I command you to flee.' I persisted until the enemy stopped bothering me in that area. I am totally free" *(A Woman's Guide to Spiritual Warfare, p. 51).*

Recently on television news I watched riot police deal with some violent demonstrators. The police had large, strong shields that protected their bodies. Similarly, as a Christian you have a spiritual shield. Keep enlarging your shield of faith by memorizing Scripture, listening to biblical sermons, becoming involved in a small-group Bible study, and learning new gospel songs.

❦ *A PRAYER FOR TODAY* ❧

Lord, help me trust only the true way of salvation and safety.

DEFENDING AND ATTACKING

*And take the helmet of salvation, and the sword of the Spirit,
which is the word of God. Eph. 6:17, NKJV.*

*M*otorcyclists must wear helmets—it's the law," the sign says as you drive into Oregon. Years ago I was riding a motorcycle when a car stopped directly in front of me. I knew that running into the back of a car at the speed I was traveling could be fatal, so I threw my motorcycle to one side and skidded on my helmet past the other side of the car. When I later looked at the damage to that protective covering, I was certainly glad that it was not my head that had hit the road. Are you wearing your helmet of salvation? It's a law of spiritual survival.

The helmet that protects the mind is the assurance of salvation which the Spirit uses to guard the thinking of a born-again Christian. If you are unsure of salvation, you will find yourself unprotected when Satan hits your head on the hard road of doubt or temptation.

While helmets still have a role in a world on the brink of the twenty-first century, swords have become obsolete. Most people, however, have seen illustrations and movies depicting pregun times and know the importance of swords as an ancient method of attack. The sword of the Spirit can chase the enemy right out of the battle, because this sword represents the Holy Spirit's enabling Christians to speak the words of God. Because God's Word is truth and the enemy's attacks are based on lies, the sword of the Spirit is always victorious.

Bible students have noticed that Paul uses *rhēma* rather than *logos* to describe the "word" of God in this verse. While we cannot make too much of the distinction between these words, as some in the charismatic movement have done, we can recognize an important point of emphasis here. The sword is not so much the Word written *[logos]* in a book as it is the Word spoken *[rhēma]*. An utterance from God, inspired by the Holy Spirit and spoken aloud by a Christian, will defeat the enemy. Very often this spoken word will include portions of the written Word, especially relating to the gospel, which have been stored in the believer's mind.

❧ *A PRAYER FOR TODAY* ❧

*Lord, hide the word of Your gospel in my mind
as a strong weapon against evil.*

HOLDING THE ROPE

*And pray in the Spirit on all occasions with all kinds of prayers
and requests. With this in mind, be alert and always keep on praying
for all the saints. Eph. 6:18, NIV.*

*D*r. Tom Lovorn tells the story of a fishing village that lay at the mouth of a turbulent river. One day a cry rang out: "Boy overboard!" A large crowd gathered quickly. Someone ran with a rope, and a strong swimmer volunteered to rescue the drowning boy. Tying one end of the rope to his waist, the swimmer threw the other end to the crowd and plunged into the raging water.

Every eye was on the man as he swam against the strong current and reached the boy. At last he grabbed the youngster in his powerful arms. "Pull the rope!" the man cried.

The villagers looked at each other. "Who's holding the rope?" they asked. Then they saw that no one was holding it! In the excitement of watching the rescue, no one had caught the rope. Its end had slipped into the water. Powerless to help, the villagers watched two precious lives drown because none of them had made it their business to hold the rope *(Why Build a House of Prayer?* p. 15).

It is absolutely essential that Christians hold the rope for each other in prayer. "I'll be praying for you" must be more than a courteous platitude. We may be swimming against the currents of evil or almost ready to drown in the turbulent waters of guilt, depression, and discouragement, but if we are certain that others are upholding us in prayer, then we will be able to survive.

The strength and persistence to hold the rope of prayer for another come from the Holy Spirit. We make our supplications, our earnest requests to God, through the moving of the Spirit within us. Often there is such urgency and fervor that our prayers for another are beyond words. Then the Spirit joins our hearts to the Father "with groanings which cannot be uttered" (Rom. 8:26). The Spirit also enables us to open our hearts to God in praise for what we believe He will do in our own life and in the lives of those who are on our rope-holding list.

❦ *A Prayer for Today* ❦

*Lord, help me to be always in connection with You in prayer, knowing that the
Holy Spirit will, in this way, bring help and strength.*

WELCOME, DELIVERER

*For I know that through your prayers and the help given by the
Spirit of Jesus Christ, what has happened to me will turn out for
my deliverance. Phil. 1:19, NIV.*

The Holy Spirit is definitely involved in a ministry of deliverance. He delivers not only from demonic bondage, slavery to sin, and guilt and fear by the blood of Jesus, but sometimes even from physical danger. If this were a trivia contest, I could ask, "Do you know the name of the U.S. president whose train ran through a house on the way to his inauguration?" Former General Conference president William A. Spicer tells about the embarrassing train experience of Zachary Taylor, his family, staff, and leading politicians.

On the evening of March 5, 1849, Mr. and Mrs. William Kitson were eating their evening meal in their house by the railroad tracks near Trenton, New Jersey, when someone shouted that the presidential train was approaching. Mrs. Kitson stood in the yard with her daughter, while Mr. Kitson remained in the house doorway with two of their sons. Suddenly Mrs. Kitson heard the word "Run!" She resisted, thinking how silly it would be to run away when nothing was happening. Again the urgent voice said "Run!" and this time she opened the gate and ran to the back of the house. At the same time a voice told Mr. Kitson to "jump out the door! Jump quickly!" He grabbed his children and jumped, rolling over a number of times on the ground.

At the moment Mr. and Mrs. Kitson obeyed the direction of the Holy Spirit, the presidential train left the tracks, ran over the very spot where Mrs. Kitson and her daughter had been standing, and crashed through the house doorway where Mr. Kitson and his two sons had been waiting.

"'You cannot convince either of us, who heard separate voices at the same time telling us to get out of the way, that God does not look after His own today just as He did in Bible times,' they said later. Mr. Kitson added, "And you can be sure that we'll always think of our living Lord and about His love for His children every time we hear those two words 'run' or 'jump'" *(The Hand That Still Intervenes,* pp. 73-75).

✦ *A PRAYER FOR TODAY* ✦

*I may not always be delivered physically, Lord, but Your Spirit
will always be ready to deliver me from any spiritual danger.*

November 8

FELLOWSHIP FRANCHISES

If you have any encouragement from being united with Christ, if any comfort from his love, if any fellowship with the Spirit, if any tenderness and compassion, then make my joy complete by being like-minded, having the same love, being one in spirit and purpose. Phil. 2:1, 2, NIV.

Christianity was never designed to be a solo religion or an impersonal, mass meeting of believers. True Christianity is people caring for people, nurturing and helping one another, reaching out and drawing others into their circle of love. This is how the *koinōnia,* or fellowship of the Spirit, works. Those who are in communication with the Holy Spirit will be His agents of grace.

Christianity has moved from being community-centered, neighborhood-centered, to being church building-centered. But the Spirit is leading Christianity back to its roots. I talked to a young pastor recently, who said, "I would like to start a new church that is based on the New Testament model. I would train 10 or 12 small group leaders and release them for ministry. We would grow many small groups and come together for a combined festival of praise in a rented building or stadium about once a month."

I like the vision of Carl F. George, director of the Charles E. Fuller Institute of Evangelism and Church Growth. "Thus the church of the future, though far bigger than a typical parish of today, will not be known for its central meeting spot, but for its small group ministry 'franchise.' In the business community, a franchiser like McDonald's provides know-how and product recognition, while the local franchisee supplies the local contact with customers. The franchiser empowers the local group as an authorized provider of desirable products and services.

"I believe pastors and church leadership will adopt a franchiser attitude toward their member-ministers in each section of a town. Members will be encouraged to start up neighborhood outlets, such as home-cell groups, throughout their church's 'service area.' They will be empowered through training from their church's leadership" *(Prepare Your Church for the Future,* pp. 22, 23).

Ask the Holy Spirit now to show you how you can be part of this movement of love that will prepare the church for our Lord's return.

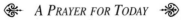

❦ A PRAYER FOR TODAY ❦

Spirit, I pray for my joy to be fulfilled in true ministry for You.

WELCOME TO SPIRIT-FILLED WORSHIP

*For we are the true circumcision, who worship in the Spirit of God
and glory in Christ Jesus and put no confidence in the flesh.
Phil. 3:3, NASB.*

The biblical words for worship always describe actions of the body. They talk of bowing down, reaching out the hands, falling down, bending the knees, and even, in the New Testament, an attitude of "kissing toward" God. True worship is difficult to describe and even more difficult to prescribe. Churches have tended to ritualize the actions and liturgy of worship so that it has become for many a formalized "confidence in the flesh" that, like an inoculation, stops them from experiencing the real thing.

Terry Law, writing in the *Power of Praise and Worship,* says: "Worship is a response to a relationship with God, but that relationship is very intimate and it is very difficult for another person to describe exactly what it is. It does involve fellowship. It does involve personal revelation of God to the individual. But it basically is the outpouring of inner thoughts to God, often accompanied by emotional and expressive actions of the body. But we always must remember that it is almost impossible to describe in words the inner sense and feeling that permeates the relationship. As the old Scotsman said, 'It is better felt than telt'" (pp. 139, 140).

The Holy Spirit will enable small groups and large congregations to create an atmosphere that is conducive to worship. Music, prayer, praise, testimony, giving, and the preaching of the Word will have a part in this. None of these things, however, is in itself worship but is merely a vehicle by which hearts may reach out in adoration to God. Attempts to mandate acceptable worship forms for another person always fail because in true worship the Holy Spirit connects individual personalities to God.

As the Holy Spirit inspires true worship He does not exalt Himself or the worshiper, but as Paul says, He glorifies Jesus. Your worship, in fact, will reflect your understanding of Jesus and the Father. While it is possible for public, manufactured worship to be an insult to the character of our God of love and joy, there is no doubt that you can worship today in Spirit and in truth.

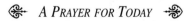

Lord, I bow down before You to worship and adore You as my God.

November 10

FILLING THE CORE

Their destiny is destruction, their god is their stomach, and their glory is in their shame. Their mind is on earthly things. Phil. 3:19, NIV.

I often wondered why Paul singled out for special condemnation people with an eating problem. Are they any worse than people whose god is money, sex, or power, for instance? The answer is obviously no. A person may overeat to help deaden a much deeper pain. In the same way, people whose gods are money, sex, or power may be trying to compensate for feelings of inferiority, failure, or rejection. Apparently, those who are finally lost have chosen to resist the Holy Spirit, who enables us to deal with root causes within rather than merely struggling with external symptoms.

Notice the helpful explanation of Canadian counselor James Moore: "Paul gives more insight into the evil desires that draw us to sin when he describes certain enemies of the gospel: 'Their god is their stomach' (Phil. 3:19). The word translated 'stomach' in this verse means deep, hollow space or empty core. According to Vine's dictionary, it refers to the 'innermost part of a man.' It is the Greek word found in John 7:38, 'out of his *inmost being* will flow streams of living water.' The image here is of an empty space that compels a person to seek to fill it with the same intensity someone dying of thirst would search for water" *(Discipleship Journal,* November-December 1992, p. 45).

As one of the philosophers has said, there is a God-shaped space in each one of us that only He can fill. Our quest to fill that space at the core of our being with anything but God leads us, like the prodigal son, into the far country. The far country is a state of mind in which there are "famine, husks, and swine" but no core satisfaction. Lust can never be satisfied, because it is impossible to obtain enough of any substitute to fill that "God-shaped space." We can be filled only at the Father's house.

As Jesus taught in John 7, it is the Holy Spirit who has been given to fill the Christian's life. Paul emphasized that through the Holy Spirit in our inner being, we are filled with all the fullness of God, and Christ dwells in our hearts by faith (Eph. 3:14-21).

❦ A PRAYER FOR TODAY ❧

Father, as Your Spirit continually fills me I know that all the other necessary things of this life fit into their rightful place.

WELCOME, MESSAGE OF LOVE

Who also declared to us your love in the Spirit. Col. 1:8, NKJV.

John Jasper was born under the yoke of slavery in Williamsburg, Virginia, in 1812 and remained a slave for more than 50 years. "In 1831, during a celebration on a public square, John heard a message which troubled his soul. Deeply convicted by the Holy Spirit, twenty-five days later he openly confessed his sins and united with a church. By God's grace he began to lose his hatred for those who had enslaved him and to love the unlovable" *(More Than Conquerors,* p. 192).

John had much reason for hatred. On the first night of his marriage to another slave, his owner sent him away so that he would never see his bride again. Although Jasper's only education was seven months of spelling from another slave, eight years after his conversion he was "convicted that the power of the Holy Spirit had been given him to preach the gospel." He believed that "whom God calls, He will also qualify," and this was confirmed in the remarkable gift of preaching that John received. Large numbers would gather to hear him speak even at funerals, where the Spirit would enable him to declare with eloquence God's love.

Of one such meeting an observer said: "He painted scene after scene. He lifted the people up to the sun and sank down to despair. He plucked them out of hard places and filled them with shouting" *(ibid.,* p. 193).

John Jasper preached the love of Jesus in the power of the Spirit for 24 years as a slave and for another 39 years as a free man. He "went from the slave house to the church house, where all who heard him—white and black, rich and poor, slave and free—were touched by the power of his preaching about a Saviour whom he faithfully served. . . . Contemporaries recognized the Holy Spirit's anointing on his preaching" *(ibid.,* p. 194).

Like Paul's friend Epaphras—and John Jasper—we may each declare our "love in the Spirit." It is not hard to do. Love is a fruit of the Spirit (Gal. 5:22), and the Spirit pours God's love into the lives of those He fills (Rom. 5:5). Love can be taught and preached, and it can be revealed in practical Christianity.

❦ *A PRAYER FOR TODAY* ❧

Dear Lord, help me see the unique way
You have for me to reveal Your love today.

November 12

WELCOME TO FULL ASSURANCE

For our gospel did not come to you in word only, but also in power, and in the Holy Spirit and in much assurance, as you know what kind of men we were among you for your sake. 1 Thess. 1:5, NKJV.

Blessed assurance, Jesus is mine!" the blind hymn writer Fanny Crosby wrote as she knelt in prayer in 1873. It is surprising how many Christians who are "born of His Spirit, washed in His blood" sing this song and yet do not have the blessed assurance of salvation. Some even speak as if it would be a sin to claim that now, through Jesus' sacrifice, they are ready for heaven.

The New Testament teaches that Christians can have full assurance by understanding the significance of the gospel (Col. 2:2). They can also have the full assurance of Jesus as their High Priest (Heb. 6:11, 19, 20) and the full assurance of faith (Heb. 10:22). If the preaching and teaching where you fellowship in a congregation or small group does not confirm full assurance in you, it could be that the gospel is coming to you, as Paul said, in "word only."

"Word only" communication gives the theory of the gospel but does not reveal its power. The *dynamis* that works miracles and changes lives is missing. This happens because the Holy Spirit has been neglected or rejected, and a church has been left with powerless word-only religion. Little wonder that in such a situation "blessed assurance" is a cliché that has no meaning, and few are, in Fanny Crosby's words, "praising [the] Saviour all the day long."

Notice the emphasis of Adventist pioneer Ellen White, who was deeply concerned that her church be filled with the Spirit. "We are to proclaim the truth to the world, not in a tame, spiritless way, but in demonstration of the Spirit and power" *(Evangelism,* p. 121). "When the free gift of Christ's righteousness is not presented, the discourses are dry and spiritless" *(Selected Messages,* book 1, p. 158). "When we have an assurance, which is bright and clear, of our own salvation we shall exhibit cheerfulness and joyfulness, which becomes every follower of Jesus Christ" *(Evangelism,* p. 630). Now that is something to sing about!

❧ A PRAYER FOR TODAY ❧

Lord, I praise You again today that my certainty of salvation depends entirely on Jesus and not on my own works.

Unshakable Inner Joy

And you became followers of us and of the Lord,
having received the word in much affliction,
with joy of the Holy Spirit. 1 Thess. 1:6, NKJV.

Gabriela had just completed a day of shopping with her children when she noticed a pain in her hip. *Perhaps walking around all day in high heels has caused this,* she thought. It was, however, one of the first symptoms of a rare spinal virus that soon paralyzed her from the chest down. After six weeks in the hospital, Gabriela came home in a wheelchair, and one year later she still needs help to walk around.

When I first met Gabriela years ago, she was a Roman Catholic, who in search of a closer walk with God, had begun to attend the Gresham Seventh-day Adventist church. Although she had faced many hard times in her childhood and marriage, Gabriela had strong faith and a determination to serve the Lord in some special ministry. Following evangelistic meetings where she "received the word," Gabriela was baptized and continued to be filled with the joy of the Spirit despite the afflictions of the enemy.

Now, about four years later, I spoke to Gabriela again and heard of her terrible illness and continual pain. Had this shaken the core of joy that the Spirit had placed in her heart? As she talked on the telephone Gabriela said, "God has been so close to me all through my illness. The Holy Spirit keeps filling me with peace and joy, even though the doctors have told me that there is no medicine or treatment for my illness. I want to be a living testimony to my great God. Our joy as Christians does not depend on being well-known, writing a book, having successful children, or earning a lot of money. Our joy is based on Jesus' love in the power of the Spirit. My one desire now is to begin a ministry for young people."

The inner core of joy cannot be shaken in the life of a believer who is filled with the Holy Spirit. The Spirit places around that core of joy the shock absorbers of the assurance of salvation, the certainty of being a child of God, and the knowledge of forgiveness and victory power. People like Gabriela are a living testimony of the inner, unshakable glory of God in the lives of His people.

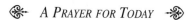

A Prayer for Today

In the midst of affliction, Father, help me reveal true joy and peace.

November 14

POWER TO DO

For God did not call us to be impure, but to live a holy life.
Therefore, he who rejects this instruction does not reject man but God,
who gives you his Holy Spirit. 1 Thess. 4:7, 8, NIV.

*I*t is helpful to receive instruction. It is even more helpful to receive the power to carry it out. Often small children are bombarded with hundreds of instructions each day, but how it is all possible is usually not discussed. "Just do what you are told," an exhausted parent may shout. Consequently, an overdose of demands can quickly lead a child into an attitude of defeat. "I can't do all that's expected of me, so why even try?"

Contrary to popular opinion, God does not make many demands on His children. He is not bossing them around all day but usually gives His people a lot of freedom in their lives. The instructions that He does give, however, are always connected to the Holy Spirit's facilitating power. Everything God asks His children to do is an opportunity to see the Spirit at work. As the familiar quotation says: "All His biddings are enablings."

"I have had enough of this church," a man informed his pastor. "It is nothing but rules and regulations. You're always asking for money, and the members have a cold, judgmental spirit. I can't live up to your demands, and I don't know who can."

The pastor had heard words like this a number of times recently and noticed that attendance was dropping at his worship services. "What's gone wrong?" he asked at our Holy Spirit Fellowship retreat.

After three days of prayer, listening to other ministers, and study in a Spirit-filled atmosphere, the pastor testified that the Lord had led him to the answer: "I can see now that I need to be teaching much more about the power of the Holy Spirit and helping my people experience this in their lives. I want to talk much more about Jesus and the certainty of salvation. At this retreat I've experienced joy in my own life, and it's made such a difference to me that I'm excited about what God can do to help me turn my ministry around."

This pastor and his congregation were not disappointed.

❧ A PRAYER FOR TODAY ❧

Thank You, Lord, for giving instructions about holy living
so that the possibilities of Holy Spirit power can be revealed
in my life through the strength that Jesus gives.

November 15

POURING WATER ON THE FIRE

Do not quench the Spirit. Do not despise prophecies. Test all things;
hold fast what is good. 1 Thess. 5:19-21, NKJV.

The Holy Spirit strengthened Gabriela with joy through more than a year of painful and debilitating illness. Often the Spirit would minister to her through spiritual gifts given to people in the two small groups that meet weekly in her home. Paul taught that Christians are to pray especially that they may prophesy so they can bring "edification, and exhortation, and comfort" to each other (1 Cor. 14:1, 3). This is done through special prayer, testimony, and spiritual counsel.

This prophetic gift is not infallible revelation but is to be tested by Scripture so that all that was good can be held onto and be used for blessing. Those who resist God's messages are in danger of pouring water on the Spirit's fire. Notice that Paul ties together quenching the Spirit, prophesying, and testing in 1 Thessalonians 5:19-21.

Each group in Gabriela's home spends time fellowshipping, praising, praying, and studying. During a Friday evening meeting, which was led by a former rabbi who is now a Christian, Gabriela was impressed by the Holy Spirit to pray for the woman next to her. She had never met Kristi before and did not know what to pray, so Gabriela initially resisted the Spirit's leading. Eventually, she held Kristi's hand as they prayed together.

When the prayer time was over, the Spirit impressed Gabriela to give her testimony. Again she resisted, but it was as if the Spirit would not let it rest. He had a message for Kristi that He wanted her to hear that Friday night. Still holding Kristi's hand Gabriela told the group about her divorce years earlier and how Satan had tried to destroy her life. She praised God for the victory and deliverance that had come to her through prayer. Finally she gave the special message of encouragement that the Lord had given her for someone in the room.

When the meeting was over, Kristi said, "Gabriela, your prayer and testimony were exactly what I needed tonight. I did not know how I was going to carry on in my situation, but the Lord has used you to give me hope."

❧ A PRAYER FOR TODAY ❧

Lord, I don't want to be one who pours cold water on Your Spirit's working.
Give me the wisdom to hold on to and share the good.

November 16

NOT A NEW METHOD OF SALVATION

But we ought always to thank God for you, brothers loved by the Lord, because from the beginning God chose you to be saved through the sanctifying work of the Spirit and through belief in the truth.
2 Thess. 2:13, NIV.

Three errors have crept into Christianity through misunderstanding Paul's words in this verse. First, did God arbitrarily, long ago, choose some people to be saved and others lost? Second, does the Holy Spirit save only those who are sanctified and holy? Third, is it necessary to believe a list of correct doctrinal truths in order to be saved?

Paul makes it clear that there is only one means of salvation—the gospel that he preached (2 Thess. 2:14). Salvation is a gift, given by God's grace and accepted by faith (Eph. 2:7-9). God's grace, justification, and righteousness are freely provided and available to all people (Rom. 5:18). "Obeying the truth" means accepting by faith Jesus Christ and His righteousness. Paul says that those who believe they can be saved by the "works of the law" are "bewitched" (Gal. 3:1-3) and could be deceived by antichrist (2 Thess. 2:9, 10).

Sonny was in doubt about his salvation. "I'm not sure if I'm one of the people God has chosen," he said to me in a spirit of hopelessness.

"It's not the people but the method of salvation that has been predestined," I replied. "The Holy Spirit desires to bring to all people the opportunity of accepting Jesus."

"I do believe in Jesus and attend church, but I certainly don't feel holy enough to be saved," Sonny continued. "I'm not even sure that I understand or believe everything that my church teaches."

"Sonny," I explained, "when you accepted Jesus as your Saviour, the Holy Spirit came into your life, and through the ministry of the Spirit, God from that moment on counted your life as sanctified, or [w]holy His [1 Cor. 6:11]. [See the September 10 reading.] Gradually the Holy Spirit leads you into deeper understandings and facets of truth. He does this not to make salvation more difficult or to change it from grace to works, but to give you more joy in the Lord and a clearer witness for Him."

Are you thanking God today for your assurance in the truth of the gospel?

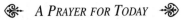

A PRAYER FOR TODAY

May I grow daily, Lord, in my ability to live the Christian life.

November 17

SOMETHING GREAT TO SING ABOUT

No one can deny how great is the secret of our religion: He appeared in human form, was shown to be right by the Spirit, and was seen by angels. He was preached among the nations, was believed in throughout the world, and was taken up to heaven. 1 Tim. 3:16, TEV.

*M*any New Testament scholars believe that Paul's words to Timothy in today's verse could have been part of an early Christian hymn that glorified the wonderful Saviour Jesus. Perhaps if you can find or compose a suitable tune, you will sing the six lines of this spiritual song, remembering how much Jesus meant to Christians in the first century. They loved to sing with "grace in [their] hearts to the Lord" (Col. 3:16).

As Jesus has been exalted in great revivals, people who have been filled with the Spirit have always burst into songs of their experience with the Lord. The Welsh revival that exerted such a dramatic influence on twentieth-century Christianity was no exception. David Matthews in his eyewitness account, "I Saw the Welsh Revival," described the services: "Such marvelous singing, quite extempore, could only be created by a supernatural power, and that power the divine Holy Spirit. No choir, no organ—just spontaneous, unctionized soul-singing. . . . Singing, sobbing, praying intermingled and proceeded without intermission" (quoted by Colin C. Whittaker in *Great Revivals,* p. 112).

As Paul said to Timothy, the Holy Spirit showed Jesus' ministry to be right and true. The Spirit worked through Jesus' teaching and miracles to convict those who observed Him that He was indeed the Saviour of the world. Many resisted the Spirit, but those who surrendered were filled with joy and peace in spite of hardship and persecution. No wonder they wanted to sing psalms, hymns, and spiritual songs (Eph. 5:18, 19).

Evan Roberts, God's instrument in the great Welsh revival, often prayed in this way: "Lord Jesus, help us through the Holy Spirit to come face to face with the cross. . . . Glorify Thy Son in this meeting. Oh, Holy Spirit, do Thou work through us and in us now." As God answered this prayer, the Welsh sang praises to Him in the same way that you can sing in the church's latter-rain revival.

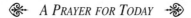

☙ *A PRAYER FOR TODAY* ❧

Father, fill my heart with songs of glory and praise to Jesus.

SAFEGUARDING THE FUTURE TODAY

The Spirit clearly says that in later times some will abandon the faith
and follow deceiving spirits and things taught by demons.
1 Tim. 4:1, NIV.

The future has not happened. It is created by today's actions and events. Only God can accurately foresee the future, and even then He apparently sees a number of scenarios that are dependent on the choices people make in the present (Deut. 28). Seeing the intensity of satanic activity and deception in the first Christian century, Paul, through the Holy Spirit, could warn the church that even Christians in the future would be deceived.

Almost 20 centuries later Vaughn Allen also issued a warning that is important to heed: "As a people, Adventists have always known that there is a controversy being fought between Christ and Satan. And we have known that the battle involves 'the church.' However, it has been easy for us to think of 'the church' as a collective and impersonal term, and forget that 'the church' is people. The church is you and me. And it is on this personal level that battles are won or lost" *(The War Is Real,* p. 18).

What can church members do today that could open them up to a future of deception? People who have succumbed to Satan's wiles reveal a number of common elements in their lives. These include a lack of the assurance of salvation; low self-image; unresolved guilt; surrender to obsessions, compulsions, and addictions; bitterness; idolatry; pride; hatred; rebellion; and occult activities.

Whenever a Christian falls into deception, deceiving spirits will try to destroy that person by the tactic of accusation. They will point to the hopelessness of the fallen Christian's future because of "God's wrath against sin." In this crisis only the Holy Spirit can help. No matter what the sinner has done, the Spirit points out that Jesus forgives sin and that He will never let one of His children go. The future is always secure for those who kneel at the foot of the cross.

❧ A PRAYER FOR TODAY ❧

Lord, I praise You for Your unfailing Word and love,
which stand as a safeguard against all satanic deception.

MAKING THE MOST OF YOUR GIFT

Do not neglect your gift, which was given you through a prophetic message when the body of elders laid their hands on you. 1 Tim. 4:14, NIV.

T he idea that a few select Christians have charisma and therefore can be more successful than others is just not true. Every born-again person has received a gift [charisma] from the Holy Spirit, and He will make the recipient able to use it mightily to God's glory. The gift is not received through the laying on of hands, but when the Spirit-filled elders laid their hands in prayer on Timothy, one with a gift of prophecy apparently helped him understand what his ministry was.

Although the Holy Spirit comes to dwell in each person's life at conversion, a number of pastors today follow the practice of laying on of hands at the conclusion of a baptismal service. They pray that those who have been baptized will become aware of their special ministry gifts. It is important to remember, however, that when a need arises, every Spirit-filled Christian can be a passage through which any of the nine supernatural gifts listed in 1 Corinthians 12 can pass.

Perhaps Timothy's special charisma was that of an evangelist. That gift, coupled to any of the nine supernatural gifts, would give tremendous power to his preaching. But Paul was concerned that Timothy would neglect his gift and lose the impact of his ministry.

Recently I heard the pastor of a church where more that 14,000 attend each weekend state that he was becoming burned out. As he prayed about the situation, the Lord helped him realize that he was neglecting his gift of evangelism and was spending most of his time in areas of ministry such as administration and counseling, where he was not gifted.

Obviously, the question to each one of us as Christians is Are we neglecting our gift? If we are, we are robbing ourselves of the tremendous satisfaction, fulfillment, and energy that come as we serve God in the way that He miraculously makes possible.

If you are not sure what your gift is, the Holy Spirit can use your pastor and fellow Christians to help you make this wonderful discovery.

❧ *A PRAYER FOR TODAY* ❧

Lord, forgive me for the sin of neglect and give me the joy of seeing my special gift from You grow and flourish.

NO TIMID SPIRIT

*For this reason I remind you to fan into flame the gift of God,
which is in you through the laying on of my hands. For God did not give
us a spirit of timidity, but a spirit of power, of love and of self-discipline.
2 Tim. 1:6, 7, NIV.*

ive me Scotland, or I die!" was the prayer of fearless Scottish reformer John Knox. The Holy Spirit had filled Knox with burning fire to see his people released from the oppression of corrupt religion and free to worship according to the simplicity of the gospel.

Some time ago I stood in the pulpit of St. Giles Cathedral in Edinburgh, and being a preacher myself with a Scottish heritage, I thought of Knox coming here for his final sermon on November 9, 1572. "So feeble was he that he had to be helped into the pulpit, but once there the old fire, which had set Scotland in a glow, once more broke out, the cathedral rang with its trumpet notes, and so vehemently did he preach that 'he was like to rend the pulpit in pieces'" (James Burns, *Revivals,* p. 265).

John Knox had never been known for a spirit of timidity. As a Catholic priest he had been converted to Protestantism in his early 40s and was soon arrested and forced to serve for 19 months as a galley slave, chained to an oar in a French boat. Barely escaping with his life, Knox found his way to England and on to Geneva. But the Lord was calling him back to Scotland, where he used in a mighty way the gift that the Spirit had given him.

"His convictions were maintained at white heat; his speech—rugged, impassioned, often when he assumed the role of the prophet, majestic—swept away the timid opposition of other men; his sincerity, which none doubted, the transparent honesty of his motives, and his utter fearlessness of consequences, appealed even to his enemies" *(ibid.,* p. 262).

Even Catholic Mary, Queen of Scots, trembled in the presence of John Knox, who on one occasion said to Her Majesty, "Madam, I pray God to purge your heart from papistry, and to preserve you from the counsel of flatterers." Miraculously Knox's life was spared, and the Holy Spirit used him as the spark of great revival.

❧ *A PRAYER FOR TODAY* ❧

*Take from me the fear of other people, Lord, so that the spiritual gift
You've given me may burn bright and clear.*

KEEP PRAYING FOR REVIVAL

That good thing which was committed to you, keep by the Holy Spirit who dwells in us. 2 Tim. 1:14, NKJV.

*W*hen John Knox returned to Scotland from Geneva on May 2, 1559, he was amazed to discover that the Spirit, who had come to dwell in his countrymen at conversion, was filling them with a deep longing for a great revival. Scotsman James Burns, writing at the beginning of this century, recounts the wonderful work of the Holy Spirit that transformed his country. If revival is to take place in our time, we must again see the Spirit whom Burns describes.

" 'If I had not seen it,' John Knox says, 'with my own eyes, in my own country, I could not have believed it. . . . The fervency here doth far exceed all others I have seen. . . . Their fervency doeth so ravish me, that I cannot but accuse and condemn my slothful coldness. God grant them their heart's desire.' 'Night and day,' again he says, he found them, 'sobbing and groaning for the bread of life.' Teachers they had practically none, but meeting together in 'assemblies,' they read the Scriptures, made confession of their sins, and united in earnest prayer. In homes not only of the humble, but in the castles of the highest of the land these 'assemblies' were held, and over the lowlands of Scotland the breath of the Spirit of God seemed to pass, awakening a nation to newness of life" *(Revivals,* pp. 270, 271).

The good things committed to us as Christians are an understanding of the gospel, the assurance of salvation, the victory power of the Holy Spirit, spiritual gifts for ministry, and the opportunities to meet with those of like faith. As the Spirit's indwelling presence keeps bringing these certainties into focus within us, an intense desire for an even greater outpouring of the Holy Spirit is created in our hearts.

Privately, in small group "assembles," as in sixteenth-century Scotland, and in large congregations, we will unite in fervent prayer, which, as Burns says, lays the foundation for revival. "Gradually, the number of people praying increases. Prayer becomes more urgent and more confident. . . . The longing for better things becomes an intense pain" *(The Laws of Revival,* p. 16).

Are we that earnest about revival today?

❧ *A PRAYER FOR TODAY* ☙

Lord, may the good things given me by the Spirit be revived and renewed so that Your church will experience life and joy.

November 22

WILL YOUR ANCHOR HOLD?

Not by works of righteousness which we have done, but according to His mercy He saved us, through the washing of regeneration and renewing of the Holy Spirit. Titus 3:5, NKJV.

*I*n the violent storms of life our anchor will hold only if it is firmly gripped by the gospel. A man whom I had respected for years as a committed Christian began to lose his assurance of salvation during his last few years of life. He and his wife had become associated with a legalistic group that had split off from the church and taught that Christians must be "good enough" to be saved. Because it is impossible to be good enough apart from the blood of Jesus, the anchor of assurance begins to slip for the legalist, and nothing but wavering uncertainty is left.

John Knox, the great Scottish reformer, did not have this uncertainty. He had experienced the new birth and knew what it meant to be renewed, or regenerated, by the Holy Spirit. The theology of the Reformation had given him a strong grasp on justification by faith so that his anchor held until the day he died.

Richard Bannatyne, Knox's assistant, recorded what happened on Knox's last day, November 24, 1572. "Early in the afternoon he [Knox] said, 'Now, for the last time, I commend my spirit, soul, and body'—pointing upon his three fingers—'into thy hands, O Lord!' Thereafter, about five o'clock, he said to his wife, 'Go, read where I cast my first anchor!' She did not need to be told, and so she read the seventeenth of John's evangel. . . . 'And this is eternal life that they might know thee.' Knox was on the bed of death, but the Book spoke of everlasting life. 'It was there,' he declared with his last breath, 'it was there that I cast my first anchor!' " (F. W. Boreham, *A Bunch of Everlastings,* pp. 112, 113).

The Spirit enables the saved to do many good works—works of righteousness—but never are these the basis of salvation. The assurance of a firm anchor is always based, as Knox said, on what happens when a sinner first accepts Jesus as Saviour. At that moment, Paul reminds us, there is rebirth into the family of God and new life through the Holy Spirit. What a sure anchor!

❧ *A PRAYER FOR TODAY* ❧

Thank You, Lord, for the certainty of my salvation, which is based entirely on Jesus and the work of the Holy Spirit.

November 23

WELCOME TO TRUE RICHES

This Spirit he poured out on us richly through Jesus Christ our Savior, so that, having been justified by his grace, we might become heirs according to the hope of eternal life. Titus 3:6, 7, NRSV.

*H*ave you noticed how Paul repeatedly connected the outpouring of the Holy Spirit with the assurance of salvation in the lives of those who are born again? He made sure that every congregation and every Christian worker to whom he wrote had this certainty. The Holy Spirit had been poured out "richly" at Pentecost as a sign of Jesus' exaltation and the full application of His sacrifice for lost humanity (Acts 2:33-36). Now, as Peter proclaimed with the gift of tongues to the crowd in Jerusalem, forgiveness of sins and the gift of the Holy Spirit have become certain possessions of all who come in surrender to Jesus.

Queen Victoria, after hearing a sermon in St. Paul's Cathedral, was troubled about her eternal salvation. Following the service, she asked her chaplain if anyone could be sure about going to heaven, and his reply contained none of the assurance that Paul gave to Titus. "I know of no way that anyone could be positive of that," the chaplain said.

A Spirit-filled London minister, John Townsend, read of the incident in the *Court News* and was concerned lest the queen be robbed of her assurance. "With trembling hands," he wrote in a note to the queen, "but a heart filled with love, and because I know that we can be absolutely sure even now of our eternal life . . . , may I ask Your Most Gracious Majesty to read the following passages of Scripture: John 3:16 and Romans 10:9, 10? There is salvation by faith in the Lord Jesus Christ for those who believe in Him and accept His finished work" (quoted in *Our Daily Bread,* Mar. 13, 1992).

If you have that assurance in your heart, the Holy Spirit will use you as an agent of certainty, just as he used Paul and John Townsend. The richness of the Spirit filling you and your understanding of the gospel's simplicity will give you a hope to share that will lead many to rejoice in Jesus.

❦ *A PRAYER FOR TODAY* ❧

Father, You know how easy it is for me to become discouraged with myself. Help me look to You, knowing that Your love is unfailing.

WELCOME, CONFIRMING GIFTS

God always has shown us that these messages are true by signs and wonders and various miracles and by giving certain special abilities from the Holy Spirit to those who believe; yes, God has assigned such gifts to each of us. Heb. 2:4, TLB.

God's plan is that His "great salvation" (Heb. 2:3) be accompanied by the witness of signs, wonders, miracles, and the gifts of the Spirit. Satan and his angels endeavor to counterfeit these confirmations of the gospel so that God's people will be suspicious of any evidence of Holy Spirit power. As a result, a large part of Christianity has become a religion of much talk but little action. It has a form of godliness but denies its power (2 Tim. 3:5).

World-famous authority on the Greek New Testament A. T. Robertson explained the significance of the words the writer of Hebrews used: *"Teras* (wonder) attracts attention, *dunamis* (power) shows God's power, *sēmeion* (signs) reveals the purpose of God in the miracles" *(Word Pictures of the New Testament,* Vol. V, p. 343). The accurate paraphrase in *The Living Bible* tells us how God will fulfill His promised plan for these wonders, miracles, and signs today. "God has always shown us that these messages are true by signs and wonders and various miracles and by giving certain special abilities from the Holy Spirit to those who believe; yes, God has assigned such gifts to each of us."

The supernatural evidences of God's power that draw attention to the church today are most apparent in small-group meetings. Here members have the opportunity to use effectively the spiritual gifts that God has given them. An overflow from this will be into the larger congregational meetings of the church. Members who have gained confidence by seeing the Spirit and truth working miracles in small groups will be open to special ministry for hurting people during and following each worship service.

"One of our small group leaders learned to pray for the sick in his small group," a pastor informed me. "He has confidence now and is always available to assist me in ministering to those with physical and spiritual problems. The Lord has used him in a way that has brought quite a number of new people to our church."

❦ *A PRAYER FOR TODAY* ❧

Lord, I pray that You'll bear witness to the power of the gospel through the spiritual gifts You've given me.

WELCOME, SIMPLE SECURITY

And since Christ is so much superior, the Holy Spirit warns us to listen to him, to be careful to hear his voice today. Heb. 3:7, TLB.

Where are you looking for truth or worthiness? Many look today in the light of modern philosophies, psychological theories, political platforms, and psycho-spiritual mysticism or introspection.

Joan Borysenko tells of a man who one night was looking for his keys under a streetlamp. "When a helpful passerby joined in the search, asking where exactly the keys had been lost, the man pointed to a vacant lot across the street. When the passerby asked the obvious question, 'Why search for the keys here, then?' the man replied, 'Because the light is better'" *(Guilt Is the Teacher, Love Is the Lesson,* pp. 23, 24).

The superiority of Jesus over every other system of religion or self-worth finds its expression in the simplicity of the gospel. Souls are lost in a dark, vacant lot until the Holy Spirit finds a born-again person who is willing to take the light to the lost and to be used to present to lost individuals, in the most understandable terms, the meaning of Jesus' life and death. The simple message of God's grace and the possibility of accepting by faith eternal life through Jesus make Christianity unique. The revelation of a life transformed by the Holy Spirit makes Christianity powerful.

Senior TWA flight attendant Margaret had searched for truth in hedonism and Eastern religions but had found no satisfaction, peace, or lasting joy. One day on a flight between Portland and Los Angeles, a passenger introduced her to Jesus and explained the simple gospel steps to eternal life. Margaret listened to the Holy Spirit speaking though this earnest Christian and that day, in a few moments of quiet prayer, accepted Jesus as her personal Saviour. The transformation in Margaret's life revealed again God's miracle-working power.

Listen for Jesus' voice speaking to you today. You will hear it as you read the Bible or as you pray with other Christians. The Holy Spirit is constantly seeking to lead you into greater light of truth and awareness of who you really are—God's child.

❧ *A PRAYER FOR TODAY* ❧

Father, please help me listen to Your voice so that I won't be confused by inferior systems of thought, belief, or action.

THE FALLEN CAN BE FORGIVEN

For it is impossible to restore again to repentance those who have once been enlightened, who have tasted the heavenly gift, and have become partakers of the Holy Spirit. Heb. 6:4, RSV.

The description of the fate of apostates (those who "fall away," Heb. 6:6) given in Hebrews has caused many Christians deep concern about their eternal destiny. It is vital to understand whom the writer of Hebrews is discussing when he says that it is impossible for some to be restored to repentance.

Apparently these people were at one time born-again Christians, because they had become partakers of the Holy Spirit, an event that takes place at conversion. But it is clear that he is not talking about backsliders or Christians who fall into sin. It is possible for them to come again to repentance, and in fact, it is the Spirit's work constantly to draw back to Jesus those who fall. That is a certainty for every saint and sinner. "Whosoever will may come" to Jesus, and those who come will not be cast out.

The book of Hebrews was addressed primarily to Jewish Christians. They were not falling away into deliberate sin, but the opposite was true. They were going back into the legalism and salvation by works of Judaism. In so doing, they were recrucifying Jesus by teaching that His sacrifice was unnecessary for their salvation. Once again they would rely on the blood of sheep, bulls, and goats and would find within themselves no desire to change their minds or repent.

One of the great martyrs of the English church was Archbishop Thomas Cranmer. It is a moving experience to stand at the monument in Oxford near where he and other protestors of Catholicism were burned at the stake in 1556. During his harsh, then indulgent, imprisonment prior to his execution, Cranmer was tricked into signing a recantation of his opposition to the heresies of Rome. Still Queen Mary was determined that he die. During his speech just before his burning he pleaded with the Lord to forgive his terrible denial of truth. Holding out his right hand to burn first, Cranmer died with the full assurance of salvation in Jesus Christ.

It is certainly not impossible for a repentant sinner to come back to God.

❧ *A PRAYER FOR TODAY* ❧

Holy Spirit, I thank You for leading me always in the certainty that You will never cast aside one of Your children.

November 27

PRESENT AGENTS OF FUTURE POWER

*[You] have tasted the goodness of the word of God and the powers
of the coming age. Heb. 6:5, NIV.*

F ollowing revival meetings in the Los Angeles area, a prayer ministry team gathered to pray for those who were seeking healing. There were requests for physical healing as well as for freedom from emotional, relational, and spiritual problems. While some were miraculously healed immediately and all were blessed spiritually, others noticed no change in their physical symptoms. The passing of a few hours or days brought to others the relief for which they had prayed, but some became aware that they would have to wait for the healing of their bodies in the age to come.

Jesus inaugurated the kingdom of God, to use George Eldon Ladd's terminology, and we await its consummation at His second coming. We live between the "already and the not yet." In this "present evil age," through the Spirit, we taste already some of the "powers" of God's kingdom. But when the joy of the "age to come" arrives, then "God will wipe away every tear from their eyes; there shall be no more death, nor sorrow, nor crying; and there shall be no more pain, for the former things have passed away" (Rev. 21:4, NKJV).

Before the prayer service for healing in Los Angeles, as in each of these situations, I reminded the people of an important consideration: "Although the Holy Spirit works healing miracles through His gifted people, the timing of the release of the sick from their ailments or injuries must be submitted to the will of God. Some will be healed immediately, some gradually, and all will be healed on the resurrection day, when the kingdom of God is consummated in the age to come. The timing of healing does not depend upon the quantity or quality of your faith but on the sovereignty of God."

Praise God for the opportunities the Holy Spirit gives us today to taste the powers of the age to come! If you haven't experienced this yet, "earnestly desire the best gifts" and see the wonders that will happen as any one of the nine supernatural gifts of 1 Corinthians 12:8-10 begins to flow from God, through you, to a specific human need.

 *A PRAYER FOR TODAY*

*Holy Spirit, help me be one of your agents in this world
for the powers of the age to come.*

WELCOME TO THE MOST HOLY PLACE

*The Holy Spirit indicating this, that the way into the Holiest of All
was not yet made manifest while the first tabernacle was still standing.
Heb. 9:8, NKJV.*

*I*n the book of Hebrews the Spirit's glorification of Jesus demonstrates
how His sacrifice and ministry are far superior to the Jewish tabernacle
and religious system. While the old system functioned, or was "still
standing," the way into the Holiest of All, the heavenly sanctuary, was not disclosed or understood. Following Jesus' death, however, the Holy Spirit shows
that every sinner has direct access into the throne room of heaven by the
blood of the Lamb of God (Heb. 10:19) and the ministry of our "great High
Priest" (Heb. 4:14).

I was teaching a Holy Spirit seminar in Glendale when a participant
handed me a book and suggested that I read about the ministry of the Holy
Spirit in the life of a rabbi. As Rabbi Isidor Zwirn had studied the Torah—
and especially the prophecies of Isaiah—the Spirit glorified Jesus, leading the
rabbi to a startling conclusion: "The name of that divine Person whom I had
so painstakingly sought and found in the pages of Torah was he, Yeshuah ha
Meshiach, Jesus Christ the Messiah of all mankind including the Jews. . . . So
it was, in that wondrously beautiful moment of mental awareness and intellectual commitment, when for the first time, I not only knew the identity of
the Messiah, but in the truest sense of the word, I knew him!" *(The Rabbi
From Burbank,* pp. 63, 64).

Soon after his conversion, as Rabbi Zwirn stood on the platform in his
synagogue to read from the Torah, police officers arrived and escorted him
out. As a Jewish Christian, he was now despised by his family and Orthodox
Jewish leaders and associates. But he rejoiced that the Spirit had made him
aware that, in Jesus, his faithful High Priest in the Holiest of All, he was righteous and qualified for ministry, especially for his Jewish people.

When we, like Isidor Zwirn, allow the Spirit to reveal to us the wonderful
meaning of Jesus' ministry in the Most Holy Place, our assurance of salvation and joy in service are multiplied greatly.

❦ A PRAYER FOR TODAY ❧

*Lord, help me look beyond the rituals of earthly religion to
the heavenly place of true worship and security.*

WELCOME, POWER OF
THE ETERNAL SPIRIT

*How much more, then, will the blood of Christ, who through the
eternal Spirit offered himself unblemished to God,
cleanse our consciences from acts that lead to death,
so that we may serve the living God! Heb. 9:14, NIV.*

*P*aul M. Sadler, of the Berean Bible Society, tells of a visit to the Pacific Garden Mission, in Chicago. Hundreds of men were present to hear him speak, and as he looked out over the group he saw the unmistakable evidence of lives that had sunken to the lowest level of "acts that lead to death." But Brother Paul knew that the power of the eternal Spirit was as available to these men as it had been to the Lord Jesus Himself.

"Mel Trotter, who was one of the former superintendents of the Pacific Garden Mission, was an alcoholic," Paul Sadler writes. "While at the Mission he told of a time when he was in such a state of despair that when his daughter died, he took her little shoes off her feet while she was in the casket and sold them to buy another drink. He said it was a time in his life when 'he was so down that he had to reach up to touch bottom'" *(Berean Searchlight,* June 1989, p. 122). The eternal Spirit, however, transformed the life of Mel Trotter and many former street people, who became staff members at the mission.

The Holy Spirit was involved in Jesus' total ministry. His conception was by the Holy Spirit (Luke 1:35). He worked His miracles and ministered in the power of the Spirit (Luke 4:18; Acts 10:38). His sinless life and sacrifice was "through the eternal Spirit" (Heb. 9:14). His resurrection was by the power of the Spirit (1 Peter 3:18).

And the same eternal Spirit is available to energize every Christian today. Even when life has reached the level of the gutter and the conscience is crippled by the accumulation of works that lead to death, the eternal Spirit can clear the mind and clean the heart for ministry.

Jesus never fell into sin. Mel Trotter did. But the eternal Spirit, who ministered through sinless Jesus, enables those who are cleansed by the Saviour's blood to serve the living God. In fact, the Holy Spirit makes it possible to do "greater works" than Jesus did (John 14:12), even at the Pacific Garden Mission.

⊱ *A PRAYER FOR TODAY* ⊰

Lord, it's such a privilege and joy to serve You, the living God!

WELCOME, AMAZING DISCOVERY

And the Holy Spirit also witnesses to us. Heb. 10:15, NKJV.

The burning desire to find treasures that no one had seen since the time of Moses led Howard Carter to dig for six years in the blazing heat and sandy rubble of Egypt's Valley of the Kings. Stories of the hidden tomb of a boy Pharaoh inspired the archaeologist, and for once, when the great discovery was made, reality was even greater than expectation.

Here's what Carter himself said about his excitement on the day of discovery: "The following day [November 26, 1922] was the day of days, the most wonderful that I have ever lived through, and certainly one whose like I could never hope to see again." A small hole was made in the wall of the tomb and, trembling with anticipation, Carter "inserted the candle and peered in." "For a moment . . . I was struck dumb with amazement, and when Lord Carnarvon, unable to stand the suspense any longer, inquired anxiously, 'Can you see anything?' it was all I could do to get out the words, 'Yes, wonderful things' " *(Discovering Tut-ankh-Amen's Tomb,* pp. 27, 28).

I have stood in the tomb of King Tutankhamen many times and have seen the dazzling treasures discovered there, but I disagree with Howard Carter. The most wonderful day in a person's life comes when the fantastic discovery is made that God remembers our sins no more (Heb. 10:16, 17)!

Carl had been watching pornographic videos. The Spirit said, "Carl, I will write God's law of love in your heart and mind, and your sins will be remembered no more."

Wendy's gossip and lies had hurt the ministry of her pastor. The Spirit said, "Wendy, I will write God's law of truth in your heart and mind, and He will remember your sins no more."

Jim had stolen company funds and was facing a jail term. The Spirit said, "Jim, I will write God's law on your heart and mind, and He will remember your sins no more."

Film star Sophia Loren once said, "I have learned what everyone learns sometime in life—prospect is better than possession." Not so for Carter at the discovery of King Tut's tomb, or when the Spirit witnesses to sinners that they are forgiven by the blood of Jesus. Reality is much better than expectation.

&⁇ A PRAYER FOR TODAY ⁇&

*Holy Spirit, clarify in my heart again the reality of God's grace
and love for me, even in my weakest moments.*

NOT INSULTING GRACE

Of how much worse punishment, do you suppose, will he be thought worthy who has trampled the Son of God underfoot, counted the blood of the covenant by which he was sanctified a common thing, and insulted the Spirit of grace? Heb. 10:29, NKJV.

*D*o you know a song that is more than 200 years old? It is likely that you do, because the most popular religious song today was written in 1779 by John Newton, a former captain of a slave trading vessel. He had trampled the Son of God underfoot and turned his back on the blood of the covenant, but he was found and saved by God's amazing grace. (See the reading for June 23.)

Amazing grace is not only God's unmerited favor; it is also the power of the Spirit that leads sinners to Jesus and capacitates saints to live for Him. When the disciples were filled with the Spirit, "great grace was upon them all" (Acts 4:33, NKJV). This is the energy that enables Spirit-filled Christians to work with signs and wonders as they are empowered with spiritual gifts of grace (see Rom. 12:6; 1 Cor. 1:4-7; 2 Cor. 9:8; Eph. 4:7).

Some Christians believe that they are saved by grace but must maintain their salvation by good works. This legalism insults the Spirit of grace, who gives the power to do good works and reveal spiritual gifts only to those who are already saved. Other Christians believe that they are saved by grace so do not need to be concerned about good works or obedience. This cheap grace insults the Spirit of grace, who glorifies Jesus through the good works, ministry, and character of His followers.

You may be surprised to learn that John Newton continued in the slave trade for some time after his conversion. He certainly understood grace as the unmerited favor of God. "But now I began to understand the security of the covenant of grace, and to expect to be preserved, not by my own power and holiness, but by the mighty power and promise of God, through faith in an unchangable Saviour" (cited in *Conversions,* p. 89). The time soon came, however, when Newton chose not to insult the Spirit of grace as the victory power in his life. He eventually became the motivating force behind William Wilberforce and the abolition of the slave trade in Great Britain.

❦ A PRAYER FOR TODAY ❦

Holy Spirit, help me not insult You by trying to do in my own strength what You only can enable me to do successfully.

WELCOME, JEALOUSY

*Or do you think that the Scripture says in vain,
"The Spirit who dwells in us yearns jealously"? James 4:5, NKJV.*

Jealousy is the language of love. But Shakespeare wrote in *The Merchant of Venice* about green-eyed jealousy, and in *Othello* he called it the green-eyed monster. The French philosopher Duc de La Rochefoucauld said that jealousy feeds on suspicion and has in it more self-love than love. Any effort to appease jealousy, like paranoia, only makes matters worse. Does this sound like a description of the Holy Spirit? Certainly not. So why does James, in his only reference to the Holy Spirit, say that He is jealous?

Jealousy is different from envy. As Chuck Swindoll has said: "Envy wants to have what someone else possesses. Jealousy wants to possess what it already has" *(Come Before Winter, p. 98)*. In this way the Holy Spirit is jealous to have the full allegiance of the heart that He has come to dwell in at conversion. When Christians fall in love with the world and give their friendship to it, then the Holy Spirit yearns jealously to bring them back to their first love for Jesus. Do you feel comfortable with that jealousy? It is good to know that we do not have a God who is casual or careless about our relationship with Him.

Some versions of the Bible have translated James 4:5 to mean that it is the human spirit in us that is greatly envious of the things of the world. While that is certainly true of our fallen human nature, it is even more true that our God is jealous for the love of His people.

"I have been a Christian all of my life," a middle-aged man informed me, "but I don't really feel any love for God. I guess my religion has just become part of the culture of my life. I'm more interested in Monday night football."

What can a jealous God do about this man's affections?

The wonder of God's love is that He not only asks us to love Him but that He also provides us with the love to make this possible. It is the Holy Spirit who pours the love of God into our hearts (Rom. 5:5), and the fruit of the Spirit is love (Gal. 5:22, 23).

God wants us filled with the Spirit every day so that loveless, cultural Christianity can be transformed by His grace.

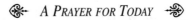

✤ A PRAYER FOR TODAY ✤

Father, may You be the center of my affections and my love.

December 3

HAPPY ABOUT HOLINESS

[Christians] have been chosen according to the foreknowledge of God the Father, through the sanctifying work of the Spirit, for obedience to Jesus Christ and sprinkling by his blood. 1 Peter 1:2, NIV.

*A*s a young Christian on the East Coast of the United States in the early part of the twentieth century, Ruth Paxton enjoyed evangelistic ministry on a number of college campuses. At age 35 the Lord called Ruth to China, where she organized missionary schools for girls and worked for the deeper Christian experience of missionaries of different denominations. Many Christians have become familiar with Ruth Paxton through her book *Rivers of Living Water,* in which she talks of the wonderful sanctification of the Spirit that is available to every child of God.

Understanding that sanctification of the Spirit means holiness of life, Ruth was often questioned about her teaching on this subject. "Every Christian is called to a holy life," she replies, "but many Christians do not want to be holy. They may want to be spiritual, but they are afraid to be holy. This may be due to a misunderstanding of what holiness is through false teaching on this subject. Holiness is not sinless perfection nor eradication of the sinful nature, nor is it faultlessness. It neither places one beyond the possibility of sinning nor removes the presence of sin.

"Scriptural holiness is blamelessness in the sight of God. We are to be 'preserved blameless' unto His coming, and we shall be 'presented faultless' at His coming (1 Thess. 5:23; Jude 24). Holiness is Christ, our Sanctification, enthroned as Life of our life. It is Christ, the Holy One, in us, living, speaking, walking" (Leona Frances Choy, *Powerlines,* pp. 211, 212).

No wonder Satan tries to keep Christians from understanding the fullness of the Holy Spirit in their lives! It is through the sanctification of the Spirit that the full significance of Jesus' life is realized in us. Through the Spirit we have victory power in Jesus and are counted in Him just as if we had never sinned.

What a deal! What holiness!

❧ *A PRAYER FOR TODAY* ☙

Father, thank You for Your perfect holiness in me. Please make victory a reality for me. May I always remember, though, that I'm not saved because of my victory, but through Jesus' sacrifice.

349

December 4

ARE TRUE PROPHETS ALWAYS RIGHT?

[The prophets tried] to find out the time and circumstances to which the Spirit of Christ in them was pointing when he predicted the sufferings of Christ and the glories that would follow. 1 Peter 1:11, NIV.

*P*eter here admits the limitations of prophets. The Holy Spirit may give a man or woman a vision or dream, but He does not necessarily give the prophet all the details of its interpretation. The prophet may have to say, "Here is what I have seen or heard from the Lord. I'm not sure what it means, but I believe that at the right time and place He will reveal its full significance."

In New Testament times Christians were told not to "treat prophecies with contempt," but to "test everything" and "hold on to the good" (1 Thess. 5:20, 21, NIV). This warning did not mean that God's people with the gift of prophecy were receiving false messages, but rather that they may place a false interpretation on them. As Wayne Grudem has said, God does not make mistakes, and He doesn't give erroneous revelations. But prophets can make mistakes in the way they report what has been revealed to them. They may not perfectly distinguish what is from God and what is their own thoughts. They may misunderstand what God is communicating. Some of their own ideas and interpretations may get mixed in with the report of the prophecy.

This certainly did not happen as far as the Bible writers were concerned, but it is a possibility with all others who exercise the spiritual gift for which all Christians are to pray (1 Cor. 14:1).

Speaking of modern prophets, Frank Demanzio warns: "A prophet as a man is liable to error, and thus his prophecy may contain error. The Lord admonishes us to judge and evaluate the prophet's word by the standard of Scripture and by the witness of the Spirit in the hearts of the believers. At the same time, the Spirit quickens the Word of Scripture in the hearts of other believers to confirm the truth of the prophet's word" *(The Prophetic Ministry,* p. 11).

What the Old Testament prophets did not fully understand, we now see clearly. The gospel of salvation by faith has been revealed in Jesus' life and death, and we can accept it personally and proclaim it with clarity to others.

❦ A PRAYER FOR TODAY ❧

Thank You, Lord, for the witness of Your sure Word in my heart.

December 5

WELCOME, GOSPEL PREACHING

It was revealed to them that they were not serving themselves but you, when they spoke of the things that have now been told you by those who have preached the gospel to you by the Holy Spirit sent from heaven. Even angels long to look into these things. 1 Peter 1:12, NIV.

*H*ow did you know to speak on the very topic that I desperately needed to hear today?" Most preachers have heard these words many times as they have shaken hands with their congregation following the Sabbath morning sermon. The amazing fact is that sometimes the Holy Spirit has impressed the preacher to change his or her topic even as he or she stood in the pulpit.

On one occasion my elders strongly requested that I preach a sermon on dress standards. I prayed for a lot of wisdom as I prepared the sermon, but was still uncomfortable. The standards were debatable and somewhat cultural, and the worship hour, I felt, was not the time to publicly embarrass "worldly" members. As I met with the elders before walking onto the platform, a church member rushed into the room. "Pastor," she said, not knowing the topic of the morning sermon, "I've brought a group of visitors with me this morning. Some of them have never been inside a church before."

I looked at my elders and said, "Brethren, the Holy Spirit is impressing me to preach a different sermon. These visitors must hear the simplicity of the gospel today." Reluctantly the elders agreed, and when the sermon was over, we discovered that the results were amazing. The visitors had filed out without much comment, but a number of the members were converted that day. At the door one of the "problem" people summed up the experience of many when she said, "Pastor, I've been fooling around with the world and have rebelled against the standards we have in this church, but today I've given my life to Jesus, and you're going to notice some big changes."

Yes, the gospel was preached by the Spirit that day, and there were some big changes as a result. These changes came not only in the lives of the members but also in the experience of the preacher. The sermon on standards I never did preach, but the Spirit used me to proclaim the gospel many times in every sermon that followed.

❦ *A PRAYER FOR TODAY* ❦

The gospel is wonderful, Lord. Even angels desire to understand it. Thank You for making it plain to sinners through the Spirit.

December 6

WELCOME, WORKS THAT PURIFY

Since you have purified your souls in obeying the truth through the Spirit in sincere love of the brethren, love one another fervently with a pure heart. 1 Peter 1:22, NKJV.

*H*ere's a wonderful verse on the obedience that the Spirit gives to Christians," I explained to a group of pastors as I read the text in my New King James Version. To my surprise, because they were using different translations, most of them could not find the word "Spirit" in the verse. While recent studies have shown that the most reliable ancient manuscripts do not refer to the Spirit in 1 Peter 1:22, its inclusion in a few sources shows that the early Christians did have a firm belief in the victory power of the Spirit.

I always found it an inspirational experience to listen to testimonies of praise from Oregon Prison Ministry leaders Noah and Leroy. The Holy Spirit gave them more than 125 baptisms in 10 years, and prison officials informed Noah and Leroy that official prison follow-up showed that 9 out of 10 of the 125 had stayed in the church, while only 1 in 10 stayed when baptized into other denominations. Noah said, "I concentrate on uplifting Jesus and showing the prisoners that they can obey all of God's truth in the power of the Holy Spirit."

On one occasion Leroy and Noah were escorted into the prison chapel by guards who listened carefully to what the two lay preachers were teaching. Two guards who were Pentecostals learned about the Sabbath and were so impressed by this truth that they took the information back to their church. Their pastor carefully studied and prayed about it, and it was not long before this whole congregation in Salem, Oregon, changed over to become a Sabbathkeeping church. They obeyed the truth in the strength of the Holy Spirit.

It is important, however, to notice Peter's explanation that the truth which purifies the soul is that which leads to the born-again experience. Through the Word, the Spirit enlightens a sinner's mind with the truth of the gospel (verse 25). And through the power of the Spirit, the sinner obeys the truth, accepting by faith the forgiveness and salvation made possible by the life and death of Jesus. This purity can never be exceeded by human works.

❦ *A PRAYER FOR TODAY* ❧

Thank You, Lord, for the purifying sacrifice of Jesus. May my works and obedience only be in gratitude for that example of love.

December 7

WHICH SPIRIT IS IT?

For Christ died for sins once for all, the righteous for the unrighteous, to bring you to God. He was put to death in the body but made alive by the Spirit. 1 Peter 3:18, NIV.

*A*s the old saying from woodstove days goes, here we find an example of "the pot calling the kettle black." Peter, who criticized Paul for writing some things that are difficult to understand (2 Peter 3:15, 16), does the same himself a number of times. First Peter 3:18, 19 is a prime illustration of this. Did the Holy Spirit raise Jesus from the dead, or did Jesus have a spirit within Him that actually did not die? Does it really matter 20 centuries later, when Christians' only concern is that we have a living Saviour and not a dead founder, as every other world religion does?

I like the way Episcopalian John Williams explains the danger of a wrong interpretation of today's verse: "Many commentators regard this as one of the most difficult passages in the New Testament and the majority tend to translate this phrase 'in spirit' rather than 'by the Spirit.' This translation again suggests the reference is to the human spirit of Jesus seen in contrast with His 'flesh.'

"However, this creates more problems than it solves, especially in relation to what follows. If we accept the reference here being to the Holy Spirit, the problem about a supposed post [or pre] resurrection appearance of Christ in Hades disappears. What Peter is saying is that just as the Holy Spirit was instrumental in Christ's resurrection, so He was in Christ's preaching to the antediluvian society of Noah's day. . . . [This repeats] Peter's idea of the Spirit of Christ testifying in the ancient prophets of Israel (1 Peter 1:10, 11)" *(The Holy Spirit—Lord and Life-Giver,* p. 63).

It is the resurrection power of the Holy Spirit, rather than a mysterious "spirit" ministry of Jesus, that Peter is teaching. The Spirit's ministry is dramatically illustrated in the lives of born-again Christians. "But if the Spirit of Him who raised Jesus from the dead dwells in you, He who raised Christ from the dead will also give life to your mortal bodies through His Spirit who dwells in you" (Rom. 8:11, NKJV).

Welcome to life in the Spirit today.

❧ *A PRAYER FOR TODAY* ❧

Thank You, Father, for the power of life that You continually give.

WHAT CAN PERSECUTION PROVE?

If you are reviled for the name of Christ, you are blessed,
because the spirit of glory, which is the Spirit of God, is resting on you.
1 Peter 4:14, NRSV.

One of the evidences that we are the true church is that we are being persecuted in so many places," two ladies at my door explained as they tried to give me one of their magazines. It is not unusual for Christian groups—whether they be Catholic, Protestant, or cultic—to use examples of persecution as a validation of their cause. But if we use persecution to prove truth, we would prove too much, because Muslims, Jews, Bahá'ís, Hindus, Buddhists, and in fact people of most religions have suffered terrible persecution.

Persecution does not prove truth, but it does prove humanity's terrible intolerance and inhumanity.

The spirit of glory that the Holy Spirit brings is not persecution, even for Christ's sake, but the glory of Jesus revealed in His followers (1Peter 4:11). Peter has explained that each Christian has received a gift (verse 10). This may be natural talent that can be used in a special way for the glory of God. On the other hand, because Peter links the gift with God's grace, he is most likely talking of the gifts of grace, the spiritual gifts, which Paul has listed in Romans 12, 1 Corinthians 12, and Ephesians 4.

As Peter explains, these gifts may involve speaking God's messages or practical Christian ministry. While practical Christianity rarely results in fiery trials (1 Peter 4:12), suffering (verse 13), or reproach (verse 14), speaking God's messages can cause opposition and even persecution. Jesus said that a person's foes may be those of his or her own household. The "household" can be family and relatives, but sometimes, unfortunately, it may be the church, the Christian community, the neighborhood, or the nation.

Never does the Holy Spirit promise to keep God's Spirit-filled children from persecution. It is inevitable in varying degrees wherever selfishness, intolerance, and inhumanity exist. But the Holy Spirit does promise strength and faith so that God's gifted people can always bring glory to Him.

❦ A PRAYER FOR TODAY ❧

Help me be kind and loving, Lord, to those who oppose my beliefs
and standards. May I never seek to hurt or destroy those who disagree with me.

December 9

WELCOME, UNDERSTANDING OF THE WORD

Knowing this first, that no prophecy of Scripture is of any private interpretation, for prophecy never came by the will of man, but holy men of God spoke as they were moved by the Holy Spirit.
2 Peter 1:20, 21, NKJV.

"What do you think this text means?" small group leader Tony asked the people who met in his home each Friday evening. Everyone had a different opinion, but in the end they all agreed with Cynthia, who did not have a lot of knowledge about the Bible but was the most persuasive. This "pooling of ignorance," as one scholar called it, is not Bible study but private interpretation.

The deductive method of Bible study can be equally dangerous if it consists of proof texts to support the preconceived ideas or traditions of the group or teacher. It is possible to find a text to support almost any belief.

The Holy Spirit, who inspired the Scripture, most effectively uses the relational and inductive methods of Bible study. Relational Bible study does not look for doctrinal truths but rather asks, What is God saying to me in this verse? How is the Holy Spirit speaking to me today in this passage of Scripture? What does this story teach me about my relationships with God, myself, others, and the world around me?

Perry came into a new relationship with God and others when he understood a little of the feeling of rejection that Jesus experienced when "He came unto his own, and his own received him not" (John 1:11).

Inductive Bible study, illuminated by the Spirit, looks at a whole passage in context and asks, with the aid of concordances and Bible dictionaries, What is this passage actually saying? Am I clear on the meaning of every word and phrase? Next, it asks, What is this passage teaching? How does it compare with other passages that use similar statements and words? What conclusions can be drawn from all that the Bible says on these topics? Finally, it asks, What am I going to do about the truths that I find here? How am I going to let the Spirit apply them to my life?

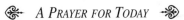
A PRAYER FOR TODAY

Speak to me from the Word, Lord, in a way that will transcend my own ideas and biases.

December 10

KNOWING THE SPIRIT OF JOY

*And this is his command: to believe in the name of his Son,
Jesus Christ, and to love one another as he commanded us. Those who
obey his commands live in him, and he in them. And this
is how we know that he lives in us: We know it by the Spirit he gave us.
1 John 3:23, 24, NIV.*

*D*o you know that Jesus is living in you and that you have eternal life? John, the last living apostle, wanted Christians to know for sure, so he used this word more than any other Bible writer. Some in John's day taught that it was possible to know because they were keeping various commandments. Others taught that they knew because they did not need to keep commandments and were morally free. But John is clear and concise: it is only through the Holy Spirit that a person can be joyfully certain of salvation.

Christians have sometimes given the impression that their religion is very pessimistic and uncertain. John, who had known Jesus personally, did not share this view. In fact, he said, "These things we write to you that your joy may be full" (1 John 1:4, NKJV). Fullness of joy is conspicuous and contagious and is the fruit of the Holy Spirit continually assuring those He fills that they have eternal life in Jesus Christ.

When John Wesley was converted in London, not only was his own heart strangely warmed, but also his public testimony that "an assurance was given me" had a dramatic affect on others in the meeting. Ralph S. Cushman writes: "The best evidence we have that Wesley's new 'discovery,' so promptly witnessed to, aroused such real excitement in the little meeting, is seen in the haste with which they hurried home to tell the news to his sick brother.

"Charles Wesley was not present in the Aldersgate meeting. Lying at home he was praying, when about ten o'clock, he heard the tramping of eager feet. The door was thrown open. In came brother John, radiant with his new consciousness of God, and surrounded by happy friends. . . . [His] diary adds, 'We sang a hymn with great joy and parted with prayer'" *(Practicing the Presence,* pp. 96, 97). That wonderful witness of joy, given by the Spirit, affected the subsequent history of Christianity.

❧ *A PRAYER FOR TODAY* ❧

*Father, help me not misrepresent Christianity by having a negative or
uncertain attitude. Thank You for the Spirit of joy.*

CONFESSING THE REAL JESUS

By this you know the Spirit of God: Every spirit that confesses that Jesus Christ has come in the flesh is of God. 1 John 4:2, NKJV.

*O*n the surface this test may appear to be superficial because even a false prophet or devil may acknowledge that Jesus took human form. But Paul has made it clear that "no one can say 'Jesus is Lord' [master of my life] except by the Holy Spirit" (1 Cor. 12:3, NRSV). In the same way, only those who are willing to accept Jesus as the Saviour of their life can, by the Spirit, confess Him as the perfect divine-human sacrifice for the sins of the world.

The Muslims see Jesus as a unique human prophet but certainly not divine. The Koran teaches that Jesus was a messenger from God but not a Saviour who made an atoning sacrifice. One so-called Christian faith reportedly teaches: "As we are, Jesus once was. As Jesus is, we will be." The New Age movement looks at Jesus from an even different perspective: "[He] is no longer said to be the only begotten Son of God, the God-man, the Lord and Saviour of the cosmos. He is merely one of the many appearances or manifestations of God throughout the millennia. . . . Jesus is thus reverentially enshrined in the pantheistic pantheon" (Douglas R. Groothuis, *Unmasking the New Age,* p. 28).

Nell had turned from her Christian upbringing to the New Age movement. Her family continued to pray earnestly for her, and on one occasion her mother gave a confession of faith to the man who had lured her into this cult: "My daughter once made a commitment to the Lord Jesus Christ, and she will come back to Him and forsake all of this garbage you have exposed her to. By the power and authority of the blood of Jesus, I bind every influence of Satan you have over my daughter" *(A Woman's Guide to Spiritual Warfare,* p. 45).

Nell was very upset about her mother's insensitive approach to her new religion. Five months later, however, in answer to many prayers, Nell walked into a Christian bookstore and purchased a book of Scripture verses that the Holy Spirit used to lead her back to her Lord Jesus Christ. Since then Nell has graduated from Bible college and has confessed her faith as she has ministered in several countries.

❧ *A PRAYER FOR TODAY* ❧

Lord, I believe in Jesus Christ, Son of God, who took humanity, lived a sinless life, and died on the cross for my salvation.

December 12

ARABIC VICTORY

You are of God, little children, and have overcome them, because He who is in you is greater than he who is in the world. 1 John 4:4, NKJV.

The Goliath-like greatness of "he who is in the world" seems almost overwhelming at times. The most devout Christians recognize that this Goliath who dominates the world has had a profound effect on their thinking also. Television, newspapers, most forms of advertising, and the conversation of associates and neighbors all have a significant impact on their standards and values. But the situation is not hopeless. Goliath can be defeated by the Holy Spirit, who represents Jesus within the Christian's life.

Chuck Swindoll says that "Goliath reminds me of the cross-eyed discus thrower. He didn't set any records . . . but he sure kept the crowd awake!" Swindoll gives two timeless truths of giant warfare: *"Prevailing over giants isn't accomplished by using their technique.* That's 'lesson one' for all of us. Goliath might have been mistaken for the battleship *Missouri* with all his noise and bronze. Not David . . . he didn't even carry a sword! His greatest piece of armor, the lethal weapon that made him unique and gave him victory, was his inner s*hield of faith.* It kept him free from fear, it made him hard of hearing threats, it gave him cool composure amidst chaos, it cleared his vision.

"Conquering giants isn't accomplished without great skill and discipline. To be God's warrior, to fight His way, demands much more expertise and control than one can imagine. Using the sling and stone of the Spirit is a far more delicate thing than swinging the club of the flesh. But oh, how sweet is the victory when the stone finds its mark . . . *and how final" (Come Before Winter,* pp. 147, 148).

I recently saw a Christian poster that showed a Middle Eastern fishing boat resting on a sandy beach. The name of the boat was *Intissar,* which is Arabic for victory, and I was interested to discover that *Issa* in the center of the word means Jesus. Perhaps the enemy has a giant problem standing in front of you today. If so, remember *Intissar*—the victory that you can have as the Holy Spirit fills you with Jesus' love and strength.

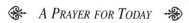

❦ *A PRAYER FOR TODAY* ❦

Help me, Lord, keep the threats of the world in perspective, knowing that they have no dominance over the mighty power of Your Spirit.

December 13

WELCOME, SPIRIT OF LOVE

No one has ever seen God; but if we love one another, God lives in us and his love is made complete in us. We know that we live in him and he in us, because he has given us of his Spirit. 1 John 4:12, 13, NIV.

*I*n this short letter John writes of love more than 30 times. Along with knowing, love is John's theme. No other book of the Bible speaks of it so much. Love is the revelation of God in His people, for "God is love," and the love of God is poured out into human hearts by the Holy Spirit (Rom. 5:5).

Ethel Waters' mother was a 12-year-old who had been raped at knifepoint. She was raised as a dead-end kid in Philadelphia and Camden by a grandmother who showed her no love. "I just ran wild as a little girl," Ethel says in her biography, *His Eye Is on the Sparrow.* "I was bad, always a leader of the street gang in stealing and general hell-raising." Eventually, at the last meeting of a children's revival, Ethel opened her heart to God, and the change was miraculous. "Love flooded my heart and I knew I had found God and that I would have an ally, a friend close by to strengthen me and cheer me on," Ethel testifies (p. 50).

The Spirit, who had filled Ethel with the love of God, used her in a special way through nearly 50 years on the stage and screen. I have been blessed along with hundreds of thousands of others who have heard Miss Waters sing her most famous song at Billy Graham crusades, "His Eye Is on the Sparrow." Ethel Waters was sure, therefore, that God was also watching her.

Even as she neared the end of her life, Ethel Waters was still filled with the love of God and was concerned that Christians allow the Holy Spirit to reveal this love through them. How did the Spirit make this possible in Ethel's life? "I have loved Jesus all of my life," she says, "but I think I had to surrender myself to Him before I knew how to love other people" *(To Me It's Wonderful,* p. 145).

John was deeply concerned at the lack of true love that was evident in the church near the end of the first century. One man loved himself so much that he was throwing others out of the church (3 John 9, 10). The answer was and is Ethel's formula: surrender to Jesus in the power of the Spirit.

 *A PRAYER FOR TODAY*

Holy Spirit, fill my heart with God's love for the unlovable.

December 14

WELCOME, FIRSTHAND WITNESS

This is the one who came by water and blood—Jesus Christ. He did not come by water only, but by water and blood. And it is the Spirit who testifies, because the Spirit is the truth. 1 John 5:6, NIV.

*A*fter the last living witness dies, every other testimony is secondhand. When I first moved to Cooranbong to attend Avondale College in 1965, I was delighted to meet an elderly gentleman who had known Ellen G. White during her years there in the late 1890s. As a young boy he had traveled with her on a number of occasions and had many inspiring stories to tell. Now in Australia there are only secondhand witnesses left to tell of Mrs. White's Spirit-filled, practical Christian ministry.

John, as he ministered in Ephesus and was in exile on Patmos, had the same concern. He was, it seems, the last living witness of the whole ministry of Jesus. All the other apostles were dead. There were no *I Witness Video* segments of Jesus' life. Sixty years after the death of Jesus, John knew that soon there would not be even one person alive who could say "I met Jesus."

But John was not discouraged. He knew the Holy Spirit, the one who would give a witness of Jesus that would be firsthand and more effective than any audiovisual testimony. Around the world in 1993 people saw on television four Los Angeles police officers beating Rodney King. There was no doubt that it happened. Similarly, when the Holy Spirit witnesses in a heart that is open to God, that person has no doubt about Jesus' sinless life and sacrificial death. The Spirit's witness is undeniable. Jesus is not dead. His witness is firsthand.

Satan is determined to keep people away from the Holy Spirit, because the Spirit of truth bears witness about Jesus. Not only individuals but whole churches have excluded the Holy Spirit. The Holy Spirit has been treated as a fearful force rather than a faithful friend. As a result, Jesus is little more than a name in cultural Christianity. Sinners are introduced to doctrines and rules, but not to Jesus, and the results are predictably pathetic. If you desire to see change in your life and church, let the Holy Spirit give a firsthand witness about Jesus. You will be amazed at what will happen.

← *A PRAYER FOR TODAY* →

Spirit, show me more about Jesus than I've ever known before.

December 15

WELCOME, TRIPLE WITNESS

The Spirit, the water and the blood; and the three are in agreement.
1 John 5:8, NIV.

*D*uring His descent like a dove at the water baptism of Jesus, throughout our Lord's sinless life of ministry, and at the time of the Saviour's sacrifice on the cross of Calvary, the Holy Spirit miraculously empowered Jesus and testified of His divinity.

All through history the Holy Spirit has witnessed to born-again Christians in the same triple way. The guilt of our discordant lives is nullified by Jesus' blood because we have the washing of regeneration and a new harmonious life with God in the power of the Spirit. Yes, the water, blood, and Spirit all convince us of the same wonderful truth: We can have assurance of salvation and ministry in Jesus.

F. B. Meyer, author of many deeply spiritual books, writes of an experience he had while at a hotel in Norway. A little girl was among the families staying as guests. She insisted on playing with one finger the piano in the drawing room, and the notes were so discordant that "everyone bolted for open air when they saw her coming." One of the finest musicians in Norway was also staying at the hotel, and on one occasion he sat beside the child and rendered a lovely accompaniment to every note she played. Soon the people streamed in from outside to enjoy the beautiful music.

"The truth this story illustrates has deeply touched my heart through the years," Meyer says. "I have been as that child at the piano of God's truth. I have tried my level best to make music come with my one finger. Again and again and again I have come away feeling that I am a terrible failure and play nothing but discords. But oh, I have also found the Holy Spirit sitting by my side. For every note of discord I have made He has struck a nobler note. Whatever you try to do for the Lord, small or great, and feel you are only making mistakes and failures and false notes, believe that the blessed Holy Spirit is by your side turning your discords into the Hallelujah Chorus!" *(Powerlines,* pp. 155, 156).

Yes, F. B. Meyer had discovered the triple witness of the Spirit.

✤ *A PRAYER FOR TODAY* ✤

Holy Spirit, again I thank You for showing me that Jesus can make something beautiful out of my discordant life.

December 16

INNER WITNESS OR LIAR?

He who believes in the Son of God has the witness in himself; he who does not believe God has made Him a liar, because he has not believed the testimony that God has given of His Son. 1 John 5:10, NKJV.

Question: How can Christians make it appear that God is a liar? Answer: By doubting their salvation. Question: How can Christians know for sure that they have eternal life?

Answer: By listening to the Spirit's inner witness.

Let me take you through some "roots" that will show how Adventists should have a hereditary advantage in answering those questions. The Moravian Christians on the estate of Count Zinzendorf in Saxony discovered the meaning of the inner witness. When the Holy Spirit was poured upon them on August 13, 1727, He gave them such a certainty of their salvation and of Jesus the Saviour that "this firm confidence changed them in a single moment into a happy people" (John Greenfield, *Power From on High,* p. 14).

When John Wesley, a minister who doubted his salvation and thus made God a liar, was questioned by Moravian bishop Spangenberg on February 7, 1736, he was asked, "Have you the witness within yourself? Does the Spirit of God bear witness with your spirit that you are a child of God?" (See the August 23 reading.) In his conversion experience on May 24, 1736, and at his baptism by the Spirit at the New Year's Eve Moravian prayer meeting, January 1, 1739, Wesley discovered the answer. He knew that "he who has the Son has life" (1 John 5:12, NKJV). No longer did he "make God a liar."

Building on her Methodist heritage, Spirit-filled Adventist pioneer Ellen White also understood the inner witness of the Spirit. Many times she referred to this inner certainty. "The Holy Spirit is a person, for He beareth witness with our spirits that we are the children of God. When this witness in borne, it carries with it its own evidence. At such times we believe and are sure that we are the children of God" *(Evangelism,* p. 616). "When we have an assurance, which is bright and clear, of our own salvation, we shall exhibit cheerfulness and joyfulness, which becomes every follower of Jesus Christ" *(ibid.,* pp. 630, 631).

John wrote that "you may know that you have eternal life." If you don't, listen again for the voice of the Inner Witness.

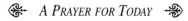 *A PRAYER FOR TODAY*

Thanks, Lord, for the undeniable certainty of eternal life and joy.

362

December 17

DESTRUCTIVE GREATNESS WITHOUT THE SPIRIT

These are the men who divide you, who follow mere natural instincts and do not have the Spirit. Jude 19, NIV.

Some names have a stigma that is difficult to erase. We do not hear of parents naming their child Hitler or Lucifer. In the same way, we would be shocked to find a Bible book entitled "Judas," so it is always called the Letter of Jude. The people Jude wrote about, however, apparently had respectable names but were the spiritual equivalents of Judas Iscariot and Hitler. Jude uses the most emotive language and worst examples of evil he can accumulate to declare the depravity of the destroyers of the faith. He does not give vague hints or subtle innuendos, but instead blasts these cheap grace antinomians with both barrels.

People who divide and destroy the church are soundly denounced in the New Testament. Paul says that church wreckers will be destroyed (1 Cor. 3:16, 17; see the September 9 reading), and Peter, using similar words to Jude's, says that such people face swift destruction (2 Peter 2:1-3:3). As Jude reached the climax of his denunciation he pinpointed the problem when he propounded his contention that these internal destroyers of the church did not have the Holy Spirit.

It seems strange that the people who have been the most destructive from within the church have often been considered as great at some time. But as Oswald Chambers once said: "We make men and women great—God does not. One essential difference between before Pentecost and after Pentecost is that from God's standpoint there are no great men after Pentecost." Every member of the church can be equally filled with the Holy Spirit after Pentecost and can minister through spiritual gifts.

Every converted person is the dwelling place of the Holy Spirit (Rom. 8:9; Eph. 1:13; Eze. 36:25-27). So the troublemakers who "do not have the Spirit" must be cultural Christians who have never been born again or who have slipped away into apostasy. Those who are filled with the Spirit will always be agents of unity in the church, growing an orchard of love, joy, peace, patience, kindness, goodness, faithfulness, gentleness, and self-control.

 *A PRAYER FOR TODAY*

Lord, bind us together in love by the power of the Holy Spirit.

363

December 18

WELCOME, CONVERSATION PRAYER IN THE SPIRIT

But you, dear friends, build yourselves up in your most holy faith and pray in the Holy Spirit. Jude 20, NIV.

When Rosalind Rinker was 15 she chose to attend a cottage prayer meeting one evening rather than go to a party with some other young people. At that prayer meeting she learned what it meant to talk in the power of the Spirit to God as a friend. Years later, as a missionary in China, Rosalind joined with another lady to pray for some students, and it was here that a principle of prayer was discovered that has helped millions of Christians.

Rosalind prayed, "Lord, art Thou trying to teach us something through this incident? Should we give Thee more opportunity while we are praying to get Thy ideas through to us? Would that give the Holy Spirit more opportunity to guide us as we pray?" *(Prayer: Conversing With God,* p. 17). As the two ladies interacted during the prayer in a natural, spontaneous way, it seemed as if they were conversing with God. They were praying "in the Spirit" as He was able to energize or "make fervent" the prayers and open the ladies' minds to the things that were important at that time.

"Do you know what?" Rosalind exclaimed to her friend Mildred. "I believe that the Lord taught us something just now! Instead of each of us making a prayer-speech to Him, let's talk things over with Him, back and forth, including Him in it as we do when we have a conversation."

Mildred agreed: "Yes, and we could bring up one person or one situation at a time, and both of us pray back and forth about it, until we feel we have touched God, and our hearts are at rest" *(ibid.,* p. 14).

Today people in small groups around the world enjoy the wonderful blessings of conversational prayer. Usually the group members begin with praise. Then they pray for needs inside the group, ministering to each other through the power and gifts of the Holy Spirit. Finally, their prayers move outside the group as they intercede for other people and situations. Each prayer is no more than a sentence or two, so that each person in the group can pray often as the Spirit moves.

❧ A PRAYER FOR TODAY ❧

Father, thank You for listening and answering as I talk to and with a group of praying friends.

WELCOME, SPIRIT OF CHANGE

I was in the Spirit on the Lord's day, and heard behind me a great voice, as of a trumpet. Rev. 1:10.

Themis last book of the Bible is the great final revelation of Jesus by the Holy Spirit. These visions lifted John from being a victim on a penal island to being a victor who saw realities beyond the confines of present circumstances. That is what vision does. It enables us to see the unseen.

Some time ago a friend shared with me a statement that I treasure: "If you can see in a given situation only what everyone else can see, you can be said to be so much a representative of your culture that you are a victim of it" (S. I. Hayakawa).

The Holy Spirit enabled John to see beyond Patmos to the ultimate triumph of the church. What are you seeing today? Imprisoning circumstances that seem to surround you? Insurmountable difficulties impeding progress? The church in a rut of Spiritless routine? If you have no vision, you will find yourself locked in a prison of spiritual, emotional, and cultural stagnation.

Was John uniquely privileged to be "in the Spirit"? Not at all. Every born-again Christian is said to be "in the Spirit, if indeed the Spirit of God dwells" within (Rom. 8:9, NKJV). And it is through that indwelling Spirit that God's people see the things that eye cannot see or ear cannot hear in the present circumstances of life (1 Cor. 2:9, 10).

At a pastors' meeting in Nova Scotia we prayed that the Holy Spirit would fill us and give us a vision of the future of His work in Canada's Maritime Provinces. Conference president Bob Lehmann pointed out that Prince Edward Island, with a population of more than 120,000, has only 40 members in a small church and company. As we prayed in the Spirit, the Lord opened up before us the possibility of a house church of at least 10 members in the 20 or more Prince Edward Island towns with populations of more than 3,000 people. For some the vision seemed an impossibility after more than 100 years of relatively fruitless work. For others it was like the trumpet John heard. "In the power of the Holy Spirit it can and will be done," they said.

And God will certainly make the vision a reality.

❦ *A PRAYER FOR TODAY* ❧

Lord, in the situations and decisions of today help me be an agent of change, not a victim of my culture and the status quo.

December 20

A Promise for Lovers

He who has an ear, let him hear what the Spirit says to the churches.
To him who overcomes I will give to eat from the tree of life, which is in
the midst of the Paradise of God. Rev. 2:7, NKJV.

For four hours each Sunday during seven weekend revival meetings in California, small groups came together to study the seven churches of Revelation. At this time they were not looking at the churches prophetically or historically, but personally. The questions were What type of Christian is represented by these churches? Which church most closely represents my present spiritual condition? How does the Spirit meet the needs of each type of Christian and provide the possibility of ultimate victory?

In this setting it is not hard to discover who the Holy Spirit is talking about in the message to the church in Ephesus. Have you ever felt like an Ephesian Christian who has lost your first love? Remember, the love of God is poured into our hearts by the Holy Spirit (Rom. 5:5). When the first love is lost, Jesus is no longer the center of life and religion. Our worship becomes formalistic and cold. A spiritual divorce has taken place, and repentance is the only solution.

Writing from Melbourne, Australia, Ellen White expressed her concern about the effect of Ephesus-type Christians in the church. "The atmosphere of the church is so frigid, its spirit is of such an order, that men and women cannot sustain or endure the example of primitive and heaven-born piety," she wrote. "The warmth of their first love is frozen up, and unless they are watered over by the baptism of the Holy Spirit, their candlestick will be removed out of its place, except they repent and do their first works" *(Testimonies to Ministers,* pp. 167, 168).

Each of the small groups in California discovered that the Holy Spirit's messages to the overcomers in Revelation are not threats but promises. The Spirit says that many who have lost their first love will be filled with the wonderful love of Jesus once again. Ultimately, for these victorious Ephesian-type Christians, there will be no more possibility of losing that love, because the Holy Spirit will lead them to the Paradise of God.

❧ A Prayer for Today ❧

I'm sorry, Lord, for losing my first love, and I ask You to pour into my life
again the overflowing love that the Holy Spirit supplies.

THE FRAGRANCE OF CRUSHED CHRISTIANS

He who has an ear, let him hear what the Spirit says to the churches.
He who overcomes shall not be hurt by the second death.
Rev. 2:11, NKJV.

*H*urting Christians. Smyrna-type Christians. They can be found in almost every congregation. They have been crushed by misunderstandings, bad decisions, the mistakes of others, opposition by relatives and church members, unfair treatment, and the list goes on. This sort of hurt fills the mind and body with pain that Tylenol cannot mask. Sometimes when a child receives a minor injury a mother will "kiss it better." But that wonderful treatment cannot mend a broken leg or a gashed head. Likewise, deeply hurting Christians cannot be healed by a quick prayer.

Danny had given up a good job to help lift a sawmilling company out of serious financial trouble. His efficiency proved remarkably successful, and in a few months the firm was back on its feet. Just before Christmas the owner of the company decided that he did not need Danny's services any longer, and terminated his employment. Now Danny had no job, no money for the Christmas holidays, and a very unhappy family. Danny struggled with deep hurt, especially on Sabbath morning when the man who had treated him so badly stood up as a leader in the same church that Danny attended.

Only the Holy Spirit can help a Smyrna-type Christian be fragrant when crushed. It is not natural; it is supernatural. But the Spirit does not do it in an abstract way. He works though the Christians He fills. He uses them to minister to the hurting, not only individually, but especially in small groups.

I saw this working most effectively at a Holy Spirit seminar I was teaching in Nova Scotia. As soon as someone would mention a hurt that was crushing his or her spirit, others would gather around to pray. The prayers were earnest and sincere and were connected to practical Christian love. The Holy Spirit has a wonderful promise for those who are crushed but who, in His strength, overcome the urge to let the hurt destroy them—they will not be hurt by the ultimate pain of the second death.

☙ *A PRAYER FOR TODAY* ❧

Lord, when pain is shared with those who care, then it's manageable.
Thank You for true friends.

December 22

POWER FOR PEOPLE IN PERGAMOS

He who has an ear, let him hear what the Spirit says to the churches.
To him who overcomes I will give some of the hidden manna to eat.
And I will give him a white stone, and on the stone a new name written
which no one knows except him who receives it. Rev. 2:17, NKJV.

While the Berlin Wall still stood I walked through Checkpoint Charlie and made my way to the famous Pergamon Museum in the eastern section of the divided city. German archaeologists in the past century brought many of the treasures of ancient Babylon here, including the massive altar of Zeus, which had been discovered in the excavations of Pergamos.

Satan, who is not omnipresent, apparently made ancient Pergamos his headquarters. Christians in this place were constantly harassed by the powers of evil, but once again the Holy Spirit promised overcoming power.

Pergamos-type Christians today find themselves in the center of evil activity. They do not face just the general exposure to sinful temptations that is common to all Christians, but are in a work, school, home, or community situation that is targeted for specific diabolical enterprise. They may be in a location that is used for drug dealership. They may be subject to satanic ritual abuse. They may be in an environment of pornographic garbage. They may be subject to violent physical attacks. The air around them may be blue with obscenities and verbal filth. Some sheltered souls may not believe that situations like this can exist, but Pergamos-type Christians know that this is reality.

Even though they may have given in to evil a number of times, the Holy Spirit has promised escape and victory to Christians in Pergamos-like situations. If you are there today, do not despair. There is forgiveness and hope for you. God has promised you a beautiful new name and eternal life in the pure environment of heaven.

If you find it hard to believe that the Holy Spirit can bring overcoming power to Pergamos-type Christians, here is a test you can apply. Ask a group of Christians, as I have done many times, how many of them have come out of Pergamos-like situations. You will then hear some testimonies of victory and praise that will amaze you. You will certainly be led to glorify El Shaddai, who is almighty.

❧ *A PRAYER FOR TODAY* ❧

Beyond all the evil of this world, I look up to You, God of hope.

WELCOME, BRIGHT STAR

And I will give him the morning star. He who has an ear, let him hear what the Spirit says to the churches. Rev. 2:28, 29, NKJV.

T hyatira-type Christians wander in the night of religious confusion, but even there the Spirit gives them glimpses of the bright morning star. Like an angel who steers a wandering child along a dangerous path, the Holy Spirit guides God's people home.

Helen dropped out of Walla Walla College and, with a friend, headed for Colorado in an old car with faulty brakes. Along the Oregon coast the brakes failed, and the car with its two frightened passengers ended up suspended on a stump at the edge of a precipice. Fortunately a "morning star" came by who not only pulled the car to safety but also gave its occupants work so that they could afford to fix the brakes.

As they journeyed on to California, Helen and her friend argued constantly, until she got out of the car with her duffel and sleeping bags and watched her only means of transportation drive off into the dusk. As she walked into town, Helen noticed a man in Army fatigues walking on the other side of the road. Soon this "morning star" crossed over and asked if he could help. In town they called the Adventist pastor, who refused assistance to the stranded girl. Fortunately, the young Christian soldier was able to introduce Helen to another group of Christians, who prayed for her, helped her with work, and cared for her until she was able to resume her journey to Colorado.

Ellen White applied the Thyatira message to the intellectuals who at the beginning of this century were trying to take her church into the religious confusion of pantheism. The brakes on the church began to fail as these Thyatira-type Christians moved it toward the precipice. Some arguing spiritual leaders began to wander in the darkness, desperately needing the light of a "morning star." Once again the Holy Spirit used Ellen White to direct His people to a place of safety where their simple faith could be renewed.

Church organizations may incorporate traditions that are confusing and beliefs that are not biblical, but the Spirit of God will light the way home for those who are seeking truth.

❦ *A PRAYER FOR TODAY* ❦

Father, in the midst of a multiplicity of religious teachings, may Your Spirit help me clearly discern and walk in the way of truth.

CAN A DEAD CHURCH LIVE?

And to the angel of the church in Sardis write, "These things says He who has the seven Spirits of God and the seven stars: 'I know your works, that you have a name that you are alive, but you are dead. . . . He who has an ear, let him hear what the Spirit says to the churches.'"
Rev. 3:1-6, NKJV.

I was recently surprised to find dozens of instances in which Ellen White applied the Holy Spirit's Sardis message to the Adventist Church. "To us today comes the message to the church in Sardis," she wrote in 1903 *(Review and Herald,* Apr. 21, 1903).

Like Christianity in general, the Adventist Church has a name that is alive, but sometimes it gives the appearance of being spiritually dead. That's what Sardis-type Christians are like. They profess to be alive, but need the resurrection-revival power of the Holy Spirit.

At a talk she gave during the 1901 General Conference session, Ellen White spoke strongly to Sardis-type Christians in leadership: "In every institution, in the publishing houses, and in all the interests of the denomination, everything that concerns the handling of the work, it requires minds that are worked by the Holy Spirit of God. . . . To have this conference pass on and close up as the conferences have done, with the same manipulating, with the very same tone, and the same order—God forbid! (Voices, 'Amen.') God forbid, brethren. (Voices, 'Amen.') He wants every living soul that has a knowledge of the truth to come to their senses. He wants every living power to arouse; and we are just about the same thing as dead men" *(Spalding and Magan Collection,* p. 163).

The Holy Spirit, the Spirit of life in Jesus Christ, can raise Sardis-type Christians from the dead. There is a problem, however. "The dead know not any thing," and most often the spiritually dead do not recognize their need. But the few who do know testify to the transforming power of God's grace, as Ellen White often emphasized. They are clothed in the white robe of Christ's righteousness and have their names forever retained in the book of life.

※ *A PRAYER FOR TODAY* ※

Father, if there's an area of spiritual deadness in my life, help me see it and allow the Holy Spirit to give me new life in every part of my being.

December 25

WELCOME, OPEN DOOR

I know your works. See, I have set before you an open door, and no one can shut it; for you have a little strength, have kept My word, and have not denied My name. . . . He who has an ear, let him hear what the Spirit says to the churches. Rev. 3:8-13, NKJV.

Philadelphia-type Christians, in the power of the Holy Spirit, step through God's open doors of opportunity, never looking back to the old ways of lifeless, loveless, lethargic inactivity.

On December 1, 1955, Rosa Lee Parks stepped through the door of a Montgomery, Alabama, bus and sat on the first available seat. Soon the whole bus was in a turmoil. The driver ordered Rosa to "Move it!" Passengers cursed her and pushed her, and soon the police came aboard and arrested her. What was Rosa's crime? This 42-year-old Spirit-filled, quiet, conservative Christian, with a good job and family, had sat in the White section of the bus and would no longer tolerate the injustice of racial segregation. That is what Philadelphia-type Christians are like. They combine love and action, faith and works, in an invincible combination.

In the strength of the Spirit, Philadelphia-type Christians step through doors of hope, doors of social concern, doors of praise, doors of intercessory prayer, and doors of spiritual vitality. They are people who nurture others in love and are involved in the small group ministries and practical outreach of the church. The reason for the strength of these Christians, who along with those in Smyrna receive no rebuke in Revelation, is clear. They have accepted the Holy Spirit's invitation to step through the door of access to the Father's throne in heaven (Eph. 2:18). As they have prayed in the Spirit (Rom. 8:26-28; Jude 20), they have come boldly to the throne of grace and have recognized God's mercy and grace to help in time of need (Heb. 4:16).

The Montgomery street where Rosa Parks was pulled off the bus in 1955 has been renamed Rosa Parks Avenue. Likewise Philadelphia-type Christians will one day receive a new name, and added to it will be God's name and the name of God's city, the New Jerusalem.

❦ *A PRAYER FOR TODAY* ❧

Father, help me step through the door of loving-kindness and positive action for Your kingdom.

THE SPIRIT WHO OPENS THE DOOR

*Here I am! I stand at the door and knock. If anyone hears my voice
and opens the door, I will come in and eat with him, and he with me. . . .
He who has an ear, let him hear what the Spirit says to the churches.
Rev. 3:20-22, NIV.*

W hile the Philadelphia-type Christians have walked through the open door and enjoy wonderful fellowship with God, those of Laodicea have closed the door and remain locked in their luke-warm self-satisfaction.

What is it that closes the door into a human heart? Sometimes it is closed by deliberate sin; sometimes by debilitating sickness; sometimes by defeat and failure; sometimes by devastating bereavement. Sometimes the door is closed by a dependency on salvation by works that results in spiritual numbness and a deceptive sense of spiritual well-being.

Often Laodicean-type Christians drift away into spiritual oblivion, and because of the lukewarmness of their fellow Laodiceans, few notice that they have gone . . . and nobody really cares. Some stay in the church only to coast along in institutionalized religion, gripped by lukewarm traditions and cold formalism.

Only through the power of the Holy Spirit can Laodicean Christians open the door and invite Jesus back into their lives. It is neither natural nor easy to turn away from the Laodicean spirit. It grips lives and churches like Super Glue.

Ellen White tells of a camp meeting in Syracuse, New York, that was inundated by Laodicean-type Christians. "The meeting was a good one; but there was not that depth and earnestness of feeling that would insure the presence of the Spirit of God, and produce lasting impressions. The people are too well satisfied with themselves, and there is a deadness that savors of spiritual paralysis. The message to the Laodiceans is applicable to them; for while congratulating themselves on their knowledge of the truth, they are destitute of true love and faith" *(Review and Herald,* Oct. 28, 1884).

There is great hope for Laodicean-type Christians. The fires of Holy Spirit revival can burn again. As a result of earnest prayer ministries, nurturing small groups, and Spirit-filled worship, the grip of Laodiceanism can be broken forever.

     ❦ *A PRAYER FOR TODAY* ❧

*Lord, shake me out of spiritual lethargy by the earthquake-like energy of Your
Spirit. Help me light a fire in Laodicea.*

December 27

WELCOME, SUPER SEVEN

At once I was in the Spirit, and there before me was a throne in heaven with someone sitting on it. . . . From the throne came flashes of lightning, rumblings and peals of thunder. Before the throne, seven lamps were blazing. These are the seven spirits of God. Rev. 4:2-5, NIV.

*D*o we conclude a year with the Holy Spirit only to discover that there are seven Spirits and not one? Revelation's symbolism makes the answer clear. Join me for a brief study on the unique ministry of the Spirit. In Revelation 4:5 it says that the Spirit is represented by seven lamps of fire. John the Baptist likened the actions of the Spirit to purifying fire (Matt. 3:11, 12). The Spirit fell like tongues of fire on the day of Pentecost (Acts 2:3), and like fire He can be quenched (Eph. 4:30).

Have you received the fire of the Spirit? Are you fueling that fire with prayer and Bible study?

In Revelation 5:6 John sees the Spirit as the seven eyes of the Lamb. These eyes represent the omnipresent insight, knowledge, and wisdom of the Holy Spirit (Zech. 3:9; 4:6, 10). There is no place where the Spirit is not present (Ps. 139:7-12). You can be absolutely confident that the Spirit is with you today. He knows where you are and will guide you through every situation of life.

The ancient prophet Isaiah also recognized the sevenfold nature of the Holy Spirit as He filled Jesus and empowered Him for ministry (Isa. 11:2; see the February 28 reading). So while there is only one Holy Spirit, the perfection of His ministry is represented by the number seven.

At a Holy Spirit revival series in Halifax I had the opportunity to watch the Spirit work in more than seven ways. At the opening service testimonies were given by people who, during our meetings earlier in the week, had received special miracles by the Spirit's power. Some had received verifiable physical healing. Others had received healing from addictions, depression, fear of ministry, an unforgiving spirit, and a lack of spiritual life. The Holy Spirit came to many as a Spirit of wisdom and revelation, opening up new understandings of the Scripture and guiding His people into all truth.

Yes, you can be sure that the Holy Spirit is your perfect friend and helper.

☙ A PRAYER FOR TODAY ❧

Lord, once again I ask You to fill me with Your Holy Spirit, who has more than seven super gifts and graces for my life and ministry.

December 28

GOOD WORKS THAT LAST

Then I heard a voice from heaven say, "Write: Blessed are the dead who die in the Lord from now on." "Yes," says the Spirit, "they will rest from their labor, for their deeds will follow them." Rev. 14:13, NIV.

*E*ven the most Spirit-filled, gospel-centered people die. Death is not a lack of faith but a fact of life. The greatest fact of spiritual life, however, is that the Holy Spirit enables the people He fills to work in ways that will have long-lasting effects, even through eternity. That's why when we talk about the work of the Spirit we can illustrate His power from the works of people who have been dead for many years. Their works are following them and have stood the test of time.

Professor Ken Hill is one whose good works will follow him. For 25 years Ken was professor of physiotherapy at Dalhousie University in Nova Scotia. In 1989, just before his retirement, he received the prestigious Edith Graham Award for the most outstanding contribution to physiotherapy in all Canada. Now, as an ADRA volunteer, he is committed to setting up physiotherapy programs to relieve the suffering of many in Kenya.

"What similarities do you see between the work of the Holy Spirit and physiotherapy?" I asked Ken recently as I enjoyed hospitality in the lovely country home that he and his wife, Hazel, built 15 years ago. "Physiotherapy, like the work of the Holy Spirit, is supportive and encouraging," he replied. "You take the people where they are, broken-down and incapacitated, and work to bring them healing. But people must cooperate and have confidence in their physiotherapist, who knows the workings of the body and its capacity to become strong and well."

Ken has served a number of terms on his conference executive committee, and for the past three years he has been the small-group ministries leader for the conference. During that time he has held training weekends on the Holy Spirit and small groups in 15 churches and has seen his own small group blessed with two baptisms.

Here is a man who is certainly not yet ready to "rest from his labors," but nevertheless already his "works do follow him."

❧ A PRAYER FOR TODAY ❧

Father, fill my life with good works, not so that people will remember me, but so that they will glorify Jesus and the Spirit's power.

CLARIFY YOUR THINKING

So he carried me away in the Spirit into the wilderness. And I saw a woman sitting on a scarlet beast which was full of names of blasphemy, having seven heads and ten horns. Rev. 17:3, NKJV.

The Holy Spirit convicts of sin and points out the devastating effects of confused religion. He knows that all confusion is disconcerting and disturbing and can lead to ultimate despair.

My family still laugh at the confusion I experienced when it was necessary for me to receive morphine during a painful episode with a kidney stone. A balloon that had been tied to my hospital bed deflated a little during the night, and I awoke thinking my bed had risen to the ceiling.

My grandfather was still walking for exercise as he neared his 100th birthday, but he became confused and could not remember his way home.

A mother was mixing a recipe that was being explained on the TV in the next room. She did not immediately realize what had happened when her small child changed the channel to an exercise program and was confused when she received the instructions to stand on her head.

An Episcopalian minister was confused when he read the fourth commandment in the Anglican Prayer Book and was instructed to pray, "Lord have mercy upon us and incline our hearts to keep this law," when his church was keeping the first day of the week.

The Holy Spirit is not the author of confusion, so He is constantly calling God's people out of Babylon. This Babylon is not a place, but a state of mind. If one thinks of Babylon primarily as an organization or institution, a Christian could feel proud that he or she is not a member of such a corrupt establishment. When, however, it is seen that Babylon may represent the religious confusion that can exist in any mind, then born-again Christians will be constantly praying that the Spirit will point out sin, reveal truth, and bring them out of confusion.

Satan is constantly working to confuse Christians concerning the Spirit Himself. If you have this problem, take time to reexamine those key passages that we have studied this year. Review the readings for John 14-16, Romans 8, and Ephesians, and these will help clarify His wonderful ministry.

❦ *A PRAYER FOR TODAY* ❧

Father, I ask You to clarify constantly my thinking and spiritual values so that all confusion can be eliminated.

WELCOME, ULTIMATE REALITY

And he carried me away in the Spirit to a great and high mountain, and showed me the great city, the holy Jerusalem, descending out of heaven from God. Rev. 21:10, NKJV.

Surgeon Bernie Seigel, M.D., once said: "Coincidence is just God's way of remaining anonymous." This year, however, as we have studied and prayed about every verse in the Bible concerning the Holy Spirit, we have discovered that He is not anonymous to the people whom He fills, but is a wonderful, personal friend. His spiritual gifts are visible demonstrations of power that transcend coincidence.

The same Spirit who showed John the New Jerusalem had filled John and Peter and the other disciples at Pentecost at the beginning of the Christian church. The same Spirit, 18 centuries later, was poured out with miraculous manifestations on the pioneers of the Adventist Church. "The old standard bearers knew what it was to wrestle with God in prayer, and enjoy the outpouring of His Spirit" *(Selected Messages,* book 1, p. 122).

Eventually the church came into tragic times in its relationship with the Holy Spirit. He was insulted and treated as an unwelcome guest. As individuals were filled with the Spirit other leaders rejected it as fanaticism *(Testimonies to Ministers,* pp. 64, 393).

But the future is bright for the revival that only the Holy Spirit can bring. Now is the time when individual church members can be filled with the Spirit and can join together in prayer for the latter rain. The results will not be coincidental or anonymous. They will be as visible and glorious as the New Jerusalem. Many will be praising God. The sick will be healed, and other miracles will take place. Thousands of homes will open up as centers of Bible study and prayer. The power of the Holy Spirit will bring genuine conversions and great blessings *(Testimonies,* vol. 9, p. 126).

In the New Jerusalem the Holy Spirit showed John the glory of the Father and the Son. John saw all the saved, who had come to Jesus through the power of the Holy Spirit. And the Spirit reveals to them Jesus' face. This is why the Spirit is eager that God's people open the way for the last great revival today. He wants to give them power now . . . and indescribable future joy.

❧ *A PRAYER FOR TODAY* ❧

Lord, Your Spirit is a welcome guest in my life today. May the last revival begin so that many will be saved and soon see the face of Jesus.

December 31

Don't Miss the Spirit's Welcome Home

And the Spirit and the bride say, "Come!" And let him who hears say, "Come!" And let him who thirsts come. And whoever desires, let him take the water of life freely. Rev. 22:17, NKJV.

*I*n 1984 Robert Fulghum sat in the Hong Kong airport, doing what comes naturally to seasoned air travelers—waiting for his plane. This day was different, however. The young lady sitting next to him was quietly sobbing. As he tried to comfort her, she told him that she had sat there for three hours in terrible grief because she had lost her ticket. Now she was stranded with no money and no friends, and her plane was about to leave.

An elderly couple joined Mr. Fulghum in trying to comfort the lady and were eventually able to talk her into accompanying them to a meal. Just as she stood up and turned around to collect her belongings, she screamed as though she had been shot. There was her ticket. She had been sitting on it for three hours (*It Was on Fire When I Lay Down on It,* pp. 189-191).

If you have accepted Jesus as your Saviour, you have your ticket to Holy Spirit power (Eph. 1:13; Acts 1:8). As John is shown in the last Holy Spirit reference in the Bible, those who accept the invitation of the Spirit to come home not only receive joy themselves but share in the wonderful privilege of Spirit-filled ministry.

Are you sitting on your ticket? Are you bewailing the spiritual lethargy of the church while at the same time you yourself are missing the flight?

When the Holy Spirit is poured out in latter-rain power, it is possible that "it may be falling on hearts all around us, and we shall not discern or receive it" (*Testimonies to Ministers,* p. 507).

Are you sure that is not happening to you now? Are you sitting on your ticket, or are you praying earnestly for more of the Spirit than ever before? God is now giving the early and latter rain (*ibid.,* p. 508).

Come now and bring others with you. You have your ticket, and the flight is ready.

❧ A Prayer for Today ❧

Lord, thank You for this year of study and prayer about my friend the Holy Spirit. Give me the ultimate joy of drinking freely of the water of life. Glorify Jesus in my life more fully than ever before.

Scripture Index

12:36	Apr. 28	16:14	June 5
13:11	Apr. 29	20:22	June 6
16:17, 18	Apr. 30		
		Acts	
Luke		1:1, 2	June 7
1:15	May 1	1:4	June 8
1:35	May 2	1:5	June 9
1:41	May 3	1:8	June 10
1:67, 68	May 4	1:16	June 11
2:25	May 5	2:1, 2	June 12
2:26	May 6	2:3	June 13
2:27	May 7	2:4	June 14
3:16	May 8	2:15	June 15
3:22	May 9	2:17	June 16
4:1	May 10	2:18	June 17
4:14	May 11	2:33	June 18
4:18, 19	May 12	2:38	June 19
10:20, 21	May 13	2:39	June 20
11:13	May 14	4:8	June 21
12:10	May 15	4:31	June 22
12:12	May 16	4:33	June 23
24:49	May 17	5:3	June 24
		5:9	June 25
John		5:32	June 26
1:32	May 18	6:3, 4	June 27
1:33	May 19	6:5, 6	June 28
3:5	May 20	6:10-15	June 29
3:6	May 21	7:51	June 30
3:8	May 22	7:55	July 1
3:34	May 23	8:15	July 2
4:24	May 24	8:16	July 3
6:63	May 25	8:17	July 4
7:37, 38	May 26	8:18	July 5
7:39	May 27	8:19	July 6
14:12	May 28	8:29	July 7
14:16	May 29	8:39	July 8
14:17	May 30	9:17	July 9
14:26	May 31	9:31	July 10
15:26	June 1	10:19	July 11
16:7	June 2	10:38	July 12
16:8	June 3	10:44	July 13
16:13	June 4	10:45	July 14